JUDICIAL REVIEW IN NORTHERN IRELAND

This book provides a detailed account of the principle and practice of judicial review in Northern Ireland. It collates and discusses the ever-burgeoning body of Northern Ireland case law and divides into eight chapters that consider: the purposes of judicial review; the nature of the public/private divide in Northern Ireland law; the judicial review procedure; the grounds for review; and remedies. Much of the case law considered here is unique to Northern Ireland, and the book identifies actual and potential differences between Northern Ireland case law and that of England and Wales. The book also integrates Human Rights Act 1998 jurisprudence as has been developed by the Northern Ireland courts and by the House of Lords; and it cross-refers much of that case law to debates about judicial review as play out in related practitioner and/or academic journals.

The book has been written primarily for practitioners of judicial review and uses numbered paragraphs for ease of reference. The book is, however, of a wider interest and it will be a valuable resource for academics and students too. Much of the Northern Ireland case law has been concerned with contentious political issues, and the courts have had to consider difficult questions of the constitutional limits to the judicial role in review proceedings. The book should therefore be of use not just to practitioners but also to those involved in the study of judicial reasoning in different jurisdictions (both within the UK and elsewhere).

Judicial Review in Northern Ireland

Gordon Anthony

Senior Lecturer,
School of Law,
Queen's University Belfast

·HART·
PUBLISHING
OXFORD AND PORTLAND, OREGON
2008

Published in North America (US and Canada) by
Hart Publishing
c/o International Specialized Book Services
920 NE 58th Avenue, Suite 300
Portland, OR 97213-3786
USA
Tel: +1 503 287 3093 or toll-free: (1) 800 944 6190
Fax: +1 503 280 8832
E-mail: orders@isbs.com
Website: www.isbs.com

Hart Publishing, 16C Worcester Place, OX1 2JW
Telephone: +44 (0)1865 517530 Fax: +44 (0)1865 510710
E-mail: mail@hartpub.co.uk
Website: http://www.hartpub.co.uk

British Library Cataloguing in Publication Data
Data Available
ISBN: 978–1–84113–617–2

Typeset by Hope Services (Abingdon) Ltd
Printed and bound in Great Britain by
TJ International Ltd, Padstow, Cornwall

*For Jill, Emily,
Louis, Ben and Toby*

Foreword

This important new work by Gordon Anthony will be of inestimable assistance to practitioners and academic commentators alike. It provides a magisterial review of developments in the field of judicial review in this jurisdiction, particularly since the coming into force in October 2000 of the Human Rights Act 1998. One of its principal themes is the increasingly important constitutional dimension of judicial review. This is of particular significance in Northern Ireland because of the recent judicial recognition in cases decided in our courts—and, on appeal from our courts, by the House of Lords—of the special status of 'constitutional statutes'. The analysis here will be of especial interest to those working in this area of the law.

The book also provides invaluable guidance on the vexed question of when resort may properly be had to the still specialised remedy of judicial review; on the evolving but perennial issue of the nature of the review that courts may conduct of impugned decisions; on the juridical basis for the various species of judicial review challenges; and on the persistently difficult subject of the appropriate level of intensity of judicial scrutiny of discretionary choices. These and many other topics are handled with great authority and clarity.

Although the emphasis of the work is on academic analysis, it contains helpful practical guidance and it is certain that this will become an indispensable reference text for those practising in judicial review in this jurisdiction and elsewhere.

Rt Hon Sir Brian Kerr, Lord Chief Justice of Northern Ireland

Preface

This is a book about the law and practice of judicial review in Northern Ireland. It has been written with the intention of providing a concise but comprehensive account of developments in Northern Ireland case law, as have occurred within the legislative framework established by, primarily, the Judicature (Northern Ireland) Act 1978 and Order 53 of the Rules of Supreme Court 1980. Although many of the principles that run through the Northern Ireland case law are at one with those in the case law of England and Wales, Northern Ireland has its own body of jurisprudence which, in a strict sense, provides the binding precedents for its courts. This book thus attempts to 'front-load' those precedents for the first time, in particular those judgments that have been delivered under the European Communities Act 1972 and the Human Rights Act 1998 (Acts that have had such profound implications for the workings of judicial review). The book at the same time pays close attention to authorities in England and Wales which have likewise been central to redefining the role of the Northern Ireland courts in judicial review proceedings.

The book has been written primarily for legal practitioners, and this is reflected in the style of analysis that has been used throughout. For instance, each chapter has been written with numbered paragraphs that include, for ease of use, extensive cross-references within and between chapters; and the analysis in individual paragraphs has been presented very much from the perspective of first principles and core propositions of the law (the chapters similarly conclude with key points by way of summary). While there are, in turn, some issues that have required fuller analysis of individual cases and/or groups of cases, there has been a deliberate attempt not to encumber the text with such analysis. It follows that more detailed comment on various points of law, or examples by way of further illustration, is typically provided in parenthesis in the footnotes, at least where the corresponding point in the text is not self-explanatory. Many important judicial statements about the law and the constitutional role of the courts can also be found in the footnotes.

The book divides into eight chapters, which range across issues of the constitutional basis of judicial review, the judicial review procedure, the grounds for review, and remedies. Chapter one—'Judicial Review in Northern Ireland: Purposes, Sources of Law, and Constitutional Context'—thus provides a background account of the nature of judicial review in the United Kingdom more generally and in Northern Ireland in particular. Starting with an analysis of the purposes served by judicial review, it identifies the various sources of law that are used in review proceedings, as well as the juridical techniques (for instance, statutory interpretation) that determine how far the sources can have an impact on the outcome of cases. The chapter also highlights the growing importance of 'common law constitutional statutes', which have recently been recognised in case law in England and Wales and which have already some impact in Northern Ireland. Such statutes—which include the European Communities Act 1972, the Human Rights Act 1998, and the Northern Ireland Act 1998—are not subject to implied repeal, and they continue to have far-reaching implications for the principle and practice of judicial review. Hence the chapter identifies the defining constitutional features of the three principal Acts, the last of which now has an added importance in Northern Ireland given political developments since the St Andrews Agreement 2006.

Chapter two—'When is the Judicial Procedure Used? The Public/Private Divide and Effective Alternative Remedies'—considers the complicated questions of the reach of judicial review and the relationship between judicial review and other remedies (which are usually, though not exclusively, found in statute). This is the first aspect of the book that highlights the uniqueness of Northern Ireland case law, as the courts have for several years used a 'public interest' test when mapping the boundaries of judicial review. This test is considerably broader in its reach than comparable tests in England and Wales, and the chapter chronicles how it has enabled judicial review in Northern Ireland to embrace a range of decision-making processes that are absent any statutory underpinning. On the other hand, the chapter considers the implications of the recent House of Lords judgment in *YL v Birmingham City Council*,[1] which suggests a lessening of the reach of public law in the context of contracting-out and the Human Rights Act 1998. Finally, the chapter analyses judicial approaches to effective alternative remedies, where case law emphasises the efficacy of alternative remedies in terms of cost and convenience.

Chapter three is titled, 'The Judicial Review Procedure'. Given that the legislative basis for the procedure is contained in the Judicature (Northern Ireland) Act 1978 and Order 53 of the Rules of Supreme Court 1980, this is inevitably an area in which there are some significant differences in the law of Northern Ireland (for instance, at the level of nomenclature and in terms of the remedies that are available). However, the Northern Ireland procedure does, at the same time, share much in common with that in England and Wales (leave/permission; delay; standing; etc), and the chapter considers some important points of principle that have been established in Northern Ireland case law but which have implications for judicial review proceedings throughout the United Kingdom. The leading example is undoubtedly that in *Tweed v Parades Commission for Northern Ireland*[2], where the House of Lords redrew the approach to discovery both in the context of cases under the Human Rights Act 1998 and in judicial review proceedings more generally.

Chapter four is 'The Grounds for Review Introduced'. As with chapter one, this is more in the form of a background chapter that examines issues of general relevance to the grounds for review. Although the grounds are often sub-divided under the headings of illegality, substantive review, and procedural impropriety, they overlap with one another and are joined by a number of important constitutional and juridical considerations. Principal among these is a judicial emphasis on the constitutional importance of judicial review and the need to safeguard the supervisory jurisdiction of the courts in the face of, most famously, ouster clauses. But there are other considerations too, for instance of the need for judicial review to be 'context sensitive' and guided by judicial restraint in appropriate cases. The chapter thus surveys a number of corresponding concepts and doctrines that are used by the courts, for instance (non)-justiciability, reviewability, deference, and 'soft-edged' review (which has been key to case law arising from the implementation of the Belfast Agreement). The chapter also considers a number of other

---

[1] [2007] 3 WLR 112.
[2] [2007] 1 AC 650.

issues that are central to the workings of the grounds, namely, the relationship between statutory powers, duties, and discretion, and the importance of 'error of law' and 'error of fact'.

Chapter five provides an analysis of 'Illegality' as a ground for review. It begins by returning to the theme of 'constitutional statutes' and considers the obligations that follow from the European Communities Act 1972, the Human Rights Act 1998, and the Northern Ireland Act 1998. The analysis here focuses not just on what the Acts entail for 'public authorities' (the term is used in the Northern Ireland Act and the Human Rights Act), but also on the implications that they have for primary legislation enacted at Westminster and in the Northern Ireland Assembly. This, in turn, raises interesting constitutional questions about the status of Acts of the Assembly, and the chapter points to literature and authority on the sustainability (or otherwise) of the orthodox understanding that Acts of the Assembly are 'subordinate' legislation. The chapter thereafter analyses the requirements of legality that govern subordinate legislation within its more conventional meaning; and it finally considers challenges to exercises of administrative discretion, whether made on the basis of the 'constitutional statutes' or with reference to the common law headings of 'relevancy', 'propriety of purpose', 'bad faith', 'non-delegation of power', and 'non-fettering of discretion'.

The sixth chapter is titled 'Substantive Review: *Wednesbury*, Proportionality, Legitimate Expectation, Equality'. In many respects, this is the ground for review that has seen most development in recent years, as the standard of *Wednesbury* review has been supplemented (query supplanted) by other, more intrusive grounds for review. This has resulted in difficult questions about the separation of powers doctrine both as relates to the review of administrative decisions and the legislative choices of the Northern Ireland Assembly and, in the context of the European Communities Act 1972 and Human Rights 1998, of the Westminster Parliament. In short, the proportionality principle—which applies in cases under the Acts of 1972 and 1998—can require courts to assess whether decisions and legislative measures have struck an appropriate balance between the objective pursued by the decision or measure and the interests affected. However, the courts in Northern Ireland have historically tended not to engage in such 'closer look' review (the point took form around the *Wednesbury* principle), and the emergence of proportionality has thereby required the courts to reassess how best to exhibit self-restraint in cases under the Acts of 1972 and 1998. The chapter thus explains how proportionality review is now often linked to a 'discretionary area of judgment' doctrine that is informed by separation of powers considerations and which has an added prominence when challenges are made to legislative choices. The chapter likewise chronicles how the more intrusive judicial scrutiny that is (potentially) associated with legitimate expectation and equality has been tempered by separation of powers concerns, as *Wednesbury* unreasonableness continues to play an (admittedly diminishing) role in cases outside the European Communities Act 1972 and Human Rights Act 1998.

'Procedural Impropriety' as a ground for review is then examined in chapter seven, which surveys the importance of procedural requirements in statute, the common law rules of fairness (the 'right to a hearing' and the 'rule against bias'), and Article 6 ECHR. The analysis here emphasises how each of these aspects of the ground can interact with one another, albeit that the interaction can sometimes be problematic. For instance, difficulties have arisen in the context of Article 6 ECHR's requirement that determinations about 'civil rights and obligations' be made by 'independent and impartial tribunals' that have 'full jurisdiction' in the matters before them. In respect of judicial review, the problem has concerned the reach of the grounds for review when an individual challenges the determination of a decision-maker who has not satisfied the requirements of Article 6 ECHR but where proceedings in the High Court may be able to ensure 'composite' compliance. The House of Lords and Northern Ireland courts have here emphasised that 'full jurisdiction' is a context dependent requirement and that it may not be necessary for a reviewing court to hear a full appeal in all cases; and it has also been emphasised that, although judicial review does not consider the merits of a decision, there remains a wide range of arguments that might be made even within the traditional grounds for review. On the other hand, it is recognised that judicial review may not be sufficient in some cases precisely because the courts cannot, among other things, reach their own conclusions on disputed questions of fact or substitute their decisions for those of the original decision-maker. This is, therefore, one area in which further development of the law may be necessary.

The final chapter addresses 'Remedies'. The starting point here, as with that in chapter 3, is the Northern Ireland specific legislation that governs judicial review and its remedies, as elaborated upon in the courts. However, the chapter also analyses EU law's remedies regime and that of the Human Rights Act 1998, which are underwritten by requirements of the effective protection of the individual. In this context, the chapter highlights how the effectiveness principle has implications for the discretionary nature of the remedies, for instance where EU law's supremacy doctrine requires that national rules or practices cede to the need to uphold EU law rights. In a different vein, the chapter discusses how the Human Rights Act 1998 is underscored by the doctrine of legislative supremacy, and how this entails that some of its remedies—specifically the declaration of incompatibility—have no formal legal effect. Finally, the chapter surveys the existing case law on damages under the Act, which has pointed towards a narrow approach that is at one with much of the more general domestic approach to damages actions against public authorities.

In terms of the layout and structure of the book, there are four further points that should be made. The first concerns the use of the language of 'constitutional statutes' in a number of chapters. Although the language may not enjoy universal support—some judges have expressed doubts about use of such a potentially open-ended term[3]—it has been integrated into the book because it provides an analytical framework that corresponds with the fact that the Acts have effected fundamental changes in the workings of judicial review. That change has, of course, followed in large part from a resulting judicial reinvention of common law principles and techniques, and case law under the Acts is therefore rightly regarded as having redefined relations both as between the individual and the State and as between the branches of the State (albeit that the Acts can still be expressly repealed or, as the enactment of the [now repealed] Northern Ireland Act 2000 attests, suspended). By using the term, the book thus merely borrows from the wording of some cases in which the courts have emphasised that the Acts enshrine certain values and obligations that the common law regards as particularly important (although the open question thereafter is what the courts might do in the event that Parliament purports to set the values aside). Use of the term also resonates with more general debates about the nature of devolution and the status of Acts made 'beneath' the level of

---

[3] Eg, *Watkins v Home Office* [2006] AC 395, 418–20, paras 58–64, Lord Rodger.

Westminster, as these debates now have an added significance in post-St Andrews Northern Ireland.

The second point concerns related academic discourse about developments in judicial review. Although the chapters incorporate references to academic literature, the book does not engage more fully with broader academic debates about common law developments in the United Kingdom as a whole or in the more particular context of Northern Ireland. This, at one level, is consonant with the fact that the book has been written primarily for practitioners, for whom broader debates may be of interest but perhaps of less immediate practical importance. However, the doctrinal analysis in this book does, at the same time, tell only one part of the story of judicial review in Northern Ireland, and there are many wider and important themes about democracy, transition and human rights. Those with an interest in those themes should consult the growing body of literature that critiques many of the legal developments analysed here.[4]

The third point is definitional and concerns the book's use of the terms 'decision-maker' and 'public authority'. In Northern Ireland, as elsewhere in the United Kingdom, the nature of public service delivery has changed fundamentally in recent years (privatisation, contracting-out, etc), and it is acknowledged that some private bodies also

---

[4] Some of the more recent contributions on Northern Ireland include: G Anthony, 'The St Andrews Agreement and the Northern Ireland Assembly' (2008) 14 EPL (forthcoming); M Requa, 'Truth, Transition, and the Inquiries Act 2005' (2007) EHRLR 404; J Morison, K McEvoy, and G Anthony (eds), *Judges, Transition and Human Rights: Essays in Memory of Stephen Livingstone* (Oxford, Oxford University Press, 2007); C McCrudden, 'Northern Ireland and the British Constitution since the Belfast Agreement' in J Jowell and D Oliver (eds), *The Changing Constitution*, Oxford University Press, 5th edn (Oxford, Oxford University Press, 2007) p 227; M Cox, A Guelke and F Stephen (eds) *A Farewell to Arms? Beyond the Good Friday Agreement*, 2nd edn (Manchester, Manchester University Press, 2006); B Dickson, 'The Northern Ireland Conflict and the House of Lords—A Sequel' (2006) 69 MLR 383; G Anthony, 'Human Rights in Northern Ireland after *In Re McKerr*' (2005) 11 EPL 5; G Anthony and J Morison, 'Here, There, and (Maybe) Here Again: The Story of Law-making for Post-1998 Northern Ireland' in R Hazell and R Rawlings (eds), *Devolution Law Making and the Constitution* (Exeter, Imprint-Academic, 2005) p 155; K McEvoy and J Morison, 'Beyond the 'Constitutional Moment': Law, Transition, and Peacemaking in Northern Ireland' (2003) 26 *Fordham International Law Journal* 961; B Hadfield, 'Does the Devolved Northern Ireland Need an Independent Judicial Arbiter?' in N Bamforth and P Leyland (eds), *Public Law in a Multi-Layered Constitution* (Oxford, Hart Publishing, 2003), p 133; C Campbell, F Ni Aolain, and C Harvey, 'The Frontiers of Legal Analysis: Reframing the Transition in Northern Ireland' (2003) 66 MLR 317; A Smith, 'Access to Intervene: The Northern Ireland Human Rights Commission and the Northern Ireland Act 1998' (2003) EHRLR 423; M Lynch, '*Robinson v Secretary of State for Northern Ireland*: Interpreting Constitutional Legislation' (2003) PL 640; F Ni Aolain, 'Truth Telling, Accountability and the Right to Life in Northern Ireland' (2002) 5 EHRLR 572; G Anthony, 'Public Law Litigation and the Belfast Agreement' (2002) 8 EPL 401; J Morison, 'Democracy, Governance and Governmentality: Civic Public Space and Constitutional Renewal in Northern Ireland' (2001) 21 OJLS 287; C Harvey (ed), *Human Rights, Equality and Democratic Renewal in Northern Ireland* (Oxford, Hart Publishing, 2001); C Harvey, 'The Politics of Rights and Deliberative Democracy: The Process of Drafting a Northern Irish Bill of Rights' (2001) EHRLR 48; R Wilford (ed), *Aspects of the Belfast Agreement* (Oxford, Oxford University Press, 2001); S Livingstone, 'The Northern Ireland Human Rights Commission' (1999) 22 *Fordham International Law Journal* 1465; S Livingstone and C Harvey, 'Human Rights and the Northern Ireland Peace Process' (1999) EHRLR 162; J Morison and S Livingstone, *Reshaping Public Power: Northern Ireland and the British Constitutional Crisis* (London, Sweet & Maxwell, 1995); S Livingstone, 'The Northern Ireland Conflict and the House of Lords' (1994) 57 MLR 333; and B Hadfield, *The Constitution of Northern Ireland* (Belfast, SLS Legal Publications, 1989). And for some of the leading contributions on developments in judicial review in England and Wales and the UK more generally see, eg, JWF Allison, *The English Historical Constitution: Continuity, Change, and European Effects* (Cambridge, Cambridge University Press, 2007); A Tomkins, *Public Law* (Oxford, Clarendon Press, 2005); M Elliott, 'Embracing "Constitutional" Legislation: Towards Fundamental Law?' (2003) 54 NILQ 25; P Craig, *Administrative Law*, 5th edn (London, Sweet and Maxwell, 2003) ch 1; CF Forsyth (ed) *Judicial Review and the Constitution* (Oxford, Hart Publishing, 2000); M Elliott, *The Constitutional Foundations of Judicial Review* (Oxford, Hart Publishing, 2000); and M Hunt, *Using Human Rights Law in English Courts* (Oxford, Hart Publishing, 1997).

exercise public law powers because of accidents of history. However, while this has led the courts to develop new tests on the reach of judicial review (considered in chapter two), the clear majority of judicial review case law is concerned with challenges to the exercise of statutory powers and/or the performance of statutory duties by government Ministers and departments, local authorities, and a variety of statutory bodies. Where the book refers in general terms to 'decision-makers' and 'public authorities', it is thus to be read as referring collectively to those decision-makers that are working within the framework of statute, notwithstanding that there may be constitutional distinctions between them. This approach has been preferred simply because the principles of law that govern the exercise of statutory powers and so on start from a common position and often apply equally, that is, irrespective of the decision-maker or authority at hand. However, where more detail on the nature of a decision-maker is required—whether for reasons of the facts of specific cases, for reasons of identifying other 'public authorities' in the modern polity, or where a constitutional distinction is of importance—the approach in the text is modified. The text is also more specific when dealing with case law on the decisions of lower courts, the Northern Ireland Assembly, and the Westminster Parliament.

Point four is likewise definitional, and concerns abstract references to applicants as 'he' or 'she' throughout the book. Applicants may, of course, include other legal personalities such as companies and local authorities, and the fuller abstraction should perhaps read 'he/she/it'. However, consistent with the more general desire not to encumber the text, the book uses 'he' or 'she' for purposes of convenience. 'It' is thus to be found between the lines.

Finally, the book has endeavoured to state the law as of 30 November 2007.

Acknowledgements

I owe a debt of gratitude to many people who, in different ways, have helped me complete this book. At university, I wish to thank Dr Dimitrios Doukas, Professor Colin Harvey, Professor John Jackson, Professor Peter Leyland, Professor Kieran McEvoy, Professor John Morison, Professor George Pavlakos, Professor Sharon Turner, Professor Sally Wheeler and Professor Tom Zwart. Particular thanks are due to Dr Jack Anderson and Professor Brice Dickson, who willingly read chapters and offered insightful and excellent comments. Remaining errors are mine.

I have also benefited greatly from the interest and generosity of members of the legal profession and of the bench. Paul Maguire QC kindly read the chapters on procedure and gave valuable advice (errors, again, are mine); and Noelle McGrenera QC and John O'Hara QC helped enormously in raising the profile of the book. The Judge-in-Residence programme at Queen's gave me unique access to members of the bench in Northern Ireland, and I wish to thank the Honourable Mr Justice Morgan and the Honourable Mr Justice Weatherup for their willingness to answer my queries. Of course, the greatest debt in this context is owed to the Lord Chief Justice of Northern Ireland, the Right Honourable Sir Brian Kerr, who kindly agreed to write the foreword for the book.

At Hart Publishing, I wish to thank Richard for giving me the chance to publish the book and for being so encouraging when doing so—he is always a pleasure to work with. Mel Hamill too was friendly, brilliantly efficient and patient, and I thank her warmly. Thanks are due to Jo Ledger for the same reasons.

Finally, I want to thank my wife Jill and our children, Emily, Louis, Ben and Toby, for all their care and consideration as I worked the book through to completion. The book is dedicated to them.

Gordon Anthony
November 2007

Contents

4. The Grounds for Review Introduced

5. Illegality

6. Substantive Review: *Wednesbury*, Proportionality, Legitimate Expectation, Equality

7. Procedural Impropriety

8. Remedies

Table of Cases

References are to paragraph numbers

UNITED KINGDOM

Northern Ireland

England and Wales

Scotland

COMMONWEALTH AND OTHER JURISDICTIONS

Antigua and Barbuda

Australia

Belize

Canada

EUROPEAN COURT OF HUMAN RIGHTS

Table of Statutes

References are to paragraph numbers

ACTS OF THE NORTHERN IRELAND PARLIAMENT AND NORTHERN
IRELAND ASSEMBLY; ORDERS IN COUNCIL MADE UNDER THE NORTHERN
IRELAND (TEMPORARY PROVISIONS) ACT 1972, THE NORTHERN IRELAND
ACT 1974, AND THE NORTHERN IRELAND ACT 2000

(On the constitutional status of Acts and Orders see [5.23]–[5.24])

Table of Statutory Rules and Statutory Instruments

References are to paragraph numbers

STATUTORY RULES

STATUTORY INSTRUMENTS

Table of International Treaties

References are to paragraph numbers

Table of Abbreviations

NIHRC	Northern Ireland Human Rights Commission
NIJB	Northern Ireland Judgments Bulletin
NILQ	*Northern Ireland Legal Quarterly*
NIQB	Northern Ireland Queen's Bench
NZLR	New Zealand Law Reports
OJLS	Oxford Journal of Legal Studies
PL	*Public Law*
PPS	Public Prosecution Service
PSNI	Police Service of Northern Ireland
QB	Queen's Bench Law Reports
RSC	Rules of the Supreme Court
RUC	Royal Ulster Constabulary
SC	Session Cases
SCR	Supreme Court Reports, Canada
SI	Statutory Instrument
SR	Statutory Rules
STC	Simon's Tax Cases
UKHL	United Kingdom House of Lords
UKHRR	United Kingdom Human Rights Reports
WLR	Weekly Law Reports

1

Judicial Review in Northern Ireland: Purposes, Sources of Law, and Constitutional Context

INTRODUCTION

[1.01]   This chapter provides an overview of the purposes of judicial review in Northern Ireland and of the constitutional doctrines and juridical techniques that underpin its development. The essentially dynamic nature of judicial review—the number of applications continues to grow and to bring forward new principles and practice[1]—is largely a function of judicial elaboration of the common law and of canons of statutory interpretation. Use of the common law and interpretive techniques has, moreover, increasingly been influenced by the demands of European Union (EU) law and the European Convention on Human Rights (ECHR) (as read with the European Communities Act 1972 and the Human Rights Act 1998 respectively) and judicial review now performs an ever more important constitutional function. This chapter thus identifies how elaboration of the common law and interpretive techniques takes form in practice and how European law is adding to that evolutionary process. Links are also made between points in this chapter and more specific developments in judicial review, as analysed in subsequent chapters.

[1.02]   The chapter begins with a section that defines judicial review and notes some of the purposes served by the corresponding procedure.[2] It next divides into three sections: the first lists the principal sources of law (viz, statute law, the common law, EU law, the ECHR, and international law) and considers judicial attitudes to them; the second considers the importance of different methods of statutory interpretation; and the third discusses the significance of common law 'constitutional statutes' (which have recently been recognised in case law in England and Wales and which have already had some impact in Northern Ireland). The conclusion offers a summary of the key points made.

[1.03]   One further point by way of introduction concerns the fact that the development of the principle and practice of judicial review often occurs against a backdrop of differing/competing judicial perspectives on the constitutional role of the courts. Applications for judicial review frequently raise the question of how far—if at all—courts should scrutinise the substantive choices of public authorities that the legislature has entrusted

---

[1] Statistics on applications for judicial review are available at http://www.courtsni.gov.uk/en-GB/Services/Statistics+and+Research/.
[2] On which see ch 3.

with a decision-making power or duty.[3] While developments in judicial review have resulted in new principles that clearly have increased the scope for judicial invigilation of decision-making processes and outcomes, judicial review remains wedded to an historical 'review, not appeal' distinction that permits the courts to assess only the legality of decisions and not their merits[4] (see [1.05]). This distinction is, in turn, founded upon the separation of powers doctrine which requires that courts should neither legislate in the place of the legislature nor interfere with the lawful discretionary choices of executive and administrative decision-makers (the legislature and subordinate decision-makers likewise should not interfere with the judicial role).[5] The wider body of judicial review case law is, in consequence, sometimes characterised by divergences in judicial opinion about the limits to legitimate development of public law principle and practice and about the importance of the separation of powers doctrine (the corresponding debate is essentially about 'judicial activism' vs 'judicial self-restraint'[6]). The juridical techniques and so on considered in this chapter should therefore not be read as prescriptive and of uniform application, but rather as the (disputed) outer markers within which judicial review develops.

WHAT IS JUDICIAL REVIEW, AND WHAT ARE ITS PURPOSES?

[**1.04**] Judicial review can be defined as the procedure through which the High Court supervises the public law actions and inactions of public authorities and other bodies that are exercising statutory powers, performing public duties, and/or taking decisions on matters of public interest.[7] A slightly different—though equally valid—definition is that judicial review is the process by which the High Court exercises its supervisory jurisdiction over the public law decisions, acts, failures to act, and other measures of inferior bodies and tribunals that are performing public functions (the High Court itself is not amenable to review[8]). Although each definition begs the difficult question of how to distinguish 'public law' from 'private law',[9] they encapsulate the understanding that judicial review is the primary means through which the courts can supervise the exercise of public powers and the performance of public duties. Moreover, the use of the terms 'matters of public interest' and 'public functions' reflects the fact that judicial review has developed to embrace powers and duties that were previously considered beyond the supervisory jurisdiction of the courts (or at least potentially so). Judicial review in the UK was historically synonymous with the ultra vires doctrine that regarded all public law powers and duties as statutory in origin and as constrained by the intentions of the legis-

---

[3] Although it is not only the decisions etc of recipients of statutory powers/duties that are amenable to judicial review: see ch 2; and [4.06]–[4.08].

[4] See, eg, *R v Secretary of State for Northern Ireland, ex p Finlay* [1983] 9 NIJB 1, 10, Hutton J; *Re Glor Na nGael's Application* [1991] NI 117, 129, Carswell J; and *Re Bow Street Mall's Application* [2006] NIQB 28, para 110 [sic], Girvan J.

[5] For a recent judicial statement of the importance of the separation of powers doctrine see *R (Anderson) v Secretary of State for the Home Department* [2003] 1 AC 837, 886, para 39, Lord Steyn.

[6] See *Department for Social Development v MacGeagh* [2006] NI 125, 136–8, paras 32–6, Kerr LCJ, surveying judicial statements about the limits to the judicial role; and see CF Forsyth (ed), *Judicial Review and the Constitution* (Oxford, Hart Publishing, 2000).

[7] *Re Wylie's Application* [2005] NI 359, 362, para 7.

[8] *Re Weir & Higgins' Application* [1988] NI 338, 351. On the range of reviewable measures see [3.05]–[3.08].

[9] See ch 2.

lature/language of the statute (see [1.12]).[10] However, while a majority of powers and duties could, and still can, be traced to statute, historical realities (the royal prerogative[11] and private monopolies of public resources[12]) and changes in modes of government (privatisation, contracting out, etc[13]) meant that there were various non-statutory powers that were potentially outwith the supervisory jurisdiction of the High Court. The terms 'matters of public interest'[14] and 'public functions'[15] (among others) have thus been used by the courts to describe non-statutory decisions that are taken to sound in public law and, for that reason, to be amenable to review.

[1.05]   Notwithstanding the wide range of decisions and other measures that are now subject to judicial review, the courts often state that their role in review proceedings is not to examine the 'merits' of a decision or other measure under challenge, but rather to scrutinise the fairness of the procedure by which it was reached and/or whether the decision is lawful.[16] This emphasis on 'review, not appeal' has long been central to the constitutional justification for judicial review and it takes form in judicial approaches to the grounds for review[17] and in the nature of the remedies that are available.[18] For instance, where a court or tribunal is hearing a full appeal in a matter it may reassess all matters of law and fact and substitute its own decision for that of the original decision-maker. This is in sharp contrast to judicial review proceedings, where there has historically been only limited scope for judicial intervention on questions of fact[19] and where the available remedies reflect upon the imperative of judicial self-restraint.[20] Although much ultimately depends upon the context to a dispute (for instance, whether a dispute engages fundamental rights), the courts in review proceedings start from the premise that they should not take decisions in the place of other bodies that the legislature has entrusted with a particular decision-making power (viz, the 'separation of powers' doctrine: see [1.03]).[21] In terms of questions of fact—for instance, how much weight should be given to a consideration and for which reason—the courts have thus traditionally stated that these relate more to the merits of the decision and that judicial intervention is permissible only where the corresponding decision is 'unreasonable' or where fundamental rights are in issue.[22] The corresponding remedies are likewise consonant with the understanding that courts should not usurp decision-making powers, as the courts cannot, in general, substitute their own findings for those of the original decision-maker[23]

---

[10] See [2.07], and [1.04] [1.05]

[11] [4.06]–[4.08].

[12] *Re Kirkpatrick's Application* [2004] NIJB 15 and *Re Wylie's Application* [2005] NI 359 (Fishermen's Co-operative Society with exclusive power to grant licences for eel fishing on Lough Neagh); and see [2.15].

[13] Ch 2.

[14] *Re McBride's Application* [1999] NI 299, 310, Kerr J.

[15] *Re Sherlock and Morris' Application* [1996] NIJB 80, 86–7; and *R v Panel on Take-overs and Mergers, ex p Datafin* [1987] QB 815.

[16] See, eg, *R v Secretary of State for Northern Ireland, ex p Finlay* [1983] 9 NIJB 1, 10, Hutton J; *Re Glor Na nGael's Application* [1991] NI 117, 129, Carswell J; and *Re Bow Street Mall's Application* [2006] NIQB 28, para 110 [sic], Girvan J.

[17] See chs 4–7.

[18] See ch 8.

[19] [4.36]–[4.44].

[20] [8.10]–[8.31].

[21] *Re Doherty's Application (No 2)* [1995] NI 144, 152, citing *R v Secretary of State for the Home Department, ex p Brind* [1991] 1 AC 696, 757–8, Lord Ackner.

[22] [6.05]–[6.11].

[23] But see too Judicature (Northern Ireland) Act 1978, s 21; and [8.15].

but can instead (and among other things) require the decision-maker to retake its decision in the light of the judgment of the court.[24]

[**1.06**]   The corresponding purposes of judicial review are often linked to the imperatives of ensuring efficiency in public decision-making processes and protecting individuals in the face of those processes. While the 'efficiency' and 'protection' imperatives need not be regarded as mutually exclusive, they can nevertheless be associated with different rationales for the principle and practice of judicial review. For instance, an emphasis on efficiency in decision-making will be underwritten by an understanding that the public at large benefits when decision-makers who are providing public services and other goods are subject to only minimal judicial invigilation and where the corresponding grounds for judicial review are not unduly intrusive. In this model, public decision-makers can thus carry out the business of government more efficiently and effectively as their decisions, once taken, can be interfered with by the courts only within closely and clearly defined parameters. On the other hand, an emphasis on the protection of the individual highlights how the public at large benefits when individuals are able, as a matter of priority, to vindicate their interests in the face of the actions or inactions of public authorities. While this does not mean that individuals can expect their interests automatically to trump those of the wider public, the essential role of judicial review here is to protect the individual by controlling those exercises of public power that impact upon the individual's interests. In this model, the parameters within which a judicial review challenge can be made to a decision or other measure would therefore be drawn more widely.

[**1.07**]   Statements to the effect that the public at large benefits when decisions may be challenged only within very specific parameters can be found in *dicta* about some of the procedural requirements that govern applications for judicial review. The requirements—contained in sections 18–25 of the Judicature (Northern Ireland) Act 1978 and RSC Order 53 (as amended[25])—are intended to ensure heightened degrees of certainty and efficiency in public decision-making by permitting challenges to decisions only where the applicant has, among other things, made the application 'promptly and in any event within three months'.[26] Although the period of three months can be extended where the court considers that 'there is good reason' for doing so,[27] emphasis has often been put on the point that applications should be made *promptly* and that they risk being dismissed for delay even if made within the three-month period.[28] The underlying rationale here is simply that the overall process of public decision-making benefits from legal certainty when potentially disruptive challenges to decisions are prohibited after a set period of time (the disruption being taken as counter to the wider public interest in 'good administration'[29]). There is thus a corresponding presumption of legality in respect of decisions that are taken but not challenged timeously in the sense that the decisions are thereafter deemed to be valid.[30]

---

[24]   See ch 8.

[25]   SR 1982/217; SR 1984/354; SR 1989/289; SR 1993/143.

[26]   RSC Ord 53, r 4; and see Lord Woolf, *Protection of the Public—A New Challenge* (Steven and Sons, London, 1990) pp 12–15.

[27]   RSC Ord 53, r 4; and see [3.27]–[3.29].

[28]   See, eg, *Re Shearer's Application* [1993] 2 NIJB 12; and *Re McCabe's Application* [1994] NIJB 27.

[29]   *Re Wadsworth's Application* [2004] NIQB 8, para 8.

[30]   See, eg, *Re Croft's Application* [1997] NI 457, 489, Girvan J; and *Re Foster's Application* [2004] NI 248, 264, Kerr J.

[**1.08**] Judicial statements about the value of protecting the interests of individuals fasten, in contrast, upon the need to constrain actual and potential abuses of power. This concern has underscored the emergence of new 'root concepts'[31] of the common law that have their origins in, among other things, the age-old concept of 'fairness'. Fairness is an open-textured, malleable concept and this allows it be used creatively by the courts as they develop and reinvent the grounds for judicial review.[32] Perhaps the best example of such use of the concept in recent years has been in respect of substantive legitimate expectations.[33] The doctrine of substantive legitimate expectation entails, at its most basic, that a public authority may not resile from a clear and unambiguous representation made to an individual where the individual has, on the basis of the representation, developed a reasonable expectation that they will receive or continue to receive some substantive benefit.[34] While the applicant's expectation must be set against considerations of the wider public interest in allowing the authority to depart from its policies or representations, the key question for the courts is whether fairness requires that the individual's expectation be upheld.[35] This, in turn, is a question that potentially involves the courts in 'closer look' review of a kind that some regard as constitutionally problematic.[36] Nevertheless, the courts have accepted that substantive legitimate expectation is now both a central doctrine in public law and an important counterweight to the 'abuse of power' by decision-makers.[37]

[**1.09**] Concern for the protection of the individual may then be at its most pronounced when fundamental rights are affected by a decision or a failure to act. Fundamental rights standards are those that are found in the common law, the ECHR (as read with the Human Rights Act 1998), and EU law, although unincorporated international human rights standards may also be of relevance where courts take them into account as 'soft law' measures or as correlates of the common law.[38] The key point in respect of such rights is that their protection can *perforce* require courts to look more closely at the justification for decisions and, where appropriate, to modify procedure and remedies.[39] While the courts will again seek to balance the individual's rights against wider conceptions of the public interest when qualified rights are in issue, there remain some rights—such as the right to life—that are in theory absolute and inviolable.[40] When those rights are in issue, it has been said that judicial review should provide for the most 'anxious scrutiny'

---

[31] *R v Department of Education and Employment, ex p Begbie* [2000] 1 WLR 1115, 1129, Laws LJ; and see [4.04]–[4.05].

[32] See chs 4–7.

[33] See [6.29]–[6.45].

[34] On legitimate expectation and its multiple forms see S Schøenberg, *Legitimate Expectations in Administrative Law* (Oxford, Oxford University Press, 2000).

[35] See *Re Neale's Application* [2005] NIQB 33.

[36] M Elliott, 'Coughlan: Substantive Protection of Legitimate Expectations Revisited' (2000) 5 *Judicial Review* 27.

[37] *R v North and East Devon Heath Authority, ex p Coughlan* [2000] 2 WLR 622, 645; and *Re Morrow and Campbell's Application* [2002] NIQB 4.

[38] *Re Adams' Application* [2001] NI 1, 24.

[39] See *Tweed v Parades Commission for Northern Ireland* [2007] 1 AC 650 (previously restrictive approach to discovery may not be appropriate in cases under the Human Rights Act 1998). See further [3.48]–[3.54].

[40] Although the position can become more complex: see, eg, *Re Scappaticci's Application* [2003] NIQB 40 (applicant challenging, as contrary to Art 2 ECHR, a government Minister's refusal to confirm or deny whether a former IRA member who was named as a British agent had been an agent: application dismissed, there had been no over-rigid adherence to the government policy of refusing to confirm or deny).

of decision-making processes and outcomes.[41] Considerations of the constitutional limits to the judicial role may therefore be different here than in other circumstances.[42]

[**1.10**]   Emphases on the interests of the decision-maker or the individual should not, however, be regarded as mutually exclusive. Both reference points arguably reduce to the proposition that the public at large benefits from the highest standards of decision-making, and they can to that extent be regarded as more complementary in form than competing. The significance in the different constitutional justifications for judicial review therefore lies not in their capacity to offer an 'either/or' rationalisation for every judicial decision (they cannot do so), but rather in the fact that they posit more or less judicial intervention in the decision-making process as the means to improve that process. An emphasis on courts safeguarding the interests of the decision-maker through the strict observation of procedural requirements would, for example, suggest that the courts should thereafter remain at the outer reaches of the substantive decision-making process and not become involved in assessing the merits of discretionary choices. But where courts focus on the interests of individuals, this would suggest less rigidity in respect of procedural requirements[43] and—as can be seen most obviously in the human rights context—closer look review.[44] The central—and overall—challenge for the courts is thus to decide how best to strike the balance between more or less intervention on a case-by-case basis.

SOURCES OF LAW

[**1.11**]   The principal sources of law of potential relevance in judicial review proceedings are: statute law (primary and subordinate); the common law (including jurisprudence from other common law systems); EU law; the ECHR; and unincorporated international treaties and customary international law. Judicial receptiveness to arguments developed with reference to these sources of law will, in turn, be crucially affected by understandings of the constitutional role of the courts and of, for instance, the relationship between UK domestic law and international law (see further [1.23]). Levels of receptiveness will often also determine the extent of any judicial intervention in administrative decision-making processes and outcomes.

Statute Law

[**1.12**]   Statute law—which is central to virtually all judicial review applications[45]—has historically been synonymous with the ultra vires doctrine whereby courts review the decisions, acts, failures to act, and other measures of public decision-makers for compli-

---

[41]   The phrase is Lord Bridge's: see *Bugdaycay v Secretary of State for the Home Department* [1987] AC 514, 531.

[42]   But see, eg, *Re A's Application* [2001] NI 335 (High Court would not order the Chief Constable of the (then) Royal Ulster Constabulary (RUC) to disclose information about ongoing inquiries into a threat to the applicant's life as the decision-maker here enjoyed an area of discretion). On the significance of the area of discretion doctrine, alternatively called the 'discretionary area of judgment' doctrine, see [6.25]–[6.26].

[43]   See, eg, *Re McBride's Application* [1999] NI 299 (on standing). On standing more generally see [3.64]–[3.66].

[44]   *Re T's Application* [2000] NI 516.

[45]   See [2.07].

ance with the primary legislation that delegates power to them or imposes a public duty to act.[46] The doctrine has its origins in understandings of the Westminster Parliament as the sovereign source of law in the UK and in that context it links judicial review to the control of decision-making processes/outcomes in the light of the sovereign legislature's intentions (the doctrine on this basis excludes judicial review of Acts of the Westminster Parliament[47]). The courts' control function is, however, here constrained by the separation of powers doctrine, as the courts recognise that Parliament has delegated power—which can include the power to make subordinate legislation—to the recipient authority and not to the courts. This means that the courts will not assess the merits of a discretionary choice—viz the historical distinction between review and appeal[48] (see [1.03] and [1.05])—and that applications for judicial review will typically be successful only where there has been a breach of procedure or a failure to observe the legal limits of the power.[49] Any scope for substantive review is, from this historical perspective, limited to that set by the standard of *Wednesbury* unreasonableness: was the decision or other measure 'so unreasonable that no reasonable authority could ever have come to it'?[50]

[1.13] Northern Ireland statute law is made both by the Westminster Parliament and by the Northern Ireland Assembly (when the Assembly was suspended at different times between 2000 and 2007 matters that fell within its competence were instead legislated for by Order in Council[51]). While this means that decisions or other measures of public bodies may be challenged on the ground that they are ultra vires the Acts of either legislature, it does not also mean that Acts of the two institutions are constitutionally equivalent. UK constitutional orthodoxy regards the Northern Ireland Assembly as a recipient of power rather than a sovereign institution,[52] and Acts of the Northern Ireland Assembly may be challenged as ultra vires the Northern Ireland Act 1998[53] (such challenges give rise to 'devolution issues' that must be resolved in the light of the procedural requirements specified in the Northern Ireland Act 1998[54]). Orthodox understandings of the nature of the Assembly and the Belfast Agreement that founded it have in turn been much criticised,[55]

---

[46] On the range of reviewable measures see [3.05]–[3.08].

[47] *Madzimbamuto v Lardner-Burke* [1969] 1 AC 645, 723, Lord Reid. But note the exception in respect of EU law: *R v Secretary of State for Transport, ex p Factortame Ltd (No 2)* [1991] 1 AC 603. And see [4.09] and [5.06]–[5.07].

[48] *R v Secretary of State for Northern Ireland, ex p Finlay* [1983] 9 NIJB 1, 10, Hutton J; *Re Glor Na nGael's Application* [1991] NI 117, 129, Carswell J; and *Re Bow Street Mall's Application* [2006] NIQB 28, para 110 [sic], Girvan J.

[49] On which see further chs 5 and 7.

[50] *Associated Provincial Picture Houses v Wednesbury Corporation* [1948] 1 KB 223, 230, Lord Greene MR. See further [6.05]–[6.11].

[51] Northern Ireland Act 2000, repealed by Northern Ireland (St Andrews Agreement) Act 2006 and Northern Ireland (St Andrews Agreement) Act 2007.

[52] Northern Ireland Act 1998, s 5(6).

[53] Northern Ireland Act 1998, s 6. See further [3.07] and [5.23]–[5.24], and, eg, *Re Landlords Association for Northern Ireland's Application* [2006] NI 16, challenging successfully the compatibility of the Housing (Northern Ireland) Order 2003 with the ECHR (the Order [SI 2003/412] had originally been introduced as a Bill in the Assembly and was carried over as an Order in Council under the Northern Ireland Act 2000).

[54] Northern Ireland Act 1998, Sch 10, and RSC Ord 120; and, eg, *Re Neill's Application* [2005] NIQB 66, [2006] NICA 5. And note that devolution issues can also arise in respect of Statutory Rules and of the acts of Northern Ireland Ministers and/or Northern Ireland Departments: sch 10 and RSC Ord 120, as read with s 24. See further [5.25]–[5.27].

[55] See C Harvey (ed), *Human Rights, Equality and Democratic Renewal in Northern Ireland* (Oxford, Hart Publishing, 2001).

and there are judicial dicta to cast doubt on the long-term relevance of that orthodoxy[56] (see [1.28]–[1.34]). However, in the absence of a devolution dispute concerned with the question of legislative competence it remains to be seen whether those dicta will become central to future judicial decision-making.[57]

The Common Law

[**1.14**]   The common law is inherently dynamic and underlies developments not just in judicial review but also across the full range of areas of public law and private law.[58] Its use in the specific context of judicial review has, however, led to the argument that the role of the courts cannot be conceived of solely in terms of the courts giving effect to the intentions of Parliament (see [1.12]).[59] The point here is simply that the courts have always used the common law creatively; that it is only the courts that can use the common law in this way; and that the development of judicial review on the basis of the common law therefore occurs independently of the intentions of Parliament. Such arguments, which draw on the historical fact that the courts' supervisory jurisdiction rested in the common law (the corresponding procedure is now contained in legislation[60]), have, in turn, proved controversial. The most obvious criticism has been that an emphasis on judicial use of the common law challenges the UK constitution's core precept of legislative supremacy by suggesting that the development of the law can occur beyond that which is expressly or impliedly authorised by Parliament.[61] Proponents of the importance of the common law nevertheless remain unconvinced, arguing that it is fictitious to relate the judge-led method of the common law to the express or implied intentions of the legislature.[62] They moreover argue that ultimate legislative sovereignty remains unaffected insofar as the legislature—here the Westminster Parliament (query the Northern Ireland Assembly too[63])—can legislate to override any judge-led development of the law that is deemed problematic.[64]

[**1.15**]   The area in which judicial use of the common law has been most apparent in the present context is that concerned with general principles of law and the grounds for judicial review.[65] It has long been recognised that the grounds for review are common law creations that determine how closely, and for which reasons, the courts will supervise public law decisions and other measures. The grounds are typically classified under the

---

[56] *Robinson v Secretary of State for Northern Ireland* [2002] NI 390, 402, para 25, Lord Hoffmann; and *Jackson v Attorney-General* [2006] 1 AC 262, 302, para 102, Lord Steyn.

[57] See further [5.23]–[5.24].

[58] See, eg, *Re Perry's Application* [1997] NI 282, 300, Girvan J: 'It is a feature of the richness of the common law that old concepts and practices in danger of becoming outdated can be dusted down, repolished and reinvigorated in the evolutionary process of case law'; and *Re T's Application* [2000] NI 516, 533, Coghlin J: 'it is important to bear in mind that history is a continuous process and that the vital dynamic of the common law has been an enduring tension between stability and creative development'.

[59] See Sir J Laws, 'Law and Democracy' (1995) PL 72.

[60] The Judicature (Northern Ireland) Act 1978, ss 18–25, and RSC Ord 53 (as amended); and see ch 3.

[61] See M Elliott, 'The *Ultra Vires* Doctrine in a Constitutional Setting: Still the Central Principle of Administrative Law' (1999) 58 CLJ 129.

[62] See P Craig, 'Competing Models of Judicial Review' [1999] PL 428.

[63] Subject to Northern Ireland Act 1998, s 6.

[64] Craig, 'Competing Models of Judicial Review' [1999] PL 428, 437–8. Although note that it is questionable whether the courts would follow all legislative overrides: see Lord Steyn's comments in [2004] 9 *Judicial Review* 107–8, discussing ouster clauses and the common law. On ouster clauses see [4.10]–[4.13].

[65] On the grounds see further chs 4–7.

headings of illegality, *Wednesbury* unreasonableness/irrationality (the starting point for substantive review), and procedural impropriety,[66] although they have long since been developed to include related sub-grounds such as substantive legitimate expectation, equality, and proportionality. While some of these grounds have in turn emerged under the (part) influence of EU law and/or the ECHR, the principal catalyst in the development of new grounds has been the common law. Indeed, the common law here has its broadest meaning, as the grounds may sometimes develop in the light of the comparative experience of other common law systems.[67]

EU Law

[**1.16**]   EU law has effect in domestic law under the terms of the European Communities Act 1972 and is on that basis statute law, albeit as constitutionally distinct in the light of the demands of the EU legal order.[68] EU law commands supremacy over domestic law whenever enacted and in whatever form,[69] and its provisions may be relied upon in domestic courts by individuals where the provisions meet the EU law requirements for direct effect.[70] The institutional competences of the EU have recently expanded to include the areas of, among others, security and foreign policy,[71] although EU law remains of primary relevance to national courts insofar as it guarantees the range of social and economic rights associated with free movement and the completion of the EU's internal market. EU law has therefore recently been used in Northern Ireland courts to challenge: nationality requirements that govern eligibility for employment in certain public service posts[72]; the levels of pay for part-time tribunal chairpersons[73]; public health legislation that placed limits on meat production[74]; the refusal to grant a road service licence to an individual for the purpose of providing a bus service[75]; aspects of planning policy[76]; and the failure of the UK government to introduce legislation to implement the Working Time Directive in Northern Ireland law.[77]

---

[66] *Council of Civil Service Unions v Minister for the Civil Service* [1985] AC 374, 408, Lord Diplock.

[67] The courts have drawn upon, among others, Canadian jurisprudence when developing proportionality as a ground of review in Human Rights Act 1998 cases: see, eg, *Brown v Stott (Procurator Fiscal, Dunfermline)* [2003] 1 AC 681. And at the level of remedies see, eg, the dissenting opinions of Lords Bingham and Steyn in *Cullen v Chief Constable of RUC* [2003] NI 375, drawing on comparative common law approaches to the right of access to a lawyer for the purposes of delimiting the tort of breach of statutory duty (the duty here found in s 15 of the Northern Ireland (Emergency Provisions) Act 1987).

[68] *Thoburn v Sunderland CC* [2003] QB 151; and [5.04]–[5.07].

[69] Case 26/62, *Van Gend en Loos v Nederlandse Aministratie der Belastingen* [1963] ECR 1; Case 6/64, *Costa v ENEL* [1964] ECR 585; and Case 106/77, *Amministrazione delle Finanze dello Stato v Simmenthal SpA* [1978] ECR 629. For UK court acceptance of the supremacy requirement see *R v Secretary of State for Transport, ex p Factortame (No 2)* [1991] 1 AC 603.

[70] Case 26/62, *Van Gend en Loos v Nederlandse Aministratie der Belastingen* [1963] ECR 1, 13.

[71] See P Craig and G de Búrca, *EU Law: Text, Cases and Materials*, 4th edn (Oxford, Oxford University Press, 2008) ch 1.

[72] *Re O'Connor's Application* [2005] NIQB 11; *Re Colgan's Application* [1996] NI 24; *Re O'Boyle's Application* [1999] NI 126.

[73] *Perceval-Price v Department of Economic Development* [2000] NI 141.

[74] *Re Eurostock's Application* [1999] NI 13.

[75] *Re McParland's Application* [2002] NI 292.

[76] *Re Friends of the Earth's Application* [2006] NIQB 48.

[77] *Re Burns' Application* [1999] NI 175. On the failure to implement Directives see too, eg, *Re Seaport Investments Ltd's Application* [2007] NIQB 62 (the Environmental Assessment of Plans and Programmes Regulations (NI) 2004 had not correctly implemented Directive 2001/42 EC in domestic law).

[**1.17**] Whenever EU law provisions are in issue there are a number of obligations that are imposed on national courts. These include: the obligation to interpret national law to be consistent with non-directly effective EU Directives that have not been implemented in domestic law (or have been implemented incorrectly)[78]; the requirement that national courts refer matters of EU law to the European Court of Justice (ECJ) in the event that the national court is uncertain as to the meaning of EU law[79]; the requirement that national courts award damages to individuals for a 'sufficiently serious' breach of their EU law rights by any of the legislative, executive, or judicial branches of the State[80]; and the requirement that national courts give effect to the general principles of EU law, which include proportionality, equality, legitimate expectation, and fundamental rights standards found in, among others, the ECHR.[81] This last requirement is of particular interest to judicial review, as it has previously resulted in national courts using general principles of law that were regarded as ill suited to the domestic constitutional context. The point was particularly true of the proportionality principle, although the more general development of that principle in domestic law has since lessened EU law's 'alien' influence.[82]

[**1.18**]   Whenever provisions of EU law are not in issue national courts are not bound by the above obligations. However, it does not follow that national court experience with EU law is wholly without relevance. There have been several important cases in which the domestic courts have drawn upon the demands of EU law to inform developments in the purely domestic context.[83] EU law can thereby have a 'spill-over effect' in judicial review in the sense that it indirectly shapes the outcome of domestic proceedings.[84]

[**1.19**]   The imagery of non-binding EU law spilling over into domestic law also has some relevance in respect of the EU Charter of Fundamental Rights.[85] The Charter contains a range of civil, political, social, and economic rights that are to be observed by the EU institutions and by the Member States 'when they are implementing EU law'.[86] While

---

[78] Known as the 'indirect effect' doctrine: see Case 14/83, *Von Colson v Land Nordrhein-Westfalen* [1984] ECR 1891 and Case C-106/89 *Marleasing SA v La Commercial Internacional de Alimentacion SA* [1990] ECR I-4153. And for acceptance of the doctrine by the House of Lords see *Webb v EMO Air Cargo (UK) Ltd (No 2)* [1995] 4 All ER 577.

[79] Art 234 EC, and RSC Ord 114. But see also Case 283/81, *Srl CILFIT and Lanificio di Gavardo SpA v Ministry of Health* [1982] ECR 3415.

[80] Known as the 'state liability' doctrine: see *Re Burns' Application* [1999] NI 175. The leading EU cases are Cases C-6/90, *Francovich and Bonifaci v Italy* [1991] ECR I-5357; Joined Cases C-46 & 48/93, *Brasserie du Pêcheur SA v Germany, R v Secretary of State for Transport, ex p Factortame Ltd* [1996] 1 ECR 1029; Joined Cases C-178–179 & 188–190/94, *Dillenkofer v Germany* [1996] 3 CMLR 469; and Case C-224/01, *Köbler v Austria* [2003] ECR I-10239. See further [8.36]–[8.38].

[81] On the general principles of law see T Tridimas, *The General Principles of EC Law*, 2nd edn (Oxford, Oxford University Press, 2006), and P Craig, *EU Administrative Law* (Oxford, Oxford University Press, 2006).

[82] J Jowell, 'Is Proportionality an Alien Concept?' (1996) 2 EPL 401. On proportionality in domestic law see now *R v Secretary of State for the Home Department, ex p Daly* [2001] 2 AC 532, and [6.12]–[6.28].

[83] The leading example remains the progression from *R v Secretary of State for Transport, ex p Factortame (No 2)* [1991] 1 AC 603 to *M v Home Office* [1994] 1 AC 377 (the availability of interim injunctions against Ministers of the Crown for purposes of protecting EU law rights extended to the non-EU context). See [3.45] and [8.34]–[8.35].

[84] For general recognition of the point see *Re Hampson's Application* [1998] NIJB 188, 193, Girvan J. And see, eg, [2.20], and *Re Sherlock and Morris* [1996] NIJB 80 (case law on 'emanations of the State' for purposes of EU law referred to when developing the reach of judicial review to include the decisions of privatised utilities).

[85] The Charter was first published in [2000] OJ C 364/01.

[86] Art 51. The rights are contained in six chapters under the headings: Freedoms; Equality; Solidarity; Citizen's Rights, and Justice (there is a seventh chapter titled 'General Provisions'; and there is also a preamble). See further the Special Issue of the *Maastricht Journal of European and Comparative Law* (2001) 8(1) ('European Charter of Fundamental Rights'); and the Special Issue of the *European Review of Public Law*

Sources of Law   11

the Charter does not at present enjoy binding force of law—it has, moreover, been agreed that the Charter should not be formally binding in the UK even in the event that it is binding in the other Member States[87]—it has nevertheless been referred to by, among other courts, the CFI and the ECtHR.[88] Such references make clear that the Charter is of potential significance in legal proceedings, notwithstanding the absence of binding legal effect. Indeed, it has been suggested in the Administrative Court in England and Wales that the Charter might 'properly be consulted' when courts are considering the content of common law and ECHR guarantees, at least 'insofar as (the Charter) proclaims, reaffirms (and) elucidates the content of those human rights that are generally recognised throughout the European family of nations'.[89]

The ECHR

[1.20]   The greater part of the ECHR has effect in domestic law under the terms of the Human Rights Act 1998. Although the ECHR had previously exerted some influence on domestic law[90]—viz as part of the general principles of EU law,[91] through courts drawing analogies with the ECHR when identifying the content of the common law,[92] and through the interpretation of ambiguous legislation in the light of the UK's international obligations[93]—the dualist nature of the constitution entailed that it could not be relied upon directly in the absence of an Act of Parliament.[94] With the enactment of the Human Rights Act 1998 the ECHR is of course now directly arguable and section 2 of the Act requires courts to 'take into account' ECHR jurisprudence in respect of the rights listed in Schedule 1 to the Act.[95] These are: the right to life (Article 2); the prohibition of torture, inhuman or degrading treatment (Article 3); the prohibition of slavery and forced labour (Article 4); the right to liberty and security (Article 5); the right to a fair trial (Article 6); no punishment without law (Article 7); the right to respect for private and family life (Article 8); freedom of thought, conscience and religion (Article 9); freedom of

---

(2002) 14(1) ('The European Union's Charter of Fundamental Rights'). Note that the Charter also constituted Part II of the ill-fated Treaty Establishing a Constitution for Europe (2004), where it had different Article numbers (eg, Article 51 of the Charter was Article II-111 of the Treaty). The text of the Constitution is available at http://europa.eu.int/constitution/index_en.htm.

[87]   See http://politics.guardian.co.uk/eu/story/0,,2191919,00.html.

[88]   The CFI referred to the Charter in, eg, Case T-211/02, *Tideland Signal v Commission* [2002] 3 CMLR 33. And for use of the Charter by the ECtHR see, eg, *Goodwin v UK* (2002) 35 EHRR 447, 480, para 100.

[89]   *A and others v East Sussex CC* [2003] All ER (D) 233, para [73], Munby J. See also Munby J's judgment in *R (Howard League for Penal Reform) v Secretary of State for the Home Department* [2003] 1 FLR 484. And see, eg, *Coppard v Customs v Excise Commissioners* [2003] 3 All ER 351; and *Sepet v Secretary of State for the Home Department* [2003] 3 All ER 304.

[90]   See generally M Hunt, *Using Human Rights Law in English Courts* (Oxford, Hart Publishing, 1997).

[91]   *R v Secretary of State for the Home Department, ex p McQuillan* [1995] 4 All ER 400.

[92]   Eg, *Re Curran and McCann's Application* [1985] NI 261 (considering Art 17 ECHR when concluding that the protective and self-defensive powers of a council to regulate its own proceedings did not include a power to exclude members of a party proclaiming a particular policy); *Attorney-General v Guardian Newspapers Ltd (No 2)* [1988] 3 All ER 545, 660, Lord Goff.

[93]   *R v Deery* [1977] NI 164. Note that this is an interpretive approach adopted in respect of all international obligations: see *Garland v British Rail Engineering Ltd* [1983] 2 AC 751, 771, Lord Diplock. But compare, in respect of unambiguous legislation, *Re Russell's Application* [1996] NI 310.

[94]   *JH Rayner v Department of Trade and Industry* [1990] AC 418, 550.

[95]   Arts 2–12 and 14 ECHR, Arts 1–3 of Protocol 1, and Arts 1–2 of Protocol 6, as read with Arts 16–18 ECHR.

expression (Article 10); freedom of association and assembly (Article 11); the right to marry (Article 12); the prohibition of discrimination (Article 14); restrictions on political activities of aliens (Article 16); the prohibition of abuse of rights (Article 17); limitation on the use of restrictions on rights (Article 18); protection of property (Article 1, Protocol 1); the right to education (Article 2, Protocol 1); the right to free elections (Article 3, Protocol 1); abolition of the death penalty (Article 1, Protocol 6); and death penalty in time of war (Article 2, Protocol 6).[96]

[1.21]   The rights within Schedule 1 are sometimes described as either substantive or procedural in form,[97] although some Articles—for instance the Article 2 ECHR right to life—have both substantive and procedural dimensions. The rights are, moreover, often subdivided into 'qualified rights' and 'absolute rights', and 'derogable rights' and 'non-derogable rights'. The difference between qualified rights and absolute rights is essentially one that is concerned with the permissibility of interference with the rights. Thus, while qualified rights such as privacy, expression, and association are open to limitation on a number of grounds associated with the public interest (subject to the demands of proportionality and legality),[98] absolute rights—such as the prohibition of torture—are not. This emphasis on the absolute nature of the rights likewise informs the distinction between derogable and non-derogable rights: while liberty and fair trial guarantees (for instance) may be derogated from at times of public emergency (subject again to proportionality and so on),[99] absolute rights are to remain unaffected.

[1.22]   The impact that the ECHR, as another body of constitutionally distinct statute law, has had on judicial review has been far-reaching and is examined more fully in subsequent chapters. However, one point of overarching importance relates to the dynamism of the ECHR and its corresponding capacity to challenge core precepts of judicial review. The ECtHR has emphasised that the ECHR is, among other things, a 'living instrument' that is unlike other international treaties,[100] 'autonomous' in terms of its meaning and content,[101] founded on the principles of democracy and respect for the rule of law,[102] and a 'constitutional instrument of European public order'.[103] While such statements must be read with the fact that provisions in the ECHR do not always

---

[96] The courts have, however, also had regard to rights not contained in the Schedule: see, eg, *R (B) v Secretary of State for Foreign and Commonwealth Affairs* [2005] QB 643 (Art 1: guarantee of the rights of any person within the jurisdiction of the UK), and *A & Ors v Secretary of State for the Home Department* [2005] 2 AC 68 (Art 15 and the power of States to derogate from certain rights at the time of a 'public emergency threatening the life of the nation').

[97] See generally A Lester and D Pannick, *Human Rights Law and Practice*, 2nd edn (London, Butterworths, 2004).

[98] Eg, the Art 8 right to respect for privacy reads: '(1) Everyone has the right to respect for his private and family life, his home and his correspondence. (2) There shall be no interference by a public authority with the exercise of this right except such as is in accordance with the law and is necessary in a democratic society in the interests of national security, public safety or the economic well-being of the country, for the prevention of disorder or crime, for the protection of health or morals, or for the protection of the rights and freedoms of others.'

[99] Art 15 ECHR. For consideration of the Article's proportionality requirement relative to anti-terrorism measures in the UK see *A v Secretary of State for the Home Department* [2005] 2 AC 68 (detention provisions in the Anti-terrorism, Crime and Security Act 2001 incompatible with the ECHR).

[100] See, eg, *Cossey v UK* (1991) 13 EHRR 622, 639, para 35, and *Ireland v United Kingdom* [1979–80] 2 EHRR 25, 103, para 239. And see *Re ES's Application* [2007] NIQB 58, para 98.

[101] See, eg, *Engel v Netherlands* (1976) 1 EHRR 647.

[102] See, eg, *Refah Partisi (the Welfare Party) v Turkey* (2003) 37 EHRR 1.

[103] *Loizidou v Turkey* (1996) 23 EHRR 99.

guarantee protection as wide as that in the common law,[104] the ECHR's general principles of law—in particular proportionality and legality—envisage increased judicial intervention in decision-making processes that affect fundamental rights. The ECHR can thereby require closer look review in cases under the Human Rights Act 1998 in the sense that courts must assess whether a decision-maker has balanced correctly all interests affected by the decision it has taken. However, to the extent that this recasts the nature of the judicial role in review proceedings, the courts have equally developed a 'discretionary area of judgment' doctrine that borrows from the ECtHR's margin of appreciation doctrine and which seeks to prevent unwarranted judicial interference with administrative and legislative choices.[105]

Unincorporated International Treaties and Customary International Law

[1.23] Two final sources of law of (potential) importance are unincorporated international treaties and customary international law.[106] Unincorporated international treaties can, for instance, have some impact where the courts are open to arguments about parallelism in the common law and the need to interpret legislation in the light of international obligations (see, in respect of the ECHR, [1.20]). However, where the courts are not open to such arguments for reasons of constitutional dualism, unincorporated international law may be deemed irrelevant.[107] Hence in *Re T's Application*[108] the High Court rejected arguments that the applicant had a legitimate expectation that the Secretary of State would make a decision about the applicant's immigration status in the light of the United Nations Convention on the Rights of the Child (the applicant, who was to be deported, had given birth to a child while residing unlawfully in Northern Ireland). Finding that such arguments would, if accepted, amount to incorporation by the 'back door', the court referred to the 'constitutional importance of the principle that international conventions do not alter domestic law except to the extent that they are incorporated into domestic law by legislation'.[109] While the application for judicial review was thus successful on other grounds, arguments made with reference to the Convention were rejected.

[1.24] The position in relation to customary international law is perhaps more complex. Customary norms are those that have 'attained the position of general acceptance by civilised nations as a rule of international conduct, evidenced by international treaties and conventions, authoritative textbooks, practice and judicial decision'.[110] Customary

---

[104] See, eg, *Re Glasgow's Application* [2004] NIQB 34 (Art 6 ECHR inapplicable in the context of a police employment dispute in which the common law rules of fairness applied), and *In Re McClean* [2005] UKHL 46 (common law rules of fairness applicable, but not the ECHR, in a dispute about the recall to prison of a prisoner released on licence).

[105] See, on the margin of appreciation, [6.20]–[6.22]; and, on the discretionary area of judgment, [6.25]–[6.26]

[106] On which see S Fatima, *Using International Law in Domestic Courts* (Oxford, Hart Publishing, 2005).

[107] *R v Secretary of State for the Home Department, ex p Brind* [1991] 1 AC 696, and *R (Hurst) v London Northern District Coroner* [2007] 2 WLR 726.

[108] [2000] NI 516.

[109] [2000] NI 516, 537, citing *Thomas v Baptiste* [2000] AC 1 (PC). But compare, eg, *Re E's Application* [2006] NICA 37, considering the Convention in the context of an application for judicial review that challenged the manner in which the police had approached a protest outside a school.

[110] *The Christina* [1938] AC 485, 497, Lord MacMillan.

norms have, as such, long been recognised as part of the common law,[111] and this allows the courts—which are solely responsible for developing the common law—to have regard to the norms even in the absence of incorporating legislation (although such use of the common law is subject to rules of precedent and to the superior force of statute[112]). However, while this offers the courts a potentially rich source of standards and values, arguments about the role of customary norms will fail where the applicant cannot establish that a norm has in fact attained customary status. Arguments may also fail where courts consider that use of the common law would involve them in disputes that are essentially political and non-justiciable.[113]

STATUTORY INTERPRETATION

[1.25]   Approaches to statutory interpretation are of particular importance when it is argued in judicial review proceedings that a decision-maker's actions or inactions constitute an 'illegality' (that is, because the decision-maker has misunderstood the law that regulates its decision-making power).[114] Although illegality and the other grounds for review overlap with one another,[115] the question whether a decision-maker has, for instance, acted in accordance with a statutory power or duty, or whether subordinate legislation is ultra vires its parent Act,[116] will depend on how the relevant statute is read by the courts. In some cases, the statute may be read 'on its own', in the sense that the question for the reviewing court is simply whether an administrative act/failure to act or subordinate legislation is consistent with the terms of the statute. However, in other cases, the courts may be required to read the statute in the light of the European Communities Act 1972 or the Human Rights Act 1998 and to gauge the legality of the decision-maker's act failure to act, or of subordinate legislation in the light of those 'constitutional Acts' (on which see [1.28]–[1.34]).[117] Under those circumstances, the courts may be required to adopt a more 'purposive' interpretive approach whereby they try to read the statute in a manner that is consistent with EU law[118] and with the ECHR[119] (as appropriate). In the event that such harmonious interpretation cannot be achieved, primary Acts that are inconsistent with EU law are to be disapplied (and subordinate legislation quashed)[120]; and those that are inconsistent with the ECHR are to be the subject

---

[111]   *Chung Chi Cheung v The King* [1939] AC 160, 168, Lord Atkin.

[112]   See, eg, *R v Bow Street Metropolitan Stipendiary Magistrate and others, ex p Pinochet Ugarte (No 3)* [2000] 1 AC 147, and *Jones v Ministry of the Interior of Saudi Arabia* [2006] 2 WLR 1424.

[113]   For further analysis see R Singh, 'The Use of International Law in the Domestic Courts of the United Kingdom' (2005) 56 NILQ 119. On justiciability see [4.14]–[4.17].

[114]   Ch 5.

[115]   *Boddington v British Transport Police* [1999] 2 AC 143, 152, Lord Irvine LC; and chs 4–7.

[116]   See, eg, *Re Cullen's Application* [2005] NIQB 9 (challenging, inter alia, the Game Preservation (Special Protection for Irish Hares) Order (Northern Ireland) 2003 made under s 7C(1) of the Game Preservation Act (Northern Ireland) 1928: application dismissed).

[117]   See too [5.04]–[5.30].

[118]   European Communities Act 1972, s 2(4), and, eg, *Perceval-Price v Department of Economic Development* [2000] NI 141 and *Garland v British Rail Engineering Ltd* [1983] 2 AC 751.

[119]   Human Rights Act 1998, s 3, considered in, eg, *Re King's Application* [2003] NI 43. And see [5.12]–[5.13] and [5.15].

[120]   *R v Secretary of State for Transport, ex p Factortame Ltd (No 2)* [1991] 1 AC 603; and see [5.06]–[5.10].

of 'declarations of incompatibility'[121] (subordinate legislation may here be quashed, save where primary legislation prevents removal of the incompatibility[122]).

[**1.26**]   The purposive approach associated with European law is often taken to require courts to look to the policy of the statute that they are interpreting and to give effect to it accordingly.[123] It is, in turn, an approach that is usually contrasted with the 'literal' approach to interpretation that has historically been preferred by courts in Northern Ireland and the rest of the UK. Under the literal approach, courts seek to give effect to the legislature's intentions by giving the words in a statute their ordinary and natural meaning (that is, the courts do not look beyond or behind the words used in the statute; the legislature for these purposes may be either the Westminster Parliament or the Northern Ireland Assembly[124]). This approach has been preferred historically because it is understood to ensure that courts 'interpret' rather than 'legislate' and that they in that way avoid usurping the role of the sovereign legislature.[125] However, even before the demands of EU law and the ECHR entailed that the courts develop more purposive approaches, the literal approach had already been modified in some important respects and/or replaced. Hence there are both older and more recent authorities that reveal a judicial willingness: to read power into legislation where that power is 'reasonably incidental' to the statute or may be reasonably implied;[126] to interpret sections in a statute with part-reference to the corresponding headings in the statute;[127] to use the age-old 'mischief rule' to look to the pre-existing common law position when deciding what the objective of legislation is;[128] to protect common law fundamental rights by requiring that any legislative interference with those rights be provided for either in express terms or by necessary implication;[129] to read legislation in the light of its historical context;[130] and to give words their broader meaning where this enables two decision-makers to exercise their powers in a complementary fashion that is consistent with the intention of the legislation.[131] Prior experience with EU law has likewise led the House of Lords to relax

---

[121] Human Rights Act 1998, s 4, and *Re McR's Application* [2003] NI 1 (Offences Against the Persons Act 1861, s 62 incompatible with Art 8 ECHR).

[122] Human Rights Act 1998, s 4(4); and see [5.12]–[5.16].

[123] *R v Secretary of State for the Environment, Transport and the Regions, ex p Spalth Holme* [2001] 2 AC 349, 397, Lord Nicholls.

[124] *Jordan v Lord Chancellor* [2007] 2 WLR 754, 778, para 44, Lord Bingham.

[125] See *Duport Steels Ltd v Sirs* [1980] 1 WLR 142, 157, Lord Diplock.

[126] See, eg, *A-G v Smethwick Cpn* [1932] 1 Ch 563.

[127] *Re French's Application* [1985] NI 310.

[128] Otherwise known as the rule in *Heydon's Case*: (1584) 3 Co Rep 7b.

[129] *R v Secretary of State for the Home Department, ex p Simms* [2000] 2 AC 115; and *Raymond v Honey* [1983] 1 AC 1, 10, Lord Wilberforce (cited in, eg, *Pettigrew v NIO* [1990] NI 179, 182, Hutton J). But for some limits to the approach see, eg, *R v Chief Constable of the RUC, ex p Begley* [1997] NI 278 (suspects have no common law fundamental right to have a solicitor present during police interviews; and the courts would not infer the right given Parliament's clear intention to exclude solicitors under the terms of the (now repealed) Prevention of Terrorism (Temporary Provisions) Act 1989, s 14(1)). And for an example of the courts inferring words that permitted of an interference with individual rights/interests see *Re Russell's Application* [1990] NI 188 (while the Prison Rules stated that each prisoner should have at least one hour of exercise in the open air every day, there was a clear necessity to imply the words 'save in exceptional circumstances' so as to permit the prison authorities to keep prisoners in their cells when it was necessary for safety and security at the prison).

[130] *R v Z* [2005] 2 WLR 1286, and *R (Quintavalle) v Secretary of State for Health* [2003] 2 AC 687, 695, para 8, Lord Bingham.

[131] *Re Shields' Application* [2003] NI 161.

more generally the exclusionary rule that prevented courts from consulting *Hansard* when trying to ascertain Parliament's intention in enacting certain provisions.[132]

[**1.27**]   The interpretive approach adopted in any one case will of course depend on the context of the case and on the corresponding judicial perception of the issues raised. However, where there is scope for the courts reasonably to adopt one or other approach (literal or purposive), it is clear that there can be very different outcomes to the case and/or judicial opinions as to the outcome. There have, for instance, been several cases in which the Northern Ireland courts and the House of Lords have read legislation differently and in ways that have had far-reaching consequences for the structures of government in Northern Ireland.[133] While such cases exist more as an exception than a rule—most issues of interpretation will not of course arise in the context of disputes about the workings of the institutions of government in Northern Ireland—they reveal how some approaches to statutory interpretation can take courts to the very fringes of political decision-making. The corresponding question—to which there is no agreed answer—is therefore whether such judicial involvement in matters of policy is to be regarded as a positive feature of judicial decision-making, or as one to be rejected.

'CONSTITUTIONAL STATUTES': THE EUROPEAN COMMUNITIES ACT 1972, THE HUMAN RIGHTS ACT 1998, AND THE NORTHERN IRELAND ACT 1998

[**1.28**]   Judicial use of the common law and more purposive interpretive techniques has resulted, most recently, in some judges recognising a category of common law 'constitutional statutes'.[134] The term denotes a class of statutes that the common law regards as superior to others because the statutes (a) condition the legal relationship between citizen and State in some general, overarching manner and/or (b) enlarge or diminish the scope of fundamental constitutional rights.[135] Such constitutional statutes are not

---

[132]   *Pepper v Hart* [1993] AC 593, drawing upon the approach adopted in, eg, *Pickstone v Freemans* [1989] AC 66. Under the rule in *Pepper v Hart* it is permissible to consult *Hansard* where: (a) the legislation is obscure or ambiguous, or leads to an absurdity; (b) the material relied upon consists of one or more statements by a Minister or other promoter of the Bill together . . . with such other Parliamentary material as is necessary to understand such statements and their effect; and (c) the statements relied upon are clear. But note that there has been considerable judicial displeasure with the ruling and there are differing judicial understandings of when recourse to *Hansard* is appropriate: see, eg, *R v Secretary of State for the Environment, Transport and the Regions, ex p Spath Holme Ltd* [2001] 2 AC 349 and *Robinson v Secretary of State for Northern Ireland* [2002] NI 390.

[133]   See, most notably, *Robinson v Secretary of State for Northern Ireland* [2002] NI 207 (NICA) and 390 (HL), where the central issue was whether a six-week time-limit in the Northern Ireland Act 1998 should be strictly observed even where such observance would have entailed fresh elections to the Northern Ireland Assembly and a corresponding political instability (Kerr J at first instance and the majority in both the Court of Appeal and the House of Lords held that the relevant provisions—ss 16(8) and 32(3)—should not be read literally but rather in the light of the Act's objective of creating stable government in Northern Ireland; Carswell LCJ and the minority in the House of Lords dissented and considered that the provisions should be read literally). And see too *Re Northern Ireland Human Rights Commission* [2001] NI 271 (NIQB and NICA), and [2002] NI 236 (HL), where the issue was whether ss 69–71 of the Northern Ireland Act 1998 should be read as giving the Northern Ireland Human Rights Commission (NIHRC) an implied power to intervene on points of human rights law in judicial proceedings (Carswell LCJ at first instance and a majority in the Court of Appeal—Kerr J dissenting—held that the power to intervene could not be read into the provisions; a majority in the House of Lords—as with Kerr J—looked to the NIHRC's overall function rather than its individual powers and on that basis held that the power to intervene could be attributed).

[134]   *Thoburn v Sunderland CC* [2003] QB 151.

[135]   [2003] QB 151, 186. Laws LJ cited as examples 'the Magna Carta, the Bill of Rights 1688, the Act of Union, the Reform Acts which distributed and enlarged the franchise, the [Human Rights Act], the Scotland Act 1998 and the Government of Wales Act 1998'.

subject to the ordinary rule of implied repeal (that is, the rule that where two statutes are in conflict and the earlier statute is not expressly repealed, the later statute prevails[136]) and they can instead be repealed only by 'express words in the later statute, or . . . words so specific that the inference of an actual determination to effect the result contended for [is] irresistible'.[137] This ascription of a higher constitutional status to some statutes is potentially very significant for judicial review, as it elevates the values that the statutes give effect to and tasks the courts with resolving disputes about them (for instance, where subsequent primary legislation is argued to be in conflict with the values or where they are interfered with by administrative choices). Although the approach in any given case will be determined by the context to the dispute,[138] a judicial use of the language of constitutional statutes might be expected to result in more activist decision-making through, for example, closer look review of administrative choices. On the other hand, a judicial preference for orthodox understandings of the constitutional role of the courts might equally be expected to lead to judicial self-restraint in the face of legislative choices and administrative decisions. Indeed, it is perhaps for this reason that there have been only relatively few references to constitutional statutes in subsequent case law,[139] with some judges identifying the definitional difficulties associated with such apparently open-ended common law constructs.[140]

The European Communities Act 1972

[**1.29**]   The term 'constitutional statute' was first used by Laws LJ in *Thoburn v Sunderland City Council* to describe the European Communities Act 1972, which provides for the primacy of EU law within the UK constitutional order.[141] Ever since, most famously, the *Factortame* case,[142] UK courts have accepted that EU law prevails over conflicting domestic primary legislation, even when that domestic legislation is enacted subsequent to the European Communities Act 1972 that gives domestic effect to EU law (on the EU law obligations that are imposed on national courts see [1.16]–[1.19]). Although this approach contradicts the doctrines of parliamentary sovereignty and implied repeal, the courts had not considered in detail the constitutional implications of EU membership but had merely stated that Parliament should use express language in subsequent legislation if the intention of the legislation is to contravene EU law.[143] *Thoburn* therefore provided a fuller justification for the reception of EU law by categorising the European Communities Act 1972 as a common law constitutional statute that attracts different domestic rules of interpretation (that is, the non-applicability of the doctrine of implied repeal). Laws LJ thereby emphasised that EU law enjoys primacy

---

[136]   See *Ellen Street Estates v Minister of Health* [1934] 1 KB 590, 597, Maugham LJ.

[137]   [2003] QB 151, 187.

[138]   See [4.14]–[4.21].

[139]   See, eg, in NI *Re Sinn Fein's Application* [2003] NIQB 27, para 31, Coghlin J, and *Robinson v Secretary of State for Northern Ireland* [2002] NI 390, 402, para 25, Lord Hoffmann; and, in England and Wales, *Levi Strauss v Tesco Stores* [2000] EWHC 1556.

[140]   *Watkins v Home Office* [2006] AC 395, 418–20, paras 58–64, Lord Rodger.

[141]   *Thoburn v Sunderland CC* [2003] QB 151, 187. But for earlier use of the term—albeit not as used in relation to the doctrine of implied repeal—see *Belfast Corporation v OD Cars* [1960] AC 490, 517, Viscount Simmonds, describing the Government of Ireland Act 1920 as a 'constitutional Act'.

[142]   *R v Secretary of State for Transport, ex p Factortame Ltd (No 2)* [1991] 1 AC 603.

[143]   An approach associated with Denning LJ's judgment in *Macarthys Ltd v Smith* [1979] 3 All ER 325, 329.

in UK courts not because EU law itself demands such status,[144] but because the common law recognises the domestic Act of Parliament that gives effect to EU law as qualitatively different from other Acts.[145]

The Human Rights Act 1998

[**1.30**]   The most significant 'other' constitutional statute identified in *Thoburn* is the Human Rights Act 1998, which gives domestic effect to most of the ECHR (see [1.20]–[1.22]). The Act is intended to ensure that there is fuller protection of fundamental rights within a framework that simultaneously consolidates key aspects of the domestic constitution, most notably the doctrine of parliamentary sovereignty. In terms of enhancing the protection of rights, the Act thus makes it unlawful for public authorities to act in manner that is incompatible with the ECHR (authorities include courts and tribunals and 'any person certain of whose functions are functions of a public nature' but exclude either House of Parliament)[146]; and it also requires courts to 'take into account all' relevant ECHR jurisprudence when hearing cases under the Act[147] and, 'so far as it is possible to do so', to interpret primary and subordinate legislation 'whenever enacted' to be consistent with the ECHR.[148] The Act's corresponding emphasis on the doctrine of parliamentary sovereignty is found in the requirement that declarations of incompatibility be made in the event that primary legislation cannot be read in a manner that is compatible with the ECHR (subordinate legislation that is incompatible can, in contrast, be struck down as ultra vires save where it has been 'made in the exercise of a power by primary legislation' and 'the primary legislation concerned prevents removal of the incompatibility'; under those circumstances, a declaration of incompatibility may issue).[149] Declarations of incompatibility do not have any legal effect on the force and validity of the legislation in respect of which they are made and they therefore have only a persuasive value.[150] The legislation in that way remains sovereign and the question whether to amend it one for Parliament.[151]

[**1.31**]   The effect that these—and other—provisions of the Human Rights Act 1998 have had on judicial review is considered in more detail in subsequent chapters.[152] There

---

[144] Case 26/62, *Van Gend En Loos v Nederlandse der Belastingen* [1963] ECR 1; Case 6/64, *Costa v ENEL* [1964] ECR 585; and Case 106/77, *Amministrazione delle Finanze dello Stato v Simmenthal SpA* [1978] ECR 629.

[145] [2003] QB 151, 189–90: 'In my judgment . . . the correct analysis of [the relationship between EU law and domestic law] requires these following four propositions. (1) All the specific rights and obligations which EU law creates are by the 1972 Act incorporated into our domestic law and rank supreme: that is, anything in our substantive law inconsistent with any of these rights and obligations is abrogated or must be modified to avoid the inconsistency. This is true even where the inconsistent municipal provision is contained in primary legislation. (2) The 1972 Act is a constitutional statute: that is, it cannot be impliedly repealed. (3) The truth of (2) is derived, not from EU law, but purely from the law of [the United Kingdom]: the common law recognises a category of constitutional statutes. (4) The fundamental legal basis of the United Kingdom's relationship with the EU rests with the domestic, not the European legal powers.'

[146] Section 6; and see [2.22]–[2.25] and [5.17]–[5.20].

[147] Section 2; and see [5.11].

[148] Section 3; and see [5.12]–[5.16]. For the definition of primary and subordinate legislation see s 21.

[149] Section 4(3)–(4).

[150] Section 4(6).

[151] Sections 4(6) and 10, and Sch 2; and see [8.46]–[8.48].

[152] See, in particular, [2.22]–[2.25] (on public authorities for the purposes of the Act); [3.67]–[3.70] (on standing under the Act); [5.11]–[5.20] (on the constitutional framework of the Act); and [8.40]–[8.48] (on remedies under the Act).

are, however, two points of overarching significance that can be made here. The first is that there have sometimes been very different judicial opinions about how the provisions of the Act should be used by the courts. This is most obviously true of the section 3 interpretive enjoinder, as there has been considerable disagreement about exactly what is 'possible' where legislation is not worded in terms that can command only one meaning.[153] Some judges have, in short, argued that the function of 'judicial interpreting' should not be allowed to become that of 'judicial legislating' and that declarations of incompatibility should instead be used so as to avoid criticisms of undue judicial activism.[154] However, other case law has equally emphasised that creative use of the interpretive obligation is the approach best suited to achieving the Human Rights Act 1998's objective of furthering the protection of fundamental rights and that Parliament entrusted the courts with that extended role by enacting section 3.[155] There are thus dicta that contradict each other; and there doubtless will be more.

[1.32] The second point is that the Act does not have retrospective effect. Even though the section 3 interpretive enjoinder applies to legislation 'whenever enacted', the House of Lords has consistently read sections 7 and 22—which govern retrospective effect—as precluding litigation in respect of events that occurred before the coming into force of the greater part of the Act on 2 October 2000.[156] The point was made most forcefully in *In Re McKerr*, where the son of a man killed in 1982 by undercover RUC officers sought, among other remedies, an order of mandamus to compel the Secretary of State to hold an Article 2 ECHR-compliant investigation into the circumstances of his father's death.[157] The application was brought on foot of the ECtHR judgment in *McKerr v UK*,[158] where it was held that the lack of an effective investigation had violated the applicant's adjectival, continuing rights under Article 2 ECHR. While the Northern Ireland Court of Appeal made a declaration to the effect that the applicant had a continuing right to an investigation,[159] the House of Lords allowed the Secretary of State's appeal on the retrospective effect point. Emphasising that they were bound first by the terms of the Human Rights Act 1998 and only second by the ECHR as read in the light of the Act, their Lordships reiterated that the Act could not apply to—or found a continuing obligation in respect of—events that occurred in 1982. The judgment was thereby founded entirely upon traditional understandings of the sovereignty of Parliament and of the

---

[153] For a judicial survey of the leading authorities see *Re ES's Application* [2007] NIQB 58, para 50 ff, Gillen J.

[154] *Re S (Minors) (Care Order: Implementation of Care Plan)* [2002] AC 291. For further reluctance to use s 3 expansively see *R (Anderson) v Secretary of State for the Home Department* [2003] 1 AC 837.

[155] See, eg, *R v A* [2002] 1 AC 45, and *Ghaidan v Mendoza* [2004] 2 AC 557.

[156] The Human Rights Act 1998 (Commencement) Order 2000, SI 2000/1851; but see also s 22(2). See, eg, *Wilson v First County Trust (No 2)* [2004] 1 AC 816 and *Wainwright v Home Office* [2004] 2 AC 406. Section 7, so far as is relevant, reads: ' (1) A person who claims that a public authority has acted (or proposes to act) in a way which is made unlawful by section 6(1) may (a) bring proceedings against the authority under this Act in the appropriate court or tribunal, or (b) rely on the Convention right or rights concerned in any legal proceedings, but only if he is (or would be) a victim of the unlawful act'; and s 22(4) reads: 'Paragraph (b) of subsection (1) of section 7 applies to proceedings brought by or at the instigation of a public authority whenever the act in question took place; but otherwise that subsection does not apply to an act taking place before the coming into force of that section'. And for a narrow reading of the s 22(4) 'public authority' exception see *R v Lambert* [2002] AC 545, and *R v Kansal* [2002] 1 All ER 257.

[157] [2004] 1 WLR 807. See too, eg, *R (Hurst) v London Northern District Coroner* [2007] 2 WLR 726, and *Jordan v Lord Chancellor* [2007] 2 WLR 754.

[158] (2002) 34 EHRR 20.

[159] *Re McKerr's Application* [2003] NICA 1.

overriding relevance of constitutional dualïsm.[160] Given this, *McKerr* is perhaps best characterised as a judgment that has not attempted to develop further any understanding of the Human Rights Act 1998 as a common law constitutional statute.[161]

The Northern Ireland Act 1998

[1.33]   The Northern Ireland Act 1998's constitutional qualities were first recognised in the *Robinson* judgment of the House of Lords.[162] The issue in this case was whether a six-week time-limit in the Act for the election by the Northern Ireland Assembly of the First and Deputy First Ministers should have been strictly observed by the Assembly and the Secretary of State (the Assembly had failed to elect the Ministers within the required time-frame, and the relevant provisions of the Northern Ireland Act 1998 required that the Secretary of State set a date for fresh elections to the Assembly[163]). In holding that the Act should be given a purposive interpretation and that the time-limit need not be observed strictly, Lord Hoffmann stated that the Belfast Agreement 'was the product of multi-party negotiations to devise constitutional arrangements for a fresh start in Northern Ireland, and that 'The 1998 Act is a constitution for Northern Ireland, framed to create a continuing form of government against the history of the territory and the principles agreed in Belfast'.[164] His Lordship's approach thereby shared much in common with that in the *Thoburn* case (see [1.29]) and his comments have since been influential in the Northern Ireland courts. Notwithstanding that the House of Lords judgment in *Robinson* was not unanimous, the case thus arguably remains as the leading example of recognition, at the highest judicial level, of the importance of common law constitutional statutes.

[1.34]   The case in which Lord Hoffmann's comments were of direct influence is *Re McComb's Application*.[165] The applicant, a former paramilitary prisoner who had been released early under the terms of the Belfast Agreement and corresponding Northern Ireland (Sentences) Act 1998, had applied to the Department of the Environment for a public service vehicle licence, but this was refused. The refusal was based, in part, on the finding that his previous conviction meant that he was a not a 'fit and proper person to hold the licence' as required by the licensing legislation.[166] The decision to refuse the licence was upheld on appeal to the Recorder of Belfast, and it was this decision that was challenged in the review proceedings. The applicant argued that a distinction should be made between prisoners released under the Agreement and other prisoners and that the decision had, as such, failed to take into account the fact that his release from prison was contingent upon the Sentence Commissioners being satisfied that he would not be a 'danger to the public'.[167] Granting the application for judicial review, Kerr J accepted

---

[160] See, in particular, Lord Nicholls' judgment at [2004] 1 WLR 807, 815.

[161] See further G Anthony, 'Human Rights in Northern Ireland after *In Re McKerr*' (2005) 11 EPL 5.

[162] *Robinson v Secretary of State for Northern Ireland* [2002] NI 390.

[163] Sections 16(8) and 32(3); and see further [7.20] considering *Robinson* with reference to 'mandatory' requirements in the statute.

[164] [2002] NI 390, 402, para [25].

[165] [2003] NIQB 47. See also, eg, *Re Parson's Application* [2002] NI 378; *Re Sinn Fein's Application* [2005] NI 412; and *Re Neill's Application* [2005] NIQB 66.

[166] Principally the Road Traffic (Northern Ireland) Order 1981, SI 1981/154 (NI 1), art 79A.

[167] Northern Ireland (Sentences) Act 1998, s 3(6).

that the 'fit and proper' test was different from the 'danger to the public' formulation but that the determination of the Sentence Commissioners was a relevant consideration that should have been taken into account (the judge did not accept that this would create a two-tier system of applicants as it was merely one consideration among others). The judge moreover referred to the Belfast Agreement, which the Recorder had described as 'aspirational only'. Citing Lord Hoffmann's comments in *Robinson*, Kerr J disagreed with the Recorder's assessment of the importance of the Agreement and concluded that, 'particular attention should be paid to the fact that a prisoner released under the terms of the Northern Ireland (Sentences) Act 1998 has been adjudged not to be a danger to the public'.[168] The decision was on this basis quashed.

CONCLUSION

[1.35] This chapter has provided an overview of: the purposes of judicial review; the main sources of law of (potential) relevance in review proceedings; the importance of approaches to statutory interpretation; and the significance of common law constitutional statutes. There are five corresponding points that may be made by way of summary:

i. Judicial review is a dynamic body of law that develops in the light of the (sometimes competing) imperatives of efficient public decision-making and of the need for individuals to be able to vindicate their rights/interests in the face of exercises of public power (see [1.04]–[1.10]).
ii. Developments in judicial review are crucially affected by judicial attitudes to the sources of law of relevance in review proceedings. These attitudes, in turn, reflect understandings of the constitutional role of the courts (see [1.11]–[1.24]).
iii. The grounds for review are common law creations that continue to develop (see [1.14]–[1.15]). The three traditional grounds of illegality, *Wednesbury* unreasonableness (the starting point for substantive review), and procedural impropriety have since developed to include new sub-categories such as substantive legitimate expectation, equality, and proportionality.
iv. The literal approach to statutory interpretation is increasingly being supplanted by the purposive approach. This change has been caused in part by the demands of European law, although the courts have also modified their interpretive techniques in cases that have not involved European law issues (see [1.25]–[1.27]).
v. Some judges now recognise a category of common law constitutional statutes (which include the European Communities Act 1972, the Human Rights Act 1998, and the Northern Ireland Act 1998). These statutes are superior to other statutes; are not subject to the ordinary rules of implied repeal; and have led the courts, in some instances, to review administrative and other decisions with reference to the wider political processes that have given rise to the Acts (see [1.28]–[1.34]).

---

[168] [2003] NIQB 47, para 31.

2

When is the Judicial Review Procedure Used? The Public/Private Divide and Effective Alternative Remedies

INTRODUCTION

[**2.01**]   This chapter considers when the judicial review procedure is, or should be, used. It focuses on the implications of (1) the public/private divide and (2) the requirement that individuals make use of effective alternative remedies in preference to judicial review (remedies which may take the form of, for instance, proceedings before a tribunal or a statutory right of appeal). This is an area of considerable conceptual and practical complexity (albeit as manifest in a relatively small number of cases) and the courts have long had difficulty, in particular, in delimiting the province of judicial review and locating the corresponding realm of public law. This chapter thus examines case law on the public/private divide in Northern Ireland law and the corresponding range of tests that the courts use when identifying matters of public law that may be heard by way of application for judicial review. The chapter also considers the implications of proceeding by way of judicial review when a dispute is one of private law; and it links that issue to the wider theme of effective alternative remedies.

[**2.02**]   The chapter begins by outlining the nature of the problem presented by the public/private divide and related procedural issues. It next examines the tests that the courts use when deciding whether a matter is amenable to judicial review, and it also considers here the significance of several statutory provisions that define and/or list 'public authorities' in a manner that has relevance for judicial review case law (the most important provision is section 6 of the Human Rights Act 1998). The chapter finally examines case law on the requirement that individuals use alternative remedies in preference to judicial review; and the conclusion provides a summary of the key points made under each heading.

THE PROBLEM OF THE PROVINCE OF JUDICIAL REVIEW

[**2.03**]   The first point to note about judicial review is that the question whether to use the judicial review procedure will not give rise to difficulty in the clear majority of cases. Judicial review has been described as concerned with 'public law issues and not private disputes involving no element of public law'.[1] Public law issues, in turn, are nearly always synonymous with the exercise or non-exercise of statutory power, or the failure

---

[1]   *Re Wylie's Application* [2005] NI 359, 362, para 7.

by a decision-maker to perform a public duty that is imposed upon it by statute[2] (public law issues may more exceptionally concern exercises of the royal prerogative[3]). Where it is self-evident that a dispute is not governed by private law, and statute does not provide for an effective alternative remedy, an application for judicial review will thus be appropriate. The issues for the court will at that stage include whether the applicant has satisfied each of the procedural requirements that govern the making of an application,[4] whether the applicant has made out the grounds for review listed in their Order 53 statement,[5] and whether the remedy sought should be granted.[6]

[**2.04**]   The question whether to use the judicial review procedure can, however, become more complex in two related ways. The first is where statutory underpinning for a decision, act, or failure to act is absent or indirect. Under these circumstances, the challenge for the courts is how to delimit the reach of public law in the face of the decision-making processes of, for instance, privatised utilities or private companies that have an historical and exclusive authority to grant licences for certain economic activities. Judicial review previously fastened upon a 'source of power' test that identified public law issues solely with decisions, acts, and failures to act in respect of statutory powers and duties[7] (the test thereby served to exclude from judicial review private law decisions taken within the framework of, most obviously, contractual relations). However, while the source of power test remains sufficient for most purposes, the courts have had to look beyond it given the argument that public law can be engaged by, among other things, employment law decisions in the public sector context and the decisions of a wide range of private bodies that now perform public functions in the place of the State (through contracting out, privatisation, etc).[8] The courts have thus had to develop a range of tests that embrace the realities of public decision-making in the modern polity, where the power of decision can be of historical or contemporary origin and have a statutory or a non-statutory basis.

[**2.05**] The second complication is procedural and concerns the implications of making an application for judicial review when it transpires that the issue is not one of public law or where the matter is not exclusively one of public law. This difficulty has its origins in *O'Reilly v Mackman*,[9] where the House of Lords emphasised the importance of a procedural public/private divide under which public law rights can be vindicated only by way of Order 53 proceedings, and private law rights by way of ordinary proceedings (further procedural arguments may then arise independently of the public/private divide, that is, where a matter is one of public law but where statute provides for an alternative remedy by way of, for instance, an appeal on a point of law). Although the practical implications of *O'Reilly* have been lessened to an extent by an 'anti-technicality' provision that allows some proceedings begun by way of judicial review to continue as if begun by way of writ[10] (see

---

[2] On statutory powers and duties see [4.22]–[4.28]; although on the relationship between statutory powers/duties and private law see, eg, *In Re Malone's Application* [1988] NI 67, 74–6.

[3] [4.06]–[4.08].

[4] Ch 3.

[5] Chs 4–7.

[6] Ch 8.

[7] Judicial review was sometimes also linked to the reach of the prerogative orders: see P Maguire, 'The Procedure for Judicial Review in Northern Ireland' in B Hadfield (ed), *Judicial Review: A Thematic Approach* (Dublin, Gill & McMillan, 1995) p 370. On the prerogative orders, see ch 8.

[8] See too [4.06]–[4.08] on the royal prerogative.

[9] [1983] 2 AC 237.

[10] RSC Ord 53, r 9(5).

[2.32])—the courts also accept that judicial review may be suited to the resolution of disputes that raise mixed issues of public law and private law[11]—the 'procedural exclusivity' rule is not without continuing relevance. Hence there have been applications in which it has been held that the applicant's Order 53 statement did not in any event lend itself to continuation under the anti-technicality provision[12]; and there have been other cases in which the courts have emphasised that judicial review is a discretionary remedy and that abuse of process may lead the court in the exercise of its discretion to refuse a remedy or to impose sanctions in costs.[13] There is, in addition, the converse difficulty of proceeding by way of writ when judicial review should have been used, as applicants here may face the particular problem of meeting the shorter time-limit prescribed for the making of an application ('promptly and in any event within three months'[14]).

TESTS FOR ISSUES AMENABLE TO JUDICIAL REVIEW

[2.06]   The principal judge-made tests that are used for purposes of delimiting the reach of judicial review are: the 'source of power' test; the 'nature of the issue' test (which was first used in the context of public sector employment disputes); the 'public interest' test (which has broadened the nature of the issue test); and the 'public functions' and 'emanation of the State' tests (which seek to identify public authorities in the modern polity). The foremost statutory provisions that refer to 'public authorities' and which are thereby of analogous value to judicial review are section 6 of the Human Rights Act 1998, section 3 of the Freedom of Information Act 2000 (as read with Schedule 1 to the Act), and section 75 of the Northern Ireland Act 1998 (as read with the Schedules to a number of other Acts[15]).

The 'Source of Power' Test: Statute

[2.07]   The source of power test is centred on the understanding that all public law decisions, acts, and failures to act can ultimately be traced to statute (although it does not thereby follow that statutory powers can only sound in public law[16]). In constitutional terms, this link between statute and public law is a correlate of the doctrine of the sovereignty of the Westminster Parliament.[17] Public law orthodoxy in the UK holds that the Westminster Parliament is the source of all legal sovereignty and that those who exercise public law powers and/or perform duties must do so in accordance with the terms of the Act of Parliament that delegates responsibility to them (the ultra vires doctrine).[18] Although

---

[11] *Re Carroll's Application* [1988] NI 153.

[12] *Re Phillips' Application* [1995] NI 322, 335.

[13] *Re Molloy's Application* [1998] NI 78; although note that this was a case in which the alternative remedy was provided for by statute (appeal by way of case stated).

[14] RSC Ord 53, r 4. See further [1.07] and [3.27]–[3.29].

[15] Viz, Sch 2 to the Parliamentary Commissioner Act 1967, Sch 2 to the Commissioner for Complaints (Northern Ireland) Order 1996, SI 1996/1297 (NI 7), and the Ombudsman (Northern Ireland) Order 1996, SI 1996/1298 (NI 8).

[16] *YL v Birmingham City Council* [2007] 3 WLR 112, 142, para 101, Lord Mance; and, eg, *Re Malone's Application* [1988] NI 67 and *Re Doherty's Application*, 30 June 1992, unreported.

[17] See [1.12]

[18] See *Boddington v British Transport Police* [1999] 2 AC 143, 171, Lord Steyn.

many now regard this orthodox view as at least in part unsatisfactory,[19] statute, which can include Northern Ireland statute law,[20] remains the source of power that is central to almost all judicial review applications.[21] The point can be seen in Table one below, which summarises the content of judicial review judgments delivered in Northern Ireland in 2007.

[2.08]   Where an applicant wishes to challenge a decision, act, or failure to act relative to the terms of statute he or she must make out one or more of the grounds for judicial review developed by the courts. The grounds were historically classified as 'illegality', 'irrationality', and 'procedural impropriety',[22] although they now include other sub-headings such as proportionality, substantive legitimate expectation, and equality.[23] Moreover, under the Human Rights Act 1998—a common law constitutional statute[24]—'it is unlawful for a public authority to act in a manner which is incompatible with a Convention right'.[25] Decisions, acts, and failures to act[26] can therefore be challenged on the ground that they are contrary to the substantive and procedural guarantees of the ECHR that have effect under the terms of the Human Rights Act 1998.[27] Decisions or other measures can also be challenged as contrary to the provisions of EU law as read with the European Communities Act 1972 (another common law constitutional statute).[28]

[2.09]   The grounds for review are examined more fully in subsequent chapters.[29] However, one point here concerns the relationship between statute as a source of power and the intensity of review conducted by the courts. Statute will give decision-makers varying degrees of discretion in an area and, while the extent of discretion is a matter for judicial interpretation of the statute,[30] the courts accept that the primary responsibility for exercising the discretion—in the sense of making substantive choices—is that of the decision-maker. This traditionally meant that the courts would not examine the legitimacy of a substantive choice if it had been made within the parameters of the power ('illegality'), if it was not outrageous in its defiance of logic or of accepted moral standards ('irrationality'), and if it adhered to statutory and common law procedural requirements ('procedural impropriety'). While judicial review has since become much more context sensitive and permitting of closer judicial scrutiny (both as a result of new grounds and the impact of EU law and the ECHR), the courts frequently emphasise the need for judicial self-restraint in the face of exercises of administrative discretion.[31] This corresponds with basic notions of the separation of powers and of the understanding that courts should neither legislate nor administer in the place of those who are lawfully entitled to do so.[32] Where the source of power is statute, judicial deliberation will there-

---

[19] Sir J Laws, 'Law and Democracy' (1995) PL 72, 78–9.

[20] See [1.13].

[21] On the constitutional position in respect of challenges to administrative decisions etc taken on the basis of Acts of the Northern Ireland Assembly see [1.13] and [5.23]–[5.24].

[22] *Council of Civil Service Unions v Minister for the Civil Service* [1985] AC 374, 408, Lord Diplock.

[23] See further M Fordham, 'The Judge Over Your Shoulder: New Principles of Governmental Accountability' [2004] JR 122.

[24] On the nature and significance of which see [1.28]–[1.34] and [5.04]–[5.30].

[25] Section 6.

[26] Section 6(6) provides that 'act' includes a failure to act (though not where the failure to act concerns the parliamentary legislative process).

[27] On the relationship between the ECHR and the Act see, eg, *In re McKerr* [2004] 1 WLR 807.

[28] See [1.16]–[1.19] and [5.06]–[5.10].

[29] Chs 4–7.

[30] See [1.25]–[1.27] and [4.22]–[4.28].

[31] See, in the human rights context, [6.25]–[6.26].

[32] *Re P* [2006] NI Fam 5, para 18, Gillen J.

fore often be characterised by a concern to avoid criticisms of unwarranted judicial intrusion given the context to the decision under challenge.[33]

Table one: Table of Judicial Review Cases, January–September 2007
(Source: NI Court Service and House of Lords websites)

Name of Case and Citation	Key Issue(s)	Judgment
Jordan v Lord Chancellor; McCaughey v Chief Constable PSNI [2007] UKHL 14 [2007] 2 WLR 754	Whether the Human Rights Act 1998 applied to a coroner's inquest into a death that occurred before the date of the coming into force of the Act (2 October 2000) but which would conclude after that date; whether s 31(1) of the Coroners (NI) Act 1959 and rr 15 and 16 of the Coroners Rules (NI) 1963 enabled the jury in an inquest into a death that occurred in 1992 to return a verdict of lawful/ unlawful killing and/or to express an opinion as to criminal or civil liability; and whether s 8 of the 1959 Act imposed on the police a continuing duty to supply the coroner with information relevant to a death that occurred in 1990	The Human Rights Act 1998 does not have retrospective effect and does not apply to inquests into pre-2000 deaths; jury could not return verdicts of lawful/unlawful killing and/or express opinions as to liability, although it could make findings of fact that point towards the existence of criminal liability; and s 8 did impose a continuing duty on the police, for reasons of the public interest in full and effective investigation of deaths
Belfast City Council v Miss Behavin' Ltd [2007] UKHL 19 [2007] 1 WLR 1420	Whether a decision to refuse an application for a sex shop licence was unlawful because of the council's failure to give express consideration to the company's rights under Art 10 ECHR and Art 1, Protocol 1 ECHR (the decision was taken on the basis of the Local Government (NI) Order 1985)	Decision not unlawful. Public authorities are not obliged to give express consideration to points of human rights law during the decision-making process so long as the final decision itself is human rights-compliant
In re Officer L [2007] UKHL 36 [2007] 1 WLR 2135	Whether an inquiry, which had been asked to grant anonymity to former police officers who were required to give evidence as witnesses to a murder, had been correct to consider only whether the giving of evidence would materially increase the risk to the lives of the officers	The test applied was correct both for the purposes of the common law and Art 2 ECHR. Having found that there was no material increase in the risk, the inquiry therefore did not need to consider whether such an increased risk, if it existed, would come up to the threshold required of a real and immediate risk to life.

---

[33] See, eg, *Re Duffy's Application* [2006] NICA 28, para 40, Kerr LCJ.

Name of Case and Citation	Key Issue(s)	Judgment
Re Hill's Application for Leave [2007] NICA 1	Whether the applicant should be permitted to challenge a grant of planning permission on the grounds that the planning authority had (a) failed to have regard to a relevant report and (b) failed to have regard to relevant parts of its own policy	Leave refused in respect of (a) and granted in respect of (b): the applicant had made out an arguable case only in respect of the latter
Re HM's Application [2007] NICA 2	Whether a grant of planning permission for the erection of mobile telephone antennae was unlawful because it, among other things, violated the applicant's right to respect for private and family life under Art 8 ECHR (the grant had been made on the basis of the Planning (NI) Order 1991)	The decision was not unlawful. The applicant was essentially arguing that the grant of permission might have a deleterious effect on her health, and there is nothing in the jurisprudence of the ECtHR which suggests that something imperceptible, intangible and having no effect on the senses can potentially infringe Art 8 ECHR
Re Wright's Application [2007] NICA 24	Whether the Secretary of State's decision to convert an inquiry established under prisons legislation into one to be held under the Inquiries Act 2005 compromised the independence of the inquiry given the Secretary of State's power to bring the inquiry to an end under s 14 of the Act	The independence of the inquiry was not compromised. The s 14 power was not unique, as the power to bring an inquiry to an end is implicit in other legislative schemes. Moreover, where an inquiry is brought to an end, the decision is challengeable by way of an application for judicial review
Re McHugh's Application [2007] NICA 26	Whether the court should make a protective costs order in favour of an applicant with multiple sclerosis who wished to challenge a health trust's refusal to make arrangements for the adaptation of her home	No order would be made, as the applicant did not satisfy the so-called *Corner House* criteria that govern the making of such orders (inter alia, that an applicant should have no private interest in the outcome of the case)
Re Young's Application [2007] NICA 32	Whether a decision of the planning authority was vitiated by apparent bias because the commissioner who had reported to the Planning Appeals Commission had participated in an earlier appeal in relation to the same planning application	There was no apparent bias. Whether there is such bias always depends on the material facts of a case as regarded by an informed and fair-minded observer, and there was nothing here to suggest that the commissioner was influenced by the earlier process

Name of Case and Citation	Key Issue(s)	Judgment
Re CD's Application [2007] NICA 33	Whether the Life Sentence Review Commissioners had applied the correct standard of proof when deciding not to release a prisoner who was alleged to have committed sexual offences while out on licence	Decision of Commissioners quashed. Where serious consequences will accrue to the person against whom allegations are made, this should be reflected in the quality of the evidence that is required. The Commissioners had here failed to consider that a more compelling quality of evidence was required
Re Magee's Application [2007] NICA 34	Whether the Secretary of State had acted unlawfully in refusing to make a payment of compensation under s 133 of the Criminal Justice Act 1988 to an individual whose conviction was deemed unsafe in the face of a finding of the ECtHR; whether a refusal to make an *ex gratia* payment was likewise unlawful	The Secretary of State had not acted unlawfully. Awards under the statutory scheme were to be made only where there was a 'miscarriage of justice', and that had not happened here. Neither would the court interfere with the exercise of discretion under the non-statutory scheme in the absence of evidence that the decision was unfair, irrational, or inconsistent
Re McCabe's Application [2007] NICA 35	Whether declarations should be made in circumstances where a prisoner's rights under Arts 5(4) and 6(1) ECHR had been violated but where he would nevertheless have remained in prison	Declarations would not be made for the reason that they would be valueless. The prisoner had suffered no damage as a result of the breaches of the ECHR
Re Downes' Application [2007] NIQB 1	Whether the court should quash the unlawful appointment of the interim victims commissioner (see [2006] NIQB 77); or whether a declaration should issue thereby allowing the commissioner—who herself was blameless in the appointment process—to conclude the work she had begun	A declaration would issue. While the normal and proper remedy in order to deprive an unlawful decision of legal effect is an order of certiorari, that principle is not an overriding one. There were thus arguments of public interest in favour of making a declaration in the instant case (inter alia, advancing the interests of victims)
Re PM's Application [2007] NIQB 2	Whether a county court judge's order that documentation should be produced to a police officer had been made in accordance with art 11 of, and sch 1 to, the Police and Criminal Evidence (NI) Order 1989 (the documentation was held by a school and related to a pupil who was being investigated for murder)	The order had been made unlawfully and would be quashed. A request under the legislation should be acceded to only where there are reasonable grounds for believing that the material is likely to be of substantial value to the investigation. On the facts, the police had not shown reasonable grounds

Name of Case and Citation	Key Issue(s)	Judgment
Re DPP's Application [2007] NIQB 3	Whether a resident magistrate's refusal to adjourn proceedings at the request of the prosecution should be quashed for reasons of the resident magistrate's alleged failure to carry out a proper inquiry into the need for an adjournment	Decision to refuse the request quashed. It is the duty of a magistrate to ensure that he or she has been sufficiently appraised of all relevant matters. In the present case, the magistrate had not discharged the duty
Re Derry City Council's Application [2007] NIQB 5	Whether the present name of the City of Londonderry is 'Derry' (the name 'Londonderry' dating from Royal Charters of 1613 and 1662); and whether, in the event that the name is not Derry, the UK government or Department of the Environment should be compelled to take steps to effect such change to the name	The name of the city remains Londonderry, as the Charter of 1662 was not affected by subsequent local government legislation. Moreover, government could not be compelled to change the name. Such change could be made only through a further exercise of the royal prerogative or through legislation
Re Thompson's Application [2007] NIQB 8	Whether a prison governor's decision to deselect a prisoner from a resettlement unit was unlawful for reasons of a lack of fairness	The decision would be quashed, as the applicant had not been given an adequate opportunity to know the case against him or to respond to that case
Re DPP's Application [2007] NIQB 10	Whether a youth court's refusal to adjourn proceedings in an assault trial and its decision to dismiss all charges when the prosecution could not proceed should be quashed	The decision would be quashed. The court had failed to enquire whether a short or lengthy adjournment would have been required to allow the case to proceed. It had therefore failed to take a relevant consideration into account
Re Zekaj's Application [2007] NIQB 13	Whether the Home Office had erred in deciding that the applicant had made a fraudulent application for asylum and that he should thereby be refused indefinite leave to remain in the UK	The Home Office had not been in error. The court was satisfied that there had been fraud on the part of the applicant
Re Zhanje's Application [2007] NIQB 14	Whether the applicant—an asylum seeker—had been unlawfully removed from the UK to the Republic of Ireland in breach of her procedural rights under, inter alia, s 82 of the Nationality, Immigration and Asylum Act 2002 (which allows an individual to remain in the UK if he or she makes a human rights claim and where the Home Secretary does notcertify that claim as clearly unfounded)	The applicant had been removed unlawfully, as she had made a human rights claim but had been removed before a certificate was issued. The court thus ordered that the applicant be allowed to return to the UK pending the resolution of her human rights claim

Name of Case and Citation	Key Issue(s)	Judgment
Re Murphy's Application [2007] NIQB 15	Whether the High Court should order discovery of documents related to the substantive issues to be raised in the application for judicial review	An order for discovery would be made in respect of some of the documents requested. These were considered necessary for the fair disposal of the matter
Re McCafferty's Application [2007] NIQB 17	Whether a prison governor's decision to award 14 days' cellular confinement to a prisoner who had already been subjected to 14 days of restricted association under rr 32 and 35 of the Prison etc (NI) Rules 1995 should be quashed (the governor had been unaware of the earlier period of time)	The decision would not be quashed but would be remitted to the governor to retake in the light of the judgment of the court. While the earlier 14-day period was not in the form of punishment (the latter was), the governor may have discounted some days when fixing the subsequent period
Re Toner's Application [2007] NIQB 18	Whether convicted prisoners who were prohibited from voting in the Northern Ireland Assembly elections of March 2007 should be given a range of remedies that would enable them to vote (the source of the prohibition was art 4 of the Northern Ireland Assembly [Elections] Order 2001, as read with, most relevantly, ss 3 and 4 of the Representation of the People Act 1983, and ss 1 and 2 of, and sch 1 to, the Elected Authorities [NI] Act 1989)	The application would be dismissed. Although it was now accepted that the blanket prohibition on prisoners voting was incompatible with the ECHR, the government was considering ways to modify the domestic legislation. There were, moreover, strong arguments of public interest against judicial intervention in the instant case where that would have the effect of postponing the elections
Re Armstrong's Application for Leave [2007] NIQB 20	Whether the Assistant Director of the Assets Recovery Agency had acted in breach of the applicant's human rights (notably under Art 8 ECHR) by refusing to remove from the Agency's website a report that named the applicant in the context of drug-related matters (the Agency had been created under the Proceeds of Crime Act 2002)	The application for leave would not be granted. The Assistant Director's actions were clearly consistent with the design of the legislation that had created the agency. Moreover, to the extent that use of the website interfered with the applicant's rights under Art 8 ECHR, this was said to be proportionate and linked to a legitimate aim (viz reducing crime)
Re Okaro's Application [2007] NIQB 21	Whether an immigrant had been unlawfully detained pending removal from the UK because of the respondent's failure to follow its own policy on the treatment of illegal entrants (removal would be effected on the basis of s 33 of, and sch 2 to, the Immigration Act 1971)	There was no illegality. The respondent had not failed to consider its own policy, and the court was satisfied that the immigration officers had exercised their discretion in accordance with the policy when determining the application

Name of Case and Citation	Key Issue(s)	Judgment
Re McHenry's Application for Leave [2007] NIQB 22	Whether the applicant had been given a fair hearing by the Planning Appeals Commission when refusing an appeal from a decision of the Planning Service	Leave would be granted, as the applicant had made out an arguable case on the issue to be raised at the substantive hearing
Re Moore's Application [2007] NIQB 23	Whether the court should make a protective costs order in favour of an applicant who was challenging the outcome of an application to the Planning Service and the Housing Executive	No order would be made because, inter alia, there were no exceptional circumstances and the case did not raise public law issues of general importance
Re McAnoy's Application [2007] NIQB 24	Whether the prison authorities had acted unlawfully—viz, contrary to r 32 of the Prison etc (NI) Rules 1995—when telling a prisoner that he could not enter the cells of other prisoners (r 32 permits of restrictions of association but contains a range of corresponding safeguards that were not observed here)	There had been no illegality. Rule 32, as conventionally understood, applied to circumstances where prisoners are placed in segregation units. In the instant case, it thus could not be read as applying to 'in cell' association
Re Bothwell's Application [2007] NIQB 25	Whether the High Court had 'full jurisdiction' for the purposes of Art 6 ECHR in circumstances where the applicant challenged the determination of a tribunal that was notArt 6 ECHR-compliant (the tribunal calculated the levels of compensation to be paid for compulsorily destroyed cattle)	Art 6 ECHR was violated. Judicial review does not extend to consideration of the merits of a decision but rather deals with challenges based on legality, procedural fairness and rationality. It is therefore unsuited to the resolution of such disputes as to individual valuations
Re Kincaid's Application [2007] NIQB 26	Whether the Public Prosecution Service had acted unlawfully at common law and under Art 2 ECHRin refusing to give fuller reasons forthe decision not to prosecute an indi-vidual who had shot the applicant	There had been no illegality. The applicant knew in outline form why proceedings had not been preferred, and the court did not consider that fuller reasons would assist the applicant's understanding of the decision. Neither was the absence of fuller reasons irrational
Re Sheridan Millenium Ltd's Application for Leave [2007] NIQB 27	Whether judicial review was the appropriate means to challenge a decision to terminate the applicant'sappointment as a preferred developer for a development programme in Belfast	Leave granted. While the respondent argued that its decision sounded in private law, it was arguable that the matter was one of public law. This was particularly so given the appli-cant's argument that the challenged decision was vitiated by unlawful motive and bad faith

Name of Case and Citation	Key Issue(s)	Judgment
Re Aiyegbusi's Application for Leave[2007] NIQB 28	Whether the applicant should be permitted to challenge a decision, made under the Immigration Act 1971, that he entered the UK by deception; that he was an illegal entrant; and that he should therefore be detained pending removal	Leave refused. The applicant had practised deception in relation to his visa application and the immigration authorities were entitled to make the decisions under challenge. Thus the applicant's case was not arguable
Re Witness A & Ors' Application [2007] NIQB 30	Whether an inquiry, which had refused to grant anonymity to individuals who were required to give evidence as witnesses to a murder, had asked itself the correct question when considering whether there was a threat to the right to life; whether the inquiry had acted unfairly by failing to disclose relevant material to the applicants when making its determination	Application granted. The inquiry had asked itself the wrong question in respect of the right to life and its decision was quashed (although judgment on this point has since been overtaken by the HL judgment in *Re Officer L*, above). There was also the possibility that the inquiry would act unfairly if it retook the decision without giving the applicants fuller access to the relevant material
Re Waide's Application [2007] NIQB 31	Whether the Criminal Injuries Compensation Appeals Panel had acted unlawfully and irrationally when refusing a claim for compensation from an individual injured as a result of being struck by a motorcycle (the corresponding compensation scheme—made under the Criminal Injuries Compensation [NI] Order 2002—precluded such awards save where the motor vehicle was used deliberately to inflict injury)	The application was dismissed, as the decision under challenge accorded with the wording of the compensation scheme. Neither could the decision be challenged as irrational. While there was evidence that the motorcyclist had driven directly at the applicant, there was also evidence that there was no intention to hit the applicant. The panel was therefore entitled to conclude that there had been no intention to inflict physical injury
Re Lockhart's Application [2007] NIQB 35	Whether the Prison Service had interfered unlawfully with the applicant's rights under Art 8 ECHR when (a) refusing to refer proposals for a programme of temporary release to the Secretary of State for determination and (b) refusing a programme of temporary release in the applicant's case	The application was dismissed because, inter alia, there was no interference with Art 8 ECHR. The schemes in question were intended to advance rather than interfere with Art 8 ECHR rights, and the point made was not well founded for that reason

Name of Case and Citation	Key Issue(s)	Judgment
Re Gallagher's Application [2007] NIQB 37	Whether the prison authorities had acted unlawfully by refusing to exercise their discretion in respect of an application for home leave so as to ignore a period of time that the prisoner had spent on bail pending a retrial for charges on which he was subsequently convicted (the application for home leave being made within the context of that conviction)	There had been no illegality. When exercising its discretion, the respondent had been entitled to take into account the fact that a decision to ignore the bail period would have been to treat the applicant more favourably than other prisoners. It was, in any event, clear that the discretion had not been exercised solely in the light of that factor
Re SH's Application [2007] NIQB 39	Whether the education authorities had acted unreasonably and contrary to the Education and Libraries (NI) Order 1986 by refusing to make provision for the applicant's transport to and from a grammar school that was further away from the applicant's house than a 'suitable' school in respect of which transport provision would be made	The authorities had not acted unreasonably. The primary responsibility for taking the decision was that of the authorities, who had to take account of parental preference, the suitability of the schools, and financial and policy considerations (among others). In those circumstances, the court did not consider that the decision was unreasonable/irrational
Re Downes' Application for Leave [2007] NIQB 40	Whether a QC who had been appointed by the Attorney-General to inquire whether government officials had interfered with the administration of justice had erred by refusing to allow the applicant to participate in his inquiry and to have access to the materials gathered by him (an earlier application for judicial review brought by the applicant had resulted in the concerns about the actions of the government officials)	Application for leave refused. The inquiry in question was non-statutory and private in form and intended to be expeditious. The decision under challenge was consonant with that framework. There was thus nothing irrational or perverse about the decision to refuse to involve the applicant more fully in the inquiry
Re Fedorovski's Application for Leave [2007] NIQB 41	Whether the immigration authorities had acted unlawfully (inter alia, in breach of sch 2 to the Immigration Act 1971) by ordering that the applicant be removed to Ukraine when he was not a citizen of that State (he did not have citizenship of any State)	Application for leave refused. The applicant originally came from that part of the USSR that is now known as Ukraine and he had avenues for obtaining citizenship there. There was therefore no arguable case

Name of Case and Citation	Key Issue(s)	Judgment
Re Ullah's Application for Leave [2007] NIQB 45	Whether costs should be awarded against the respondent for the reason that it had changed its decision on the applicant's immigration status only after an application for leave had been made, notwithstanding the clarity of the issues raised in the applicant's pre-action correspondence	An order for costs would be made. Although the early resolution of cases will not, as a general rule, lead to an award of costs, this was an exceptional case where the respondent had failed to concede a well-founded argument
Re Stewart's Application [2007] NIQB 48	Whether a prisoner released on licence had been unlawfully convicted of an offence under art 27 of the Criminal Justice (NI) Order 1996, that is, of failing to observe licence conditions or to provide a 'reasonable excuse' for not doing so	Conviction quashed. The magistrate had erred in finding that there had been no reasonable excuse as the applicant had been willing to comply with the conditions but had been unable to do so because of force of circumstance. In that instant, there was reasonable excuse
Re Purcell's Application [2007] NIQB 50	Whether there was apparent bias on the part of a police disciplinary panel that had had access to a document that summarised how panels should address arguments based on a leading authority in the field of police discipline	Application dismissed. The document in question was general guidance that was not case-specific and the court was satisfied that the content of the document was not in the minds of the members of the panel when dealing with the case before it
Re Beattie's Application [2007] NIQB 51	Whether a prison disciplinary adjudication was flawed for reason of insufficient evidence to support the finding that the applicant had breached the Prison Rules by bringing drugs in on his person after a period of leave (drugs were found in the prisoner's cell after he had returned to it)	The adjudication would be remitted to the governor to be heard again, as the evidence relied upon had not confirmed the absence of an item in the cell before the applicant re-entered it. Thus, while all the evidential rigour of a criminal trial was not required, fuller evidence was needed given the potential consequences for the applicant
Re Delaney's Application [2007] NIQB 55	Whether Belfast Improved Housing Association's policy of refusing to sell two-bedroom bungalows to its clients unlawfully fettered its discretion (the policy was operated by reason of art 3A of the Housing [NI] Order 1983); whether the policy was irrational; and whether the policy violated the applicant's rights under Art 1, Protocol 1 ECHR	Application dismissed. There was no fettering of discretion, as the policy was set by statute and there was no scope for discretion; the policy was not irrational as it was intended to protect housing stock in the public sector; and there was no violation of Art 1, Protocol 1 ECHR as the applicant had no right to buy

Name of Case and Citation	Key Issue(s)	Judgment
Re JR10's Application [2007] NIQB 56	Whether the High Court should give judgment in the case notwithstanding that the matter before it had become academic (that is, the applicant had been questioned about offences but had been released without charge); whether the High Court should issue a declaration that the police had acted unlawfully in conducting an identity parade under the Terrorism Act 2000 where the applicant had withdrawn his consent to the parade	It was right that the court should hear the case as the issues raised would likely arise again in the future. However, no declaration would be made. In circumstances such as those in the case, the question of prejudice to the individual could better be dealt with by the court that hears any charges, where art 76 of the Police and Criminal Evidence (NI) Order 1989 would allow the court to exclude evidence in the interests of justice
Re ES's Application [2007] NIQB 58	Whether the manner of making emergency protection orders under, inter alia, art 64(8) of the Children (Northern Ireland) Order 1995 is incompatible with Arts 6 and 8 ECHR (orders made under art 64(8) cannot be challenged in court for 72 hours)	Incompatibility established. The 72-hour provision constitutes an unnecessary and disproportionate response to the self-evidently legitimate aim of protecting children. Court invited further submissions on appropriate relief
Re Omagh District Council's Application [2007] NIBQ 61	Whether a new statement of planning policy introduced by the Minister for Regional Development was ultra vires art 4 of the Strategic Planning (NI) Order 1999 insofar as the policy addressed in the statement fell within the responsibility of the Department of the Environment under art 3(1) of the Planning (NI) Order 1991	The policy was unlawful, as the Department for Regional Development had attempted to usurp the Department of the Environment's function. While the court would not quash the policy—this could result in adverse public consequences—it would make a declaration as to the policy's illegality
Re Seaport Investment's Application [2007] NIBQ 62	Whether the Environmental Assessment of Plans and Programmes Regulations (NI) 2004 had correctly implemented Directive 2001/42 EC in domestic law	The Directive had not been implemented fully. This was because of, inter alia, an incorrect designation of a consultation body and the absence of appropriate time-frames
Re S's Application [2007] NIQB 63	Whether the Public Prosecution Service had acted unlawfully in not seeking medical notes and counselling records in relation to the alleged victim of an indecent assault where solicitors for the accused wished to examine the records for the presence of any inconsistency in the accounts given by the complainant	The refusal was not unlawful. The Public Prosecution Service has a 'margin of consideration' when deciding whether to request material that might reasonably be capable of undermining the prosecution case. Notwithstanding that the refusal was based partly on an erroneous assumption about whether the materials existed, the court would not intervene

Name of Case and Citation	Key Issue(s)	Judgment
Re Christian Institute & Ors' Application [2007] NIQB 66	Whether the Equality Act (Sexual Orientation) Regulations (NI) 2006 were susceptible to challenge on the ground of procedural impropriety; whether the regulations violated, inter alia, Art 9 ECHR	The regulations were partly flawed because of lack of consultation, and the corresponding provisions would be quashed. However, the remaining provisions were unaffected and their validity could not, in any event, be addressed properly in the instant application. Any violation of Art 9 ECHR was therefore a matter for case-by-case resolution
Re LM's Application [2007] NIQB 68	Whether the Compensation Agency had acted unlawfully in ruling that an application for a review of a refusal of compensation was time-barred by virtue of having been made outside the 90-day limit specified in the Criminal Injuries Compensation Scheme 2002	The finding that the application was time-barred was not unlawful. It was clear from the legislation that applications had to be made within 90 days, albeit that the limit could be extended on the basis of the exceptions noted in the scheme
Re Tweed's Application [2007] NIQB 69	Whether a Parades Commission decision that imposed conditions upon an Orange Order procession was unlawful for the reason, inter alia, that it interfered with the applicant's rights under Arts 9, 10 and 11 ECHR	The decision was not unlawful. Rights under Arts 9, 10 and 11 ECHR are qualified rights, and the rights of the applicant had to be balanced with the rights of the police and the general public. The decision thus aimed to prevent disorder (a legitimate objective), and the measures adopted were proportionate
Re RK and Ors' Application [2007] NIQB 71	Whether a school had acted unlawfully relative to the Education (NI) Order 1997 by operating a policy of not examining the addresses of applicants for places at the school when the school's entry criteria centred on a Northern Ireland residence requirement and when the school had general knowledge that false addresses were being used to secure places; whether corresponding decisions of the Admissions Appeal Tribunal were unlawful	The school and Tribunal had acted unlawfully. The policy of not checking addresses meant that the school was not applying properly the statutory criteria that gave priority to Northern Ireland residents. The Tribunal had in turn erred by accepting the policy of the school rather than treating it as an incorrect application of the admissions criteria. The decisions of the Tribunal in respect of the applicants were quashed and admission to the school ordered

The 'Nature of the Issue' Test and Public Sector Employment Disputes

[**2.10**]　The source of power test (see [2.07]–[2.09]) is predicated on the now outdated understanding that public law powers and duties can have their origins solely in statute. One corollary of this is that private law relations—for instance those based on contract—have traditionally been excluded from judicial review precisely because the source of power is non-statutory and found on the private law side of the public/private divide.[34] For example, in *Re Lyle's Application*,[35] judicial review was sought of the decision of the Executive Committee and the Disciplinary Committee of the Ulster Unionist Council to disaffiliate North Down Constituency Association. In holding that the dispute was not amenable to judicial review, Carswell J held that 'there is no statutory regulation of the constitution or membership of political parties . . . they remain private associations regulated by private law'.[36] The dispute was therefore contractual, notwithstanding that 'political parties are very closely involved in elections and that their affairs and activities are a matter in which the public have considerable interest'.[37] Case law in England and Wales has likewise affirmed that the existence of a contract will normally prove decisive, even where it is argued that the contractual relationship in question is not truly consensual.[38]

[2.11]   The question whether a matter is one of public law or private law can, however, become more complex in the context of public sector employment disputes and the courts have here developed a 'nature of the issue' test. Although public sector employees are ordinarily in the same position as private sector employees—that is, their employment law disputes are matters of private law[39]—the courts accept that judicial review proceedings may be appropriate in some circumstances. Hence in *Re Phillips' Application*[40] Carswell LJ suggested that, when a public sector employment dispute comes before the court on an application for judicial review, the court should 'consider the nature of the issue itself and (ask) whether it has characteristics which import an element of public law'.[41] In identifying when public law issues may arise, Carswell LJ referred to the points of principle outlined by the Court of Appeal in England and Wales in *McClaren v Home Office*.[42] The first of these was, again, that employment disputes involving public sector employees would normally be matters of private law and that proceedings should be begun in the ordinary way. However, judicial review may be appropriate where a body established under the royal prerogative or statute hears disputes in proceedings that are neither domestic nor wholly informal,[43] as judicial review has long been available in respect of the decisions of such inferior bodies (subject to the non-availability of an effective alternative remedy). The Court of Appeal in England and Wales also considered that judicial review may be appropriate where an employee of the Crown or other public body is adversely affected by an employment decision that is of

---

[34] See, eg, *Re TSI (Ireland) Ltd's Application* [2005] NIQB 87 (government tendering process in respect of its private telephone network not subject to judicial review).

[35] [1987] 1 NIJB 24.

[36] [1987] 1 NIJB 24, 34.

[37] [1987] 1 NIJB 24, 34–5. For an example of a party political dispute being heard by way of private law proceedings see *Donaldson and ors v Empey and ors* [2003] NIQB 52.

[38] See, most famously, *R v Jockey Club, ex p Aga Khan* [1993] 1 WLR 909 (applicant unable to challenge a determination of the Jockey Club's disciplinary panel because of the existence of a contract and notwithstanding the argument that the contract was not truly consensual, ie the Jockey Club enjoyed a monopoly over the regulation of horse racing and the applicant could not race his horses in the absence of a contract). See too *R (Mullins) v Appeal Board of the Jockey Club* [2005] LLR 151.

[39] See, eg, *Re Wislang's Application* [1984] NI 63; *Re Malone's Application* [1988] NI 67; and *Re Deman's Application*, 19 January 1996, unreported.

[40] [1995] NI 322.

[41] [1995] NI 322, 334.

[42] [1990] ICR 824.

[43] On 'domestic' decision-makers see [4.35].

general application and which can be argued to be *Wednesbury* unreasonable.[44] The key, under these circumstances, is to distinguish between decisions that are made in respect of an individual (a private law matter) and decisions that are 'taken as a matter of policy, not in relation to a particular member of staff, but in relation to staff in general'.[45] Decisions of this latter kind 'could be the subject of judicial review'.[46]

[2.12] *Phillips* clearly represented a move away from a rigid source of power test towards one that focuses on the nature of the decision at issue. While the case is for that reason significant, the fact that only a few employment disputes may fall within the *McClaren* exceptions[47] does, however, mean that the case also has limitations (it is notable that on the facts in *Phillips*, where the applicant challenged his dismissal from his post with the Ministry of Defence, it was held that no public law issue arose[48]). The point here is that a decision to proceed by way of application for judicial review when that is the wrong procedure may subsequently present practical difficulties for the applicant. Although RSC Order 53, rule 9(5) allows some applications for judicial review to continue as if commenced by way of writ—the courts may also allow an application to proceed where there are mixed issues of public law and private law[49]—much will depend on the remedy sought in the Order 53 statement. In *Phillips* the court thus refused to allow the proceedings to continue because it considered that the case had been built around the public law objective of having the dismissal quashed (the court thought that the applicant's case would thereby need to be substantially recast before it would be suited to private law proceedings). The applicant was on that basis prejudiced at two levels, as the application for judicial review had proven ill advised (the court considered that there would, in any event, have been no grounds for granting the relief sought) and he was unable to proceed under Order 53, rule 9(5). The significance of this procedural point is considered more fully at [2.30]–[2.33].

[2.13] One further public sector employment case of relevance is *Re Aitken's Application*,[50] which confirms that judicial review will often be available where an individual has no other remedy. The applicant here was a full-time member of the Royal Ulster Constabulary Reserve who was employed on a three-year contract. Although the contract was renewable, the Chief Constable—whose power of appointment derived from statute[51]—refused to renew it in the light of concerns about the applicant's association with suspected members of a terrorist organisation. The Chief Constable's power to refuse or renew a contract had not, however, been included in the terms of the applicant's contract, and the applicant initiated judicial review proceedings. While the application

---

[44] On which see *Associated Provincial Picture Houses v Wednesbury Corporation* [1943] KB 223, and [6.05]–[6.11].

[45] [1990] ICR 824, 836–7.

[46] [1990] ICR 824, 836–7; and see, eg, *Re Shields' Application* [2003] NI 161 (Force Order in respect of promotion within the RUC unsuccessfully challenged as ultra vires its parent legislation).

[47] For a recent case that did fall within the *Phillips* and *McClaren* public law criteria see *Re McQuillan's Application* [2004] NIQB 50 (a decision as to a council employee's pay was challengeable by way of judicial review as the challenge had as its effective target a general policy on pay during suspension from employment). And for an earlier case that drew upon *McClaren* see *In Re McGrotty's Application*, 22 June 1994, unreported.

[48] And see *Re Coroner for South Down's Application* [2004] NIQB 86 (no public law issue involved in a pay dispute that raised, inter alia, arguments about discrimination as between full-time and part-time coroners).

[49] *Re Carroll's Application* [1988] NI 153.

[50] [1995] NI 49.

[51] Police Act (Northern Ireland) 1970, s 9 and reg 10 of the Royal Ulster Constabulary Reserve (Full-time) (Appointments and Conditions of Service) Regulations 1988, SR 1988/36.

was to be dismissed both for reasons of delay and merits, Kerr J nevertheless emphasised that judicial review had been open to the applicant. Highlighting that the Chief Constable's powers of appointment were statutory and that they had not been written into the applicant's contract, the judge considered that a decision to renew or refuse a contract amounted to an exercise or non-exercise of statutory power that sounded in public law. The judge also noted the absence of private law rights that the applicant could pursue by way of civil proceedings, as well as the absence of the possibility of bringing proceedings for unfair dismissal.[52]

The 'Public Interest' Test

[**2.14**]   The 'nature of the issue' approach in *Re Phillips' Application* has since been used to found a much wider 'public interest' test of amenability to judicial review. This test was first used in *Re McBride's Application*,[53] where a challenge was made to a decision of an army board not to discharge from service two soldiers who had been convicted in a civilian court of murder (the applicant was the mother of the victim of the murder). The question for the court, among others, was whether this decision was an employment decision that affected only the soldiers in respect of whom it was made, or whether it was a decision that was amenable to judicial review. In holding that it was amenable, Kerr J referred to Carswell LJ's judgment in *Phillips* and said:

> It appears to me that an issue is one of public law where it involves a matter of public interest in the sense that it has an impact on the public generally and not merely on an individual or group. That is not to say that an issue becomes one of public law simply because it generates interest or concern in the minds of the public. It must affect the public rather than merely engage its interest to qualify as a public law issue. It seems to me to be equally clear that a matter may be one of public law while having a specific impact on an individual in his personal capacity.[54]

The impugned decision was on this basis open to review because 'the public has a legitimate interest in whether those who have been convicted of murder should be allowed to continue to serve as members of the armed forces'.[55] While the judge at the same time said that the position would be different where a decision was, for example, taken to retain an office worker in the service of a private company, the distinction here was clear: 'Whether an individual be retained in employment dedicated to the service of the public is, to my mind, self evidently a matter of public law.'[56]

[**2.15**]   The width of the public interest test—both potential and actual—has been apparent in a number of subsequent cases. For instance, in *Re Kirkpatrick's Application*[57] the court considered that the Lough Neagh Fishermen's Co-operative Society's decision to refuse the applicant a licence for eel fishing would have been amenable to judicial review had the applicant not had an effective alternative remedy.[58] Although the Co-operative

---

[52] Applying *R v Secretary of State for the Home Department, ex p Benwell* [1985] QB 554.
[53] [1999] NI 299.
[54] [1999] NI 299, 310, cited with approval by the NICA in *Re McBride's Application (No 2)* [2003] NI 319, 336, Carswell LCJ.
[55] [1999] NI 299, 310.
[56] [1999] NI 299, 310.
[57] [2004] NIJB 15.
[58] Namely, discrimination proceedings before a Fair Employment Tribunal under the Fair Employment and Treatment (Northern Ireland) Order 1998, (SI 1998/3162) (N121).

Society is a private organisation, it has an historical and exclusive right to grant licences for eel fishing on Lough Neagh, and the judge considered that 'the public has a legitimate concern as to how fish stocks are maintained and how fishing activities are regulated in this substantial and important natural asset . . . But for the historical accident that fishing rights are privately owned by the Society one would expect that such an important natural resource would be controlled by a public agency accountable to government and ultimately the public.'[59] The test was also used in *Re Wadsworth's Application*,[60] where it was held that the Northern Ireland Railways Company Ltd's decision to exclude a taxi driver from a designated rank at Belfast's Central Station was a matter of public law. This was because 'the provision of taxi services at Central Station affects the public interest where those members of the public using public transport provided by the statutory railway authority have a legitimate interest in the continuity of those services with incidental transport arrangements'.[61] And in *Re City Hotel (Derry) Ltd's Application*[62] it was held that a dispute between a property company and the Department of Social Development about costing for the development of lands owned by the Department likewise fell within the public interest test. Although the Department argued that the dispute was commercial, Weatherup J adopted the 'affects' and 'impacts' approach developed through *Phillips*, *McBride*, and *Kirkpatrick*:

> The decision under challenge is not a decision made directly in connection with the contractual relationship between the applicant and the Department . . . The issue concerns the terms on which public lands might be developed and disposed of . . . The site is publicly owned and the public have a right to expect that the development and disposal of the site will be undertaken by the Department in the public interest.[63]

[2.16] Such use of the public interest test is of importance for two reasons. First, by elaborating upon the precise nature of the public interest in the issues in *McBride*, *Kirkpatrick*, *Wadsworth*, and *City Hotel (Derry) Ltd*, the courts have used the test in a way that should in part alleviate concerns about the use of the term 'public interest'. The term is one that is both potentially vague and value laden,[64] and its use in other contexts has been criticised as shielding judicial policy preferences and facilitating judicial involvement in disputes that are essentially political.[65] By linking the 'public interest' in the various cases to concrete—though not incontestable—considerations the test has thus arguably been used in a manner that observes minimum requirements of transparency. On other hand, it might also be said that the test gives individual judges too much discretion in cases before them and that this can only engender uncertainty as to the test's future applicability.

---

[59] [2004] NIJB 15, 21, para 26, Kerr J. See also *Re Wylie's Application* [2005] NI 359.

[60] [2004] NIQB 8.

[61] [2004] NIQB 8, para 16.

[62] [2004] NIQB 38.

[63] [2004] NIQB 38, para 14. See too *Re Sheridan Millennium's Application for Leave* [2007] NIQB 27 (court granting leave to challenge a decision to terminate the applicant's appointment as a preferred developer for a development programme in Belfast, as it was arguable, following *McBride*, that the case raised public law issues).

[64] For judicial consideration of the potential width of the term see *Re DD's Application* [2006] NIQB 19, paras 24–8, Morgan J (considering the term within the context of legal aid provision).

[65] Eg, in respect of the interpretation of standing rules to permit public interest applications: see C Harlow, 'Public Law and Popular Justice' (2002) 65 MLR 1. On standing see [3.64]–[3.70].

[**2.17**]   The second reason relates to the test's ability to embrace the decision-making processes of the varied and de facto forms of governmental power in the modern era. While the source of power test traditionally traces all public power to statute (see [2.07]), historical accidents (*Kirkpatrick*) and the increased contractualisation of government (privatisation, contracting out, etc[66]) mean that public law decisions may in fact be taken by a wide range of non-statutory and/or private bodies. Under the public interest test, applications for judicial review may therefore now (potentially) be brought in respect of the decision-making processes of such bodies, whether their power is of historical or contemporary origin. The public interest formulation on that basis provides the most expansive—and perhaps important—of all of the tests for amenability to review.

'Public Functions' and 'Emanations of the State'

[**2.18**]   The public function test—which is now central to judicial review in England and Wales[67]—is another to have been developed in the light of the diffuse and de facto forms of governmental power. The test is most famously associated with the judgment of the Court of Appeal in England and Wales in *R v Panel on Take-overs and Mergers, ex p Datafin*.[68] In that case it was held that the decisions of a self-regulating unincorporated association that oversees the take-overs of listed public companies could be subject to judicial review, notwithstanding that the body had no direct statutory, prerogative, or common law powers (statute did, however, play an indirect role relative to sanctions for breach of the Panel's code). For the Court, it was no longer appropriate to consider solely the source of a body's power, but also its nature. Hence where a body is 'exercising public law functions, or if the exercise of the functions have public law consequences, then that may . . . be sufficient to bring the body within the reach of judicial review'.[69] This, in turn, was an open-ended formulation that was premised upon the need to identify 'a public element, which can take many different forms',[70] and it has since given rise to a number of related tests and questions that include: 'whether (the body) operates as an integral part of a system which has a public law character, is supported by public law . . . and performs what might be described as public law functions'[71]; whether there is sufficient statutory penetration of the decision-maker's functions[72]; whether the body is under an express or implied public duty to perform its tasks[73]; or whether government would, 'but for' the existence of the non-statutory body, create a statutory body to oversee the area in question.[74]

---

[66] See P Leyland and G Anthony, *Textbook on Administrative Law*, 5th edn (Oxford, Oxford University Press, 2005) ch 3.

[67] Part 54.1 of the Civil Procedure Rules (CPR) reads: 'A' claim for judicial review" means a claim to review the lawfulness of (i) an enactment or (ii) *a decision, action or failure to act in relation to the exercise of a public function*' (emphasis added).

[68] [1987] QB 815.

[69] [1987] QB 815, 847, Lloyd LJ.

[70] [1987] QB 815, 838, Sir John Donaldson MR.

[71] [1987] QB 815, 836, Sir John Donaldson MR; and see, eg, *R (Beer) v Hampshire Farmers Market Ltd* [2004] 1 WLR 233, and *R (Al Veg Ltd) v Hounslow London Borough Council* [2004] LGR 536.

[72] *R v Governors of Haberdashers' Aske's Hatcham College Trust, ex p T* [1995] ELR 350, and *R v Cobham Hall School, ex p S* [1998] ELR 389. Cf *R v Muntham House School, ex p R* [2000] LGR 255, and *R v Servite Houses, ex p Goldsmith* [2001] LGR 55.

[73] [1987] QB 815, 852, Nicholls LJ.

[74] [1987] QB 815, 835, Sir John Donaldson MR. And see, eg, *R v Advertising Standards Authority Ltd, ex p The Insurance Service Plc* (1990) 2 Admin LR 77, 86 (government inevitably would intervene); *R v Chief Rabbi of the United Hebrew Congregations of Great Britain and the Commonwealth, ex p Wachmann* [1992] 1 WLR

[**2.19**]   Case law in Northern Ireland has also referred to the public function test, although it is arguable that it would in any event now be subsumed within the public inter-est test considered above ([2.14]–[2.17]). One such reference was made in *Re Sherlock and Morris's Application*,[75] where Kerr J held that judicial review was available to challenge a decision of Northern Ireland Electricity (NIE) to disconnect the permanent electricity supply to two residences. Although the judge noted that NIE was a privatised company that was accountable to its shareholders and in which the government was not a majority shareholder, he held that the performance of NIE's functions was a matter of public law. Finding first that 'it could not have been argued that the supply of electricity was not a public law function' before NIE was privatised, the judge emphasised that 'it is the pub-lic nature of the function which is discharged which provides the primary, if not the exclu-sive, guide to the question of whether (a decision) is amenable to judicial review'.[76] Having thus analysed NIE's core responsibilities in respect of the provision of electricity to the public—NIE holds a licence for this purpose under the Electricity (Northern Ireland) Order 1992[77]—Kerr J concluded that 'It would be inconceivable . . . that the dis-charge of these duties should be outside the common law control of public functions'.[78]

[**2.20**]   Kerr J also decided that NIE's decision should be amenable to review by draw-ing comparisons with the reach of EU law's 'emanation of the State' doctrine. Under this doctrine, individuals can invoke the terms of directly effective Directives in proceedings against the State or a body 'which has been made responsible, pursuant to a measure adopted by the State, for providing a public service under the control of the State and has for that purpose special powers beyond those which result from the normal rules appli-cable in relations between individuals'[79] (the purpose of the doctrine is to ensure that understandings of the 'State' are drawn as widely as possible in the face of the ECJ's *Marshall* ruling, which established that Directives can only be relied upon in proceedings involving the State and not those between private parties[80]). In cross-referring to the doc-trine, Kerr J noted that a privatised water utility in England had already been held to be an emanation of the State for the purposes of EU law.[81] Given that he considered NIE to discharge similar duties to those of the water authority, Kerr J reasoned that it 'would be anomalous if NIE . . . were to be regarded as a state authority but was considered to be immune from judicial review'.[82] EU law thereby 'spilled over' in *Sherlock and Morris* and influenced the judgment of the court in a purely national law dispute.[83]

[**2.21**]   The 'emanation of the State' test should, however, be partly distinguished from the 'nature of the issue' and 'public interest' tests that are alternatively used by the courts

1036, 1041 (government would not intervene); *R v Football Association, ex p Football League Ltd* [1993] 2 All ER 833, 848 (no evidence that government would intervene); *R v Jockey Club, ex p Aga Khan* [1993] 1 WLR 909, 923 and 932 (members of Court of Appeal disagreeing on whether government would intervene).

[75] [1996] NIJB 80.
[76] [1996] NIJB 80, 86–7.
[77] SI 1992/231 (NI 1).
[78] [1996] NIJB 80, 87.
[79] Case C-188/89, *Foster v British Gas* [1990] ECR I-3313, 3348–9, para 20.
[80] Case 152/84, *Marshall v Southampton and South-West Hampshire Area Health Authority* [1986] ECR 723, 749, para 48. On the corresponding significance of the emanation of the State formulation and related doctrines see G Anthony, *EC Law for Northern Ireland Practitioners* (Belfast, SLS Legal Publications, 1999) pp 103–17.
[81] *Griffin v South West Water Services Ltd* [1995] IRLR 15.
[82] [1996] NIJB 80, 87.
[83] On 'spill-over' see [1.18].

([2.10]–[2.17]). This is because the question whether a body is an emanation of the State is in one sense anterior to the question whether a decision taken by the body sounds in public law (the point could also be made if the question posed is whether a particular body *is able to perform* a public function). In other words, while the emanation of the State test may help to determine whether a body is, in effect, a repository of public power, the body will still make a variety of public law and private law decisions (for example, to cut off the electricity supply, and to discipline an employee, respectively). In respect of an individual decision taken by, for instance, a private company it is thus likely that the key question will remain whether the decision is in the nature of a public law decision or comes within the terms of the public interest test. It is, moreover, significant that the courts have, in any event, emphasised the need for judicial caution when reviewing the 'public law' decisions of such bodies[84]: while judicial review is available, the courts plainly wish to avoid over-active invigilation of decisions taken in quasi-commercial contexts where such invigilation may have unforeseen implications for parties beyond those before the court.

Section 6 of the Human Rights Act 1998

[2.22]   Definitions, descriptions, and/or lists of public authorities can also be found in a variety of statutory provisions and these too may be considered by the courts when delimiting the reach of judicial review. One of the most important provisions is section 6 of the Human Rights Act 1998, which reads:

> 6. (1) It is unlawful for a public authority to act in a way which is incompatible with a Convention right.
> . . .
>
> (3)   In this section 'public authority' includes—
>
>   (a) a court or tribunal, and
>   (b) any person certain of whose functions are functions of a public nature,
>
> but does not include either House of Parliament or a person exercising functions in connection with proceedings in Parliament.
>
> . . .
>
> (5)   In relation to a particular act, a person is not a public authority by virtue only of subsection (3)(b) if the nature of the act is private.

This section, which is to be interpreted by the courts on a case-by-case basis (the Act does not contain a formal list of authorities), is understood to impose human rights obligations upon 'pure' or 'obvious' public authorities and 'mixed function' or 'hybrid' authorities.[85] Pure/obvious public authorities are those that are synonymous with the State and which include central government departments, local authorities, and the police.[86] The human rights obligations imposed upon such authorities are all-embracing in the sense

---

[84] See, eg, *R v Panel on Take-overs and Mergers, ex p Datafin* [1987] QB 815, 842, Sir John Donaldson MR, and *Re Kirkpatrick's Application* [2004] NIJB 15, 23, para 36.
[85] See further D Oliver, 'Functions of a Public Nature under the Human Rights Act' [2004] PL 329.
[86] See 314 HC 406, 408.

that the authorities must comply with section 6 whether they are acting in either a public law or a private law capacity.[87] The position in respect of 'mixed function' authorities is, however, different. Mixed function/hybrid authorities are those bodies that are private in form but which may nevertheless perform public functions (it was suggested in advance of the Act coming into force that these might typically include privatised utilities and private companies performing contracted-out government functions[88]). When such a body is performing a public function, it must do so in an ECHR-compliant manner.[89] However, where the nature of the act is private, section 6 does not apply and the ECHR does not bind the decision-maker. The only possible exception to this rule is where the courts—which are pure/obvious public authorities for the purposes of the Act—accord horizontal effect to the Act by developing private law causes of action in the light of the ECHR.[90]

[**2.23**]   In terms of delimiting the reach of judicial review, the key issue in respect of mixed function authorities is when their acts are to be regarded as public and when they are to be regarded as private. Although the reach of section 6 and of judicial review are more generally distinct,[91] the question of when a private body is performing a public function for the purposes of the Act is often taken as equivalent to the question of when non-statutory decisions should be amenable to judicial review.[92] Indeed, the overlap between the two led to an expectation, in advance of the Act's coming into force, that an expansive reading of section 6(3)(b) would prompt analogous developments in judicial review. Courts in England and Wales had, for instance, previously rejected the argument that decisions taken by private bodies performing some contracted-out government functions should be amenable to judicial review. While the courts accepted that this was unsatisfactory given the modern nature of government, they nevertheless considered themselves constrained by the existence of a contractual relationship between government and the service provider (on the limiting influence of contract see [2.10]). The result was for individuals to be left without any meaningful remedy in some cases because: (a) judicial review was not available against the private body; (b) the individuals often did not have any private law relationship with the private body that could found a private law cause of action; and (c) judicial review proceedings against the public authority that had entered into the contractual relationship with the private body would be futile given that the actual decisions under challenge had been taken by the private body that was party to the contractual relationship.[93]

[**2.24**]   Case law under the Act in England and Wales has not, however, resulted in an expansive approach to section 6(3)(b) and, by analogy, to judicial review. The leading

---

[87] Subject to s 6(2); and see [5.20].

[88] 314 HC 406, 409–10.

[89] Subject to s 6(2).

[90] See M Hunt, 'The 'Horizontal Effect' of the Human Rights Act' [1998] PL 423, and *Campbell v Mirror Group Newspapers* [2004] 2 AC 457.

[91] For instance, the courts are to delimit the reach of the Act with reference to the case law of the ECHR (Human Rights Act 1998, s 2), while no such obligation exists in respect of judicial review. Another difference concerns the role of, eg, local authorities and city councils as litigants: while local authorities and councils may bring judicial review proceedings, they may not, as per s 7 of the Act and Art 34 ECHR, bring proceedings under the Act. See [3.70].

[92] *R (Beer) v Hampshire Farmers Markets Ltd* [2004] 1 WLR 233.

[93] See, most strikingly, *R v Servite Houses, ex p Goldsmith* [2001] LGR 55 (private body's decision to close a residential care facility that it provided on the basis of a contractual relationship with Wandsworth London Borough Council was not amenable to review).

authority on the point is *YL v Birmingham City Council*.[94] In that case, a majority in the House of Lords held that a privately owned, profit-earning care home that provided accommodation for publicly funded residents was not a public authority for the purposes of section 6(3)(b). The issue had arisen when an individual who had been placed with the care home under the terms of a contract between the home and a local authority that had a statutory duty to make arrangements for accommodation for the individual[95] sought to rely upon the ECHR when challenging the care home's decision to move her from the home. In holding that arguments based on the ECHR were not open to the individual because the care home was not embraced by section 6, the House of Lords held that there was an important distinction to be drawn between the act of the local authority in making arrangements for the accommodation of the individual (which corresponded with the performance of a public function under the Act) and the subsequent actions of the care home in providing the accommodation under the terms of the contract (which had a commercial basis and thereby fell outwith section 6(3)(b)). Although the minority in the House felt that the existence of, among other things, public funding and the wider public interest in the provision of care services meant that the care home should be regarded as performing a public function, the majority placed the activities of the care home squarely on the private law side of the public/private divide. Moreover, to the extent that it was acknowledged that this approach may lessen the scope for the protection of rights within the framework of the Act, the majority suggested that any extension of the Act was a matter for Parliament rather than the courts. On the facts, the individual therefore retained public law rights only against the local authority.

[2.25]   This judgment of the House of Lords would clearly suggest that, where cases fall within the Human Rights Act 1998, a more narrow approach to the meaning of 'public authority' should be adopted by Northern Ireland courts[96] (that is, while the Northern Ireland courts are not formally bound by House of Lords judgments in cases originating in England and Wales, such 'precedents' are typically followed in practice[97]). However, less clear are the judgment's analogical implications for judicial review cases that do not raise issues under the Human Rights Act 1998. Here, it is arguable that the broad approach of the Northern Ireland courts to the reach of judicial review should remain largely unaffected by *YL*, notwithstanding that the House of Lords judgment might be argued to have narrowed more generally the scope of 'public law' matters. In other words, while *YL* has reiterated that the existence of contract renders a matter one of private law, this says little about whether the broader 'public interest' test of amenability to review should, on its own terms, now be regarded as too expansive (on the test see [2.14]–[2.17]). At its highest, *YL* may therefore be decisive simply of the approach to be adopted when an application for judicial review arises in the context of contracting out, where there is already some Northern Ireland authority to indicate that judicial review will not lie.[98]

---

[94] [2007] 3 WLR 112. See too *Aston Cantlow v Wallbank* [2004] 1 AC 546; *Poplar Housing Association v Donoghue* [2002] QB 48; and *R (Heather) v Leonard Cheshire Foundation* [2002] 2 All ER 936.

[95] National Assistance Act 1948, s 21.

[96] For cases that considered section 6 before *YL* see, eg, *Re Delaney's Application* [2007] NIQB 55; *Re Wylie's Application* [2005] NI 359; and *Re Wadsworth's Application* [2004] NIQB 8.

[97] See B Dickson, *The Legal System of Northern Ireland*, 5th edn (Belfast, SLS Legal Publications, 2005) p 90.

[98] *Re TSI (Ireland) Ltd's Application* [2005] NIQB 87 (government tendering process in respect of its private telephone network not subject to judicial review).

The Northern Ireland Act 1998 and the Freedom of Information Act 2000

[2.26]   Formal lists of public authorities can also be found in section 75 of the Northern Ireland Act 1998 (as read with the Schedules to a number of other Acts[99]) and in section 3 of the Freedom of Information Act 2000 (as read with Schedule 1 to the Act). Neither list is, in turn, closed, as each Act permits the relevant Secretary of State to amend the lists by order.[100] This is perhaps in recognition of the fact that some public authorities may have been omitted from the original list. It undoubtedly also reflects the fact that public authorities in the modern era escape easy or comprehensive definition.

[2.27]   If a body is listed in either the Northern Ireland Act 1998 or the Freedom of Information Act 2000, the body will of course be a public body and its *public law decisions* will in general be subject to judicial review (though likely not those decisions in respect of section 75 and the working of the 2000 Act themselves, as the Acts provide for alternative remedies and the courts will usually require that those are exhausted first[101]). The fact that a body may be a public authority for the purposes of the Northern Ireland Act 1998 and/or the Freedom of Information Act 2000 does not, however, mean that all decisions that fall beyond the remedial structures of the Acts (or other legislation) will be amenable to review. Such bodies may also make private law decisions—for example, in their capacity as employers—and such decisions will ordinarily fall on the private law side of the public/private divide ([2.10]–[2.13]). Inclusion in the Acts therefore only answers the anterior question of whether a body's decisions *may* sound in public law. The answer to the question of whether a decision does so sound will then be found in the application of one or more of the source of power, nature of the issue, or public interest tests that are used by the courts ([2.07]–[2.17]).

PROCEDURAL EXCLUSIVITY AND EFFECTIVE ALTERNATIVE REMEDIES

[2.28]   The above paragraphs have outlined the range of tests that are used to delimit the reach of judicial review. This section considers related case law on the consequences of making an application for judicial review when it transpires that the judicial review procedure is the wrong procedure. There are two main ways in which this can happen. The first is where the courts consider that a decision under challenge sounds only in private law, the above range of tests notwithstanding.[102] Under those circumstances, the rule of procedural exclusivity as originally established in *O'Reilly v Mackman*[103] meant that the applicant would have to 'start over' and bring private law proceedings. While the introduction of an 'anti-technicality' provision[104] and increased judicial flexibility on

---

[99] Viz Sch 2 to the Parliamentary Commissioner Act 1967, Sch 2 to the Commissioner for Complaints (Northern Ireland) Order 1996, SI 1996/1297 (NI 7), and the Ombudsman (Northern Ireland) Order 1996, SI 1996/1298 (NI 8).

[100] Northern Ireland Act 1998, s 75(3)(d); Freedom of Information Act 2000, ss 3–4.

[101] See, in respect of s 75, *Re Neill's Application* [2006] NICA 5, and [5.28]–[5.29]; and on the structure of the Freedom of Information Act 2000 see [3.56]–[3.58].

[102] *R v Secretary of State, ex p Magee and McKeown*, 8 July 1994, unreported (decision to appoint an individual to a position with the Post Office was a matter of private law).

[103] [1983] 2 AC 237.

[104] RSC Ord 53, r 9(5).

matters of procedure have since reduced the impact of *O'Reilly*,[105] the rule can still result in an applicant having to commence private law proceedings afresh. This can create obvious problems of expense, albeit that longer limitation periods and the absence of a leave requirement in private law proceedings will mean that the individual is not unduly prejudiced.

[**2.29**]   The second circumstance that may render it wrong to use the judicial review procedure is where a matter is one of public law but where the applicant has an alternative remedy through, for instance, tribunal proceedings or other statutory means of recourse (such as an appeal on a point of law or by way of case stated). The basic position here is that judicial review should be regarded as a remedy of last resort and that individuals should avail themselves of the alternative remedy.[106] While this has sometimes led the courts to emphasise that use of the judicial review procedure may result in them exercising their discretion to refuse a remedy and/or to impose sanctions in costs[107]—the courts may also pre-empt such outcomes by setting aside a grant of leave[108]—the requirement that the alternative remedy be used is subject to some important qualifications. These relate primarily to the need for the remedy to be effective and to the need to balance the costs and convenience of an application for judicial review against those involved in using the alternative remedy.[109]

Procedural Exclusivity and the 'Anti-technicality' Provision

[**2.30**]   The rule of procedural exclusivity introduced in *O'Reilly v Mackman* was intended to consolidate a public/private divide under which public law rights would be vindicated only by way of public law proceedings and private law rights by way of private law proceedings. The case arose when prisoners at Hull Prison brought private law proceedings for the purposes of obtaining declarations that decisions of the prison's board of visitors had been made in breach of the rules of natural justice. In holding that the prisoners could not proceed by way of private law proceedings as the affected interests sounded in public law, Lord Diplock considered that it would 'as a general rule be contrary to public policy and . . . an abuse of the process of the court to permit a person seeking to establish that a decision of a public authority infringed rights to which he was entitled to protection under public law to proceed by way of an ordinary action and by this means to evade the provisions of Order 53 for the protection of such authorities'.[110] *O'Reilly* thus established that the judicial review procedure was not only intended to enable individuals to vindicate their public law rights; it was also intended to protect public law decision-makers by requiring individuals to observe statutory requirements of leave, delay, standing, and so on.[111]

---

[105] Increased flexibility has been particularly notable in England and Wales: see *Clark v University of Lincolnshire and Humberside* [2000] 1 WLR 1988, and T Hickman, '*Clark*: The Demise of *O'Reilly* Completed?' (2000) 5 JR 178.

[106] *Re Kirkpartick's Application* [2004] NIJB 15, and *Re Dax's Application* [2007] NIQB 96, para 22.

[107] *Re Molloy's Application* [1998] NI 78.

[108] *Re Savage's Application* [1991] NI 103.

[109] *Re Ballyedmond Castle Farm Ltd's Application; Re DPP for Northern Ireland's Application* [2000] NI 174.

[110] [1983] 2 AC 237, 285.

[111] On which requirements see ch 3. On the rationale for offering such protection to public law decision-makers see [1.06]–[1.07].

[**2.31**]   It was to be recognised almost immediately that overly strict adherence to the rule in *O'Reilly* had the potential to work to the significant disadvantage of individuals.[112] The central criticism was that it may not always be clear to an individual when a matter is one of public law (the point can seen in the largely open-ended tests for amenability to judicial review, considered at [2.10]–[2.25]); and it was also noted that disputes may sometimes raise mixed issues of public law and private law and that this could in turn make choice of procedure difficult (for example, should judicial review always be available in such disputes, or should it be available only where the public law element is the dominant element?). Although such problems were in part alleviated in England and Wales by an 'anti-technicality' provision that allowed private law matters commenced by way of application to be continued as if begun by writ,[113] the Rules of Court in Northern Ireland did not originally contain a comparable provision. This thus meant that applicants who ill-advisedly initiated judicial review proceedings in respect of a private law matter could be required to start private law proceedings afresh, notwithstanding the corresponding considerations of expense.[114] The only apparent scope for flexibility was in those cases that raised mixed issues of public law and private law, as there were dicta here to suggest that the courts should be 'slow to refuse to hear a claim in proceedings for judicial review where part of it is properly based on an issue of public law . . . to hear [such a] matter as an application for judicial review does [not do] any great violence to public policy'.[115]

[**2.32**]   Order 53, rule 9, as amended, does, however, now provide for the transfer of proceedings that have been erroneously commenced by way of application for judicial review.[116] While this obviously works to the advantage of litigants, existing case law on the rule has made clear that transfer may not follow automatically. Much depends, instead, on judicial perception of the applicant's objectives in bringing the proceedings, and the court may consider that the application is not suited to transfer even where the remedies sought include declarations, injunctions, and damages. Hence in *Re Phillips' Application*[117] Carswell LJ refused to allow proceedings to continue as if begun by writ because he considered that the application centred on the remedy of certiorari. Given the point, the judge considered that the applicant's affidavit/pleadings would need to be substantially recast before they would be suited to private law proceedings (see further [2.11]–[2.12]).

---

[112] See, eg, *Cocks v Thanet District Council* [1983] 2 AC 286, critiqued in HWR Wade and CF Forsyth, *Administrative Law*, 9th edn (Oxford, Oxford University Press, 2004) p 666.

[113] RSC Ord 53, r 9(5) (but note that the judicial review procedure in England and Wales is now governed by Part 54 of CPR, with provision for transfer being made by CPR r 54.20 [out of Part 54] and by CPR r 30.5 [into Part 54]). The term 'anti-technicality' was used by Sir John Donaldson MR in *R v East Berkshire Health Authority, ex p Walsh* [1985] QB 152, 166.

[114] See *Re Malone's Application* [1988] NI 67, 83–5, Kelly LJ.

[115] *In Re Carroll's Application* [1988] NI 153, 165, Carswell J.

[116] The rule now reads: 'Where the relief sought is a declaration, an injunction or damages and the Court considers that it should not be granted on an application for judicial review but might have been granted if it had been sought in an action begun by writ by the applicant at the time of making his application, the Court may, instead of refusing the application, order the proceedings to continue as if they had been begun by writ; and Ord 28, r 8, shall apply as if the application had been made by summons.' RSC Ord 28, r 8(1) in turn reads: 'Where, in the case of a cause or matter begun by originating summons, it appears to the Court at any stage of the proceedings that the proceedings should for any reason be continued as if the cause or matter had been begun by writ, it may order the proceedings to continue as if the cause or matter had been so begun and may, in particular, order that any affidavit shall stand as pleadings, with or without liberty to any of the parties to add thereto or to apply for particulars thereof.'

[117] [1995] NI 322.

[**2.33**]   A related point about choice of procedure concerns the converse—and rare—circumstance where private law proceedings are initiated in respect of a public law matter (as in *O'Reilly*). Under these circumstances, the Rules of Court do not provide for transfer precisely because continuation of proceedings by way of application would be likely to run contrary to key aspects of the judicial review procedure, for instance, the requirement that applications be made 'promptly and in any event within three months'.[118] While it would follow from this that proceedings in respect of a matter that is solely one of public law would have to be dismissed, the position may be more complex where the proceedings raise mixed matters of public law and private law. Here, there is House of Lords authority to suggest that it may be possible to consider the point of public law as a collateral issue in the private law proceedings and, in that way, to avoid an over-rigid adherence to procedure at the expense of the merits of the individual's case.[119] This is an approach that has since been consolidated in England and Wales under the Civil Procedure Rules,[120] and the Northern Ireland courts have also recognised the need for flexibility on questions of procedure when mixed issues of public and private law are in dispute[121] (see [2.31]). So long as the private law element to the dispute is the dominant element, it may therefore be that the courts would not consider there to be any 'abuse of process' where mixed issue cases come before the courts by way of private law proceedings.[122]

Effective Alternative Remedies

[**2.34**] The requirement that individuals pursue alternative remedies in preference to judicial review has both a constitutional and a practical underpinning (the alternative remedies will typically—though not always[123]—be found in statute). In constitutional terms, the rationale is simply that, where statute provides for a remedy by way of, for example, tribunal proceedings or rights of appeal, that manifestation of legislative intent is to be prioritised.[124] The corresponding practical justification focuses on the nature of the judicial review procedure as compared to other forms of procedure, and emphasises how the process and remedies available on review may be more limited than those available in tribunal proceedings (for instance). The judicial review procedure—considered in chapter three—is centred on a distinction between review and appeal that generally prevents the court from enquiring into the facts of a dispute and, moreover, offers only limited scope for awards of damages.[125] In contrast, while the functions of tribunals vary according to the provisions of their underlying statutes, a tribunal may nevertheless be able to enquire into disputed facts, to resolve the issues according to its own assessment of the merits, and to award a remedy in damages (among others). In *Re Kirkpatrick's*

---

[118] RSC Ord 53, r 4; and see [1.07] and [3.27]–[3.29].

[119] *Roy v Kensington and Chelsea Family Practitioner Committee* [1992] 1 AC 624. On collateral challenges see too [5.35].

[120] See Hickman, '*Clark*: The Demise of *O'Reilly* Completed?' (2000) 5 JR 178.

[121] *In Re Carroll's Application* [1988] NI 153, 165, Carswell J.

[122] See further HWR Wade and CF Forsyth, *Administrative Law*, 9th edn (Oxford, Oxford University Press, 2004) p 674 ff.

[123] Eg, the non-statutory Queen's Regulations that provide for appeals to the Army Board where a soldier is to be discharged from the armed forces; and see *Re BW's Application* [2004] NIQB 39.

[124] For discussion in the context of damages actions see, eg, *Marcic v Thames Water Utility* [2004] 2 AC 42.

[125] [1.05]. On review for error of fact see [4.36]–[4.44]; and on damages see [8.21]–[8.29].

Application[126] Kerr J thus dismissed an application for judicial review of the Lough Neagh Fishermen's Co-operative Society's decision to refuse the applicant a licence for eel fishing. Although the judge accepted that the matter was one of public law (see [2.15]), he considered that the live issue was discrimination and that the matter would thereby better and more effectively be pursued before the Fair Employment Tribunal under the terms of the Fair Employment and Treatment (Northern Ireland) Order 1998.[127] The judge also accepted that the court in review proceedings would, in any event, inevitably refrain from granting an order of mandamus to compel that a licence be given. This was both because it was likely the court would be unable to conclude that but for the discrimination the applicant would have been allowed a licence, and also because the court would be slow to order the grant of a licence when this could have repercussions for other candidates for licences who had superior claims to that of the applicant.[128]

[2.35]   There are, however, exceptions to the rule on alternative remedies and these centre upon the need for the remedy to be effective[129] and efficient in terms of cost and convenience. The leading authority on the point is *Re Ballyedmond Castle Farm Ltd's Application; Re DPP for Northern Ireland's Application*.[130] The issue here was whether the Director of Public Prosecutions (DPP) should be allowed to use judicial review to challenge a magistrate's decision to award costs against the DPP, notwithstanding that the Magistrates' Courts (Northern Ireland) Order 1981[131] provided for an appeal on a 'point of law involved in the determination of the proceeding' by way of case stated.[132] The DPP argued that there had been recourse to judicial review only because it was unclear whether costs constituted 'a point of law involved in the determination of the proceeding' and because failure to use judicial review first could result in a subsequent application being dismissed as outside the judicial review time-limit. In finding that judicial review should be available on the facts of the case, the High Court noted the need for flexibility on matters of procedure in the light of all the interests to be affected by the proceedings. While the court emphasised that each case should be considered individually and in context, it identified guidelines to aid courts in deciding whether to require that an alternative remedy be pursued. Principal among these were that a court should look for 'special circumstances' before allowing judicial review to be used ahead of an alternative statutory remedy; that the court should recognise that there a number of factors that may constitute 'special circumstances' and be astute not to abdicate its supervisory

---

[126] [2004] NIJB 15.

[127] SI 1998/3162 (NI 21).

[128] See too, eg, *Re BW's Application* [2004] NIQB 39 (challenge to the fairness of the procedure leading to the applicant's discharge from the armed services: although the procedure was unfair no remedy was granted as the applicant had a right of appeal to the Army Board; upheld on appeal, NICA, unreported); *Re McNally's Application* [1993] 4 NIJB 64 (challenge to decision of county court judge in a criminal matter: application dismissed for other reasons, with Hutton LCJ considering that the matter should in any event have been challenged by way of case stated); and *Re Gribbon's Application*, 11 July 1990, unreported (challenge to a school's refusal to admit a pupil: application dismissed for other reasons, with Carswell J stating that tribunal proceedings would have been more effective).

[129] See, eg, *R v Chief Constable, ex p McKenna* [1992] NI 116 (individual arrested by the police was entitled to bring review proceedings to challenge a decision to delay access to his solicitor: while the Crown Court had power to exclude any confession made by a suspect who had been wrongfully prevented from consulting with his solicitor, such a remedy might well be inadequate and ineffective because an arrested person could, among other things, be kept in custody awaiting trial because of an unlawfully obtained confession when he might otherwise have been released).

[130] [2000] NI 174.

[131] SI 1981/1675 (NI 26).

[132] Art 146.

role; and that, in deciding what is the most efficient and convenient means to resolve a dispute, the court should have regard not only to the interests of the applicant and respondent, but also to the wider public interest in the overall working of the legal system. It was, moreover, suggested that a court should consider the scope of the enquiry needed to resolve a dispute effectively (for instance, whether fact-finding would be better carried out by an alternative tribunal) and also whether the expense of the alternative remedy and/or delay may constitute special circumstances.[133]

Satellite Litigation

[**2.36**]   One final point related to the issue of alternative remedies concerns a judicial aversion to 'satellite litigation'. This term is used to refer to the circumstance where an individual who is involved in other proceedings—usually criminal or disciplinary—seeks to raise an issue of public law relevant to those proceedings by way of an application for judicial review. The existing case law has emphasised that it is only in 'exceptional circumstances'[134] that judicial review should be used in this way and that public law issues should, where possible, be dealt with within other forums that are suited to their resolution. In the criminal context, the courts have thus stated that issues should ordinarily be dealt with at trial or on appeal as this will avoid undue delay in the conduct of criminal proceedings[135]; and it has been said that issues in disciplinary proceedings should be addressed through those proceedings and any available appeal before an application for judicial review is considered.[136] On the other hand, it has also been acknowledged that earlier review proceedings may be appropriate where the disputed issue is fundamental to a particular disciplinary structure[137] and, by analogy, the workings of the criminal system. Under those circumstances, the point of law to be resolved may be of much wider relevance.

CONCLUSION

[**2.37**]   The above issues are complex and the corresponding case law continues to evolve. However, there are four overarching points that may be made by way of conclusion:

i.   Judicial review is concerned with the province of public law issues and not private disputes involving no element of public law. Public law issues are nearly always synonymous with the exercise or non-exercise of statutory powers, or the failure by a decision-maker to perform a public duty that is imposed upon it by statute. Where the source of authority is statute and an individual has no other remedy, judicial review will normally lie (see [2.03] and [2.07]–[2.09]).

---

[133] [2000] NI 174, 178–9, quoting M Belhoff and H Mountfield, 'There is no Alternative' [1999] JR 143. For further consideration of the guidelines see, eg, *Re Smyth's Application* [2001] NI 393, 399–400.

[134] *Re O'Connor's and Broderick's Application* [2006] NI 114, 124, para 23, Weatherup J.

[135] *R v DPP, ex p Kebilene* [2000] 2 AC 326, 371, Lord Steyn; and, eg, *Re Taggart's Application* [2003] NI 108 and *Re O'Neill's Application* [2004] NIQB 55.

[136] *Re O'Connor's and Broderick's Application* [2006] NI 114, 124, para 23, Weatherup J.

[137] *Re O'Connor's and Broderick's Application* [2006] NI 114, 124, para 23, Weatherup J (question of bias in respect of police disciplinary proceedings affected the whole system of adjudication, and the application for judicial review was granted).

ii. The source of power test is no longer the sole test for amenability to review. There are many other tests that have been developed in the light of the fact that public law decisions are taken by a wide range of bodies, some of which are not working within the framework of statute. The most important of these is the 'public interest' test (see [2.10]–[2.25]).

iii. Purely private law matters cannot be subject to judicial review. If an application for judicial review is made in respect of a private law matter, the court may order that the proceedings continue as if begun by writ (subject to the nature of the dispute lending itself to continuation). However, public law matters pursued by way of private law proceedings cannot be ordered to continue as if commenced by way of application as this would undermine the procedural protections contained in the Order 53 procedure. The courts will, however, be more flexible where private law proceedings raise mixed matters of public law and private law and where the private law matter is dominant. The public law matter may here be considered as a collateral issue (see [2.05] and [2.28]–[2.33]).

iv. Judicial review is a remedy of last resort. Where statute provides an individual with an alternative remedy, that remedy should ordinarily be pursued. This requirement is, however, qualified by the need for the alternative remedy to be effective and efficient. The courts will thus consider issues of cost, delay, the nature of the inquiry needed, and the overall interests of the legal system when deciding whether an application for judicial review should be allowed to proceed (see [2.34]–[2.36]).

3

The Judicial Review Procedure

INTRODUCTION

[**3.01**]   This chapter examines the procedure that governs applications for judicial review in Northern Ireland. The procedure, which covers the two stages of leave and the substantive hearing of an application, remains that contained in sections 18–25 of the Judicature (Northern Ireland) Act 1978 and Order 53 of the Rules of the Supreme Court (Northern Ireland) 1980 (hereafter RSC). Although the corresponding procedure in England and Wales has been modified significantly in recent years,[1] the Northern Ireland procedure has been the subject of only relatively minor amendment since it was first introduced.[2] Northern Ireland case law thus continues to use the original terms of 'leave' and 'application' (among others) that have been replaced in England and Wales by, respectively, the terms 'permission' and 'claim'.[3] The Northern Ireland procedure still also refers to the prerogative orders of 'certiorari', 'mandamus', and 'prohibition', which are now known as 'quashing orders', 'mandatory orders', and 'prohibiting orders' in England and Wales.[4]

[**3.02**]   The fact that the formal rules and provisions governing the judicial review procedure have remained largely unchanged should not, however, be taken to mean that procedural issues have been more generally static. The rules and provisions are, of course, open to judicial interpretation, and the procedure can—and has—evolved on that basis (there are also a number of related practice directions[5]). The procedure is, moreover, subject to the demands of EU law and the ECHR, as read with the European Communities Act 1972 and the Human Rights Act 1998; and it is clear that other 'constitutional statutes' such as the Freedom of Information Act 2000 are of increasing relevance too.[6] While the procedure may therefore be largely settled, aspects of it may still be reconsidered and reinterpreted on a case-by-case basis.

[**3.03**]   The chapter begins by outlining a number of prior considerations that are relevant to deciding whether to make an application for judicial review. It thereafter divides into sections that consider key issues regarding: the leave stage; interim issues of

---

[1] Notably by virtue of Part 54 the Civil Procedure Rules (CPR): see T Griffiths, 'The Procedural Impact of Bowman and Part 54 of the CPR' (2000) 5 JR 209, and M Fordham, *Judicial Review Handbook*, 4th edn (Hart Publishing, Oxford, 2004) p 12ff.
[2] SR 1982/217; SR 1984/354; SR 1989/289; SR 1993/143.
[3] CPR rr 54.1 and 54.4.
[4] CPR r 54.1.
[5] Eg, *Judicial Review: Practice Note 01/2006*, available at http://www.courtsni.gov.uk.
[6] On constitutional statutes see [1.28]–[1.34] and [5.04]–[5.30].

remedies, discovery, and cross-examination; the substantive hearing; and the availability of final remedies (each section also integrates consideration of the role of EU law and the ECHR, and so on). The conclusion provides a summary of the central points made.

DECIDING TO PROCEED

[**3.04**]   There are three interlinked issues that should be considered in advance of deciding to proceed by way of application for judicial review (in addition to obvious practical matters of cost). These are (a) whether there is a decision, act, failure to act, or other measure that (b) sounds in public law and which (c) may appropriately be challenged by way of judicial review (that is, is there an alternative remedy?; would judicial review proceedings be premature?; and so on).

Is there a Decision, Act, Failure to Act, or Other Measure?

[**3.05**]   There is a wide range of measures that may be challenged by way of judicial review. The target of a challenge will, however, often be a decision contained in a decision letter that has been addressed to the potential applicant (the rule of law requires notice of a decision before it can have legal effect; the requirement has added force when existing rights/interests are affected[7]). A decision, in turn, may identify a number of outcomes and/or proposed courses of action that will point to the remedies that may appropriately be sought in any subsequent application for judicial review. For instance, a decision may: affect the interests of the individual by refusing him or her a licence for a particular activity[8] or by refusing to renew an existing licence[9]; state that the decision-maker will act in a particular way in the light of the individual's inquiry/request[10]; or state that the decision-maker is not going to take any course of action beyond issuing the decision letter in question (which decision may project a future failure to act).[11] Under such circumstances, there will often be a core remedy that will be sought by the individual, with the appropriateness of other remedies depending on the fuller context of the dispute. Hence where a decision affects existing interests—for example, the refusal to renew a licence—the core remedy is likely to be an order of certiorari, as this will have the effect of quashing the decision and requiring it to be retaken. However, where a decision-maker proposes to act in a particular way that the individual considers would be unlawful, an order of prohibition or an injunction may be sought, as these will prevent the proposed course of action. An order of mandamus may in turn be appropriate where a decision is to the effect that no further act will be performed, as this remedy will compel the decision-maker to perform its public duty. Mandamus may also be appropriate

---

[7] *R (Anufrijeva) v Secretary of State for the Home Department* [2004] 1 AC 604 (Home Office failure to inform the applicant that her asylum application had been unsuccessful meant that the decision was without force of law until notice of it was given).

[8] Eg, *Re McComb's Application* [2003] NIQB 47 (application for a public service vehicle licence refused).

[9] Eg, *Re Eastwood's Application* [1997] NI 73 (refusal to renew a bookmaker's licence).

[10] Eg, *Re UK Waste Management's Application* [2002] NI 130 (Department of Environment issuing a variety of opinion notices in relation to the applicant's application for planning permission but not reaching any final decision).

[11] *Re Scappaticci's Application* [2003] NIQB 56 (government Minister refused to confirm or deny whether a former IRA member who was named as a British agent had been an agent).

where there is an unreasonable delay in a decision-maker's reply to a formal request[12] (on the remedies see [3.72]–[3.87][13]).

[**3.06**]   It is not, however, always necessary for there to be a formal decision addressed to an individual for the purposes of judicial review, and there are many examples of challenges to other types of measures. While such challenges will often follow from some prior communication between the applicant and respondent (which may result in a decision that a subsequent challenge goes 'behind'), others may not be preceded by communication and the courts must decide whether a matter is one that should be heard and the grievance of the individual remedied. Some of the measures challenged thus include: statements[14]; policies[15]; a school's entrance criteria[16]; regulations[17]; non-exercises of the royal prerogative[18]; failures to act[19]; preliminary decisions[20]; a council vote to defeat a motion[21]; the validity of appointments to a Commission established by statute[22]; bye-laws[23]; schemes[24]; circulars[25]; resolutions[26]; the operational choices of the police[27]; and the findings, during proceedings, of coroner's courts.[28]

[12] See, eg, *R v Secretary of State for the Home Department, ex p Phansopkar* [1976] QB 606 (order of mandamus granted given the Home Office's unreasonable delay in processing the individuals' immigration applications).

[13] And ch 8.

[14] Eg, *Re Williamson's Application* [2000] NI 281 (challenge to Secretary of State's statement and related decision to the effect that the IRA was maintaining a ceasefire for the purposes of the Northern Ireland (Sentences) Act 1998: application dismissed).

[15] Eg, *Re Byer's Application* [2004] NIQB 23 (applicant challenging a prison policy that prevented Republican prisoners from, inter alia, wearing Easter Lilies: application dismissed).

[16] *Re Anderson's Application* [2001] NI 454 (students who obtained 'A' grades in their 11-plus examination but who were refused entry to the school of their choice challenged the school's corresponding sub-criteria: application dismissed).

[17] *Re Kelly's Application* [2000] NI 103 (challenge to the lawfulness of Law Society Regulations that govern/limit access to a professional legal studies course: application dismissed).

[18] *Re Hannaway's Application* [1995] NI 159: (Secretary of State for Northern Ireland refused to exercise the prerogative of mercy to allow the remains of an IRA man who had been executed and buried within Crumlin Road prison to be removed and commemorated by the Republican Movement: application granted).

[19] *Family Planning Association of Northern Ireland v Minister for Health, Social Services and Public Safety* [2005] NI 188 (challenge to the department's failure to issue guidelines and advice on the law of abortion in Northern Ireland: application granted on appeal).

[20] *MacManus & Ors v Northern Ireland Housing Executive*, 3 July 1997, unreported (challenge to a finding in respect of the applicant's 'preliminary inquiry' regarding eligibility for a housing grant, which finding did not have legal force and did not preclude a further and full application for a grant: one of the applications granted).

[21] *Re O'Neill's Application* [1995] NI 274 (challenge to the lawfulness of a vote in Cookstown District Council in respect of a motion to promote the Sunday opening of recreational facilities: application granted).

[22] *Re White's Application* [2000] NI 432 (applicant challenging the composition of the Parades Commission—which had no women members—as contrary to the requirement in para 2(3) of Sch 1 to the Public Processions (Northern Ireland) Act 1998 that the Commission be representative of the community in Northern Ireland: application dismissed); and *Re Duffy's Application* [2006] NICA 28 (applicant challenging appointment to the Parade's Commission of two members of the loyal orders: application dismissed on appeal).

[23] *Belfast Corporation v Daly* [1963] NI 78 (collateral challenge to the lawfulness of a bye-law in a criminal prosecution: challenge failed before the Court of Appeal in proceedings by way of case stated).

[24] *Re Benson's Application* [2005] NIQB 39 (challenge to a Voluntary Severance Scheme developed by the Police Service of Northern Ireland (PSNI) and Northern Ireland Office: application dismissed).

[25] *Re Conlon's Application* [2005] NI 97 (challenge to a Departmental Circular dealing with release of persons convicted of certain offences against children: application granted).

[26] *Re Cook's Application* [1986] NI 242 (challenge to a majority resolution of Belfast City Council to suspend forthcoming meetings of the council and to delegate its functions to the town clerk in protest at the signing of the Anglo-Irish Agreement of 1985: application granted).

[27] *Re E's Application* [2004] NIQB 35, [2006] NICA 37 (challenge to the mode of policing of the 'Holy Cross' dispute: application dismissed).

[28] Eg, *Re Devine's Application* [1990] 9 NIJB 96 (whether the admission of written statements of soldiers involved in the death of the deceased was contrary to natural justice: application dismissed).

[**3.07**]   Judicial review can also be used to challenge various forms of subordinate legislation (primary legislation—most obviously Acts of the Westminster Parliament[29]—cannot be challenged save where it conflicts with EU law[30] and/or to the limited extent associated with declarations of incompatibility under section 4 of the Human Rights Act 1998[31]). For instance, subordinate legislation made under Acts of the Westminster Parliament can be challenged as ultra vires its parent Act or as otherwise unlawful[32]; and Statutory Rules made under Acts of the Northern Ireland Assembly or its predecessors can likewise be reviewed.[33] Moreover, those same Acts of the Assembly (or Orders in Council made when the local institutions have been suspended[34]) can be challenged as ultra vires the Northern Ireland Act 1998 that devolves power to the Assembly. Although there is debate about whether Acts of the Assembly/Orders in Council should properly be regarded as subordinate legislation,[35] it remains the position that such legislation can be made only within the terms of section 6 of the Northern Ireland Act 1998.[36] Where the lawfulness of an Act of the Assembly is raised in proceedings, this thus gives rise to a 'devolution issue' that must be resolved in accordance with additional procedural requirements[37] (similar requirements apply when a challenge to Statutory Rules gives rise to a 'devolution issue'[38]). Those requirements are outlined at [3.23].

[**3.08**]   It is also possible to challenge the lawfulness of EU Regulations and Directives in the High Court by bringing review proceedings against the government department that is responsible for giving domestic effect to the measures. A challenge here will argue that

---

[29] But see too the wider definition in Human Rights Act 1998, s 21.

[30] *R v Secretary of State for Transport, ex p Factortame Ltd (No 2)* [1991] 1 AC 603; and [1.16], [4.09], and [5.06]–[5.07].

[31] On s 4 see [8.46]–[8.47]; and *Re McR's Application* [2003] NI 1 (Offences Against the Persons Act 1861, s 62 incompatible with Art 8 ECHR); and for an unsuccessful human rights challenge to legislation see *Re Sinn Féin's Application* [2004] NICA 4 (s 12 of the Political Parties, Elections and Referendums Act 2000 not incompatible with Art 10(1) ECHR and Art 3 of Prot 1, ECHR, as read with Art 14 ECHR).

[32] See, eg, *Re Christian Institute and Ors Application* [2007] NIQB 66 (challenge to the lawfulness of the Equality Act (Sexual Orientation) Regulations (Northern Ireland) 2006, SR 2006/439, that had been made under s 82 of the Equality Act 2006: application granted in part for lack of adequate consultation); and [5.31]–[5.32].

[33] See, eg, *Re Cullen's Application* [2005] NIQB 9 (challenging, inter alia, the Game Preservation (Special Protection for Irish Hares) Order (Northern Ireland) 2003 made under s 7C(1) of the Game Preservation Act (Northern Ireland) 1928 Act: application dismissed).

[34] Most recently under the Northern Ireland Act 2000, s 1 and Sch 10 (now repealed by the Northern Ireland (St Andrews Agreement) Act 2006 and Northern Ireland (St Andrews Agreement) Act 2007).

[35] See [5.23]–[5.24].

[36] Section 6 reads: (1) A provision of an Act is not law if it is outside the legislative competence of the Assembly. (2) A provision is outside that competence if any of the following paragraphs apply: (a) it would form part of the law of a country or territory other than Northern Ireland, or confer or remove functions exercisable otherwise than in or as regards Northern Ireland; (b) it deals with an excepted matter and is not ancillary to other provisions (whether in the Act or previously enacted) dealing with reserved or transferred matters; (c) it is incompatible with any of the Convention rights; (d) it is incompatible with Community law; (e) it discriminates against any person or class of person on the ground of religious belief or political opinion; (f) it modifies an enactment in breach of section 7'. Convention rights for the purposes of the section are to be read in the light of the Human Rights Act 1998 (s 98); and s 7 lists entrenched enactments that, subject to s 7(2), may not be modified by Act of the Assembly or subordinate legislation (these are the European Communities Act 1972, the Human Rights Act 1998, and ss 43(1)–(6) and (8), s 67, ss 84–6, s 95(3) and (4), and s 98 of the Northern Ireland Act 1998 (s 7(2) permits modification of s 3(3) or (4) or s 11(1) of the European Communities Act 1972)). For an example of challenge to an Assembly measure see, by analogy, *Re Landlords Association for Northern Ireland's Application* [2006] NI 16, challenging successfully the compatibility of the Housing (Northern Ireland) Order 2003 with the ECHR (the Order [SI 2003/412] had originally been introduced as a Bill in the Assembly and was carried over as an Order in Council under the Northern Ireland Act 2000).

[37] Northern Ireland Act 1998, Sch 10; and RSC Ord 120.

[38] Northern Ireland Act s 24 and Sch 10, para 1; and RSC Ord 120, r 2.

a Regulation or Directive is contrary to the EC Treaty and/or its general principles of law,[39] and, if the court thinks that the measure might be unlawful, the domestic court must make an Article 234 EC reference to the ECJ as the court responsible for determining 'the validity and interpretation of acts of the [EU] institutions'.[40] Such challenges in the national courts will, moreover, be likely to give rise to the question whether an injunction should issue to prevent the implementation and operation of the EU measure or domestic measure that gives effect to it and, if so, which standard—domestic or EU—should govern the granting of relief.[41] The relevant domestic and EU law on injunctions under such circumstances is considered at [3.43]–[3.46].

Does the Decision or Other Measure Sound in Public Law?

[3.09]   Judicial review is concerned with 'public law issues and not private disputes involving no element of public law',[42] and an application for leave should therefore not be made if the matter in question is one of private law. While it will often be clear that a matter falls within the realm of public law and is amenable to judicial review, difficult questions about the public/private divide still remain and the courts have fashioned a variety of tests—examined in detail in chapter two—that seek to map the boundaries of public law. The most important of these is the 'public interest' test, which holds that 'an issue is one of public law where it involves a matter of public interest in the sense that it has an impact on the public generally and not merely on an individual or group'.[43] Related tests include the 'source of power' test,[44], and the 'public functions' and the 'emanation of the State' tests[45]; and further guidance on the reach of public law—or certainly on public authorities whose decisions may sound in public law—can be found in case law under section 6 of the Human Rights Act 1998 and in the lists of public authorities used by the Northern Ireland Act 1998 and the Freedom of Information Act 2000.[46]

Would Review Proceedings be Appropriate (in light of alternative remedies, prematurity, and so on)?

[3.10]   Even where a dispute can be characterised as one of 'public law', judicial review proceedings may be inappropriate where the individual has an alternative remedy (for

---

[39] On the relevant principles of law see G Anthony, *EC Law for Northern Ireland Practitioners* (Belfast, SLS Legal Publications, 1999) p 123ff (discussing, by analogy, challenges to measures before the Court of First Instance).

[40] Art 234 EC, para 1(b); and RSC Ord 114. See also Case 314/85, *Foto-Frost v Hauptzollamt-Lübeck-Ost* [1987] ECR 4199, and Case C-344/04, *R (International Air Transport Association) v Department for Transport* [2006] 2 ECR 403.

[41] The domestic test is found in *American Cyanamid Co v Ethicon Ltd* [1975] AC 396; the EU test is associated with Cases C-143/88 and C/92/89, *Zuckerfabrik Süderdithmarschen AG v Hauptzollamt Itzhoe* [1991] ECR I-415, and Case C-465/93, *Atlanta Fruchthandelsgesellschaft mbH v Bundesamt fur Ernahrung und Forstwirtschaft* [1995] ECR I-3761.

[42] *Re Wylie's Application* [2005] NI 359, 362, para 7.

[43] See [2.10]–[2.13]; and *Re McBride's Application* [1999] NI 299, 310, Kerr J. For subsequent application see, eg, *Re Kirkpatrick's Application* [2004] NIJB 15; *Re Wadsworth's Application* [2004] NIQB 8; *Re City Hotel (Derry) Ltd's Application* [2004] NIQB 38; and *Re Wylie's Application* [2005] NI 359.

[44] See [2.07]–[2.09].

[45] See [2.18]–[2.21].

[46] See [2.22]–[2.27].

instance, a statutory right of appeal). The requirement that individuals avail themselves of such remedies first—while not absolute and subject to considerations of effectiveness and efficiency[47]—reflects the constitutional assumption that remedies regimes established by the legislature should ordinarily enjoy priority over those developed by the courts. There are, however, practical justifications for the requirement too, and the courts have emphasised that appeals or tribunal hearings (for example) may be more suited to the nature of dispute at hand, both in terms of procedures and the remedies available. Applications for judicial review may therefore be dismissed where such alternative means of redress have not been exhausted.[48]

[3.11] Judicial review proceedings may also be inappropriate if deemed 'premature', or where the issue at hand is not considered 'ripe for review'.[49] These concepts correspond to the argument that governmental and administrative decision-making processes should not be unduly constrained by the prospect of review proceedings, particularly where the decision-making process has not reached its conclusion in the sense of a final decision being taken and relayed to an individual.[50] While a decision that affects the interests of an individual will therefore typically be open to review (subject to requirements of delay, standing, and so on), the position may be different where no formal decision has yet been made or where an individual wishes to challenge a preliminary determination in the overall decision-making process.[51] Under those circumstances, courts may prefer for the legal issue to mature and to be challenged as a formal decision that has legal effect.[52]

[3.12] Case law in Northern Ireland does, however, also point to some competing considerations that may permit of challenges at an earlier stage in the decision-making process. The courts have, for instance, recognised that challenges to recommendations and preliminary decisions are in theory possible where those measures are an integral part of an overall process that will affect the individual's legal interests or rights.[53] The courts have, moreover, noted the value of pragmatism in the administrative decision-making process and have allowed challenges to preliminary determinations where those determinations are part of a wider scheme that seeks to save time and expense on the part of both the individual and the decision-maker. For example, in *MacManus v Northern Ireland Housing Executive*[54] the applicant had used the respondent's 'preliminary inquiry' system whereby the authority gave an indication whether an individual would be eligible for a renovation grant for their residence. The outcomes of such inquiries had no statutory effect and did not prevent the individual from making a formal application for a grant, although the result of any formal application usually mirrored that of the preliminary inquiry. In allowing the applicant to challenge the finding of the preliminary inquiry, the court observed that the scheme in place was 'pragmatic and sensible' as it

---

[47] *Re Ballyedmond Castle Farm Ltd's Application; Re DPP for Northern Ireland's Application* [2000] NI 174.

[48] Eg *Re Kirkpatrick's Application* [2004] NIJB 15; and [2.34].

[49] See J Beatson, 'The Need to Develop Principles of Prematurity and Ripeness for Review' [1998] JR 79; and, eg, *Re Ferris' Application*, 22 June 2000, unreported.

[50] See *Re Kinnegar Residents' Action Group's Application* [2007] NIQB 90, para 24.

[51] On preliminary decisions and fairness see [7.11].

[52] See, eg, *R (Burkett) v Hammersmith and Fulham LBC* [2002] 3 All ER 97, 111, para 43, Lord Steyn observing that 'a court might as a matter of discretion take the view that it would be premature to apply for judicial review as soon as [a] provisional decision is announced'.

[53] *Re Sterritt's Application* [1980] NI 234, 237–8, citing, among others, *R v Electricity Commissioners, ex p London Electricity Joint Committee Company (1920) Ltd* [1924] 1 KB 171.

[54] 3 July 1997, unreported.

enabled the individual to avoid the expenditure of a further application for a grant (which would require an additional decision on the part of the authority).[55] Seen from this perspective, judicial review of the preliminary finding therefore complemented the pragmatic nature of the decision-making process, notwithstanding that the finding in question lacked formal legal force.

[**3.13**]   One further point about preliminary decisions concerns the question of when time-limits run for the purposes of review proceedings. Under RSC Order 53, rule 4(1), applications for leave to apply for judicial review 'shall be made promptly and in any event within three months from the date when the grounds for the application first arose unless the Court considers that there is good reason for extending the period within which the application shall be made' (see [3.27]–[3.29]. In *R (Burkett) v Hammersmith and Fulham LBC*[56]—a planning dispute—the House of Lords had to consider whether time ran from the moment that there was a preliminary determination that was reviewable (in this instance a council resolution that authorised a grant of planning permission subject to conditions precedent) or whether it ran from the date that the final decision was made (the formal grant of permission on fulfilment of the conditions precedent). The application for leave/permission in this case had been made seven months after the date of the resolution (which was the target of the challenge) and one month before the final decision was made, and the respondent argued that the application thereby fell outside the corresponding time-limits in England and Wales.[57] Rejecting the argument, the House held that there were strong reasons of policy for holding that time ran from the date when planning permission had actually been granted rather than from the date of the resolution. These included the need for certainty and simplicity in terms of ascertaining dates for the purposes of proceedings and the need for individuals to be able to vindicate their rights and, where appropriate, the corresponding interests of the community. The House, on this basis, likewise rejected the argument that the proceedings could only relate to the resolution as the application had been made before the decision in question had in fact been taken. Such an argument, it was held, served only to elevate a procedural difficulty to a position of prominence when the emphasis in public law should be placed more on matters of substance than form.

PRE-ACTION PROTOCOL

[**3.14**]   Where it is apparent that a matter is one of public law and that the individual has no effective alternative remedy etc, an application for leave to bring an application for judicial review will be appropriate. However, before the application for leave is made, applicants must observe some points of 'pre-action protocol'. These points are intended to prevent disputes coming to court, where possible, by facilitating the independent resolution of a dispute by the parties to it. Pre-action protocol in that way provides a case management mechanism that seeks, among other things, to limit costs.

---

[55]   The court here used Girvan J's description of the system in *Re Kelly's Application*, 14 January 1997, unreported.

[56]   [2002] 3 All ER 97.

[57]   RSC Ord 53, r 4(1), as later replaced by CPR, r 54.5(1).

[**3.15**]   The leading authority on the need to observe pre-action protocol is *Re Cunningham's Application.*[58] In that case, Girvan J stated that practitioners should ordinarily observe the type of 'reasonable, fair preliminary procedure set out in the English Pre-action Protocol' (there is no recorded Protocol that applies in Northern Ireland). The judge also said that, where there is a failure to observe the elements of the Protocol, the courts should be slow to grant leave.

[**3.16**]   The salient features of the English Protocol are:

i.   Before making an application, the applicant should send a pre-action letter to the respondent.[59] This letter should identify the issues in dispute and establish whether litigation can be avoided.

ii.   The letter should contain the date and details of the decision, act, or failure to act being challenged and a clear summary of the facts on which the application is based. It should also contain the details of any relevant information that the applicant is seeking and an explanation of why it is considered relevant.

iii. The letter should normally contain the details of any interested parties known to the claimant. They should be sent a copy of the letter before the request for information.

iv.   The application for leave should not normally be made until the proposed reply date given in the pre-action letter has passed, unless the circumstances of the case require more immediate action to be taken.

v.   Respondents should normally reply within 14 days.[60] Failure to do so will be taken into account by the court, and sanctions may be imposed unless there are good reasons for the failure.

vi.   Where it is not possible to reply within the proposed time-limit the respondent should send an interim reply and propose a reasonable extension. Where an extension is sought, reasons should be given and, where required, additional information requested. This will not affect the time-limit for making an application for judicial review (on which see [3.27]–[3.29]) nor will it bind the applicant where he or she considers this to be unreasonable. However, where the court considers that a subsequent application is made prematurely it may impose sanctions.

vii. If the matters raised in the applicant's letter are being conceded in full, the reply should say so in clear and unambiguous terms.

viii. If the matters raised in the applicant's letter are being conceded in part or are not being conceded at all, the reply should say so in clear and unambiguous terms, and should (a) where appropriate, contain a new decision, clearly identifying which matters are being conceded and which are not, or give a clear time-scale within which a new decision will be issued; (b) provide a fuller explanation for the decision, if considered appropriate to do so; (c) address any points of dispute, or explain why they cannot be addressed; (d) enclose any relevant documentation requested by the applicant, or explain why the documents are not being enclosed; and (e) where appropriate, confirm whether or not the respondent will oppose any application for an interim remedy (on which remedies see [3.42]–[3.47]).

---

[58]   [2005] NIJB 224.

[59]   For the suggested standard format for the letter under the English Protocol see: http://www.dca.gov.uk/civil/procrules_fin/menus/protocol.htm.

[60]   For the suggested standard format for the letter of response under the English Protocol see: http://www.dca.gov.uk/civil/procrules_fin/menus/protocol.htm.

ix.   The response should be sent to all interested parties identified by the applicant
      and contain details of any other parties who the respondent considers to have an
      interest.

THE LEAVE STAGE

[3.17]   Leave to make an application for judicial review is required in all cases, save
where there is an application for certiorari by the Attorney-General acting on behalf of
the Crown.[61] The corresponding function of the leave stage is to filter out unmeritorious
or frivolous applications and in that way to safeguard decision-makers from unnecessary
legal proceedings[62] (the filter also enables the court to control its calendar). An application for leave must therefore demonstrate that the applicant: has an arguable case; has
acted with promptitude; and has standing for the purposes of the application (although
the question of standing is generally regarded as unproblematic and, where it is in issue,
it is more often resolved at the substantive hearing). Applications must also be made in
accordance with related guidance in case law and practice notes, as a failure to follow
that guidance may result in costs orders against the applicant and/or in the application
being dismissed.[63]

Making the Application

[3.18]   Applications for leave are made ex parte to the High Court and by lodging in the
Central Office (1) an ex parte docket, (2) an Order 53 statement, and (3) affidavit evidence[64] (a fee of £52 is payable, which will be credited against the fee for a subsequent
originating motion in the event that leave is granted). The Order 53 statement must set
out the name and description of the applicant, the relief sought (including any application for a protective costs order: see [3.34]), and the grounds for that relief. The Order 53
statement should not, however, include evidence or arguments, and it should be as precise as possible, as a lack of clarity and focus may result in later difficulties, for instance
in obtaining an order for discovery.[65] The applicant's affidavit(s), which should be
drafted in 'clear and unambiguous language',[66] should in turn: set out the evidence (but
not the arguments); explain any delay in applying promptly (if appropriate); refer to the
applicant's book of exhibits by document number and page number if necessary; and be
accompanied by an index where there is more than one affidavit.[67] As the application is
made ex parte, the applicant should, moreover, make full and frank disclosure as false
disclosure/non-disclosure may result in refusal of a remedy[68] (applicants and respondents are both under a more general duty of candour—and see [3.49]). The Court of

---

[61]   Judicature (Northern Ireland) Act 1978, s 18(2)(a); and RSC Ord 53, r 3(1).
[62]   *R v Secretary of State for Trade and Industry, ex p Eastaway* [2000] 1 WLR 2222, 2227, Lord Bingham.
[63]   For the most recent guidance see *Judicial Review: Practice Note 01/2006*, 16 January 2006, available
through http://www.courtsni.gov.uk.
[64]   RSC Ord 53, r 3(2); and *Judicial Review: Practice Note 01/2006*, Part A.
[65]   *Re Austin's Application*, 25 November 1994, unreported, Kerr J.
[66]   *Re Downes' Application* [2006] NIQB 77, para 31, Girvan J.
[67]   On the preparation of affidavits see also *Preparation of Affidavits and Exhibits: Practice Direction 5/2005*.
[68]   *Re D's Application* [2003] NI 295.

Appeal has also stated that, where affidavits contain substantive facts, they should be sworn by persons with first-hand knowledge of those facts and not by solicitors or other persons deposing to such facts. In the event that such evidence is not prepared and filed properly, the Court of Appeal has said that leave to apply for judicial review should not be given and nor should legal aid be granted.[69]

[3.19] The corresponding book of exhibits should be prepared in accordance with the guidance contained in *Judicial Review: Practice Note 01/2006*.[70] This states that there should be one indexed and paginated book of exhibits containing all material relied on by the applicant, and that this should include a separate section that contains all relevant correspondence in chronological order. The Practice Note also states that affidavits and exhibits can be presented in one file or more depending on the volume of material, albeit that continuing page numbering should be used throughout (any later affidavits and exhibits can then be added to the earlier affidavit(s) and exhibits, and the indexes for affidavits and exhibits amended accordingly). Key documents should be marked in the exhibits index with an asterisk, although it is only necessary documents that are to be exhibited. Copies of legislation should therefore not be included in the exhibits, and relevant extracts should be included only where they are appropriate. Use of superfluous materials may lead the Court to disallow costs.[71]

[3.20] The papers will be referred to a judge,[72] who may direct that the applicant appear before him or her before a decision to grant leave on the papers is taken. Where the judge is minded to refuse leave, the rules of court require that such a direction be given.[73] However, the judge may otherwise consider that a hearing is desirable, and notice of the hearing should, where possible, be given to the proposed respondent or respondents (the applicant's solicitor is responsible for identifying the appropriate respondent(s) and their legal representatives).[74] A decision to grant leave here—as with a decision on the papers—will depend on the issues of arguability, delay, and standing (see [3.24]–[3.30]). Section 18(2)(b) of the Judicature (Northern Ireland) Act 1978 and RSC Order 53, rule 3(6) also require that the court ask whether the remedy applied for is one that may be granted 'having regard to the nature of the persons and bodies' against whom the relief is sought. These latter provisions have not, however, featured prominently in the case law.[75]

Criminal Causes

[3.21]   Applications for leave to make an application for judicial review in respect of a criminal cause or matter will also be determined by a judge in chambers[76] (review pro-

---

[69] See *Re D's Application* [2003] NI 295, 301, para 11, Carswell LCJ.

[70] Available through http://www.courtsni.gov.uk.

[71] *Re Doherty's Application* [2006] NIQB 33, paras 28–9.

[72] RSC Ord 53, r 3(3). It is also possible for an application for leave to be heard by a Master, albeit that this occurs only rarely in practice: see RSC Ord 32, rr 11–12.

[73] RSC Ord 53, r 3(10): 'Upon consideration of an application for leave the Court may direct the applicant to appear before it and no application for leave shall be refused without first giving the applicant an opportunity of being heard'.

[74] *Judicial Review: Practice Note 01/2006*, Part A.

[75] For discussion of the provisions see P Maguire, 'The Procedure for Judicial Review in Northern Ireland' in B Hadfield (ed), *Judicial Review: A Thematic Approach* (Dublin, Gill & MacMillan, 1995) pp 371, 373–4.

[76] RSC Ord 53, rr 2(1) and 3(3), and RSC Ord 32, r 11.

ceedings fall to be described as concerned with a criminal cause where they are ancillary or incidental to other substantive proceedings that are criminal[77]). Where the judge is minded to refuse the application for leave, the applicant must be given an opportunity to be heard and such hearing will be held before a two- or three-judge court.[78] Where leave is granted, the substantive application will either be heard by three judges sitting together,[79] by two judges where the Lord Chief Justice so directs,[80] or by a single judge where both parties consent[81] (the corresponding decision of the court may only be appealed, with leave and where there is a point of law of general public importance, to the House of Lords[82]). Where an application for leave is refused but the Divisional Court certifies the issue as being of public importance, the proposed appellant can petition the House of Lords for leave (the Divisional Court may also grant leave).[83] If the issue is not certified as being of public importance, that is the end of the matter.

The Human Rights Act 1998; and 'Devolution Issues'

[**3.22**]   Where an application for leave is founded wholly or partly on one or more of the ECHR provisions that have effect under the Human Rights Act 1998, RSC Order 121, rules 5(1)(c) and 5(2) require that the applicant's Order 53 statement give details of the right or rights which it is alleged have been (or would be) infringed and details of the alleged infringement and of the relief sought. An application may, most obviously, challenge an administrative decision, act, and/or failure to act relative to the ECHR,[84] and the appropriate judicial remedy—certiorari, mandamus, and so on—should therefore be requested (although remedies will not be available where the decision, act, or failure to act is rendered lawful by primary legislation[85]). An application may, however, also involve a challenge to primary and/or subordinate legislation[86] and, where the remedy sought is a declaration of incompatibility, the Order 53 statement must give details of the legislative provision (or provisions) alleged to be incompatible and the grounds on which it is (or they are) alleged to be incompatible.[87] While declarations of incompatibility are most usually associated with primary legislation (they are the only available remedy),[88]

---

[77] *Re Shuker's Application* [2004] NI 367, 379, para 37. See too *Re Coleman's Application* [1988] NI 205, 208, citing *R v Hull Visitors, ex p St Germain* [1979] QB 425, 453: 'to stamp proceedings as being of a criminal nature there must be in contemplation the possibility of trial by a court for some offence'.

[78] RSC Ord 53, r 3(10), (11) (as read with r 2).

[79] RSC Ord 53, r 2(2).

[80] RSC Ord 53, r 2(3).

[81] RSC Ord 53, r 2(6), as read with Judicature (Northern Ireland) Act 1978, s 16(5) ('Except where a statutory provision otherwise provides, any jurisdiction of the High Court or a division thereof shall be exercised by a single judge'). Note too that r 2(3) provides that a single judge may hear an application in vacation 'where necessary'.

[82] Judicature (Northern Ireland) Act 1978, s 41(2).

[83] Judicature (Northern Ireland) Act 1978, s 41(2).

[84] Human Rights Act 1998, s 6. Although note also the possibility of proceedings in respect of judicial acts: see Human Rights Act 1998, s 9; and RSC Ord 121, r 5 (2)(f). See also *Judicial Review: Practice Note 01/2006*, Part B.

[85] Human Rights Act 1998, s 6(2); and *R (Hooper) v Secretary of State for Work and Pensions* [2006] 1 All ER 487. See [5.20].

[86] Human Rights Act 1998, ss 3–6. Primary and subordinate legislation for the purposes of the Act are defined in s 21.

[87] RSC Order 121, r 5(2)(d).

[88] Human Rights Act 1998, s 4(1)–(2). See, eg, *Re McR's Application* [2003] NI 1 (Offences Against the Persons Act 1861, s 62 incompatible with Art 8 ECHR).

they will also be made in respect of subordinate legislation where primary legislation prevents removal of incompatibility in the subordinate legislation and where it is not possible to read the subordinate legislation compatibly with the ECHR (subordinate legislation that is not vouchsafed by primary legislation may likewise be the subject of a standard declaration or, in the alternative, struck down as ultra vires[89]). Order 53 statements that may lead a court on an application for judicial review to consider the compatibility of primary and subordinate legislation should therefore specify clearly all particulars as these will serve as the foundation of any subsequent Notice issued to the Crown by the court in accordance with section 5 of the Human Rights Act 1998 and RSC Order 121, rules 2 and 3A.[90]

[3.23]   An application for judicial review will in turn give rise to a 'devolution issue' where it raises: (a) a question whether any provision of an Act of the Northern Ireland Assembly is within the legislative competence of the Assembly; (b) a question whether a purported or proposed exercise of a function by a Minister or a Northern Ireland department is, or would be, invalid by reason of the section 24 of the Northern Ireland Act 1998; (c) a question whether a Minister or a Northern Ireland department has failed to comply with any of the Convention rights, any obligation under Community law, or any order under section 27 of the Northern Ireland Act so far as relates to such an obligation; or (d) any question arising under the Northern Ireland Act 1998 about excepted or reserved matters.[91] A party raising a devolution issue must specify in a notice filed in the Central Office and served on each of the parties to the proceedings the facts, circumstances, and points of law that provide the basis for the alleged devolution issue.[92] This will not of itself determine that the proceedings give rise to a devolution issue, as it is for the court to decide whether the assertion is well founded or merely frivolous or vexatious.[93] However, where the court decides that the assertion of a devolution issue is valid, it must, as per Schedule 10, paragraph 5 to the Northern Ireland Act 1998 and RSC Order 120, rule 3, give notice of the issue to the Attorney-General, the Attorney-General for Northern Ireland, and the appropriate Northern Ireland Minister or department.[94]

---

[89]   Human Rights Act 1998, s 4(3)–(4). The interpretive obligation is contained in s 3.

[90]   *Judicial Review: Practice Note 01/2006*, Part B. Human Rights Act 1998, s 5(1) reads: 'Where a court is considering whether to make a declaration of incompatibility, the Crown is entitled to notice in accordance with rules of court'. RSC Ord 121, r 2 is titled 'Declaration of Incompatibility: Notice to the Crown'; r 3A is titled 'Subordinate Legislation: Notice to the Crown'.

[91]   Northern Ireland Act 1998, Sch 10, para 1 (note that the Judicial Committee of the Privy Council is the final court of appeal on such matters). The competences of the Assembly are delimited in the Northern Ireland Act 1998, s 6 (see n 36 above); and s 24 of the Act provides: '(1) A Minister or Northern Ireland department has no power to make, confirm, or approve any subordinate legislation, or to do any act, so far as the legislation or act: (a) is incompatible with any of the Convention rights; (b) is incompatible with Community law; (c) discriminates against any person or class of person on the ground of religious belief or political opinion; (d) in the case of an act, aids or incites another person to discriminate against a person or class of person on that ground; or (e) in the case of legislation, modifies an enactment in breach of section 7. (2) Subsection (1)(c) and (d) does not apply in relation to any act which is unlawful by virtue of the [Fair Employment and Treatment (Northern Ireland) Order 1998], or would be unlawful but for some exception made by virtue of [Part VIII of that Order]'; and s 27 deals with quotas for purposes of international obligations. For the lists of excepted and reserved matters as they relate to the competence of the Assembly see Northern Ireland Act 1998, Schs 2 and 3, respectively.

[92]   RSC Ord 120, r 2; and *Judicial Review: Practice Note 01/2006*, Part C.

[93]   *Judicial Review: Practice Note 01/2006*, Part C.

[94]   Devolution issues have been taken to arise in, eg, *Re McBride's Application* [2002] NIQB 64 (regulations challenged as contrary to Convention rights: application dismissed) and *Re Neill's Application* [2005] NIQB 66 and [2006] NICA 5 (Anti-social Behaviour (Northern Ireland) Order 2004, SI 2004/1998 (NI 12) challenged, inter alia, as having been introduced beyond the powers of the Northern Ireland Assembly as exercised by Her Majesty in Council under the Northern Ireland Act 2000: application dismissed).

The Onus of Proof and the 'Arguable Case' Threshold

[**3.24**]   The onus of proof throughout judicial review proceedings is on the applicant[95]—save where there is a prima facie case of illegality[96]—and he or she must demonstrate at the leave stage that they have an 'arguable case'.[97] This has been described as a 'modest hurdle',[98] and the Court of Appeal has stated that where a matter (generally an issue of law) is sufficiently difficult to require argument from both parties, it is ordinarily appropriate for leave to be given if the matter cannot be clearly resolved against the applicant.[99] The application of the test of arguability will, however, depend on the material available at the leave stage[100] and on the view of the judge hearing the application, and the corresponding modesty of the hurdle may vary accordingly.[101] For instance, in *Re Morrow and Campbell's Application for Leave*, Kerr J considered that two Democratic Unionist Party (DUP) Ministers of the Executive Committee of the Northern Ireland Assembly had failed to demonstrate that they had an arguable case in respect of a decision of the First and Deputy First Ministers to withhold certain Committee documents from them in advance of committee meetings (the decision to withhold documents had been taken in the face the DUP's refusal to be bound by confidentiality in respect of Committee deliberations).[102] However, the Court of Appeal disagreed with this conclusion and considered that the application should proceed to a full hearing. The substantive issues were thus heard by the High Court, where Coghlin J granted the application for judicial review in the light of the unlawful frustration of the applicants' substantive legitimate expectation that they would be provided with some of the documents at issue.[103]

[**3.25**]   Where leave has been granted a respondent or a notice party (on which see [3.36]–[3.37]) may apply to have a grant of leave set aside precisely because the case is not, in their view, arguable[104] (grants of leave may be set aside on the basis of RSC Order

[95] *Re McGuigan's Application* [1994] NI 143, 154, Hutton LCJ; *Re SOS's Application* [2003] NIJB 252, 259, para 19; and *Re Downes' Application* [2006] NICA 24, para 14.

[96] *R v Secretary of State for the Home Department, ex p Khawaja* [1984] AC 74.

[97] *Re Hill's Application for Leave* [2007] NICA 1, para 23, and *Re Morrow and Campbell's Application for Leave* [2001] NI 261, 270, Kerr J. See too, eg, *Re Jones' Application*, 10 July 1996, unreported, Campbell J: the test for the grant of leave is whether the judge is satisfied 'that there is a case fit for further investigation and a full *inter partes* hearing of the substantive application for judicial review'; and *Omagh District Council v Minister for Health, Social Services and Public Safety* [2004] NICA 10, para 5: a 'court will refuse permission to claim judicial review unless satisfied that there is an arguable ground for judicial review on which there is a realistic prospect of success'.

[98] *Re Morrow and Campbell's Application for Leave* [2001] NI 261, 270, Kerr J.

[99] *Re UK Waste Management's Application* [2002] NI 130, 139.

[100] See *Re Armstrong's Application* [2007] NIQB 20, para 9, Gillen J: there may be 'circumstances where an enhanced arguability threshold may be imposed even at the leave stage . . . I consider that there is much merit in the views expressed by Keene J in *R v Cotswold District Council, e p Barrington* [1998] 75 P and CR 515 where he said: "Where the court seems to have all the relevant material and have full argument at the (permission) stage on an inter partes hearing, the court is in a better position to judge the merits than as usual on a (permission) application. It may then require (a claimant) to show a reasonably good chance of success if he is to be given (permission)".' See too *Re Downes' Application* [2007] NIQB 40, paras 7–8.

[101] For examples of leave being refused for the absence of an arguable case see, eg, *Re Madden's Application* [1991] 1 NIJB 99; *Re O'Callaghan's Application* [2004] NI 248; and *Re Northern Ireland Commissioner for Children and Young People's Application* [2004] NIQB 40.

[102] [2001] NI 261.

[103] *Re Morrow and Campbell's Application* [2002] NIQB 4. On substantive legitimate expectations see [6.29]–[6.45].

[104] On the position of notice parties in this context see *Re Secretary of State for Northern Ireland's Application* [2002] NIQB 26.

32, rule 8 or with reference to the inherent jurisdiction of the High Court[105]). The existing case law does, however, emphasise that such applications should be acceded to only sparingly and when legal argument makes it clear that there is no basis for the application[106] (the courts have thus sometimes refused to set aside leave where the factual basis for an application has changed but where the court considers that wider points of public interest remain to be resolved[107]). Examples of leave having been set aside include cases where a challenge was to be made to certificates which were legally determinative of all matters of fact and law contained in them,[108] and where an applicant had initiated private law proceedings in tandem with an application for judicial review.[109]

[3.26]   A respondent may also argue that the application should be dismissed on the basis of the *res judicata* doctrine; that is, because a previous application in respect of the matters now before the court had already been dismissed.[110] Such arguments are, however, rare in the case law, and it has, in any event, been doubted whether the *res judicata* doctrine has any relevance in the context of judicial review.[111]

Delay

[3.27]   RSC Order 53, rule 4(1) requires that applications for leave are 'made promptly and in any event within three months from the date when the grounds for the application first arose unless the Court considers that there is good reason for extending the period within which the application shall be made' (this provision is, however, without prejudice to any statutory provision which has the effect of limiting the time within which an application must be made[112]). Time, for these purposes, will in general run only from the date of a formal decision with legal effect[113] or, for instance, from the date of judgment in subordinate proceedings[114] (although the fact that a wide range of measures may be challenged in review proceedings may mean that different considerations will apply in

---

[105] RSC Ord 32, r 8 reads: 'The Court may set aside an order made *ex parte*'.

[106] See *Re Ballyedmond's Application; Re DPP's Application* [2000] NI 174, 176. See also *Re Savage's Application* [1991] NI 103, 106–7.

[107] Eg, *Re E's Application* [2003] NIQB 39 (court refused to set aside the grant of leave to challenge the policing of the Holy Cross dispute in North Belfast as there were important public issues to be resolved notwithstanding that the mode of policing had since changed).

[108] *Re Savage's Application* [1991] NI 103 (the certificates had been issued under s 40(2)(b) & (3) of the Crown Proceedings Act 1947 and had the effect of preventing civil actions against the Ministry of Defence in respect of the shooting dead of three IRA members in Gibraltar). But note that the case pre-dates the Human Rights Act 1998 and that the courts must now approach 'conclusive' certificates in the light of Art 6 ECHR; and see, eg, *Tinnelly & McElduff v UK* [1998] 27 EHRR 249, and *Devenney v UK* [2002] 35 EHRR 24.

[109] *Re Ruane's Application; Re Belfast City Council's Application* [2001] NIQB 4.

[110] See, eg, *Re Wadsworth's Application* [2004] NIQB 8, para 6, Weatherup J.

[111] W Wade and C Forsyth, *Administrative Law*, 8th edn (Oxford, Oxford University Press, 2000) p 255ff.

[112] RSC Ord 53, r 4(3).

[113] *R (Burkett) v Hammersmith and Fulham LBC* [2002] 3 All ER 97. See also, eg *Re Wadsworth's Application* [2004] NIQB 8, para 7, Weatherup J.

[114] RSC Ord 53, r 4(2) reads: 'Where the relief sought is an order of certiorari in respect of any judgment, order, conviction or other proceeding, the date when grounds for the application first arose shall be taken to be the date of that judgment, order, conviction or proceeding'. But see also RSC Ord 53, r 3(7): 'Where leave is sought to apply for an order of certiorari to remove for the purpose of its being quashed any judgment, order, conviction or other proceeding which is subject to an appeal and a time is limited for the bringing of the appeal, the Court may adjourn the application for leave until the appeal is determined or the time for appealing has expired.'

different cases; and on the range of reviewable measures see [3.05]–[3.08]). Case law in Northern Ireland has, in any event, long emphasised that an application should be made *promptly* once time starts to run and that applications made within the three-month period may still be deemed out of time for lack of promptitude.[115] The corresponding rationale for the strict application of the time-limit has been linked to the interests of good administration[116] and also to the need for respondents to be able effectively to defend proceedings (that is, within a time-frame that ensures that individuals involved in the decision can remember the decision and its context).[117] A further justification is that of the need for protection of the interests of third parties who may have benefited from an original decision but who may suffer a detriment if the decision is later deemed unlawful[118] (subject to any detriment being meaningful relative to the third party's circumstances and actions[119]).

[3.28]   On the other hand, the time-limit can be extended where there is 'good reason' for doing so. 'Good reason' is a context-driven criterion, and the courts sometimes prefer to decide whether there has been good reason for delay at the substantive hearing rather than at the preliminary leave stage.[120] In determining the issue the court will enquire: whether there is reasonable and objective justification for the late application; whether permission to proceed would be prejudicial to third party interests or the interests of good administration; and whether the public interest requires that the application should be allowed to proceed.[121] Corresponding examples of good reason in the case law include: the fact that delay was caused by prior attempts to obtain legal aid[122]; the fact that counsel for the applicant was hospitalised[123]; the absence of an adverse impact on good administration or the interests of a third party[124]; and the fact that the issue before the court on a delayed application was one that could be brought before the court again in substantially the same form in a subsequent application.[125] The case law does,

---

[115] Eg, *Re Shearer's Application* [1993] NIJB 12, and *Re McCabe's Application* [1994] NIJB 27. See too *Re Hill's Application* [2007] NICA 1, para 33, and *Re McHenry's Application* [2007] NIQB 22, para 3(3).

[116] *Re Wadsworth's Application* [2004] NIQB 8. On this justification see further [1.07].

[117] *Re McCabe's Application* [1994] NIJB 27 (challenge to a disciplinary decision of a prison governor almost two years after the event was dismissed for reasons of delay as the governor had since retired and the precise details of the adjudication process were not recalled within the prison service: application dismissed).

[118] *Re McKevitt's Application* [2005] NIQB 56 (argued that a challenge to the legality of a legislative measure in the field of legal aid would have far-ranging implications for third parties who had already benefited under the measure: the argument was rejected on the evidence before the court, and the application for judicial review was granted).

[119] See *Re Murphy's Application* [2004] NIQB 85, Weatherup J (application for judicial review here challenged the lawfulness of a grant of planning permission that had already led to some work being undertaken by the third party developer: held, at para 11, that although 'there would be some measure of financial and operational prejudice if the decision to permit this development were to be set aside . . . such prejudice is limited when account is taken of the scale of the (third) party's operation and the undertaking of works while aware of the opposition to the proposed development, and the possibility of statutory objection or proceedings for judicial review'. The application for judicial review was, in any event, dismissed).

[120] See *Re Leeper's Application*, 29 November 1991, unreported.

[121] *Re Zhanje's Application* [2007] NIQB 14, para 7, Gillen J, citing *R v Secretary of State for Transport and Industry, ex p Greenpeace* [2000] Env LR 221.

[122] *Re McKevitt's Application* [2005] NIQB 56; *Re Murphy's Application* [2004] NIQB 85; *Re Wadsworth's Application* [2004] NIQB 8; and *Re Mullen's Application*, 18 January 1999, unreported

[123] *Re Wadsworth's Application* [2004] NIQB 8, para 8.

[124] *Re Wadsworth's Application* [2004] NIQB 8, para 8.

[125] *Re O'Neill's Application* [1995] NI 274 (challenge to the lawfulness of a vote in Cookstown District Council, whereby a motion proposing the opening of a leisure centre and swimming pool facilities on a Sunday was discussed and defeated: Kerr J thought that a further motion would likely be put before the council in the event that the present proceedings were dismissed and the corresponding vote challenged).

wever, also make clear that, where there have been several periods of delay in the mak-
g of the application, the applicant must lay sufficient evidence to account for each of
those periods.[126] An application may thus fail—whether at leave or at the substantive
hearing—when an applicant's explanation for delay is only partial.[127]

[**3.29**]   One final point about the delay provision concerns its potential inconsistency
with EU law and the ECHR. In *R (Burkett) v Hammersmith and Fulham LBC*[128] Lord
Steyn suggested that the requirement that applications be made promptly may be contrary to the doctrine of certainty in EU law and to the ECtHR's Article 6 jurisprudence
on the right to a fair hearing within a reasonable time. While his Lordship did not doubt
the validity of the three-month limit—applications for judicial review of measures of the
EU institutions must in comparison be brought within two months[129]—he did state that
'there is at the very least doubt whether the obligation to apply "promptly"' corresponds
to the demands of European law.[130] The point made therefore was that uncertainty may
follow from the fact that applications may be dismissed for lack of promptitude even if
brought within three months and that this may be inconsistent with the rights of individuals under both EU law and the ECHR. His Lordship's comments were, however, obiter,
and they have yet to be given express consideration by the Northern Ireland courts.
Subsequent case law in England and Wales has also referred to ECHR authority that
regards the delay requirement as ECHR-compliant.[131]

Standing

[**3.30**]   The requirement for standing to bring an application for judicial review is
contained in section 18(4) of the Judicature (Northern Ireland) Act 1978 and RSC Order
53, rule 3(5), both of which state that an applicant must have 'a sufficient interest in the
matter to which the application relates'. RSC Order 53, rule 3(5) also links standing
specifically to the leave stage of proceedings,[132] although the courts will here form only
a preliminary view of standing so as to exclude applications made by 'cranks, busybod-
ies or mischief makers'.[133] The courts thereafter regard standing as a matter to be determined in the full legal and factual context to a dispute and they thus more typically
resolve the issue at the substantive hearing of an application for judicial review.[134] The
corresponding case law and the reasons for the shift away from an emphasis on standing

---

[126]   *Re Wilson's Application* [1989] NI 415, 416, Carswell LJ.

[127]   See, eg, *Re McCabe's Application* [1994] NIJB 27, and *Re Aitken's Application* [1995] NI 49.

[128]   [2002] 3 All ER 97.

[129]   Article 230(5) EC.

[130]   [2002] 3 All ER 97, 114, para 53.

[131]   Eg, *R (I-CD Publishing Ltd) v Office of the Deputy Prime Minister* [2003] EWHC 1761, citing *Lam v UK*
(App No 41671/98), 5 July 2001. See further R Taylor, 'Time Flies Like the Wind: Some Issues that Burkett Did
Not Address' [2005] JR 249.

[132]   The rule reads: 'The Court shall not, having regard to section 18(4) of the Act, grant leave unless it considers that the applicant has a sufficient interest in the matter to which the application relates'; and s 18(4)
reads: 'The Court shall not grant any relief on an application for judicial review unless it considers that the
applicant has a sufficient interest in the matter to which the application relates.'

[133]   *Re Ward's Application for Leave* [2006] NIQB 67, para 5, Girvan J, citing *R v Inland Revenue
Commissioners, ex p National Federation of Self-Employed and Small Businesses Ltd* [1982] AC 617.

[134]   *R v Inland Revenue Commissioners, ex p National Federation of Self-Employed and Small Businesses
Ltd* [1982] AC 617; and *Re McBride's Application* [1999] NI 299.

at the leave stage are considered at [3.64]–[3.66]. Consideration is there also given to the related question of standing under section 7 of the Human Rights Act 1998.

Urgent Cases

[**3.31**] Where the issues raised on an application for leave are deemed urgent and the court considers that the applicant has an arguable case and so on, the application for leave can be heard as the substantive case.[135] Whether an application is 'urgent' is, in turn, a matter for the court, although it appears that the court will proceed to hear the substantive application only with the agreement of the parties.[136] An example of an urgent case is *Re LL's Application*,[137] where the issue was whether the rights and duties in respect of the burial of a terminally ill child who had been in the care of a health and social services trust remained with the trust at the time of death or whether they reverted to the child's biological parents. The court held that they remained with the trust.

Where Leave is Granted

[**3.32**] Where the court grants leave to make an application for judicial review, the applicant is confined to the ground(s) for challenge in the Order 53 statement[138] in respect of which leave is granted, subject to the court's powers of amendment at both the leave stage and the substantive hearing.[139] Where leave is granted in respect of only some of the grounds in the Order 53 statement, the applicant may appeal that partial grant of leave to the Court of Appeal. However, one corresponding point of procedure that remains unclear is whether leave to appeal is required in such circumstances. Although Order 53, rule 10(a) states that leave to appeal is not required where an application for leave to bring an application for judicial review is dismissed, it was contended in *Re Downes' Application* that leave to appeal should be required in respect of partial grants of leave as these constitute interlocutory orders that can, as per section 35(2)(g) of the Judicature (Northern Ireland) Act 1978, only be appealed with leave.[140] The Court of Appeal in *Downes* did not, however, consider the point at length and it stated that, if leave to appeal was required in the instant case, it should be granted.

---

[135] For guidance on making urgent applications see *Judicial Review: Practice Note 01/2006*, available at http://www.courtsni.gov.uk.

[136] *Re LL's Application* [2005] NIQB 83, para 2.

[137] [2005] NIQB 83.

[138] RSC Ord 53, r 5(1).

[139] RSC Ord 53, r 3(4) reads: 'Without prejudice to its powers under section 18(2) of the [Judicature (Northern Ireland)] Act and Order 20, rule 8, the Court hearing an application for leave may direct or allow the applicant's statement to be amended, whether by specifying different or additional grounds or otherwise, on such terms, if any, as it thinks fit'; and RSC Ord 53, 6(2) reads: 'The Court may on the hearing of the motion direct or allow the applicant to amend his statement, whether by specifying different or additional grounds or relief or otherwise, on such terms, if any, as it thinks fit and may allow further affidavits to be used by him'. But note that, where the applicant intends to ask to be allowed to amend his statement or to use further affidavits, he/she must give notice of that intention and of any proposed amendment to every other party: RSC Ord 53, r 6(3). And see too, eg, *Re Delaney's Application* [2007] NIQB 55 (court refusing to allow the applicant to argue new grounds at the substantive hearing for reasons of fairness to the other parties).

[140] Section 35(2)(g) provides: '(2) No appeal to the Court of Appeal shall lie: . . . (g) without the leave of the judge or of the Court of Appeal, from any interlocutory order or judgment made or given by a judge of the High Court'.

[**3.33**]   Once leave has been granted an originating motion, which carries a fee of £123 (less the £52 fee paid at the leave stage), must be issued and served on the respondent(s) within 14 days. An affidavit of service of the notice of motion must also be filed in the Central Office within the same time period, after which period of time leave to make the application will lapse (where leave has lapsed an application for extension of time or for a further grant of leave must be made by summons and an affidavit that explains the failure to issue and serve the notice of motion in time; the court may order costs against the party who has failed to comply with the time-limits).[141] The notice of motion should specify the relief and grounds in respect of which leave has been granted, and it should be accompanied by the applicant's Order 53 statement (as amended by the grant of leave), the affidavits and exhibits, and the Order granting leave.[142] The respondent's affidavit(s), which must be drafted in 'clear and unambiguous language'[143] and prepared within a suggested time-frame of 21 days,[144] must then set out the evidence (but not the arguments) and refer to both the respondent's and applicant's book of exhibits (the respondent's book of exhibits—as with the applicant's—should be prepared in line with the guidance in *Judicial Review: Practice Note 01/2006*[145]). The applicant's rejoinder must in turn be made within a suggested time-frame of 14 days and a date for a pre-hearing review of the case fixed.[146]

Costs

[**3.34**]   Where an application for leave is granted, costs, which are in the discretion of the court,[147] will ordinarily be reserved until after the substantive hearing of the application ('costs follow the event'). However, applicants in 'public interest' cases (see [3.64]) may, at the leave stage, also apply to the court for a protective costs order that will limit the extent of any potential costs order against (the 'flip-side' to such orders would be 'security for costs' orders requested by respondents[148]). Such orders have been of growing significance in England and Wales in recent years,[149] and they have also started to feature in Northern Ireland case law.[150] The case law in England and Wales centres on

---

[141] RSC Ord 53, r 5(3), (5) and (6); and *Judicial Review: Practice Note 01/2006*, Part A.

[142] *Judicial Review: Practice Note 01/2006*, Part A.

[143] *Re Downes' Application* [2006] NIQB 77, para 31, Girvan J.

[144] *Judicial Review: Practice Note 01/2006*, Part A.

[145] Viz, Part A, which reads: 'Respondent's book of exhibits: (1) There should be <u>one</u> indexed and paginated book of exhibits containing any additional material relied on by the respondent. Where necessary this may be divided into more than one file, with continuing pagination. (2) Material contained in the applicant's book of exhibits should not be copied into the respondent's book of exhibits. References to material contained in the applicant's book of exhibits should be to the document number and page number if necessary. (3) Key documents should be marked in the exhibits index with an asterisk. (4) If there are two or more respondents *represented by the same solicitor*, there should be one respondents' book of exhibits. (5) Similarly if there are notice parties or interveners filing affidavits *where they are represented by the respondent(s) solicitor*, there should be one respondents' book of exhibits if possible. (6) Only necessary documents should be exhibited. Copies of legislation should not be included in the exhibits. (7) Relevant extracts only should be included where appropriate. The Court may disallow costs where superfluous materials are included' (emphasis in the Practice Note). On the applicant's book of exhibits see [3.19].

[146] *Judicial Review: Practice Note 01/2006*, Part A.

[147] Judicature (Northern Ireland) Act 1978, s 59. And see RSC Ord 62; and *Re Eshokai's Application* [2007] NIQB 75, para 19.

[148] On which see RSC Ord 59, r 10(5); and *Re SOS's Application* [2003] NIJB 252, 255, para 8 ff.

[149] See R Stein and J Beagent, 'Protective Costs Orders' (2005) 10 JR 206.

[150] See, eg, *Re McHugh's Application* [2007] NICA 26, and *Re Moore's Application* [2007] NIQB 23.

the so-called '*Corner House* principles',[151] which hold that a protective order may be made at any stage in the proceedings—and subject to such conditions as the court thinks fit—if the court in its discretion is satisfied that: (i) the issues raised are of general public importance; (ii) the public interest requires that those issues should be resolved; (iii) the applicant has no private interest in the outcome of the case; (iv) having regard to the financial resources of the applicant and the respondents(s) and to the amount of the costs that are likely to be involved it is fair and just to make the order; and (v) if the order is not made the applicant will probably discontinue the proceedings and will be acting reasonably in doing so (the principles are also linked to an understanding that, where those acting for the applicant are doing do so *pro bono*, this will be likely to enhance the argument in favour of an order). The *Corner House* principles thereby reflect a concern that matters of public interest should not escape judicial scrutiny for reasons of the financial limitations of the applicant,[152] although important questions about the principles remain. These include the meaning of 'no private interest in the outcome of the case',[153] as the vast majority of applicants will have a private interest and may for that reason not qualify for a protective order (an obvious exception to the private interest requirement would be an environmental pressure group that challenges a decision or other measure as contrary to environmental law). Another unresolved issue is the position in respect of proceedings under the Human Rights Act 1998: while the *Corner House* principles require that an applicant has no 'private interest', it is typically only applicants with such an interest who may initiate proceedings under section 7 of the Human Rights Act 1998[154] and it would thus seem that there would be limited scope for protective costs orders in cases under the Human Rights Act 1998 (on section 7 see [3.67]–[3.70]).[155]

[3.35]   Where the application for leave is dismissed (see [3.40]), the applicant will have to cover his or her own costs (subject to the availability of legal aid). On the other hand, unsuccessful applicants will not normally be required to pay costs to the respondent as the leave stage is ex parte and the respondent will make submissions to the court only if they wish to do so.[156] Moreover, should proceedings be discontinued, the issue of costs will depend on the reasons for the discontinuance. Hence where the reason is the respondent's change of position in the light of the challenge, the applicant will have a reasonable expectation of costs.[157] An order for the applicant will also be made if the reason for discontinuance is a change of the respondent's position for the purpose of pre-empting the application.[158]

---

[151] Named after the case in which they were identified: *R (Corner House) v Department of Trade and Industry* [2005] 1 WLR 2600.

[152] See also, eg, *R v Lord Chancellor, ex p CPAG* [1991] 1 WLR 347.

[153] See, eg, *Re McHugh's Application* [2007] NICA 26 (applicant with multiple sclerosis applied for judicial review of a decision of a trust not to make arrangements to provide her with assistance for adaptation of her home: held that the applicant could not obtain a protective costs order as the issues raised were not of general public importance and she had a personal interest in the outcome of the case).

[154] But see now also, eg, the Justice and Security (Northern Ireland) Act 2007, s 14, giving the Northern Ireland Human Rights Commission a power to bring proceedings under the Human Rights Act 1998. And see [3.68].

[155] For consideration see, eg, *R (Smeaton) v Secretary of State for Health and Schering plc* [2002] EWHC 866 (Admin) (costs ordered against applicant who was supported by the Society for the Protection of the Unborn Child).

[156] *Re SOS (NI) Ltd's Application* [2003] NIJB 252, 256, para 11.

[157] *R v Royal London Borough of Kensington and Chelsea, ex p Ghebregiogis* (1994) 27 HLR 602.

[158] On costs see further J Larkin and D Schofield, *Judicial Review in Northern Ireland: A Practitioner's Guide* (Belfast, SLS Legal Publications, 2007) ch 16. And see *Re Ullahs Application* [2007] NIQB 45, at n 379 below.

Notice Parties

[**3.36**] ¡Where leave has been granted, the applicant's originating motion must also be served on notice parties. Notice parties are typically defined as 'all parties directly affected' by the proceedings,[159] although RSC Order 53, rule 5(7) allows other parties to be joined as notice parties where the court is of the opinion that they should be joined.[160] The corresponding purpose of such notification is to place the affected parties in a position that will enable them to make representations to the court, albeit that the extent to which they may do so is ultimately a matter for the discretion of the court.[161] A failure to serve the originating motion on a notice party is in turn regarded as a serious omission, although it need not entail that the court cannot hear the matters before it (much will instead depend on the nature of the issue and the remedy sought).[162] The scope for failure to notify should, in any event, be limited where the applicant has observed the Pre-Action Protocol as this requires potential applicants to copy their pre-action letter to interested parties (see [3.14]–[3.16]).

[**3.37**] \Where leave is granted in an application that raises a devolution issue and/or may lead the court to make a declaration of incompatibility under the Human Rights Act 1998, statute contains a number of additional notification requirements (see [3.22]–[3.23]). Hence where the proceedings give rise to a devolution issue the court must, as per Schedule 10, paragraph 5 to the Northern Ireland Act 1998, and RSC Order 120, rule 3, give notice of the issue to the Attorney-General, the Attorney-General for Northern Ireland, and the appropriate Northern Ireland Minister or department[163]; and where the court is considering whether to make a declaration of incompatibility a notice should be issued to the Crown by the court in accordance with section 5 of the Human Rights Act 1998 and RSC Order 121, rules 2 and 3A.[164]

Third Party Interveners

[**3.38**] \Where leave is granted it is sometimes perceived that the legal issues to be raised at the substantive hearing are of a wider importance in the sense that they have implications for parties other than the applicant, respondent, and notice parties (where

---

[159] RSC Ord 53, r 5(3).

[160] See J Larkin and P Schofield, *Judicial Review in Northern Ireland: A Practitioner's Guide* (Belfast, SLS Legal Publications, 2007) p 159*ff*.

[161] RSC Ord 53, r 9(1); and *Re Secretary of State for Northern Ireland's Application* [2002] NIQB 26.

[162] *Re Secretary of State for Northern Ireland's Application* [2006] NIQB 10 (no notification had been given to the recipient of an award of compensation when the Secretary of State sought to establish that the approach adopted by the Criminal Injuries Compensation Appeals Panel was procedurally and legally flawed: while notice should have been given, the fact that the Secretary of State was not seeking to quash the actual award of compensation made the presence of the third party unnecessary).

[163] Devolution issues have been taken to arise in, eg, *Re McBride's Application* [2002] NIQB 64 (regulations challenged as contrary to Convention rights: application dismissed) and *Re Neill's Application* [2005] NIQB 66, [2006] NICA 5 (Anti-social Behaviour (Northern Ireland) Order 2004, SI 2004/1998 (NI 12), challenged, inter alia, as having been introduced beyond the powers of the Northern Ireland Assembly as exercised by Her Majesty in Council under the Northern Ireland Act 2000: application dismissed).

[164] *Judicial Review: Practice Note 01/2006*, Part B. Human Rights Act 1998, s 5(1) reads: 'Where a court is considering whether to make a declaration of incompatibility, the Crown is entitled to notice in accordance with rules of court'. RSC Ord 121, r 2 is titled 'Declaration of Incompatibility: Notice to the Crown'; r 3A is titled, 'Subordinate Legislation: Notice to the Crown'. And see, eg, *Re ES's Application* [2007] NIQB 58 (Department of Health and Social Services and Public Safety given notice in proceedings concerning the compatibility with Arts 6 and 8 ECHR of art 64 of the Children (Northern Ireland) Order 1995, SI 1995/755 (NI 2): application granted).

applicable). Under such circumstances, third parties such as private organisations or statutory bodies may wish to intervene to bring further arguments to the attention of the court[165] (some bodies, for instance the Northern Ireland Human Rights Commission, have a statutory power to apply to intervene in judicial proceedings[166]). The arguments made by the intervener may lend specific support to the submissions of the applicant or the respondent, or they may alternatively seek to highlight other points of more general relevance (the ordinarily partisan nature of the third party intervention means that the role performed is different from that of an amicus curiae, who provides the court with an impartial overview and opinion on an aspect of the law).[167] In any event, interventions are taken to have the potential to enhance the judicial decision-making process by providing the court with a much wider range of arguments on germane legal points.[168] Courts must therefore decide how best to reconcile the benefits which may be derived from a third party intervention with the possible inconvenience, delay, and expense that the intervention may cause to the existing parties.[169]

[**3.39**] Leave to intervene is at the discretion of the court, although RSC Order 53, rule 9(1) also provides that the court may receive submissions from any 'proper person' who wishes to be heard in opposition to an application for judicial review.[170] The corresponding case law on interventions suggests that they should in the first instance be limited to the presentation of written submissions, as the court can then consider the written submission at a later stage in proceedings and decide whether oral argument from the intervener would be of further assistance.[171] The case law also makes clear that interventions—whether written or oral—should be strictly confined 'to relevant and apposite matters which directly address the issues before the court'.[172] However, this is a requirement that may cause some uncertainty, most notably when human rights law is in issue. This is because human rights arguments are often developed with reference to international instruments that have not yet been incorporated into UK domestic law[173] and, even though some recent decisions have demonstrated an increased receptiveness to arguments based upon unincorporated norms,[174] binding precedent has emphasised that

---

[165] See, eg, *Re Christian Institute and Ors' Application* [2007] NIQB 66 (challenge to the lawfulness of the Equality Act (Sexual Orientation) Regulations (Northern Ireland) 2006, SR 2006/439: interventions by the Archbishop of Armagh and Primate of All Ireland, the Northern Ireland Human Rights Commission, the Equality Commission for Northern Ireland, and the Coalition on Sexual Orientation)

[166] *Re Northern Ireland Human Rights Commission* [2002] NI 236, interpreting Northern Ireland Act 1998, s 69 as including a power to apply to intervene. See further [1.27], n 133; and see now also the Justice and Security (Northern Ireland) Act 2007, s 14.

[167] For recent cases where third party interventions were made to the courts see, eg, *Family Planning Association of Northern Ireland v Minister for Health, Social Services and Public Safety* [2005] NI 188, and *Re Neill's Application* [2006] NICA 5. On the role of an amicus curiae see *Re Northern Ireland Human Rights Commission* [2002] NI 236, 261, para 72, Lord Hobhouse.

[168] See JUSTICE/Public Law Project, *A Matter of Public Interest: Reforming the law and practice on interventions in public interest cases* (London, 1996).

[169] *Re Northern Ireland Human Rights Commission* [2002] NI 236, 246, para 32, Lord Woolf.

[170] 'On the hearing of any motion under rule 5, any person who desires to be heard in opposition to the motion, and appears to the Court to be a proper person to be heard, shall be heard, notwithstanding that he has not been served with notice of the motion.'

[171] *Re White's Application* [2000] NI 432, 435–6.

[172] *Re White's Application* [2000] NI 432, 445.

[173] See further [1.23]–[1.24].

[174] *A v Secretary of State for the Home Department* [2005] 2 AC 68; *A v Secretary of State for the Home Department (No 2)* [2006] 2 AC 221; and *Re E's Application* [2006] NICA 37. But compare, eg, *In Re McKerr* [2004] 1 WLR 807.

such standards do not enjoy the force of (domestic) law.[175] Understandings of what is 'relevant and apposite' may therefore vary accordingly.

Where Leave is Refused: Appeals

[3.40]   Where an application for leave is refused, the refusal may be appealed to, or renewed before, the Court of Appeal (on refusals in criminal causes see [3.21]).[176] While both appeals and renewals may result in an application for leave being granted, the Court of Appeal has emphasised that an appeal can be procedurally advantageous.[177] The point here is that it is possible for the Court of Appeal in a suitable case on appeal—but not on the renewal of an application for leave—to hear and determine the substantive application under RSC Order 53, rule 5(8).[178] This point should, however, be read with the Court of Appeal's related statement that leave should ordinarily be granted in the High Court where a matter cannot be clearly resolved against the applicant, as this will result in any subsequent appeal having the benefit of fuller evidence and submissions from the substantive hearing at first instance.[179]

[3.41]   It should finally be noted that it is only applicants who have rights of appeal at the leave stage. Therefore, respondents and notice parties who wish to challenge the grant of leave cannot do so by way of appeal but must apply to the High Court to have the grant of leave set aside (see [3.25]). In the event that such application is unsuccessful, the decision of the High Court may be appealed, with the leave of the High Court or the Court of Appeal, to the Court of Appeal.[180] Such appeals must be made within 21 days.[181]

INTERIM MATTERS

Remedies

Stays, Interim Declarations, and Interim Injunctions

[3.42]   The granting of interim remedies is governed by section 19 of the Judicature (Northern Ireland) Act 1978 and by RSC Order 53, rule 3(13). Under section 19, the court may 'grant a stay of proceedings or of enforcement of an order or may grant such interim relief as it considers appropriate pending final determination of the application'; and RSC Order 53, rule 3(13)(a) provides that, where the relief sought is an order of prohibition or

---

[175] *R v Secretary of State for the Home Department, ex p Brind* [1991] 1 AC 696; and *R (Hurst) v London Northern District Coroner* [2007] 2 WLR 726; and, eg, *Re McCallion's Application* [2005] NICA 21; *Re T's Application* [2000] NI 516; and *Re White's Application* [2000] NI 432.

[176] RSC Ord 53, r 10 states: 'Leave shall not be required for an appeal to the Court of Appeal from (a) an order refusing an application for leave under rule 3'. Applications for leave may be renewed in accordance with RSC Ord 59, r 14.

[177] *Re Rice's Application* [1998] NI 265, 268; and *Re SOS's Application* [2003] NIJB 252, 254, para 5.

[178] This rule reads: 'Except in a criminal cause or matter, the Court of Appeal may hear and determine an application for an order under this rule where the Court has granted leave under rule 3 on appeal from the refusal of such leave by the Court.'

[179] *Re UK Waste Management's Application* [2002] NI 130, 139.

[180] Judicature (Northern Ireland) Act 1978, s 35(2)(g).

[181] RSC Ord 59, r 4(1)(a).

certiorari, the Court may direct that the grant of leave 'shall operate as a stay of the proceedings to which the application relates until the determination of the application or until the Court otherwise directs' (authority in England and Wales suggests that the power to stay is not limited to judicial/quasi-judicial proceedings but includes any procedure by which a public law decision is reached[182]). RSC Order 53, rule 3(13)(b) then makes provision in respect of other remedies and reads: 'if any other relief is sought, the Court may at any time grant in the proceedings such interim relief as could be granted in an action begun by writ'. Such remedies include, most obviously, interim injunctions. Interim declarations—whereby the court specifies the legal position that is to be observed pending the final hearing of the application for judicial review—may be also available.[183]

[**3.43**]   If the court is considering whether to grant an interim injunction—for instance to prevent a course of administrative action or to prevent the coming into force or maintaining in force of subordinate legislation that is challenged as ultra vires—it will determine the matter in accordance with a 'balance of convenience' test.[184] This test is typically associated with private law disputes in which a plaintiff must establish that there is a serious issue to be tried, at which stage the court will decide whether damages would be an adequate remedy for either party or whether the balance of convenience favours the award of an injunction. In public law proceedings, the application of the test varies according to the context of the case and in the light of corresponding public law considerations. Several such considerations were apparent in *Re Eurostock's Application*, where a meat producer had challenged subordinate public health legislation as contrary to EU law's free movement of goods provisions (the interim matter was not in fact whether an injunction should be granted but whether an order of the High Court that had quashed the legislation should be stayed pending an Article 234 EC reference to the ECJ).[185] The Court of Appeal emphasised that, where the public interest is engaged by a dispute, the likelihood of irreparable financial damage to a private party must be set against factors that include the importance of upholding national legislation and the risk to public health if the legislation in question is quashed.[186] The court on this basis held that the order of the High Court should be stayed, save in respect of that part of the order that quashed the provisions of the legislation that had direct implications for the private party's economic activities.

[**3.44**]   Interim and final injunctions are available against all public bodies and also against Ministers of the Crown. In respect of Ministers of the Crown, this is the result of the House of Lords judgment in *M v Home Office*,[187] which held that section 21 of the Crown Proceedings Act 1947 does not apply to judicial review.[188] Section 21 prevents the grant of injunctions against the Crown in civil proceedings,[189] but the House considered

---

[182] *R v Secretary of State for Education, ex p Avon CC* [1991] 1 All ER 282.

[183] See P Maguire, 'The Procedure for Judicial Review in Northern Ireland' in B Hadfield (ed), *Judicial Review: A Thematic Approach* (Dublin, Gill & MacMillan, 1995) pp 371, 381. Provision for such declarations is now made in England and Wales: see CPR, r 25.1(b).

[184] On which see *American Cyanamid Co v Ethicon Ltd* [1975] AC 396.

[185] [1999] NI 13. The legislation in question was the Specified Risk Material Order (Northern Ireland) 1997, SR 1997/551.

[186] See also *R v Secretary of State for Transport, ex p Factortame Ltd (No 2)* [1991] 1 AC 603.

[187] [1994] 1 AC 377.

[188] The principle of the case has recently also been extended to Scotland: see *Davidson v Scottish Ministers* (2006) SC (HL) 41.

[189] For earlier application of the section see *McKernan v Governor of HM Prison* [1983] NI 83.

that judicial review should be regarded as distinct from civil proceedings and that injunctions should be available in limited circumstances for the purposes of constraining government Ministers. In reaching this conclusion, the House noted how the prerogative orders had long been available against Ministers of the Crown and that injunctions would merely complement the existing remedial options. The House moreover noted that declarations and injunctions are linked to the prerogative orders under the judicial review procedure and that the governing legislation does not distinguish between the scope of injunctions and other remedies (except for damages).[190] The grant of injunctions against government Ministers would therefore not offend any constitutional principle—the courts would grant such relief only sparingly—and it would ensure that rights and interests under domestic law enjoyed protection equal to that available in EU law cases (on which see [3.45]).

The European Communities Act 1972 and EU Law

[3.45]   It is a core requirement of the EU legal order that individuals have access to effective national remedies for the purposes of protecting their EU law rights and that any national rule of law that would prevent such effective protection must cede to the superior force of EU law.[191] This is true both in terms of the availability of final remedies (see [3.77])[192] and in terms of the interim protection of rights. Hence in *Factortame (No 2)*, the House of Lords held that section 21 of the Crown Proceedings Act 1947—which prevents the grant of injunctions against the Crown in civil proceedings—did not apply where EU law rights were in issue. This finding, which later 'spilled over' in *M v Home Office*[193] ([3.44]), was made in the context of proceedings that challenged the lawfulness of the Merchant Shipping Act 1988 vis-à-vis the nationality, establishment, and capital provisions of the EC Treaty.[194] The injunction granted in the case therefore had the effect of preventing the Secretary of State for Transport from enforcing the terms of an Act of Parliament that was enacted after the European Communities Act 1972 that gives domestic effect to EU law. This was an outcome that was widely understood to have contradicted the UK constitution's fundamental precepts of parliamentary sovereignty and implied repeal.[195]

[3.46]   Should an individual challenge the lawfulness of an EU Regulation or Directive in the High Court, the question will arise whether an interim injunction should issue to prevent the operation of the EU measure and/or national regulations or other legislation that give(s) effect to the EU measure. Domestic courts may not, as such, rule on the law-

---

[190] The provision at issue in the case was the Supreme Court Act 1981, s 31, which corresponds to the Judicature (Northern Ireland) Act 1978, s 18 and RSC Ord 53, r 1. On the position in respect of damages see [3.75] and [8.21]–[8.29].

[191] See, eg, Case 33/76, *Rewe-Zentralfinanz eG and Rewe-Zentral AG v Landwirtschaftskammer für das Saarland* [1976] ECR 1989; Case 47/76, *Comet v Produktschap voor Siergewassen* [1976] ECR 2043; Case 158/80, *Rewe Handelsgesellschaft Nord mbH v Hauptzollamt Kiel* [1981] ECR 1805; Case C-213/89, *R v Secretary of State for Transport, ex p Factortame* [1990] ECR I-2433; Case 326/88, *Anklagemyndigheden v Hansen & Sons I/S* [1990] ECR I-2911; and Case C271/91, *Marshall v Southampton and South West Hampshire Area Health Authority (No 2)*, [1993] ECR I-4367. And see, in the NI courts, *Johnston v Chief Constable of the RUC* [1998] NI 188.

[192] See also [8.32]–[8.39].

[193] [1994] 1 AC 377; and on 'spill-over' see [1.18].

[194] Viz, ex Art 7 EC (now repealed); Arts 43 and 48 (ex Arts 52 and 58) EC; and Art 294 (ex Art 221) EC.

[195] See [5.04]–[5.07].

fulness of an EU measure—the issue should be referred to the ECJ under the Article 234
EC reference procedure[196]—although they may grant injunctions pending the ECJ's decision on the legality of the EU measure.[197] Where the EU measure under challenge is
already in force—that is, national legislation has been introduced to give effect to an EU
Directive within the prescribed time-frame—the test for granting an injunction will be
the 'serious doubt' and 'serious and irreparable damage' formulation of the ECJ (the
'doubt' relates to the validity of the measure; the 'damage' to that to be suffered by the
applicant). Less clear, however, is the test to be applied when the time-limit for giving
effect to a Directive has not passed but where a challenge is made to national legislation
that has already been introduced to give effect to the Directive. Here, some judges have
suggested that it is the domestic test that should govern the grant of an interim injunction
against national legislation (on which see [3.43]) rather than the test developed by the
ECJ.[198] However, the comments in question were made in a case in which the issue ultimately became academic, and the greater weight of opinion would suggest that, in the
absence of an Article 234 EC reference on the matter, injunctions should issue on the
basis of the EU law formulation.[199]

The Human Rights Act 1998

[3.47]   Section 8(1) of the Human Rights Act 1998 reads: 'In relation to any act (or
proposed act) of a public authority which the court finds is (or would be) unlawful, it
may grant such relief or remedy, or make such order, within its powers as it considers
just and appropriate'. The interim remedies available where leave to bring an application
for judicial review has been granted will therefore also be available should that application be founded wholly or partly on any of the ECHR provisions that have effect under
the Human Rights Act 1998. It is, however, also true that the remedies will not be available in respect of primary legislation[200] as the Act does not enable the courts to strike
down such legislation as unlawful. The courts may instead only declare such legislation
to be incompatible with the ECHR[201] and, as such declarations have no legal effect on
the legislation in respect of which they are made,[202] it is clear that an interim injunction
could not issue.

---

[196] See, most recently, Case C-344/04, *R (International Air Transport Association) v Department for
Transport*, [2006] ECR 403.

[197] Cases C-143/88 and C/92/89, *Zuckerfabrik Süderdithmarschen AG v Hauptzollamt Itzhoe* [1991] ECR
I-415, and Case C-465/93, *Atlanta Fruchthandelsgesellschaft mbH v Bundesamt fur Ernahrung und
Forstwirtschaft* [1995] ECR I-3761.

[198] See, in the Court of Appeal in England and Wales, *R v Secretary of State for Health, ex p Imperial
Tobacco Ltd* [2000] 1 All ER 572, 594*ff* (Laws LJ dissenting); and in the House of Lords [2001] 1 All ER 850,
856*ff* (Lord Hoffmann).

[199] Viz, the majority in the Court of Appeal in England and Wales in *R v Secretary of State for Health, ex
parte Imperial Tobacco Ltd* [2000] 1 All ER 572. And see also *R (ABNA) v Secretary of State for Health* [2004]
2 CMLR 39.

[200] Defined in Section 21.

[201] Section 4.

[202] Section 4(6); and see [5.14] and [8.46].

Discovery

The General Position

[**3.48**]   Discovery in judicial review proceedings is, in general, ordered only exceptionally and, where it is ordered, it is often more limited in its extent than that which would typically be ordered in private law proceedings.[203] Indeed, while the courts now look at the issue on the merits of individual cases rather than on the basis of a near-blanket presumption against discovery (particularly in cases under the Human Rights Act 1998—see [3.53]–[3.54]), it would appear that orders for discovery will remain as an exception rather than a rule.[204] The reason for this follows both from the costs and inconvenience involved in full discovery and from the role of the courts in judicial review proceedings. Courts, on an application for judicial review, are characteristically concerned with issues of law, and facts will either not be in dispute or will be relevant only insofar as they show how the issue of law arises. An order for discovery is thus usually regarded as unnecessary.[205]

[**3.49**]   The time for seeking discovery is after leave has been granted and affidavit evidence completed,[206] as the respondent will by that stage have set out fully the circumstances leading to the decision including, where appropriate, references to any documents generated and/or upon which reliance has been placed in the decision-making process. Respondents need not disclose every document upon which reliance is placed and/or which is referred to in the replying affidavit, although it must as a matter of law disclose fairly the decision making process.[207] This corresponds to a 'duty of candour'[208] that is imposed on both parties to proceedings but which has a pronounced importance in respect of public decision-makers who 'hold the cards' and who must act in the light of the need for 'trust between the governed and the government'.[209] Should a respondent fail to observe the duty of candour, this may therefore promote the need for discovery if there is any resultant obscurity in relation to the facts. Failure to observe the duty may also lead the court to draw inferences against the decision-maker on points that remain obscure[210] and, in extreme cases, to refer to the Attorney-General the concern that the decision-maker may have interfered with the administration of justice.[211]

[**3.50**]   Interlocutory applications for discovery are determined by a judge in chambers,[212] whose decision can be appealed to the Court of Appeal.[213] While the High Court has the power to order discovery of any documents in the respondent's possession[214]

---

[203] See *Re AM Developments UK Ltd's Application* [2006] NIQB 9, para 3.
[204] *Tweed v Parades Commission for Northern Ireland* [2007] 1 AC 650, 673–4, para 56, Lord Brown.
[205] *Tweed v Parades Commission for Northern Ireland* [2007]1 AC 650, 655, para 2, Lord Bingham.
[206] *Re Gilgan Ltd's Application*, 20 February 1991, unreported.
[207] *Re Tweed's Application* [2005] NICA 42, para 19.
[208] *Re Duffy's Application* [2006] NIQB 29, para 3, Morgan J.
[209] *Re Downes' Application* [2006] NIQB 77, para 21.
[210] *Re Downes' Application* [2006] NIQB 77, para 30.
[211] *Re Downes' Application* [2006] NIQB 79, paras 3–7.
[212] RSC Ord 53, r 8(1).
[213] RSC Ord 58, r 4.
[214] RSC Ord 24, r 3(1), which reads: '. . . the Court may order any party to a cause or matter (whether begun by writ, originating summons, or otherwise) to make and serve on any other party a list of documents which are or have been in his possession, custody or power relating to any matter in question in the cause or matter, and may at the same time or subsequently also order him to make and file an affidavit verifying such a list and to serve a copy thereof on the other party'.

(subject to arguments of, for instance, public interest immunity: see [3.55]), it will, as per RSC Order 24, rule 9, refuse to make an order if it is of the opinion that discovery is not necessary at that stage either for disposing fairly of the matter or for saving costs.[215] The court will also not permit the applicant—on whom the onus of proof rests—to benefit from contingent (or 'Micawber') discovery.[216] Although the House of Lords has held that the applicant need no longer show that there is a demonstrable contradiction or inconsistency or incompleteness in the respondent's evidence, it has at the same time emphasised that disclosure orders are likely to remain exceptional in judicial review proceedings and that the courts should guard against purely speculative claims for discovery.[217] Discovery on foot of those would be 'by way of a fishing licence' and would be oppressive.[218]

[3.51]   The corresponding judicial approach to a specific claim for discovery will depend on how far—if at all—the court considers that discovery would be required to enable it to resolve an issue that arises in the application. Much here will fall to be determined with reference to the grounds for judicial review in the case, as reflect upon the constitutional role of the courts in review proceedings.[219] Although the grounds for review elide into one another and overlap, they are often subdivided under the headings of illegality, substantive review (which was previously synonymous with *Wednesbury* unreasonableness), and procedural impropriety.[220] Hence where a decision is, for instance, challenged as *Wednesbury* unreasonable, discovery may not be considered necessary as the issue for the court will be whether a decision is lawful in the sense that it is not 'so unreasonable that no reasonable' decision-maker could have taken it.[221] This is a question that is concerned with the final decision itself rather than the process by which it was reached and, as *Wednesbury* has traditionally entailed that the courts do not consider the merits of a final decision (subject now to the influence of the Human Rights Act 1998—see [3.53]–[3.54]), discovery will be unnecessary.[222] On the other hand, the applicant may be able to point to material which suggests that the decision-maker has acted unfairly or was guided by irrelevant considerations in the decision-making process, and the court may here consider that further disclosure would be necessary.[223] However, where there is no dispute as to the facts governing the procedure[224] or the applicant merely has a suspicion that the decision-maker was influenced by (for example) irrelevant considerations, discovery may again be deemed unnecessary and/or inappropriate.

---

[215] RSC Ord 24, r 9 reads: 'On the hearing or an application for an order under Rule 3 . . . the court, if satisfied that discovery is not necessary, or not necessary at that stage of the cause or matter, may dismiss, or as the case may be, adjourn the application and shall in any case refuse to make such an order if and so far as it is of the opinion that discovery is not necessary either for disposing fairly of the cause or matter or for saving costs.'

[216] *Re Glor Na nGael's Application* [1991] NI 117, 132.

[217] *Tweed v Northern Ireland Parades Commission* [2007] 1 AC 650, 673–4, para 56, Lord Brown.

[218] *Re McGuigan's Application* [1994] NI 143, 153, Hutton LCJ, quoting Nolan LJ in *R v Secretary of State for the Environment, ex p London Borough of Islington*, 19 July 1991, unreported; and see *Tweed v Northern Ireland Parades Commission* [2007] 1 AC 650, 673–4, para 56, Lord Brown.

[219] See [1.04]–[1.10]; and ch 4.

[220] See chs 4–7.

[221] *Associated Provincial Picture Houses v Wednesbury Corporation* [1948] 1 KB 223, 230, Lord Greene MR.

[222] On *Wednesbury* unreasonableness see [6.05]–[6.11].

[223] See *Re Austin's Application*, 25 November 1994, unreported.

[224] See, eg, *Re Glor Na nGael's Application* [1991] NI 117.

[**3.52**]   It should finally be emphasised that the courts now consider requests for discovery very much on the basis of the case before them. This is the result of the House of Lords judgment in *Tweed v Parades Commission for Northern Ireland*,[225] before which case there existed a strong presumption against orders for discovery.[226] In *Tweed*, the House thus held that the judicial approach to applications for discovery should in future be guided by 'a more flexible and less prescriptive principle, which [gauges] the need for disclosure in accordance with the requirements of the particular case, taking into account the facts and circumstances'.[227] While *Tweed* will, in turn, be likely to have its fullest impact in cases under the Human Rights Act 1998[228] (see [3.53]–[3.54]), it remains of more general significance insofar as it marks a move away from the pre-existing, and narrow, approach to discovery. The House of Lords has therefore accepted that the previous approach was not without criticism and that requests for particular documents—though not for general discovery—should in future be treated on their merits.[229] On the other hand, the House of Lords also stated that it did not envisage that the need for further discovery would arise in most applications for judicial review[230] and that courts should continue to guard against 'fishing expeditions'.[231] Their Lordships also held that, where a judge considers that there may be a need for further discovery, he or she should first assess the relevant documents and then decide whether discovery is necessary for the fair disposal of the case.[232]

The Human Rights Act 1998

[**3.53**]   Where an application for judicial review is made wholly or partly under the Human Rights Act 1998, it is now accepted that the nature of the issues and corresponding general principles of law involved may mean that further discovery is necessary[233] (the point can also arise in EU law cases[234]). Under section 6 of the Act, courts must review public authority actions and inactions for compliance with the provisions of the ECHR that are contained in Schedule 1 to the Act (acts, failures to act, and so on, will not, however, be unlawful where they are authorised by primary legislation[235]). When doing so, the courts must 'take into account' the ECHR's general principles of law, which include the proportionality principle that requires a reviewing court to assess whether the correct balance has been struck between the reason for a decision and the impact that that decision has had—or would have—on an individual.[236] Although the courts have

---

[225] [2007] 1 AC 650.

[226] See, eg, *Re Belfast Telegraph's Application* [2001] NI 178, 184.

[227] *Tweed v Parades Commission for Northern Ireland* [2007] 1 AC 650, 664, para 32, Lord Carswell.

[228] *Tweed v Parades Commission for Northern Ireland* [2007] 1 AC 650, 655, para 3, Lord Bingham.

[229] *Tweed v Parades Commission for Northern Ireland* [2007] 1 AC 650, 664, para 32, Lord Carswell.

[230] *Tweed v Parades Commission for Northern Ireland* [2007] 1 AC 650, 664, para 32, Lord Carswell.

[231] *Tweed v Parades Commission for Northern Ireland* [2007] 1 AC 650, 673–4, para 56, Lord Brown.

[232] *Tweed v Parades Commission for Northern Ireland* [2007] 1 AC 650, 656, para 5, Lord Bingham, and 674, para 58, Lord Brown. And for subsequent application of *Tweed* see, eg, *Re X's Application* [2007] NIQB 74 (discovery of documents not ordered); *The Northern Ireland Commissioner for Children and Young People v Secretary of State* [2007] NIQB 52 (discovery of documents not ordered); and *Re Murphy's Application* [2007] NIQB 15 (ordering discovery of some of the documents requested).

[233] *Tweed v Parades Commission for Northern Ireland* [2007] 1 AC 650.

[234] *Re AM Developments UK Ltd's Application* [2006] NIQB 9, para 11, Girvan J.

[235] Section 6(2); and see *R (Hooper) v Secretary of State for Work and Pensions* [2006] 1 All ER 487. And see [5.20]

[236] Human Rights Act 1998, s 2; and *R v Secretary of State for the Home Department, ex p Daly* [2001] 2 AC 532. See further [6.18]–[6.28].

also developed a 'discretionary area of judgment' doctrine that seeks to ensure that use of the proportionality principle does not result in the courts assuming the place of the original decision-maker,[237] the principle is nevertheless understood to demand heightened judicial scrutiny of decision-making processes and outcomes (it is thereby often taken to contrast with the *Wednesbury* approach to substantive review—see [3.51]).[238] In terms of discovery, the corresponding point is thus that a court may be able to subject a decision to heightened scrutiny only where it is able to assess fully all documents that relate to a decision under challenge. Limited discovery, on this rationale, can only frustrate proportionality review.

[3.54] The leading authority on discovery in human rights cases, as with those that do not raise human rights points (see [3.52]), is the House of Lords judgment in *Tweed v Parades Commission for Northern Ireland*.[239] The applicant here had been granted leave to challenge, as contrary to Articles 6, 9, 10, and 11 ECHR, a decision of the Parades Commission that placed conditions on a parade organised by the applicant (the Article 6 point concerned the applicant's inability to contest confidential evidence given to the Commission in advance of its determination; the Articles 9, 10, and 11 points went to the proportionality of the interference with the qualified religion, expression, and association guarantees in those Articles). The applicant thereafter made an application for discovery of various documents held by the Commission, which resisted the application for the reason that much of the information in question had been provided on a confidential basis. However, the House of Lords considered that discovery of some of the documents was necessary in the case, precisely because of the demands of the proportionality principle. While their Lordships did not at the same time accept that fuller discovery would follow in every case that involved the proportionality principle,[240] they accepted that discovery was needed here and that the judge should first examine the documents to assess whether they would be needed for the disposal of the case. The House also held that, should the judge decide that disclosure to the applicant was thereafter necessary, the possibility of redaction should be considered and, after that, any argument of public interest immunity.[241] In the event that the judge decided that discovery was not necessary, it was said that all other points would be moot.

Public Interest Immunity

[3.55]   Where an order for discovery is made a respondent may argue that certain of the listed documents or materials should not be disclosed because they attract public interest immunity. Where such arguments are made, it is for the court to decide whether the public interest in non-disclosure outweighs the applicant's interest in obtaining the information.[242]

---

[237] The term was coined by Lord Hope in *R v DPP, ex p Kebilene* [2000] 2 AC 326, 381. For application in Northern Ireland see, eg, *Re Stewart's Application* [2003] NI 149, 159, para 26 (planning authorities enjoy a 'discretionary area of judgment' when setting the property rights of an individual against the wider public interests in permitting the appropriate development of property). And see [6.25]–[6.26].

[238] See, for analysis, *Re Boyle's Application* [2005] NIQB 41, para 15, Weatherup J.

[239] [2007] 1 AC 650.

[240] *Tweed v Parades Commission for Northern Ireland* [2007] 1 AC 650, 669, para 38, Lord Carswell, and 672, para 51, Lord Brown.

[241] *Tweed v Parades Commission for Northern Ireland* [2007] 1 AC 650, 670, para 41, Lord Carswell, and 674, para 58, Lord Brown.

[242] *Re Ministry of Defence's Application* [1994] NI 279, considering *Conway v Rimmer* [1968] AC 910.

The court's approach will here depend upon the context of the case and the nature of the evidence, and the court may be more inclined to accede to public interest immunity arguments where, for instance, the evidence would not give substantial support to the applicant's case or where disclosure would be prejudicial to national security. On the other hand, the court may be less likely to accept arguments of public interest immunity where the applicant's human rights are involved, for example, where proceedings relate to actual or possible criminal liability.[243] In cases of this latter kind (and others), both the common law and the ECHR recognise that there is an enhanced need for transparency and that any determination of a claim for immunity should account for that.[244]

The Freedom of Information Act 2000

[**3.56**]   An applicant may also be able to gain access to documents and so on held by a public authority under the Freedom of Information Act 2000 (public authorities for these purposes are listed in Schedule 1 to the Act, as read with sections 3–5[245]). A request for such access may be made in advance of an application for leave—for instance in tandem with a letter written in accordance with Pre-Action Protocol (see [3.14]–[3.16])—or it may be made while judicial review proceedings are ongoing.[246] Requests under the Act are made on the basis that any person is entitled to be informed in writing by the public authority whether it holds information of the description specified in the request (the so-called 'duty to confirm or deny') and, if so, to have that information communicated to them.[247] While an authority is not obliged to disclose information and/or to confirm or deny its existence when the information is exempt from disclosure[248]—it may also refuse a request where it considers that the cost of compliance would exceed 'the appropriate limit'[249] or where the request is repetitive or vexatious[250]—it must accede to or refuse the request within 20 working days.[251] Its response to the request may, however, be made contingent upon a 'fees notice' that will require that the applicant pay the amount specified in the notice before the authority will comply with its obligations under the Act.[252] Under those circumstances, the corresponding working days between the date of the fees notice and payment are to be disregarded when calculating the 20 working day time-limit.[253]

---

[243] See, eg, *R v H* [2004] 2 WLR 335.

[244] On public interest immunity see further HWR Wade and CF Forsyth, *Administrative Law*, 9th edn (Oxford, Oxford University Press, 2004) p 842*ff*.

[245] See further [2.26]–[2.27] on how the Sch to the Act may aid in delimiting the reach of judicial review. Note too that requests for information in respect of the environment may be made under the Environmental Information Regulations 2004, SI 2004/3391. See further P Birkinshaw, *Government & Information: The Law Relating to Access, Disclosure and their Regulation*, 3rd edn (Sussex, Tottel Publishing, 2005).

[246] P Coppel, 'Access to Information in Public Law Cases' [2004] 9 JR 266, 274–7.

[247] Section 1. Requests for information must be in writing, state the name of the applicant and an address for correspondence, and describe the information requested: s 8.

[248] Section 2.

[249] Section 12. The 'appropriate limit' is £600 for public authorities in Part I of Sch 1 to the Act and £450 for all other public authorities: see the Freedom of Information and Data Protection (Appropriate Limit and Fees) Regulations 2004, SI 2004/3244.

[250] Section 14.

[251] Sections 10 and 17 (although the period of 20 days may be extended where a refusal is contemplated: s 17(2)).

[252] Section 9; and the Freedom of Information and Data Protection (Appropriate Limit and Fees) Regulations 2004, SI 2004/3244.

[253] Section 10(2).

[**3.57**] Refusals of requests—or to confirm or deny that the authority holds the information in question—will most often be made on the ground that the information is governed by a provision of the Act which confers either an 'absolute' or a 'qualified' exemption[254] (these exemptions also correspond in large part with the Act's understanding that certain 'classes' of information should not be disclosed [the absolute exemption][255], and with the Act's prejudice test that requires the authority to consider whether disclosure would, or would be likely to, prejudice particular interests or processes [the qualified exemption][256]). Where the requested information attracts absolute exemption, refusal of the request will follow automatically[257]; and the refusal of a request relating to information that has qualified exemption will depend on the authority concluding that the public interest in maintaining the exemption outweighs the public interest in disclosure[258] (this will be in addition, where appropriate, to any assessment of prejudice). Should an applicant wish to challenge a refusal to confirm or deny or to disclose information, they must first use the authority's internal complaints procedures,[259] after which stage he or she may bring the matter to the Information Commissioner. Should the Commissioner's office consider that the authority is in breach of the Act, it will serve on the authority a 'decision notice' that specifies the steps to be taken to comply with the Act (the Commissioner's office may alternatively give the applicant—called 'the complainant' in the Act—a reasoned notification that no decision has been taken).[260] The applicant or public authority may then appeal the decision notice to the Information Tribunal, which may 'allow the appeal or substitute such other notice as could have been served by the Commissioner; and in any other case the Tribunal shall dismiss the appeal'.[261] Appeals from the Tribunal are to the High Court on a point of law.[262]

[**3.58**] In some circumstances—principally those concerned with national security—requests for information may alternatively be dealt with by way of conclusive evidence

---

[254] Section 2; and Part II. The term 'qualified' is not used in the Act, but is used in literature: see, eg, J Wadham and J Griffiths, *Blackstone's Guide to the Freedom of Information Act 2000*, 2nd edn (Oxford, Oxford University Press, 2005). And note that some provisions of the Act confer a mixture of both absolute and qualified exemptions: see ss 36 and 40 ('prejudice to effective conduct of public affairs' and 'personal information', respectively).

[255] All but one of the absolute exemptions—the s 36 exemption in respect of information held by the House of Commons or the House of Lords, disclosure of which would prejudice the effective conduct of public affairs—are class-based exemptions.

[256] Although note that some provisions contain elements of both the class-based and prejudice-based exemptions: see, eg, s 27 and international relations.

[257] Section 2(3) cross-refers to the provisions of the Act that confer absolute exemption, namely: s 21 (information reasonably accessible by other means); s 23 (information from, or relating to certain security bodies); s 32 (information contained in court records); s 34 (information which would breach parliamentary privilege); s 36 (information held by the House of Commons or the House of Lords, disclosure of which would prejudice the effective conduct of public affairs); s 40 (some personal information); s 41 (information provided in confidence); and s 44 (information covered by prohibitions on disclosure).

[258] Section 2. The relevant provisions here are: s 22 (information intended for future publication); s 24 (national security); s 26 (defence); s 27 (international relations); s 28 (relations within the UK); s 29 (the economy); s 30 (investigations and proceedings); s 31 (law enforcement); s 33 (audit functions); s 35 (formulation of government policy); s 36 (prejudice to the effective conduct of public affairs); s 37 (communications with Her Majesty); s 38 (health and safety); s 40 (some personal information); s 42 (legal professional privilege); s 43 (commercial interests).

[259] Section 50(2)(a).

[260] Section 50(4).

[261] Section 58.

[262] Section 59.

certificates issued by a Minister of the Crown or by the Law Officers[263]; and 'decision notices' of the Commissioner may, in some other circumstances, be made the subject of a ministerial override certificate.[264] Where a conclusive evidence certificate is issued, the Commissioner cannot question that certificate and the matter must be appealed, at the initiative of either the Commissioner or an applicant, to the Information Tribunal[265] (the Tribunal can, depending on the nature of the certificate, either quash it[266] or hold, with reference to grounds applied by the High Court judicial review proceedings, that the Minister did not have reasonable grounds for issuing the certificate[267]). The Act does not, in contrast, make provision for appeals against ministerial override certificates, and the remedy here will be an application for judicial review.[268] The government has, however, stated that such certificates will be used only in extreme circumstances.[269]

Cross-examination and Interrogatories

[3.59]   An applicant may also make an interlocutory application, under RSC Order 38, rule 2(3) and RSC Order 53, rule 8, to obtain an order to compel the attendance of a deponent for the purposes of cross-examination. As with the courts' more general approach to discovery ([3.48]–[3.52]), much will depend on the issues before the court and whether 'the party seeking cross-examination [can] make out a case that in the particular circumstances there is something specific which requires such further investigation'.[270] The court may, moreover, prefer to rule on the application at the substantive hearing rather than at the interlocutory stage, as the particular issues for the court may then be clearer.[271] This may also be true even where rights under the ECHR and Human Rights Act 1998 are central to the application for judicial review.[272]

[3.60]   Interrogatories are also available in judicial review proceedings (RSC Order 26 and RSC Order 53, rule 8). The court, on an application for this interlocutory facility, will here too be guided by the principles that govern discovery.

---

[263] See s 23(2) (regarding requests for information supplied by, or relating to, bodies dealing with security matters) and s 24(3) (regarding national security). But see also certificates that may issue in respect of parliamentary privilege and information held by either House of Parliament (ss 34(3) and 26(7)). On conclusive evidence certificates see [4.19].

[264] Section 53.

[265] Section 60.

[266] Certificates issued under s 23(2)—regarding requests for information by, or relating to, bodies dealing with security matters—may be quashed where the Tribunal finds that the information in question was not exempt by virtue of s 23(1): see s 60(2).

[267] Viz, where a s 24(3) national security certificate is issued: s 60(3). On judicial review and national security see [4.18]–[4.19].

[268] Parliamentary certificates—see n 263 above—may likewise only be challenged by way of judicial review, subject to judicial concerns about interference in the parliamentary process. See, eg, Lord Browne-Wilkinson's comments in *Prebble v Television New Zealand Ltd* [1995] 1 AC 321, 332.

[269] *Hansard*, HL, 25 Oct 2000, col 436.

[270] *Re McCann's Application*, 13 May 1992, unreported.

[271] *Re McCann's Application*, 13 May 1992, unreported.

[272] See, by analogy, *Tweed v Parades Commission for Northern Ireland* [2007] 1 AC 650, at [3.54]. For an example of cross-examination being ordered in a human rights case see, in England and Wales, *R (Wilkinson) v Broadmoor Hospital Authority* [2002] 1 WLR 419.

THE SUBSTANTIVE HEARING

Papers for the Hearing

[**3.61**] Papers for the hearing should be prepared and filed in accordance with Part E of *Judicial Review: Practice Note 01/2006*.[273] This states that the applicant must file a paginated and indexed set of papers containing all relevant documents required for the hearing of the judicial review at least five working days before the hearing date and that the papers should include those documents required by the respondent(s) and any other party who is to make oral or written representations at the hearing. The Practice Note also states that the papers filed at the leave stage may serve as the papers for the hearing (see [3.18]–[3.19]), although these must be supplemented by updated indexes and skeleton arguments and related documents. Skeleton arguments, in turn, are compulsory in the substantive hearing of a judicial review and must be prepared in accordance with *Practice Direction 4/2005: Skeleton Arguments and Related Documents*.[274]

[**3.62**]   The Practice Note also states that, in cases where the materials filed in the exchanges of affidavits are not all necessary for the hearing, the court may order at a pre-hearing review of the case that a 'core' bundle should be prepared for the hearing. Unless the court directs otherwise, this core bundle should be paginated and indexed, with sections comprising: the applicant's affidavit(s); the applicant's exhibits; the respondent'(s') affidavit(s); the respondent'(s') exhibits; and any notice party's affidavit(s) and exhibits (on notice parties see [3.36]–[3.37]). While the contents of the 'core' bundle will be directed specifically or in general outline by the court, the Practice Note emphasises that the applicant is responsible for preparing and filing the 'core' bundle in accordance with the directions of the court. Failure to act in accordance with the directions of the court may have implications in costs.[275]

The Grounds for Review

[**3.63**] Before the court will grant a remedy—remedies are discretionary (see [3.81]–[3.87][276]—the applicant must establish that the decision, act, failure to act, or other measure is contrary to one or more of the grounds for judicial review. These grounds, which overlap with one another, have long been divided under the headings of illegality, *Wednesbury* unreasonabless/irrationality (the starting point for substantive review), and procedural impropriety.[277] They have, however, also long since developed within and beyond this three-way classification and they now include proportionality, equality, legitimate expectation, and error of fact (among others). Each of the grounds for review is considered in more detail in chapters four to seven.

---

[273] Available at http://www.courtsni.gov.uk.
[274] This Direction is appended to *Judicial Review: Practice Note 01/2006*.
[275] *Re Doherty's Application* [2006] NIQB 33, paras 28–9.
[276] And [8.08]–[8.09]
[277] *Council of Civil Service Unions v Minister for the Civil Service* [1985] AC 374, 408, Lord Diplock, and *In Re Glor Na nGael's Application* [1991] NI 117, 130, Carswell J.

Standing

The General Position

[**3.64**]   The test for standing—at least in cases outside the Human Rights Act 1998—is whether the applicant has a 'sufficient interest in the matter to which the application relates'.[278] Although RSC Order 53, rule 3(5) states that leave should be granted only where the applicant satisfies this test, it is solely hopeless or meddlesome applications that will be dismissed at the leave stage, and the issue is more typically considered at the substantive stage in the light of the full legal and factual context of the case[279] (the test applies equally and irrespective of the remedy sought; the relevant facts will usually be those at the time when the application for judicial review was instituted, not when it was heard[280]). In the vast majority of cases, the application will be made by an individual who claims to be directly affected by a decision or other measure, and the question for the court will be whether he or she has the requisite sufficiency of interest.[281] However, the courts have also developed a 'liberal' approach to standing and accepted that representative applicants, statutory bodies and/or pressure groups should sometimes be taken to have standing to challenge a respondent's action or inaction.[282] The courts have likewise allowed private individuals to bring applications for judicial review in respect of matters of 'public interest'[283]; and they have also held that it is not an abuse of process for a community that is affected by a decision to name one applicant who may qualify for legal aid ahead of another applicant who would not, so long as the named applicant has standing in the legal and factual context of the case.[284]

---

[278] Judicature (Northern Ireland) Act 1978, s 18(4); and RSC Ord 53, r 3(5). Although note that legislation may also provides that named parties can apply to the High Court for judicial review, subject to the requirement of leave: see, eg, Local Government (NI) Order 2005, SI 2005/1968 (NI 18), art 21 (power of local government auditor to apply for judicial review).

[279] *R v Inland Revenue Commissioners, ex p National Federation of Self-Employed and Small Businesses Ltd* [1982] AC 617; *Re Hogan's Application* [1985] 5 NIJB 81; and *Re Ward's Application for Leave* [2006] NIQB 67, para 5.

[280] *Re D's Application* [2003] NI 295, 302, paras 16–17.

[281] See, eg, *Re Cook and Other's Application* [1986] NI 242 (application made by three members of Belfast City Council and an individual ratepayer who challenged the lawfulness of Belfast City Council's adjourning of meetings in protest at the Anglo-Irish Agreement: held that each of the applicants had standing to obtain declarations that the council was acting unlawfully and orders of mandamus to compel it to hold meetings and to discharge its obligations but that the individual ratepayer did not have standing to obtain an injunction in respect of other actions of the council). And see too *Re Ward's Application for Leave* [2006] NIQB 67.

[282] The term 'liberal' was used by the Court of Appeal in *Re D's Application* [2003] NI 295, 302, para 15; and see, eg, *Family Planning Association of Northern Ireland v Minister for Health, Social Services and Public Safety* [2005] NI 188 (applicant was a charity that works to improve the sexual health and reproductive rights of individuals); and *Re Friends of the Earth's Application* [2006] NIQB 48 (application brought by a pressure group challenging the Water Service's grant of consents and the making of agreements under the Water and Sewerage Services (Northern Ireland) Order 1973 for reasons of non-compliance with the requirements of the Urban Waste Water Treatment Regulations (Northern Ireland) 1995: application granted).

[283] Eg, *Re McBride's Application* [1999] NI 299 (mother of a man killed by two soldiers who were subsequently convicted of his murder held to have standing to challenge a decision not to discharge the soldiers from the armed services; although note that the approach of the court was later doubted in the Court of Appeal—see *Re McBride's Application (No 2)* [2003] NI 319, 337, para 27, Carswell LCJ).

[284] *Re Murphy's Application* [2004] NIQB 85, paras 5–7. Cf *Re Anderson (a minor)'s Application* [2001] NI 454, 468 (although children have standing to challenge decisions about the refusal of admission to schools of their parents' choosing, applications brought in the name of a child for legal aid reasons may be an abuse of process).

[**3.65**]   The willingness of the courts to accept representative and/or public interest applications is not without controversy, and it is sometimes said that public interest litigation can result in courts becoming involved in essentially political disputes.[285] However, the liberal approach is, in turn, often justified with reference to the need to vindicate the rule of law and to ensure that government illegality does not escape appropriate scrutiny in the courts.[286] The point here is simply that judicial scrutiny of exercises of public power is a constitutional fundamental and that the courts' ability to exercise such control should not be frustrated by the absence of an applicant with a directly affected interest. While applications for judicial review will thus ordinarily be made by individuals who have such directly affected interests, the wider public interest in the rule of law means that this may not necessarily always be so.[287] The courts, in other words, will be reluctant 'to decline jurisdiction to hear an application for judicial review on grounds of [the lack of standing of] any responsible person or group seeking, on reasonable grounds, to challenge the validity of government action'.[288]

[**3.66**]   The leading statement of the liberal approach—and of the justification for it—is contained in the Court of Appeal's judgment in *Re D's Application*.[289] The applicant in this case was an anonymous wheelchair user who sought to challenge a number of decisions of the Department of Regional Development relating to the unlawful erection of an Orange Order Arch in Glengormley. Although it was ultimately held that the applicant did not have standing—there had been a lack of candour at first instance and the applicant had also failed to provide sufficient evidence to the Court of Appeal to justify his claim for anonymity—the Court listed four 'generally valid' propositions about the current judicial approach to standing. These were: (1) that standing is a relative concept, to be deployed according to the potency of the public interest content of the case; (2) that the greater the amount of public importance that is involved in the issue before the court, the more ready the court should be to hold that the applicant has the necessary standing; (3) that the focus of the courts is more upon the existence of a default or abuse on the part of a public authority than the involvement of a personal right or interest on the part of the applicant; and (4) that the absence of another responsible challenger is frequently a significant factor, so that a matter of public interest or concern is not left unexamined.[290]

Section 7 of the Human Rights Act 1998

[**3.67**]   Where an application for judicial review is made partly or wholly with reference to the guarantees in the ECHR, the test for standing in respect of the ECHR is different from the sufficiency of interest test that otherwise applies. The test here, instead, is that contained in section 7 of the Human Rights Act 1998, which states that an individual may rely on the ECHR in domestic proceedings only where he or she is, or would be,

---

[285]   See C Harlow, 'Public Law and Popular Justice' (2002) 65 MLR 1

[286]   *R v Inland Revenue Commissioners, ex p National Federation of Self-Employed and Small Businesses Ltd* [1982] AC 617, 644, Lord Diplock.

[287]   See JUSTICE/Public Law Project, *A Matter of Public Interest: Reforming the law and practice on interventions in public interest cases* (London, 1996).

[288]   *Family Planning Association of Northern Ireland v Minister for Health, Social Services and Public Safety* [2005] NI 188, 233, para 45, citing H Woolf, J Jowell and AP Le Sueur, *de Smith, Woolf and Jowell Principles of Judicial Review* 5th edn (London, Sweet and Maxwell, 1999) p 47.

[289]   [2003] NI 295.

[290]   [2003] NI 295, 302, para 15.

a 'victim' of the decision or other measure in question.[291] The term 'victim' corresponds to that used in Article 34 ECHR, which governs standing before the ECtHR,[292] and the courts are obliged to 'take into account' the ECtHR's case law on that Article when determining questions of standing under the Human Rights Act 1998.[293] That case law has long been characterised by a restrictive approach to access to the ECtHR, and it is clear that an applicant must have suffered and/or will suffer in some concrete way before they will satisfy the Article 34 ECHR standard (although the close relatives of persons affected may bring proceedings on their behalf where the affected person is in a 'vulnerable position'[294]; the next of kin of a deceased person may also act in their place[295]). Indeed, while there may be some ECtHR authority to suggest that abstract review of State action/inaction is possible,[296] that authority exists very much as an exception to a well-established rule. Victims for the purposes of proceedings before the ECtHR and for the purposes of section 7 must therefore ordinarily be able to demonstrate that they have been, or will be, 'actually affected by the violation' alleged.[297]

[3.68]   In terms of judicial review, there are three points of note about section 7. The first is that representational and/or public interest applications of the kind seen outside the Human Rights Act 1998 (see [3.64]–[3.66]) are not generally possible within the framework of the Act (that is, representative bodies and so on will be able to rely on the ECHR only where their own interests are concretely affected). Although there have been some cases that have tended towards abstract review on the basis of the ECHR[298]—particular statutes may also provide that a body such as the Northern Ireland Human Rights Commission need not satisfy the victim requirement when bringing proceedings in its own name[299]—there have been many more cases in which applicants have been found not to have standing under section 7. These have included applications made by a representational body that sought clarification of the law on abortion in Northern Ireland (the body in question conceded that it had no standing to raise points under the Human Rights Act 1998[300]) and by an independent organisation that sought to rely upon Article

---

[291]   Section 7, so far as is relevant, reads: ' (1) A person who claims that a public authority has acted (or proposes to act) in a way which is made unlawful by section 6(1) may (a) bring proceedings against the authority under this Act in the appropriate court or tribunal, or (b) rely on the Convention right or rights concerned in any legal proceedings, but only if he is (or would be) a victim of the unlawful act . . . (3) *If the proceedings are brought on an application for judicial review, the applicant is to be taken to have a sufficient interest in relation to the unlawful act only if he is, or would be, a victim of that act*'. (Emphasis added).

[292]   Section 7(7) reads: 'For the purposes of this section, a person is a victim of an unlawful act only if he would be a victim for the purposes of Article 34 of the Convention if proceedings were brought in the [ECtHR] in respect of that Act'; and Art 34 ECHR reads: 'The Court may receive applications from any person, non-governmental organisation or group of individuals claiming to be the victim of a violation by one of the High Contracting Parties of the rights set forth in the Convention or the protocols thereto. The High Contracting Parties undertake not to hinder in any way the effective exercise of this right.'

[293]   Human Rights Act 1998, s 2.

[294]   *Re E's Application* [2006] NICA 37 para 76, considering *Ilhan v Turkey* (2002) 34 EHRR 36 and *YF v Turkey* (2004) 39 EHRR 34.

[295]   See, eg, *McCann, Farrell and Savage v UK* (1996) 21 EHRR 97.

[296]   See T Zwart, 'Comparing Standing Regimes from a Separation of Powers Perspective' (2002) 53 NILQ 391, 405, discussing, among others, *Open Door and Dublin Well Woman v Ireland* (1992) 15 EHRR 244. See too the analysis in *Re ES's Application* [2007] NIQB 58, paras 9–13.

[297]   *Klass v Germany* (1980) 2 EHRR 214, 227, para 33.

[298]   See, eg, *R (Rusbridger) v Attorney General* [2004] 1 AC 357 (newspaper that could, in theory, be subject to criminal proceedings for publishing a story that advocated Republicanism could rely on the ECHR).

[299]   Justice and Security (Northern Ireland) Act 2007, s 14.

[300]   *Family Planning Association of Northern Ireland v Minister for Health, Social Services and Public Safety* [2005] NI 188, 245, para 97.

2 ECHR when requesting further information from the Police Service of Northern Ireland and Police Ombudsman about ongoing investigations into the murder of one of the organisation's members.[301] On the other hand, the courts have held that an individual who is 'particularly vulnerable' may be represented by another family member, albeit that the application should name the injured person as the applicant and be accompanied by a letter of authority that allows the other family member to act on his or her behalf.[302] Such an application is in that way made with the consent of the victim of the alleged breach and does not fall to be described as an *actio popularis*.[303]

[3.69] The second point concerns cases where an individual has successfully brought proceedings before the ECtHR and then initiates a further application for judicial review in the High Court in order to obtain additional remedies. This happened in *In Re McKerr*,[304] where the son of a man killed in 1982 by undercover officers of the (then) RUC sought, among other remedies, mandamus to compel the Secretary of State for Northern Ireland to order an Article 2 ECHR-compliant investigation into the circumstances of his father's death (the application for judicial review was brought in the light of the ECtHR judgment in *McKerr v UK*[305]). One of the questions on appeal before both the Court of Appeal and the House of Lords was whether Mr McKerr had ceased to be a victim for the purposes of the Act once judgment had been entered in his favour in Strasbourg. Although the point was ultimately rendered secondary by the House of Lords' finding that the Human Rights Act 1998 does not have retrospective effect and that Mr McKerr could therefore not rely upon it,[306] the House emphasised that the applicant would otherwise have been a victim within the meaning of Article 34 and section 7. This was because the ECtHR ruling had not resolved all issues relevant to Article 2 ECHR, in particular as related to the proportionality of the use of force by the police.[307] The case on that basis suggests that individuals will, subject to arguments of retrospectivity, remain as 'victims' for so long as their concrete interests are affected by the State's failure fully to discharge its continuing obligations under international law.

[3.70] The third point concerns public authorities. Article 34 ECHR states that 'any person, non-governmental organisation or group of individuals claiming to be the victim of a violation by one of the High Contracting Parties' may institute proceedings before the ECtHR. The wording of this Article has long been understood to preclude proceedings brought by a State and/or by its manifestations[308] and it is clear that 'core' public authorities for the purposes of section 6 of the Human Rights Act 1998 cannot be victims for the purposes of section 7[309] (although such authorities may still bring judicial review proceedings in cases outside the Act). Less clear, however, is the position in respect of 'mixed function' public authorities. Mixed function authorities are those persons 'certain of whose functions are functions of a public nature' and who are bound by the Human

[301] *Re CAJ and Martin O'Brien's Application* [2005] NIQB 25.

[302] *Re E's Application* [2006] NICA 37, paras 75–7, quoting, eg, *Ilhan v Turkey* [2002] 34 EHRR 36.

[303] And see, by analogy, RSC Ord 80(2), which provides for persons under a disability to sue etc by their next friend or *guardian ad litem*.

[304] [2004] 1 WLR 807.

[305] (2002) 34 EHRR 20.

[306] See [1.32].

[307] [2004] 1 WLR 807, 815–16, Lord Nicholls.

[308] Although a State may make an Inter-State complaint to the ECtHR: see Article 33 ECHR and, eg, *Ireland v UK* (1979–80) 2 EHRR 25.

[309] *Aston Cantlow v Wallbank* [2004] 1 AC 546. On 'core' public authorities see [2.22].

Rights Act 1998 when performing public functions but not when they are performing private acts.[310] Some commentators have argued that the courts should be slow to recognise bodies such as charities, privatised utilities and companies as section 6 mixed function authorities, as this would mean that the bodies would not be able to rely on the ECHR in other cases as they would no longer exist as 'non-governmental organisations' and so on.[311] The logic of that argument has, however, since been doubted in the House of Lords, where it has been suggested that a body may be classified as a mixed function authority in one case but still be able to avail of its rights under the ECHR in another when it is acting in a private capacity.[312] The fact that the comments were *obiter* nevertheless means that there is, as yet, no definitive authority on the interplay between sections 6 and 7.

Third Party Interveners

[3.71]   Third party applications to intervene in proceedings will be made after the leave stage of the relevant proceedings when the court, in its discretion, may grant leave for a written intervention by a third party (the court will then decide at the substantive hearing whether it wishes to receive fuller oral submissions from the intervener: see further [3.38]–[3.39]). Interventions, whether written or oral, must be strictly confined 'to relevant and apposite matters which directly address the issues before the court', and the courts have sometimes criticised interventions for raising unsuitable points of law.[313] The corresponding uncertainty that the terms 'relevant and apposite' may give rise to is considered at [3.39].

REMEDIES

[3.72]   Where an applicant successfully makes out an argument of illegality in respect of a public authority's actions/inactions, he or she may be granted the remedy or remedies sought in their Order 53 statement. The word 'may' is here to be emphasised, as the remedies in judicial review are, at least when EU law and/or the ECHR is not in issue, discretionary.[314] There is thus a wide range of reasons why a court may decline to award a remedy to an applicant or may substitute a different remedy to that requested. Awards of damages will, on account of judicial approaches to the liability of public service providers, also be exceptional (although the position may be different if the illegality sounds in respect of rights under EU law and/or the ECHR).

---

[310] Section 6(3)(b) and (5). See further [2.22]–[2.24].

[311] D Oliver, 'The Frontiers of the State: Public Authorities and Public Functions Under the Human Rights Act' (2000) PL 476, cited with approval in the Administrative Court in *R (Heather) v Leonard Cheshire Foundation*: see [2001] EWHC Admin 429, para [105]. And for the current, restrictive approach see *YL v Birmingham City Council* [2007] 3 WLR 112; and [2.24].

[312] *Aston Cantlow v Wallbank* [2003] 3 WLR 283, 288, para 11, Lord Nicholls. For consideration of *Aston Cantlow* in NI courts see, eg, *Re Wylie's Application* [2005] NI 359.

[313] *Re White's Application* [2000] NI 432, 445.

[314] See Sir Thomas Bingham, 'Should Public Law Remedies be Discretionary?' (1991) PL 64.

The Range of Remedies

[3.73] The remedies available on an application for judicial review have three principal sources, namely: the Judicature (Northern Ireland) Act 1978 and RSC Order 53, rules 1 and 7; EU law, as read with the European Communities Act 1972; and the ECHR, as read with the Human Rights Act 1998.

The Judicature (Northern Ireland) Act 1978 and RSC Order 53: The Prerogative Orders, Declarations, and Injunctions

[3.74] Section 18 of the Judicature (Northern Ireland) Act 1978 and RSC Order 53, rule 1 both provide that on an application for judicial review an application:

> may be made to the (High) Court for one of more of the following forms of relief, that is to say, relief by way of—
>
> (a) an order of mandamus;
> (b) an order of certiorari;
> (c) an order of prohibition;
> (d) a declaration;
> (e) an injunction.

The nature and extent of these remedies are examined in more detail in chapter eight, although their effects may be summarised as: (a) an order of mandamus compels a decision-maker to perform a public duty; (b) an order of certiorari quashes a decision or other measure of an inferior court, tribunal, or other body amenable to judicial review (but see also [3.76]); (c) an order of prohibition prevents a decision-maker from acting in an ultra vires manner in the future; (d) a declaration—which is a non-coercive remedy—clarifies the legal position between the parties and/or their respective rights and obligations; and (e) an injunction prevents or compels a future course of action and/or issues to stop an ongoing state of affairs. Declarations and injunctions—as opposed to the prerogative orders of mandamus, certiorari, and prohibition—are also available as private law remedies, and the court on an application for judicial review may consider that it would not be appropriate to grant the remedies in public law proceedings (for example, where the issues raised on the application are matters of private, rather than public, law). Under those circumstances—and also where an application for judicial review includes a claim for damages—the court may order that the proceedings be continued as if begun by writ.[315] An order to continue will not, however, be made unquestioningly, and much will depend on how the issues have been presented in the application for judicial review and on whether the court considers that they lend themselves to continuation as private law proceedings.[316]

---

[315] RSC Ord 53, r 9(5).
[316] *Re Phillips' Application* [1995] NI 322; and see further [2.12] and [2.30]–[2.33]. And for an example of a case that began by way of application but which continued as a private law action see *Martin v Prison Service of Northern Ireland* [2006] NIQB 1 (applicant who challenged the lawfulness of HMP Magilligan's sanitary conditions instead claimed damages for the alleged breach by the Prison Service of Arts 3 and 8 ECHR taken separately or together with Art 14 ECHR) .

The Judicature (Northern Ireland) Act 1978 and RSC Order 53: Damages

[3.75] / Awards of damages are governed by section 20 of the Judicature (Northern Ireland) Act 1978 and by RSC Order 53, rule 7. These provisions state that damages may be made in lieu of or in addition to any other relief where (a) the applicant has included with his application for leave a claim for damages arising from any matter to which the application relates and (b) the court is satisfied that, if the claim had been made in a separate action begun by the applicant at the time of making his application, he would have been entitled to damages./This corresponds to the rule that an ultra vires act per se will not give rise to damages[317] and that an applicant must instead be able to satisfy the court that the relevant facts would sound in, for instance, negligence, an actionable breach of statutory duty, or misfeasance in public office. Private law actions against public authorities are, however, often rendered problematic by a judicial concern to avoid imposing undue financial burdens upon public decision-makers that are providing public services through the exercise of statutory powers and the performance of statutory duties.[318] The corresponding principles and case law are considered in chapter eight.

The Judicature (Northern Ireland) Act 1978 and RSC Order 53: Other Disposals

[3.76]   The Judicature (Northern Ireland) Act 1978 and RSC Order 53 also provide for a number of other disposals. For instance, where the remedy sought is an order of certiorari and the court is satisfied that there are grounds for quashing the decision, it 'may, instead of quashing the decision, remit the matter to the lower deciding authority concerned, with a direction to reconsider it and reach a decision in accordance with the ruling of the Court or may reverse or vary the decision of the lower deciding authority'[319] (the High Court also has a power to vary sentence on an application for certiorari[320]). The court may, moreover, issue declaratory judgments under section 23 of the Judicature (Northern Ireland) Act 1978; that is, judgments that pronounce on matters of general public interest in the abstract or where the judgment cannot affect the decision in respect of which it is made or where the party who initiated proceedings no longer has a direct interest in proceedings[321] (the courts have, however, also emphasised that it is not the

---

[317]   See, eg, in England and Wales, *R (Quark Fishing) v Secretary of State for Foreign and Commonwealth Affairs* [2003] EWHC 1743, para 14.

[318]   See G Anthony, 'The Negligence Liability of Public Authorities: Was the Old Law the Right Law?' (2006) 57 NILQ 409.

[319]   Judicature (Northern Ireland) Act 1978, s 21; and RSC Ord 53, r 9(4). And see, eg, *Re Zhanje's Application* [2007] NIQB 14 (decision to certify a human rights claim as unfounded for the purposes of para 5(4) of Sch 3 to the Asylum and Immigration (Treatment of Claimants etc) Act 2004 remitted to the Home Secretary); *Re McLean's Application*, 25 November 1994, unreported (decision in respect of a bookmaker's licence remitted to resident magistrate); *Re Ward's Application*, 4 June 1993, unreported (decision in respect of a payment from the Social Fund remitted to Social Fund Inspector); *Re McAuley's Application* [1992] 4 NIJB 1 (High Court granted legal aid to the applicant because it considered that the magistrate had failed to have regard to a relevant consideration); and *R (Att-Gen) v Belfast Justices* [1981] NI 208 (convictions of shoplifters who had given false names remitted to the magistrates' court so that it could, if satisfied that the offenders were the persons who were convicted, amend the convictions by substituting their real names).

[320]   Judicature (Northern Ireland) Act 1978, s 25.

[321]   See *Re McConnell's Application* [2000] NIJB 116, 119–20; and [8.17]–[8.18]. Section 23 reads: '(1) No action or other proceeding shall be open to objection on the ground that a merely declaratory judgment or order is sought thereby. (2) The High Court may make binding declarations of right in any action or other proceeding whether or not any consequential relief is or could be claimed therein. (3) Notwithstanding that the events on which a right depends may not have occurred, the High Court may in its discretion make a binding

function of the court to give advisory opinions to public bodies[322]). Section 24 of the Act finally gives the High Court the power to issue injunctions concerning 'public office', which for the purposes of the section means 'any substantive office of a public nature and permanent character which is held under the Crown or has been created by or under a statutory provision of royal charter'. Injunctions under the section may issue to prevent a person in such an office acting unlawfully or to declare the office to be vacant.

The European Communities Act 1972 and EU Law

[3.77] It is a core requirement of the EU legal order that individuals enjoy effective protection of their EU law rights.[323] The ECJ has, as such, long emphasised that EU law rights are to be protected through national law remedies and procedures, although it has also held that those procedures must ensure effective protection and that the protection given to EU law rights should be no less favourable than that given to national law rights.[324] Each of the remedies available on an application for judicial review should therefore be available in the EU law context and they should be applied with a view— where appropriate—to ensuring the primacy of EU law rights.[325] Access to the remedies may on that basis also raise the question of how far, if at all, aspects of the judicial review procedure—for instance time-limits—can be enforced at the expense of the protection of EU law rights (see [3.29]).

[3.78] Applicants may also make a claim for damages where their EU law rights have been breached by a legislative, administrative, or judicial act that is contrary to provisions of the EC Treaty or other EU measure (for instance, where the State has failed to implement a Directive within the prescribed time-frame[326]). The ECJ's understanding that national remedies are to be used to protect EU law rights is, however, here at its most strained, as the ECJ has developed its own State liability doctrine that national courts

---

declaration of right if it is satisfied that—(a) the question for decision involves a point of general public importance or that it would in the circumstances be unjust or inconvenient to withhold the declaration; and (b) the interests of persons not parties to the proceedings would not be unjustly prejudiced by the declaration.' For cases in which a point of general interest has been taken to arise notwithstanding that the concrete issues before the court have been rendered academic see, eg, *Re E's Application* [2003] NIQB 39, [2004] NIQB 35 and [2006] NICA 37 (challenge to the mode of policing at the 'Holy Cross' dispute—which had since ended—allowed because of the matters of general interest involved) and *Re McBurney's Application* [2004] NIQB 37 (patient in a mental health facility who was awaiting a tribunal decision on whether to discharge her brought proceedings in respect of an earlier decision not to discharge: held that, while the earlier dispute was now academic, the corresponding application raised questions of general interest about the involvement of a lay representative in the decision-making process); and for a case in which the court concluded that there was no point of general interest see, eg, *Re Nicholson's Application* [2003] NIQB 30 (application in respect of a prison adjudication dismissed as academic, as the prisoner had since been released and it was unlikely that the resolution of the issues in the application would provide guidance to the Prison Service in future cases).

[322] *Re McConnell's Application* [2000] NIJB 116, 120.

[323] See, in Northern Ireland, *Johnston v Chief Constable of the RUC* [1998] NI 188.

[324] See, eg, Case 33/76, *Rewe-Zentralfinanz eG and Rewe-Zentral AG v Landwirtschaftskammer für das Saarland* [1976] ECR 1989; Case 47/76, *Comet v Produktschap voor Siergewassen* [1976] ECR 2043; and Case 158/80, *Rewe Handelsgesellschaft Nord mbH v Hauptzollamt Kiel* [1981] ECR 1805.

[325] See, most famously, *R v Secretary of State for Transport, ex p Factortame Ltd (No 2)* [1991] 1 AC 603 (injunction granted to prevent Minister of Crown enforcing terms of the Merchant Shipping Act 1988 pending resolution of the question of its compatibility with EU law).

[326] See, in Northern Ireland, *Re Burns' Application* [1999] NI 175.

must give effect to.[327] This doctrine entails that the State may be liable in damages for the actions/inactions of any of its legislative, administrative, or judicial branches where the action/inaction constitutes a 'sufficiently serious' breach of an individual's EU law rights.[328] Claims for such sufficiently serious breaches of EU law rights may perhaps best be framed as actions for breach of statutory duty (the relevant statute is the European Communities Act 1972, as read with corresponding provisions of EU law).[329]

The Human Rights Act 1998 and the ECHR

[**3.79**]   Section 8(1) of the Human Rights Act 1998 provides that the remedies available on an application for judicial review are likewise to be available under the Act.[330] Although this means that the prerogative orders, declarations, and injunctions will issue for the same reasons and purposes under the Act as they do in other proceedings, the courts' approach under the Act should also be guided by the ECHR's effectiveness principle. The effectiveness principle has long been central to the case law of the ECtHR, and it requires that the rights under the ECHR are protected in a way that is 'real' rather than 'illusory'.[331] While the corresponding Article 13 ECHR guarantee of the right to an effective remedy is not included in Schedule 1 to the Human Rights Act 1998—sections 7–9 of the Act are intended to provide for effective remedies[332]—section 2 of the Human Rights Act requires the courts to 'take into account' the effectiveness principle in proceedings that raise points under the ECHR. Judicial approaches to the availability of the remedies under the Human Rights Act 1998 should therefore be conditioned as much, if not more, by the 'real, not illusory' distinction as they are by the considerations that determine when the courts will exercise their discretion to grant a remedy (on which see [3.81]–[3.87]).[333]

[**3.80**]   Awards of damages are also available under the Human Rights Act 1998 and they are made in the light of the ECtHR's Article 41 ECHR case law.[334] In contrast to damages actions against public authorities outside the Act, there is no need to establish that the action complained of is also actionable in (for instance) tort law, as the violation of the right may itself suffice for damages. The existing House of Lords case law on damages under the Human Rights Act 1998 does, however, suggest that awards of damages under the Act may be more limited than those that would be available at common law.[335]

---

[327]   Introduced in Joined Cases C-6/90, *Francovich and Bonifaci v Italy* [1991] ECR I-5357, and subsequently developed in: Cases C-46 & 48/93, *Brasserie du Pêcheur SA v. Germany, R v Secretary of State for Transport, ex p Factortame Ltd* [1996] 1 ECR 1029; Case C-392/93, *R v HM Treasury, ex p British Telecommunications plc* [1996] ECR I-1631; Case C-5/94, *R v Ministry of Agriculture, Fisheries and Food, ex p Hedley Lomas (Ireland) Ltd* [1996] ECR I-2553; Joined Cases C-178–179 & 188–190/94, *Dillenkofer v. Germany* [1996] 3 CMLR 469; and Case C-224/01, *Köbler v Austria* [2003] ECR I-10239.

[328]   The term was first used in *Brasserie du Pêcheur SA v Germany, R v Secretary of State for Transport, ex p Factortame Ltd* [1996] 1 ECR 1029.

[329]   *R v Secretary of State for Transport, ex p Factortame (No 7)* [2001] 1 CMLR 1191. But see too [8.38].

[330]   Section 8(1) reads: 'In relation to any act (or proposed act) of a public authority which the court finds is (or would be) unlawful, it may grant such relief or remedy, or make such order, within its powers as it considers just and appropriate'.

[331]   *Airey v Ireland* (1979) 2 EHRR 305, 316, para 26.

[332]   For a parliamentary statement to this effect see *Hansard* 583 HL 475 (1997); and on ss 7–9 see further A Lester and D Pannick, *Human Rights Law and Practice*, 2nd edn (London, Lexis Nexis Butterworths, 2004) p 48 ff.

[333]   And see further [8.42].

[334]   Human Rights Act 1998, s 8(4).

[335]   *R (Greenfield) v Home Secretary* [2005] 2 All ER 240.

The House of Lords has also held that human rights claims should be brought under the Act rather than on the basis of modified common law causes of action.[336]

The Prerogative Orders, Declarations, and Injunctions: Their Discretionary Nature

[3.81] The remedies available under the Judicature (Northern Ireland) Act 1978 and RSC Order 53 are discretionary and there are four main considerations that, subject to European law requirements of effectiveness,[337] guide the courts when exercising their discretion to award any of the remedies available on an application for judicial review. These considerations—which are not exhaustive and which may elide into one another—are: (a) the utility of the remedy; (b) the conduct of the applicant; (c) delay (which embraces related considerations of good administration and the interests of third parties); and (d) the availability of alternative remedies.

Utility

[3.82] In some cases—most notably those where the decision has been impugned for lack of procedural fairness—the courts may conclude that an order of, for instance, certiorari would be of limited/no value. This is because the court may consider that, even if the decision were to be taken again and in accordance with the correct procedures, the final decision would not be different from the decision that was quashed. Rather than 'beat the air' in such circumstances,[338] the courts may therefore simply decline to make an order.[339] The courts may alternatively consider that the judgment itself is sufficient given the context of the case, albeit that the applicant is not given a formal remedy.[340]

[3.83] The courts may also consider that there would limited utility in granting a remedy where a matter is, or has become, academic (for instance, where there is a material change in the facts that gave rise to a dispute or where the applicant has suffered no

---

[336] *D v East Berkshire Community Health NHS Trust* [2005] 2 AC 373; and *Watkins v Home Office* [2006] 2 AC 395.

[337] See [8.39] (EU law) and [8.42] (ECHR).

[338] *R (McPherson) v Ministry of Education* [1980] NI 115, 121, Lord MacDermott.

[339] See, eg, *Re Wylie's Application* [2005] NI 359 (the court was satisfied that, even though there had been procedural shortcomings in respect of the decision not to grant the applicant a boat owner's licence, any representations made by the applicant would not have affected the outcome), and *R (Campbell College) v Department of Education* [1982] NI 123 (no benefit could arise from quashing the Department's decision in respect of the school's proposed admission policy as, in the circumstances of the case, a reconsideration of the proposal in accordance with proper legal principles would inevitably have led to the same result). But compare, eg, *R (Snaith) v The Ulster Polytechnic* [1981] NI 28 (where the rules of fairness are breached by persons acting as judge in their own cause then certiorari should ordinarily issue, notwithstanding that a properly constituted body would probably have come to the same decision or would do so in the future); *R (Smyth) v Coroner for County Antrim* [1980] NI 123 (the court has power to issue certiorari where the rules governing a coroner's inquest are broken notwithstanding that it is arguable that no benefit would accrue—it is important in the interests of both the next of kin and the public more generally that a verdict is reached by considered and regular inquiry); and *R (Hennessey) v Department of the Environment* [1980] NI 109 (while the court may refuse to exercise its discretion to quash a decision vitiated by procedural unfairness where the result would be of no consequence, it must be a very rare case where on a failure to give a hearing on an appeal the applicant would not be entitled to review by way of certiorari).

[340] *Re McCabe Ltd's Application* [2003] NIQB 77 (High Court considered that no need to interfere with the decision of the Industrial Court as the respective rights of the parties had in effect been declared in the judgment).

injustice or prejudice).[341] Under these circumstances, the court may again decline to grant a remedy, or it may alternatively grant a declaration as to the relevant legal principles (the court's willingness to do so will, however, depend on the context of the case and whether it gives rise to a matter of general interest[342]). The courts may likewise consider that there would be little merit in granting a remedy if it would be contrary to the interests of 'good administration' to do so,[343] although arguments of administrative inconvenience will not of themselves automatically lead the court to refuse relief.[344] Section 18(5) of the Judicature (Northern Ireland) Act 1978 in similar vein provides that the court may refuse a remedy where the illegality in question is a technical irregularity that has caused the applicant no substantial wrong or a miscarriage of justice[345]; and the courts may in 'exceptional circumstances'[346] also decline a remedy where, for instance, there has been insufficient consultation but where the court is of the opinion that proper consultation would not have made a difference to the course of action that the applicants took and that they had thereby suffered no significant unfairness.[347]

Conduct of Applicant

[3.84]   Applicants are expected to behave with candour and integrity and the courts may refuse to grant a remedy where an applicant fails to do so (lack of candour/integrity may also be relevant at the leave stage[348] and in respect of standing[349]: see [3.18] and [3.66]). The courts have thus said that remedies should not be granted where an applicant has misled the court.[350] On the other hand, the case law suggests that there must be some element of intent on the part of the applicant and that the courts may not censure an applicant for a simple, and largely inconsequential, oversight.[351]

Delay

[3.85]   Applications for judicial review must be made promptly and in any event within three months,[352] and the courts have long held that a failure to observe this delay requirement may be fatal to an application[353] (see [3.27]–[3.29]). The corresponding points of

---

[341] See, eg, Re Nicholson's Application [2003] NIQB 30 (application in respect of a prison adjudication dismissed as academic, as the prisoner had since been released and it was unlikely that the resolution of the issues in the application would provide guidance to the Prison Service in future cases).

[342] R v Secretary of State for the Home Department, ex p Salem [1999] 1 AC 45; and see [8.18].

[343] Re Police Association's Application [1990] NI 258, 285; and Re Russell's Application [1990] NI 188.

[344] R v Chief Constable, ex p McKenna [1992] NI 116, 123, Hutton LCJ.

[345] See, eg, Re Gribben's Application [1987] NI 129 (failure to read aloud written statements that had been adduced in evidence in a case where the applicant had been convicted of failure to provide a specimen of blood or urine contrary to art 144 of the Road Traffic (Northern Ireland) Order 1981 had not, in the context, given rise to any unfairness and no remedy would issue).

[346] Re Hove's Application [2005] NIQB 24, para 22; and Re Zhanje's Application [2007] NIQB 14.

[347] See, eg, Re National Union of Public Employers and Confederation of Health Service Employees' Application [1988] NI 255 (held that, although the applicant unions had a legitimate expectation of consultation in respect of hospital closures and the reorganisation of certain general medical services, they would not have addressed themselves to the merits or demerits of the proposals, even if they had been furnished with fuller financial and staffing information).

[348] Re Ruane's Application; Re Belfast City Council's Application [2001] NIQB 4.

[349] Re D's Application [2003] NI 295.

[350] Re O'Neill's Application [1990] 3 NIJB 1.

[351] Re EOC's Application [1988] NI 278.

[352] RSC Ord 53, r 4(1).

[353] Re Shearer's Application [1993] NIJB 12; and Re McCabe's Application [1994] NIJB 27.

justification for refusing a remedy for reasons of delay are manifold and include: the interests of good administration[354]; the need for respondents to be able effectively to defend proceedings[355]; and the need to protect the interests of third parties who may have benefited from an original decision but who may suffer a detriment if the decision is later deemed unlawful.[356] Refusal of a remedy for reasons of delay is not, however, inevitable and the courts accept that there may be 'good reason' for a lack of promptitude.[357] The applicant must nevertheless be able provide evidence of good reason for all periods of the delay if the application is not to be deemed out of time.[358]

Alternative Remedies

[**3.86**]   Where an applicant has an alternative remedy, the remedies sought on an application for judicial review will likely be refused if the alternative remedy is effective and efficient and where the wider public interest in the overall working of the legal system would be better served by refusing the application.[359] The courts have thus refused relief where they have considered that specially constituted tribunals would provide a more effective means to resolve a dispute or where there was a statutory appeal by way of case stated[360]; and they have also set aside a grant of leave where an applicant had initiated private law proceedings in tandem with the application for judicial review.[361] Case law has, however, also seen the courts reject arguments about alternative remedies where the nature of the alternative proceedings would not be suited to resolving a public law issue of illegality,[362] and where the alternative remedy was one that was not immediately open to the applicant.[363]

[354] *Re Wadsworth's Application* [2004] NIQB 8. On this justification see further [1.07].

[355] *Re McCabe's Application* [1994] NIJB 27 (a challenge to a disciplinary decision of a prison governor almost two years after the event was dismissed for reasons of delay as the governor had since retired and the precise details of the adjudication process were not recalled within the prison service).

[356] *Re McKevitt's Application* [2005] NIQB 56 (argued that a challenge to the legality of a legislative measure in the field of legal aid would have far-ranging implications for third parties who had already benefited under the measure: the argument was rejected on the evidence before, and the submissions to, the court). But see also *Re Murphy's Application* [2004] NIQB 85, para 11: detriment should be meaningful relative to the third party's circumstances and actions.

[357] See, eg, *Re Murphy's Application* [2004] NIQB 85, and *Re McKevitt's Application* [2005] NIQB 56 (delay in both caused by prior attempts to obtain legal aid); and *Re Wadsworth's Application* [2004] NIQB 8, para 8 (counsel for the applicant had been hospitalised).

[358] *Re Wilson's Application* [1989] NI 415, 416, Carswell LJ.

[359] See *Re Ballyedmond Castle Farm Ltd's Application; Re DPP for Northern Ireland's Application* [2000] NI 174; and [2.35].

[360] See, eg, *Re Kirkpatrick's Application* [2004] NIJB 15 (arguments about religious discrimination could be dealt with more effectively by the Fair Employment Tribunal); *Re BW's Application* [2004] NIQB 39 (challenge to the fairness of the procedure leading to the applicant's discharge from the armed services discussed: although the procedure was unfair, no remedy was granted as the applicant had a right of appeal to the Army Board); *Re McNally's Application* [1993] 4 NIJB 64 (challenge to decision of county court judge in a criminal matter: application dismissed for other reasons, with Hutton LCJ considering that the matter should in any event have been challenged by way of case stated); and *Re Gribbon's Application*, 11 July 1990, unreported (challenge to a school's refusal to admit a pupil: application dismissed for other reasons, with Carswell J stating that tribunal proceedings would have been more effective).

[361] *Re Ruane's Application; Re Belfast City Council's Application* [2001] NIQB 4.

[362] *R v Chief Constable, ex p McKenna* [1992] NI 116 (respondent argued that the applicant's challenge to a police officer's decision to defer access to a solicitor could be remedied before the Crown Court at any subsequent trial: held that the criminal trial would offer an ineffective forum for resolving the matter).

[363] *Re Cook and Other's Application* [1986] NI 242 (order of mandamus sought to compel a local council to set rates: held that judicial review was appropriate as the alternative remedy canvassed—a central government default power—would provide neither an effective nor an appropriate remedy).

[**3.87**]   A decision to make an application for judicial review when there is an alternative effective remedy may also be disposed of under RSC Order 53, rule 9(5). This provision enables the court to order that public law proceedings continue as if begun by writ where the remedy sought is a declaration, injunction, and/or damages, and where the court considers that the issues raised are more suited to private law proceedings.[364] An order to continue will not, however, follow automatically, and much will depend on how the issues have been presented in the application for judicial review and on whether the court considers that they are suited to continuation as private law proceedings.[365]

Appeals

[**3.88**]   Where an application for judicial review is dismissed or granted, the applicant or respondent in a civil matter may respectively appeal the decision of the High Court to the Court of Appeal without leave[366] ('leap-frog' appeals to the House of Lords are also possible in limited circumstances, although the leave of the House is here required[367]). Appeals are normally on one or other of the points of law at issue in the proceedings before the High Court, although new arguments are possible with the permission of the Court of Appeal, and new points of pure law may be allowed where the other party is not prejudiced.[368] New evidence may also be admitted on an appeal where: the evidence could not with reasonable diligence have been obtained for the substantive hearing at first instance; where the evidence will probably have an important influence on the result; and where the evidence appears credible[369] (although these conditions need not always be satisfied if the public interest requires that fresh evidence be admitted[370]). An applicant may also amend their statement of case on appeal with the permission of the court to seek a different/additional remedy. Where the statement of case is amended to add the new relief the notice of motion should also be amended by making a similar addition.[371]

[**3.89**]   Appeals should ordinarily be initiated within six weeks of the grant or refusal of the application for judicial review.[372] However, where an appeal is brought out of time, the Court of Appeal may exceptionally exercise its discretion to grant leave to bring an appeal. One such recent example is *Re E's Application*, where the Court of Appeal granted leave to bring an out-of-time appeal against the dismissal of an application for judicial review because 'there was good reason in the public interest' for doing so (the case concerned a challenge to the mode of policing of the 'Holy Cross' school dispute).[373]

[**3.90**]   It should finally be noted that appeals in criminal cases may be heard solely by the House of Lords. Such appeals will be heard only where the High Court certifies that

---

[364] See further [2.30]–[2.33].
[365] *Re Phillips' Application* [1995] NI 322; and see further [2.12] and [2.32].
[366] RSC Ord 53, r 10(b).
[367] Administration of Justice Act 1969, ss 12–16. The limited circumstances are where the judge certifies that: (i) the parties consent; (ii) the decision involves a point of law of public importance relating to interpretation of statute or rules, or the subject of a binding decision of the Court of Appeal or the House of Lords; and (iii) a sufficient case for appeal has been made out.
[368] *Pittalis v Grant* [1989] QB 605, 611.
[369] *Ladd v Marshall* [1954] 1 WLR 1489.
[370] *R v Secretary of State for the Home Department, ex p Momin Ali* [1984] 1 WLR 663.
[371] *Re McConnell's Application* [2000] NIJB 116.
[372] RSC Ord 59, r 4(1)(c).
[373] [2006] NICA 37.

the proceedings raise a point of law of general importance and where the High Court or the House of Lords grants leave to appeal[374] (see further [3.21]).

Costs

[**3.91**]   Costs are in the discretion of the court and orders will usually follow the event.[375] Costs orders will, as such, ordinarily be made to an applicant who is successful on an application for judicial review, although the court may make an order of costs against the applicant where there are good grounds for doing so[376] (an order may also take account of an applicant's failure to prepare their papers for the case properly and/or to observe time-limits once leave has been granted[377]). The corollary of this position is that, where an application is dismissed or the court refuses in its discretion to grant relief, a costs order will be made for the respondent or at least not against it[378] (where there is more than one respondent a single costs order will be made against the applicant). Where the issue of costs arises on the discontinuation of the application, the order will then be made against an applicant who withdraws for reasons of likelihood of failure. However, an order for the applicant will be made where the reason for discontinuance is a change of the respondent's decision or other measure for the purpose of pre-empting the application.[379]

[**3.92**]   Applicants in 'public interest' cases may also apply to the court for a protective costs order that will limit the extent of any potential costs order against them.[380] Applications for such orders will ordinarily be made and resolved earlier in proceedings and will be determined in the light of the '*Corner House* principles'.[381] Those principles are listed and considered at [3.34].

CONCLUSION

[**3.93**]   There are four points that may be made by way of conclusion on the judicial review procedure that is contained in the Judicature (Northern Ireland) Act 1978 and RSC Order 53:

i.   The judicial review procedure should be used only where there is (a) a decision, act, failure to act, or other measure that (b) sounds in public law and which (c) may

---

[374] Judicature Act (Northern Ireland) 1978, s 41; and see, eg, *Neill v North Antrim Magistrates Court* [1992] 1 WLR 1220.

[375] Judicature (Northern Ireland) Act 1978, s 59. And see RSC Ord 62; *Re Eshokai's Application* [2007] NIQB 75, para 19.

[376] *Re Morris's Application*, 30 April 1997, unreported.

[377] See *Re Doherty's Application* [2006] NIQB 33, paras 28–9; and *Judicial Review: Practice Note 01/2006* 16 January 2006, available through http://www.courtsni.gov.uk.

[378] *Re Quigley's Application* [1997] NI 202.

[379] J Larkin and D Schofield, *Judicial Review in Northern Ireland: A Practitioner's Guide* (Belfast, SLS Legal Publications, 2007) ch 16. And see, eg, *Re Ullah's Application for Leave* [2007] NIQB 45 (costs awarded against respondent for the reason that it had changed its decision on the applicant's immigration status only after an application for leave had been made, notwithstanding the clarity of the issues in the applicant's pre-action correspondence).

[380] R Stein and J Beagent, 'Protective Costs Orders' (2005) 10 JR 206.

[381] *R (Corner House) v Department of Trade and Industry* [2005] 1 WLR 2600.

appropriately be challenged by way of judicial review. Judicial review should, in general, therefore not be used where a matter is one of private law or where the individual has an effective alternative remedy in (typically) statute. Applicants should also seek to avoid bringing judicial review proceedings prematurely and they should observe the key points of the Pre-Action Protocol (see [3.04]–[3.13]).

ii. Applicants should observe the various procedural requirements at the leave stage and at the substantive hearing of an application for judicial review. Although the courts have shown some flexibility on aspects of procedure (see, for example, [3.64]–[3.66] on standing, and [3.89] on out-of-time appeals), they typically emphasise the importance of adhering to the procedure (see, for example, [3.27]–[3.29] on delay; although the courts may also be flexible here where there is 'good reason' for any delay).

iii. Various points of guidance on the judicial procedure can be found in the case law of the courts and in related Practice Directions.[382] Failure to act in accordance with this guidance can result in an application for leave being refused or, where leave is granted, in the dismissal of the substantive application. Failure to follow guidance may, depending on context, alternatively have implications in costs.[383]

iv. The remedies available on an application for judicial review are discretionary. The courts may thus decline to grant a remedy where they consider, among other things, that: (a) the remedy would be of limited utility; (b) the conduct of the applicant is not deserving of the remedy sought; (c) there has been undue delay in bringing the application; and (d) effective alternative remedies are available (see [3.81]–[3.87]).

---

[382] *Judicial Review: Practice Note* 01/2006, available at http://www.courtsni.gov.uk.
[383] See, eg, *Re D's Application* [2003] NI 295, 301, para 11, Carswell LCJ; and *Re Doherty's Application* [2006] NIQB 33, paras 28–9.

4

The Grounds for Review Introduced

INTRODUCTION

[4.01] The purpose of this chapter is to identify the public law precepts that underpin the grounds of illegality, substantive review, and procedural impropriety that may be argued in an application for judicial review.[1] The grounds, which determine how closely and for which reasons the courts will scrutinise public law decisions and so on,[2] correspond to debates about the constitutional role of the courts, and the relevance of doctrines such as the separation of powers.[3] Judicial review in Northern Ireland and elsewhere in the UK was previously synonymous with a 'review, not appeal' distinction that entails that the courts do not take substantive decisions in the place of bodies that Parliament has entrusted with a particular statutory function.[4] However, while the courts often emphasise that the imperative of judicial self-restraint remains,[5] they have also modified the grounds for judicial review—whether with reference to the common law and/or to EU law and the ECHR[6]—to permit closer look review where the context of a case is taken to require such review (judicial review is now also available for purposes of challenging various forms of non-statutory power—see [4.06]–[4.08][7]). In identifying the precepts that underlie these variable and context-sensitive grounds for review this chapter thus examines: the constitutional purposes of, and limits to, the grounds; the approach of the courts to statutory powers, duties, and discretion (an issue which is central to the workings of the separation of powers doctrine); and the approach of the courts to errors of law and errors of fact on the part of subordinate decision-makers.

[4.02] One further point by way of introduction concerns the overlapping nature of the grounds for judicial review. Although the grounds may be listed as illegality, substantive review and procedural impropriety (principles such as proportionality, legitimate expectation, and so on, then exist within these), a decision that is challengeable under one heading will often also be challengeable under another.[8] The case law considered in this

---

[1] See chs 5–7 for detailed discussion.

[2] On the range of reviewable measures see [3.05]–[3.08].

[3] On which see [1.03] and [1.05].

[4] See *R v Secretary of State for Northern Ireland, ex p Finlay* [1983] 9 NIJB 1, 10, Hutton J; *Re Glor Na nGael's Application* [1991] NI 117, 129, Carswell J; and *Re Bow Street Mall's Application* [2006] NIQB 28, para 110 [sic], Girvan J.

[5] See, eg, *Re Duffy's Application* [2006] NICA 28(1), para 40, Kerr LCJ.

[6] See further [1.14]–[1.15].

[7] And ch 2.

[8] See, eg, *Boddington v British Transport Police* [1999] 2 AC 143, 152, Lord Irvine LC: the categories are 'not watertight compartments because the various grounds for judicial review run together. The exercise of power for an improper purpose may involve taking irrelevant considerations into account, or ignoring relevant

chapter should therefore not be read as of relevance to only one or other of the grounds, but rather as of more general importance to developments in judicial review.

THE CONSTITUTIONAL PURPOSES OF, AND THE LIMITS TO, THE GROUNDS FOR REVIEW

[**4.03**]   The variable and context-sensitive nature of the grounds for review is the consequence of a judicial awareness, on the one hand, of the constitutional importance of judicial review and, on the other, of the fact that there are desirable limits to the judicial role. For instance, in terms of the constitutional importance of judicial review, the courts have not only emphasised that the grounds for review perform an important function through constraining exercises of public power; they have also read legislation in a way that safeguards the supervisory jurisdiction of the courts. While this perhaps posits a tendency towards judicial activism, the courts have at the same time accepted that some matters are essentially ill suited to the judicial process in the sense that they are non-justiciable or non-reviewable. The courts have similarly accepted the need for judicial self-restraint when decisions that straddle the elusive line between law and politics are in issue, where the context-sensitive nature of the grounds is manifest in judicial use of a 'soft-edged' standard of review.

'Root Concepts' of the Common Law and the 'Rule of Law'

[**4.04**]   Judicial review's capacity to constrain, or control, the exercise of public power is largely dependent upon judicial development and application of common law concepts such as fairness, abuse of power, reasonableness, proportionality, and propriety of purpose (the common law may here evolve independently or in the light of EU law and/or the ECHR[9]). While the imagery of judicial review 'controlling' decision-making processes and outcomes offers only a partial perspective on its constitutional purpose(s),[10] use of the common law's 'root concepts' of fairness and so on has long been central to judicial oversight of decisions and other measures.[11] 'Abuse of power', for instance, has underscored the development of common law notions of 'improper purpose' and 'unreasonableness',[12] and 'fairness' has been central to the emergence of the doctrine of substantive legitimate expectation.[13] The protection of human rights—

considerations; and either may lead to an irrational result. The failure to grant a person affected by a decision a hearing, in breach of principles of procedural fairness, may result in a failure to take into account relevant considerations'. On relevancy see [4.40]–[4.41] and [5.40]–[5.43]; on irrationality/unreasonableness see [6.05]–[6.11]; and on fair hearing guarantees see [7.30]–[7.57].

[9]   See, on the spill-over of EU law, [1.18].

[10]   See [1.04]–[1.10].

[11]   The term 'root concept' was used by Laws LJ to describe abuse of power: see *R v Department of Education and Employment, ex p Begbie* [2000] 1 WLR 1115, 1129.

[12]   See *R v Department of Education and Employment, ex p Begbie* [2000] 1 WLR 1115, 1129, Laws LJ; and *Re Croft's Application* [1997] NI 457, 491, Girvan J. And on improper purpose and unreasonableness see further [5.44]–[5.46] and [6.05]–[6.11].

[13]   See *Re Treacy's Application* [2000] NI 330, 362 ff, Kerr J, analysing *R v North and East Devon Health Authority, ex p Coughlan* [2000] 2 WLR 622; and, eg, *Re Neale's Application* [2005] NIQB 33. See further [6.29]–[6.45].

whether on the basis of the common law and/or under the Human Rights Act 1998—is also consonant with any/all of the concepts of fairness, abuse of power, and so on, and the courts here review decisions with reference to the 'fundamental principle'[14] of 'anxious scrutiny'.[15]

[**4.05**] Judicial use of these concepts can, in turn, be traced to the related notion of the 'rule of law'.[16] The rule of law here means that all those who exercise public power must be subject to the demands of legality, whether developed with reference to specific concepts like abuse of power or to some other formulation (for example, a straightforward misunderstanding of the nature of a power or duty)[17]. The rule of law has, as such, also led the courts to emphasise that *any* decision, or other measure, of a subordinate body that is founded upon statute and characterised by a misapprehension of the law is, in general, unlawful; and they have on this basis further emphasised that the ultra vires doctrine—whereby a decision or other measure is deemed unlawful where it is 'outside the power'—should be given its broadest meaning.[18] Thus, while the courts previously distinguished between errors of law that went to the jurisdiction of a subordinate body and those that were made within the body's jurisdiction, any error of law is, subject to only very few exceptions, now taken to affect the jurisdiction of the decision-maker and to render a decision or other measure unlawful (see [4.30]–[4.35]). The rule of law has here also been strengthened by the courts' rejection of the former distinction between decisions that are 'void' and those that are 'voidable', as the broader ultra vires doctrine requires that any decision that is unlawful can only ever be deemed void[19] (although the courts may at the same time decline to grant a remedy[20]).

Non-statutory Power and the Rule of Law: The Royal Prerogative

[**4.06**] The rule of law can also found challenges to decisions or other measures that are taken on the basis of non-statutory power. Such power includes the royal prerogative,[21] which has been described as 'a residue of miscellaneous fields of law in which the executive government retains decision-making powers that are not dependent on any statutory authorisation but nevertheless have consequences' for the rights of individuals[22] (the executive for these purposes can include Northern Ireland Ministers, who may, as respects transferred matters, exercise 'the prerogative and other executive powers of Her

---

[14] *R (Yogathas) v Secretary of State for the Home Department* [2003] 1 AC 920, 927, para 9, Lord Bingham.

[15] *R v Secretary of State for the Home Department, ex p Bugdaycay* [1987] AC 514, 531, Lord Bridge; and see [6.10].

[16] On the wider constitutional positioning of which see Constitutional Reform Act 2005, s 1: 'This Act does not adversely affect (a) the existing constitutional principle of the rule of law, or (b) the Lord Chancellor's existing constitutional role in relation to that principle'.

[17] On the various forms of illegality see ch 5; and for other uses and meanings of the 'rule of law' see [6.29]–[6.45] (legitimate expectations).

[18] *Boddington v British Transport Police* [1999] 2 AC 143.

[19] *Boddington v British Transport Police* [1999] 2 AC 143, 154, Lord Irvine. On void vs voidable see *Re North Down Borough Council's Application* [1986] NI 304, 315.

[20] See [3.81]–[3.87]; [5.36]; and [8.08]–[8.09].

[21] And see ch 2 for other forms of non-statutory power that may be subject to judicial review.

[22] *Council of Civil Service Unions v Minister for the Civil Service* [1985] AC 374, 409–10, Lord Diplock. *Defining* it is, however, more difficult: see the NICA's analysis in *Re W's Application* [1998] NI 219, 226–7. But note that delimiting the prerogative is, in any event, a matter for the courts: *A-G v De Keyser's Royal Hotel* [1920] AC 508.

Majesty in relation to Northern Ireland'[23]). In historical terms, decisions taken on the basis of the prerogative were not subject to judicial review as the powers were regarded as essentially political in form,[24] and the role of the courts was limited to enquiring into whether a particular power existed and, if so, its extent.[25] In making this enquiry the courts would consider whether legislation had been enacted in the area in question, as it had long been accepted that legislation would extinguish the non-statutory power, or place it in abeyance.[26] This rule—which remains of contemporary importance[27]—has its origins in the doctrine of the sovereignty of the Westminster Parliament and it corresponds to the basic democratic principle that Acts of elected legislatures should trump executive power. Legislatures for this purpose also include the Northern Ireland Assembly, as it has since been established that the prerogative can be extinguished by the 'constitutional laws' of Northern Ireland[28] (viz lawful Acts of the Assembly/Orders in Council made at times of suspension[29]).

[4.07]   The fact that the prerogative can have a direct impact on the interests of individuals subsequently led the courts to modify their approach to the availability of judicial review, and exercises or non-exercises of the prerogative are now subject to the supervisory jurisdiction of the courts where the issues raised are 'justiciable'.[30] This means that certain prerogative decisions fall within the constitutional jurisdiction of the courts and that judicial scrutiny is thereby legitimate. While the concept can at the same time be criticised for placing some decisions beyond the scope of judicial invigilation (see [4.16]), its use has moved the courts towards the fuller review of a significant range of executive powers. The courts thus now distinguish between non-justiciable matters of 'high policy' (which include making treaties, the dissolution of Parliament, and mobilising the armed forces),[31] and justiciable 'other matters' (for instance, a decision not to issue a passport to a suspected criminal living outside the UK).[32] The courts, moreover, accept that these categories are open rather than closed and that the justiciability of matters can be reconsidered in the light of 'modern conditions'.[33] Exercises of the prerogative of mercy are, as

---

[23] Northern Ireland Act 1998, s 23(2), as read with Sch 2 to the Act. And see too s 23(3): 'As respects the Northern Ireland Civil Service and the Commissioner for Public Appointments for Northern Ireland, the prerogative and other executive power of Her Majesty in relation to Northern Ireland shall be exercisable on Her Majesty's behalf by the First Minister and Deputy First Minister acting jointly'.

[24] See B Hadfield, 'Judicial Review and the Prerogative Powers of the Crown' in M Sunkin and S Payne (eds), *The Nature of the Crown: A Legal and Political Analysis* (Oxford, Oxford University Press, 1999) p 197.

[25] *A-G v De Keyser's Royal Hotel* [1920] AC 508.

[26] *A-G v De Keyser's Royal Hotel* [1920] AC 508, and, eg, *Re Downes' Application* [2006] NIQB 77, para 32.

[27] *R v Secretary of State for the Home Department, ex p Fire Brigade's Union* [1995] 2 AC 513.

[28] Interpretation Act (Northern Ireland) 1954, s 7; considered in, eg, *Re Derry City Council's Application* [2007] NIQB 5, paras 25–8. And see, eg, *Re W's Application* [1998] NI 219 (Secretary of State for Northern Ireland had no prerogative power to make an *ex gratia* payment of compensation to an individual who had applied 'out of time' under the Criminal Injuries (Compensation) (Northern Ireland) Order 1988, SI 1988/793).

[29] On which see [1.13] and [5.23]–[5.24].

[30] *Council of Civil Service Unions v Minister for the Civil Service* [1985] AC 374.

[31] See, eg, *Ex p Molyneaux* [1986] 1 WLR 331 (not the function of the court to inquire into the exercise of the prerogative in either entering into or implementing the Anglo-Irish Agreement 1985).

[32] The distinction was made by Taylor LJ in *R v Secretary of State for Foreign and Commonwealth Affairs, ex p Everett* [1989] 1 All ER 655, 660.

[33] *Re McBride's Application (No 2)* [2003] NI 319 (while the administration of the affairs of the army was historically a matter for the sovereign, decisions of an Army Board—here to retain in service two soldiers convicted of murder in a civilian court—was properly subject to review in the modern era).

a result, no longer regarded as wholly immune from review[34]; and case law in England and Wales has seen the courts both review Orders in Council made on the basis of the prerogative[35] and analyse executive decisions in a manner that has taken the courts to the margins of matters of high policy.[36]

[4.08]   The extent to which specific exercises of the prerogative will be subject to the rule of law then depends on how the courts use the grounds for review in any given case. Here, it is established that the various grounds of review are each available but that much will depend on the context to a dispute, including the fact that the power in question is a prerogative power[37] (on context-sensitivity see further [4.14]–[4.21]). For instance, should a dispute centre on whether a Minister has a prerogative power in respect of a particular matter and, if so, on how it should be exercised, a court may merely confirm that the power exists and expressly decline to comment on how it should be used.[38] On the other hand, the courts may consider that the width of a prerogative power has been qualified by the practices, conduct, and representations of executive government and that these can found a challenge to the lawfulness of a decision. The point here is simply that the arbitrary nature and width of prerogative powers can be regarded as 'somewhat anomalous in modern society where the concept of arbitrariness is alien to the commonly accepted features of the rule of law'.[39] Should government therefore indicate that it will, for instance, exercise the prerogative power to make public appointments in accordance with values of non-discrimination and transparency, there are dicta to suggest that the government should be held to those assurances. Such an approach, it is said, would be a 'legitimate and logical development of the law'.[40]

---

[34] Compare *Council of Civil Service Unions v Minister for the Civil Service* [1985] 1 AC 374, 418, Lord Roskill (prerogative of mercy not justiciable) and *R v Secretary of State for the Home Department, ex p Bentley* [1993] 4 All ER 443 (Home Secretary's decision not to recommend a posthumous free pardon for a youth reviewed on the ground that the Home Secretary had considered only an unconditional pardon and had not taken account of other possibilities). And see also, eg, *Lewis v A-G of Jamaica* [2000] 1 WLR 1785.

[35] *R (Bancoult) v Secretary of State for Foreign and Commonwealth Affairs* [2007] EWCA 498 (the British Indian Ocean Territory (Constitution) Order 2004 and the British Indian Ocean Territory (Immigration) Order 2004 found to be without legal force as they had been made in breach of the applicants' legitimate expectations and, as such, constituted an abuse of power).

[36] *R (Abbasi) v Secretary of State for Foreign and Commonwealth Affairs* [2003] UKHRR 76 (Foreign Office policy documents gave a British citizen held at Guantanamo Bay a legitimate expectation that the Secretary of State would consider making representations on his behalf to the US government. The court could thus inquire whether the Secretary of State had given such consideration to the plight of the prisoner, without thereby reviewing any corresponding decision about how best to balance factors such as the gravity of the injustice to the individual and reasons of foreign policy which may lead the Secretary of State to decline to intervene).

[37] See *Re Croft's Application* [1997] NI 457, 486–7, Girvan J: '[W]here a decision is made on foot of ministerial or more accurately the royal prerogative it may be that somewhat different considerations apply in relation to a judicial review of such decision as compared to other ministerial or administrative decisions.'

[38] Eg, *Re Hannaway's Application* [1995] NI 159 (Secretary of State for Northern Ireland refused to exercise the prerogative of mercy to allow the remains of an IRA man to be removed from Crumlin Road prison because he was of the opinion that the prerogative of mercy did not apply as burial within prison was not part of the punishment: held that burial was part of the punishment and that the prerogative of mercy was available but that the court would express 'no view whatever as to whether or not the Secretary of State should exercise the prerogative to order the removal of the remains. There are arguments for and against such a course and the decision whether to exercise the prerogative in this case is one for the Secretary of State and not for this court').

[39] *Re Downes' Application* [2006] NIQB 77, para 40.

[40] *Re Downes' Application* [2006] NIQB 77, para 40.

The Rule of Law and Parliamentary Sovereignty

[4.09]   One final issue related to the rule of law concerns the status of Acts of the Westminster Parliament. The rule of law here has a more complex connotation, as the doctrine of parliamentary sovereignty has historically meant that the courts will not review the constitutionality of primary legislation and will accept as supreme the most recent statement of Parliament's intentions[41] (the role of judicial review is thus limited to ensuring that decision-makers—including a functioning Northern Ireland Assembly—act in accordance with the terms of primary legislation that delegates powers to them, or imposes on them a duty to act: see [4.05]). However, while the absolute sovereignty of the Westminster Parliament is, in theory, still central to the constitution,[42] judicial interpretation of legislation in such a way that, for instance, permits interference with common law fundamental rights only where such interference is provided for expressly or by necessary implication suggests that there are some increasingly important common law limitations to Parliament's powers.[43] Constitutional orthodoxy is, moreover, complicated by challenges to primary legislation on the ground that it is contrary to EU law and/or to the limited extent associated with declarations of incompatibility with the ECHR: while the rule of law that here 'binds' Parliament can be said to be that which Parliament has set for itself under the terms of the European Communities Act 1972 and the Human Rights Act 1998, the fact that these Acts are regarded as common law 'constitutional statutes' would suggest that the rule of law that binds Parliament may yet develop to take further account of judge-made conceptions of abuse of power, and so on.[44]

Ouster Clauses and Time-limits

[4.10]   The courts' recognition of the constitutional importance of judicial review is per-haps most famously associated with their approach to absolute 'ouster' clauses. Such

---

[41] *Ellen Street Estates v Minister of Health* [1934] 1 KB 590, 597, Maugham LJ.

[42] But see now also Lord Steyn's comments in *Jackson v Attorney-General* [2006] 1 AC 262, 302, para [102]: 'This is where we may have to come back to the point about the supremacy of Parliament. We do not in the United Kingdom have an uncontrolled constitution as the Attorney General implausibly asserts. In the European context the second *Factortame* decision made that clear. The settlement contained in the Scotland Act 1998 also points to a divided sovereignty. Moreover, the European Convention on Human Rights as incor-porated into our law by the Human Rights Act 1998 created a new legal order. One must not assimilate the European Convention on Human Rights with multilateral treaties of the traditional type. Instead it is a legal order in which the United Kingdom assumes obligations to protect fundamental rights, not in relation to other states, but towards all individuals within its jurisdiction. The classic account given by Dicey of the doctrine of the supremacy of Parliament, pure and absolute as it was, can now be seen to be out of place in the modern United Kingdom. Nevertheless, the supremacy of Parliament is still the *general* principle of our constitution. It is a construct of the common law. The judges created this principle. If that is so, it is not unthinkable that cir-cumstances could arise where the courts may have to qualify a principle established on a different hypothesis of constitutionalism.'

[43] Eg, *R v Secretary of State for the Home Department, ex p Leech* [1993] 4 All ER 539 (prison rules that permitted authorities to interfere with correspondence between prisoners and lawyers save where proceedings had been initiated were ultra vires Prison Act 1952, s 47, as they impeded access to a lawyer for purposes of con-sidering whether to bring proceedings). Although for judicial caution in respect of delimiting the content of common law constitutional rights see *Watkins v Home Office* [2006] 2 AC 395, 417–18, para 58, Lord Rodger.

[44] See M Elliott, 'Embracing "Constitutional" Legislation: Towards Fundamental Law?' (2003) 54 NILQ 25; and *Jackson v Attorney-General* [2006] 1 AC 262, 304, para 107, Lord Hope: 'The rule of law enforced by the courts is the ultimate controlling factor on which our constitution is based.' On constitutional statutes see fur-ther [1.28]–[1.34] and [5.04]–[5.30].

clauses typically provide that, once a decision has been reached by a decision-maker, the decision is to be regarded as final in the sense that it cannot be challenged in a court of law.[45] While there are dicta to suggest that Parliament may limit access to the courts through use of express language to that effect,[46] the prevailing approach of the courts is identified with the seminal *Anisminic* judgment of the House of Lords.[47] In that case it was held that an ouster clause that sought to prevent challenges to determinations of a compensation commission had effect only where the determination in question was a lawful determination.[48] Distinguishing between lawful determinations and determinations that were vitiated by an error of law, the House of Lords held that the latter were merely 'purported determinations' that fell beyond the wording of the statute.[49] The House in that way ensured that the decision-making processes of subordinate bodies remained constrained by the rule of law, notwithstanding Parliament's apparent intention to place certain decisions beyond judicial scrutiny.[50]

[**4.11**]   The courts are, however, more inclined to accept that judicial review has been ousted where a statute contains a time-limited ouster clause[51] that is regarded as reasonable.[52] In this context, a statute may (a) provide for a remedy in the face of a determination but (b) require that the remedy be availed of within the specified period of time, after which time the decision of the subordinate body may not be challenged in proceedings.[53] The courts' willingness to accept that the jurisdiction of the High Court can here be ousted is essentially unproblematic from a rule of law perspective, as judicial assessment of the legality of a decision can still be achieved through the statutory remedy (a remedy may even provide for a full appeal, which will allow the court to assess the merit of a decision). However, by accepting that the courts' jurisdiction is thereafter ousted, the courts ensure that decision-makers enjoy the degree of certainty that the time-limit seeks

---

[45] See, eg, the Criminal Justice (Serious Fraud) (Northern Ireland) Order 1988, SI 1988/1846 (NI 16), art 3(3): 'A designated authority's decision to give notice of transfer shall not be subject to any appeal or liable to be quashed in any court'.

[46] *R v Registrar of Companies, ex p Central Bank of England* [1986] QB 1114, 1169, Lawton LJ: there is an 'overriding rule that Parliament can by a statutory provision exclude recourse to the courts. The courts must, in consequence, refuse to entertain matters in respect of which Parliament by clear words or by necessary implication has enacted that they should not have jurisdiction.' But compare, eg, *Jackson v Attorney-General* [2006] 1 AC 262, 318, para 159, Baroness Hale: 'The courts will treat with particular suspicion (and might even reject) any attempt to subvert the rule of law by removing governmental action affecting the rights of the individual from all judicial powers.'

[47] *Anisminic Ltd v Foreign Compensation Commission* [1969] 2 AC 147.

[48] Foreign Compensation Act 1950, s 4(4).

[49] And see, eg, *Re Bates' Application* [2004] NIQB 84, para 40, Deeny J, stating that any determination on an appeal under art 12 of the Pollution Control and Local Government (Northern Ireland) Order 1978, SI 1978/1049 (NI 19), must be a real determination and not a purported determination.

[50] See, eg, *R v McGill & Ors* [2006] NICC 6, para 6, Deeny J, reading art 3(3) of the Criminal Justice (Serious Fraud) (Northern Ireland) Order 1988, SI 1988/1846) (NI 16), in the light of *Anisminic*.

[51] See, most famously, *Smith v East Elloe RDC* [1956] AC 736; followed in, eg *Re Bowden; JGS Services Ltd; Re Scalene Investments Ltd* [2004] NIQB 32. And see also the Judicature (Northern Ireland) Act 1978, s 22: '(1) Any statutory provision to the effect that any order or determination shall not be called into question in any court, or which by similar words excludes any of the powers of the High Court, shall not operate so as to (a) prevent the removal of the proceedings into the High Court by order of certiorari; or (b) prejudice the powers of the High Court to make orders of mandamus. (2) *This section does not apply to . . . (b) any statutory provision specially authorising applications to the High Court within a time limited by that provision*; or (c) a statutory provision passed on or after 1 August 1958.' (Emphasis added.)

[52] See W Wade and C Forsyth, Administrative Law, 9th edn (Oxford, Oxford University Press, 2004) p 732.

[53] See, eg, Local Government Act (Northern Ireland) 1972, Sch 6, para 5(1)(a)–(c), considered in *Re Bowden; JGS Services Ltd; Re Scalene Investments Ltd* [2004] NIQB 32.

to provide and that 'good administration' is taken to require.[54] Acceptance and prioritisation of the statutory scheme established by Parliament would also be consistent with
the doctrine of legislative supremacy, although this rule in respect of partial ouster
clauses arguably sits in contrast to that adopted in respect of clauses that are absolute (see
[4.10]).[55]

[4.12]   There are two further points of importance about ouster clauses. The first concerns the difference between statutory remedies that are linked to time-limited ouster
clauses (which the courts accept as preventing recourse to judicial review) and statutory
remedies that are not linked to time-limit clauses (the existence of which remedy does not
necessarily prevent recourse to judicial review). Although it is well established that individuals must ordinarily exhaust alternative remedies (whether in statute or in a private
law cause of action), the wider body of case law on alternative remedies is underwritten
by considerations of pragmatism and the wider interests of justice.[56] While time-limits
are thus taken to oust the jurisdiction of the High Court (that is, because the statute
requires that the remedy be availed of within a set time-frame), it does not follow that a
failure to use an alternative statutory remedy that is not couched in time-limited terms
will mean that judicial review proceedings would be inappropriate. Much will instead
depend upon the wider context of the case and of the court's perception of how far judicial review may play a residual role in providing a remedy and safeguarding the rule of
law.[57]

[4.13]   The second point concerns the compatibility of absolute and time-limited ouster
clauses with Article 6 ECHR's guarantees in respect of 'civil rights' (see also [4.19]
regarding 'conclusive evidence' certificates). Article 6 ECHR specifies a range of procedural requirements that centre upon the right of access to a court,[58] and the case law of
the ECtHR emphasises that any limitations on rights of access must be proportionate and
that they cannot provide public bodies with 'immunity' from proceedings.[59] Absolute
ouster clauses would, subject to arguments about the effect of *Anisminic* (see [4.10]), on
that basis appear to be incompatible with the ECHR; and time-limited ouster clauses
would likewise appear to be open to challenge if the time-limit does not strike an appropriate balance between the objective it pursues and the rights of the affected individual.[60]
However, before such arguments might successfully be made out, an applicant would
have to establish that any clause in question is procedural in form rather than one that
determines whether the individual has a substantive cause of action in domestic law
(a distinction that is fraught with difficulty[61]). The individual would further need to

---

[54]   On which see further [1.07].

[55]   For a judicial reconciliation of the approach to time-limited and absolute ouster clauses see *R v Secretary
of State for the Environment, ex p Ostler* [1977] 1 QB 122; now doubted in England and Wales in, eg,
R (Richards) v Pembrokeshire County Council [2004] EWCA 1000.

[56]   See [2.34]–[2.35].

[57]   See, eg, *Re Neill's Application* [2006] NICA 5, paras 30–31 (while the remedy for a breach of s 75 of the
Northern Ireland Act 1998 will usually be that contained in Sch 9 to the Act, judicial review is not automatically precluded).

[58]   *Z v UK* (2002) 34 EHRR 97.

[59]   *Perez de Rada Cavanilles v Spain* (1998) 29 EHRR 109, 120, paras 44–5.

[60]   Compare, by analogy, *Stubbings v UK* (1997) 23 EHRR 213 (limitation period in a personal injury claim
did not violate Art 6 ECHR: such limitation periods serve important purposes such as providing legal certainty
and finality, and the essence of the applicant's right of access to a court had not been impaired).

[61]   See *Matthews v Ministry of Defence* [2003] 1 AC 1163; and T Hickman, 'The "Uncertain Shadow":
Throwing Light on the Right to a Court under Article 6(1)' [2004] PL 122.

establish that they have a recognised civil right within the meaning of Article 6 ECHR, which does not apply to 'public law' rights.[62]

Context-sensitivity: Justiciability, Reviewability, and Deference

[**4.14**] The courts' acceptance that the grounds for review should be applied in a context-sensitive manner (see [4.03]) can be seen in their use of the concept of justiciability. For instance, the courts have, on the one hand, drawn upon the concept to justify review where they have considered that the subject-matter of a decision falls within the constitutional jurisdiction of the courts and that judicial scrutiny is thereby legitimate. Such development of the law has occurred most notably in relation to the royal prerogative, where the courts accept that some decisions should now be subject to review notwithstanding the historical exclusion of that review (see [4.06]–[4.08]). In terms of reconciling the change with an awareness of context, the courts have relied upon the fact that some exercises of the prerogative can have implications for the rights and interests of individuals and that judicial control in such circumstances is apposite.[63]

[**4.15**] On the other hand, the concept of justiciability has been used to place certain categories of decisions beyond the reach of the courts. The concept in these circumstances assumes the negative connotation 'non-justiciability', which entails that some decisions are not 'subject to the jurisdiction of the courts'[64] and are thereby effectively immune from review. Use of the concept in this negative form has been particularly prominent in relation to some prerogative powers (see [4.07]), although it has been used in other areas too.[65] For instance, where public authorities have been sued directly in negligence by individuals who claim to have suffered loss as a result of discretionary choices taken in the light of resource considerations (see [4.28]), the courts have said that such disputes can sometimes give rise to non-justiciable matters of 'policy'.[66] While case law on the point has at the same time become more complex in recent years,[67] the non-justiciability approach corresponds to the understanding that judicial involvement in matters of policy would involve the courts in taking decisions in the place of authorities that the legislature has entrusted with the power of decision (a separation of powers argument[68]). The courts are here also guided by the concern that frequent awards of damages against public authorities could diminish the quality of services that are provided on the basis of finite resources and for the benefit of the public as a whole.[69]

---

[62] See, eg, *Re Glasgow's Application* [2004] NIQB 34 (Art 6 ECHR not applicable to employment contracts of police officers); and *Re Shuker's Application* [2004] NI 367, considering *Runa Begum v Tower Hamlets London Borough Council* [2003] 2 AC 430 (Art 6 ECHR did not govern a prosecution decision of the Attorney-General as the rights involved in the case were firmly rooted in public law and were not similar to private law rights of the kind governed by Art 6 ECHR). On the reach of Art 6 ECHR, and its relationship with public law rights, see [7.14]–[7.16].

[63] *Council of Civil Service Unions v Minister for the Civil Service* [1985] AC 374, 409–10, Lord Diplock.

[64] *Re Shuker's Application* [2004] NI 367, 370, para 7.

[65] For discussion see A Le Sueur, 'Justifying Judicial Caution: Jurisdiction, Justiciability, and Policy' in B Hadfield (ed), *Judicial Review: A Thematic Approach* (Dublin, Gill & MacMillan, 1995) p 228.

[66] *Barrett v Enfield LBC* [2001] 2 AC 550; and [8.23]–[8.25].

[67] G Anthony, 'The Negligence Liability of Public Authorities: Was the Old Law the Right Law?' (2006) NILQ 409.

[68] On which see [1.03].

[69] See, eg, *Brooks v Metropolitan Police Commissioner* [2005] 2 All ER 489.

[**4.16**]   Use of the concept of justiciability within this latter meaning has, however, often been criticised as having the potential to close off certain decision-making areas entirely from judicial scrutiny, and the trend in more recent case law has been to move away from the concept. The courts have, instead, preferred to find that a particular decision is justiciable but that the manner in which the grounds for review are to be used in a case should be modified to reflect the content of the decision under challenge. The leading Northern Ireland authority on this approach—which may termed as the 'reviewability' approach—is *Re Shuker's Application.*[70] The High Court there held that, while a decision of the Attorney-General not to 'de-schedule' certain offences under the Terrorism Act 2000 was justiciable, not all of the grounds for review were open to the applicant. Holding in particular that the decision in question was not reviewable on the basis that it failed to comply with requirements of procedural fairness, the court added that the decision had involved the evaluation of material that was of a sensitive nature and that the court should thereby be reluctant to intrude in the decision-making process. The court, moreover, noted that Parliament had entrusted the decision-making power to the Attorney-General and that the court should for that further reason exhibit restraint.[71]

[**4.17**]   This reviewability approach is clearly conditioned by an awareness of the need for judicial invigilation to be available in as many cases as possible while at the same time remaining sensitive to the context of those cases. The corresponding restraint of the kind exhibited in *Shuker*—the context of other cases may equally lead the courts to engage in 'closer look' review[72]—has previously been referred to as 'judicial deference'. Although the House of Lords has grown increasingly sceptical about 'deference' as a term to describe the judicial role in review proceedings,[73] the term, as originally conceived, was regarded as consonant with the separation of powers doctrine and the understanding that the courts should not usurp the functions of either the legislature or the executive (and neither should either of those branches of the State usurp the judicial function).[74] The need for judicial self-restraint, however described, is therefore often taken as central to the workings of the grounds for review, particularly as relate to the substantive choices of decision-makers. The need for restraint may likewise inform judicial approaches to statutory interpretation, whether for purposes of delimiting the powers and duties of a decision-maker ([4.22]–[4.28]) or when reading legislation in the light of the ECHR.[75]

National Security

[**4.18**]   The nature of the shift from justiciability to reviewability/deference can be seen most clearly in the context of challenges to decisions taken with reference to national

---

[70] [2004] NI 367.

[71] See also, eg, *R v DPP, ex p Kebeline* [2000] 2 AC 326; and *Re Kincaid's Application* [2007] NIQB 26, para 19*ff.* But note that the approach of the courts may be different where an application for judicial review is made in respect of a decision taken by an individual whom the Attorney General has appointed to, for instance, inquire whether a public body has interfered with the due administration of justice: see *Re Downes' Application* [2007] NIQB 40, para 10(viii).

[72] See [6.10]–[6.11].

[73] See, most recently, *Huang v Secretary of State for the Home Department* [2007] 2 AC 167. And for a survey of some of the earlier judicial opinions see *Department for Social Development v MacGeagh* [2006] NI 125, 136–8, paras 32–6, Kerr LCJ.

[74] On the relevance of the separation of powers to judicial review more generally see [1.03] and [1.05].

[75] Human Rights Act 1998, s 3; and, eg, *Ghaidan v Mendoza* [2004] 2 AC 557.

security considerations. Matters of national security were previously and *par excellence* regarded as non-justiciable and the courts accorded the executive an absolute discretion in the area.[76] More recent case law has, however, seen an acceptance that decisions of ministers should now be subject to judicial review.[77] While any such review will typically be linked to a presumption in favour of restraint[78] (which presumption may be reflected in, for instance, lessened procedural protections[79]), the courts accept that some decisions, for instance a deportation decision that has implications for an individual's right to life or general well-being, are demanding of closer scrutiny.[80] Judicial consideration of the rights of individuals has also resulted in courts in England and Wales examining closely the effect of control orders that limit the movements of suspected terrorists.[81]

[4.19]   Much of the impetus for this move towards reviewability has its origins in ECHR case law, which requires that national security considerations are balanced against the rights of individuals (the requirement also underpins aspects of EU law[82]). Where the rights in issue are found in Article 2 ECHR (life) and/or Article 3 ECHR (prohibition of torture), judicial scrutiny should be more exacting given the absolute nature of those rights.[83] However, even where absolute rights are not in issue, judicial scrutiny of decisions may still be necessary to ensure compliance with fair trial guarantees in Article 6 ECHR (that is, where an individual's 'civil rights' within the autonomous meaning of the ECHR are affected by a decision[84]). This is a point that previously took form around government use of conclusive evidence certificates that confirmed that a particular decision—for instance, not to award a contract to a particular individual—had been taken for purposes of safeguarding national security or of protecting public safety or public order.[85] Such certificates had the effect of preventing tribunals and other bodies from questioning the validity of the certificate[86] and, while the decision to issue the certificate was amenable to judicial review, the High Court tended to focus on whether there was evidence of bad faith on the part of the decision-maker rather than whether there had been a failure, for instance, to take account of relevant considerations.[87] This limited approach to judicial review, coupled with the absence of any subsequent role for tribunals, was criticised by the ECtHR as contrary not just to the Article 6 ECHR right of access to a court but also to the Article 13 ECHR right to an effective remedy.[88] Legislation that permits national security certificates to be issued therefore now often provides for a means to challenge certificates before specially constituted

---

[76]   *The Zamora* [1916] 2 AC 77.

[77]   See *Secretary of State for the Home Department v Rehman* [2003] 1 AC 153, 187, para 31, Lord Steyn.

[78]   *Secretary of State for the Home Department v Rehman* [2003] 1 AC 153, 187, para 31, Lord Steyn; and, eg, *Re Scappaticci's Application* [2003] NIQB 56, para 18.

[79]   See, by analogy, *Re Shuker's Application* [2004] NI 367.

[80]   *Secretary of State for the Home Department v Rehman* [2003] 1 AC 153, 193, para 54, Lord Hoffmann.

[81]   Eg, *Secretary of State for the Home Department v E* [2007] EWCA Civ 459 and [2007] UKHL 47. See too *Home Sec v JJ* [2007] UKHL 45 and *Home Sec v MB* [2007] UKHL 46.

[82]   See, eg, Case 222/84, *Johnston v Chief Constable of the Royal Ulster Constabulary* [1986] ECR 1651.

[83]   See, eg, *Chahal v UK* (1996) 23 EHRR 413 (re: deportation orders). On absolute rights see [1.21].

[84]   On the meaning of 'civil rights' see [7.14].

[85]   See, most famously, *Tinnelly & McElduff v UK* (1999) 27 EHRR 249 (certificate issued under s 42 of the Fair Employment (Northern Ireland) Act 1976).

[86]   See, eg, *R v Secretary of State, ex p Devlin*, 6 September 1995, unreported.

[87]   See *R v Secretary of State, ex p Gilmore*, 10 April 1987, unreported. On bad faith see [5.47]–[5.48]; and on relevancy see [5.40]–[5.43].

[88]   Eg, *Tinnelly & McElduff v UK* (1999) 27 EHRR 249; and *Devenney v UK* [2002] 35 EHRR 24.

tribunals[89]; and more general changes in the judicial review case law have reflected the need for more demanding scrutiny to be available on a case-by-case basis.[90]

Law, Politics, and 'Soft-edged' Review

[4.20]   One further tool that reflects the context-sensitive nature of judicial review is the so-called 'soft-edged' standard of review. This standard, which is founded on the assumption that there will sometimes be 'a higher degree of knowledge and expertise on the part of the decider' and that the courts should defer to that knowledge 'so long as the [decision is taken] in accordance with the proper principles',[91] is used by the courts when they consider that judicial restraint would be appropriate. The standard thus corresponds, in an accentuated form, to the orthodox understanding that courts, on an application for judicial review, are not concerned with the merits of a decision and that they should grant a remedy in respect of a substantive choice only where the decision is perverse or of such a kind that no reasonable decision-maker could have taken it (viz *Wednesbury* unreasonableness and the distinction between 'review' and 'appeal'[92]). The standard has been used in England and Wales in the context of challenges to decisions of economic 'policy',[93] and the Northern Ireland courts have also drawn upon it in cases that have been taken to involve challenges to 'political' decisions. Many of these cases have arisen in the context of the implementation of the Belfast Agreement,[94] where the courts have emphasised that they do not wish to step outside 'their proper function of review'.[95] The soft-edged standard has thus been invoked and/or referred to where challenges have been made to: the Secretary of State's assessment of the state of the IRA ceasefire[96]; the decision of First Minister not to nominate Sinn Féin Ministers to meetings of the North/South Ministerial Council[97]; and the Secretary of State's decision as to the appropriate date for Assembly elections in Northern Ireland.[98] The essence—though not the language—of the standard has recently also been apparent in an application for judicial review that challenged the Secretary of State's decision to appoint two members of the Loyal Orders to the Parades Commission.[99]

[89] See, eg, Northern Ireland 1998, ss 90–92 and Sch 11 (discrimination certificates issued by the Secretary of State can be challenged before the tribunal established under s 91); and Freedom of Information Act 2000, ss 18, 23–4 and 60 (national security certificates issued under ss 23 and 24 can be challenged before the Information Tribunal; although note also that some certificates may be issued under s 53 of the 2000 Act, which are not open to challenge before the Information Tribunal and in respect of which the remedy is judicial review).

[90] For analysis see *Norman Baker MP v Secretary of State for the Home Department* [2001] UKHRR 1275.

[91] *Re Williamson's Application* [2000] NI 281, 303–4, Carswell LCJ.

[92] See, on *Wednesbury*, [6.05]–[6.11]; and on the distinction between review and appeal, [1.05].

[93] Eg, *R v Secretary of State for the Environment, ex p Nottinghamshire CC* [1986] AC 240, and *R v Secretary of State for the Environment, ex p Hammersmith LBC* [1991] 1 AC 521, where the courts used what is sometimes referred to as the 'super-*Wednesbury*' test in respect of national economic policy decisions.

[94] See further G Anthony, 'Public Law Litigation and the Belfast Agreement' (2002) 8 EPL 401.

[95] *Re Williamson's Application* [2000] NI 281, 304, Carswell LCJ.

[96] *Re Williamson's Application* [2000] NI 281, 303–4, Carswell LCJ.

[97] *Re De Brun and McGuinness's Application* [2001] NIQB 3.

[98] *Re Robinson's Application* [2001] NIQB 49.

[99] *Re Duffy's Application* [2006] NICA 28(1), para 40, Kerr LCJ: 'the decision considered in this case was *par excellence* a political one. Regrettably, it appears that there is still a widespread misconception that the merits of such a decision fall under scrutiny where a judicial review challenge is made. It is important that this misconception be dispelled. The courts may only entertain a challenge to a decision such as that taken by the Secretary of State on well-established judicial review grounds. I am not concerned with the wisdom of the decision made—either on political grounds or otherwise. The role of the courts is to examine the procedures by which the decision has been made and the rationality (in the legal context) of the decision. It goes no further.'

[**4.21**]   Soft-edged review, as with justiciability and reviewability, is consonant with the need for judges to recognise that there are constitutional limits to the role of the courts and to ensure that those limits are meaningful in practice. It is, however, a standard that is also open to variable application and inconsistency in judicial reasoning, particularly as its existence is founded upon an assumed distinction between law and politics or between issues that are suited to judicial control and those that are not (so-called matters of 'policy'[100]). Individual judges may, in short, have different opinions as to whether a case raises issues of law or issues of politics, and the extent to which a decision may be susceptible to review will be determined accordingly.[101] In other words, while judicial acceptance that a decision raises issues of law will allow the court to review the decision with reference to the requirements of legality, relevancy, reasonableness, propriety of purpose, and so on, the understanding that a decision is one for political value judgment will result in the exercise of judicial self-restraint. The likelihood of success in an application for judicial review may thus be crucially affected by the answer that the court gives to the prior question of where a decision falls relative to the law/politics divide.

POWERS, DUTIES, AND DISCRETION

[**4.22**]   Applications for judicial review will often centre on the lawfulness of a decision-maker's exercise of discretion (discretion here denoting the power lawfully to choose between different courses of action/inaction). The discretion, which will have been given to the decision-maker by statute, will typically take the form of a statutory power to act in a particular way, although it may also exist in a statutory duty (see [4.26]–[4.28]). In terms of the grounds of illegality, substantive review, and procedural impropriety, an applicant may thus argue that the decision-maker has misunderstood the nature of their discretion (illegality), exercised their discretion in a way that is unreasonable or disproportionate (substantive review), or exercised their discretion without having due regard for the rules of fairness or some other procedural requirement that is specified in statute (procedural impropriety). Where such arguments are made, much will depend on how the courts choose to interpret the legislation that underpins the discretion. Courts can, for instance, adopt literal or purposive approaches to statutory interpretation (among others),[102] and the approach adopted in any given case will be determined by judicial perception of the nature of legislation[103] and of the context to the dispute (as well as by overarching considerations of the constitutional role of the courts). A court may therefore choose: to read a power into legislation where that power can be said to be reasonably incidental to the statute's existing powers[104]; to read words 'out' of a statute to ensure

---

[100]   On 'policy' see [6.03]. But for an alternative use of the term—viz in the context of decision-makers adopting policies to guide them in the exercise of their discretion—see [5.52].

[101]   Compare and contrast, eg, the decisions of the High Court and the Court of Appeal in *Re Duffy's Application*, which concerned the lawfulness of the appointment to the Parades' Commission of two members of the loyal orders: see [2006] NIQB 31 (decision unlawful) and [2006] NICA 28 (appeal allowed).

[102]   See [1.25]–[1.27].

[103]   *McEldowney v Forde* [1970] NI 11, 48, Lord Pearce.

[104]   *Re Northern Ireland Human Rights Commission* [2002] NI 236 (House of Lords reading ss 69–71 of the Northern Ireland Act 1998 as giving the Northern Ireland Human Rights Commission an implied power to intervene on points of human rights law in judicial proceedings).

that the supremacy of EU law is unaffected[105]; to give words their broader meaning where this enables two decision-makers to exercise their powers in a complementary fashion that is consistent with the intention of the legislation[106]; to find that the wider statutory context of a provision does not require that the decision-maker give effect to a procedural provision contained in the statute[107]; and to conclude that a power to act in a particular way must be provided for in express terms or exist by way of necessary implication.[108] Where an application for judicial review is made under the Human Rights Act 1998, the courts must, moreover, attempt, 'so far as it is possible to do so', to construe powers in legislation as compatible with the provisions of the ECHR that have effect under the Act.[109]

Powers and Duties

[**4.23**]   Legislation will ordinarily be read as granting a decision-maker a statutory power to do something or not to do something where it uses permissive terms such as 'may' or 'as the decision-maker considers appropriate' (the permissive is to be contrasted with the mandatory 'shall'[110]). Where permissive terms are interpreted as giving the decision-maker wide discretionary powers, this will reduce the scope for judicial intervention, particularly on the ground of substantive review (save where there is, for instance, bad faith[111]). The separation of powers doctrine entails that, where the legislature

---

[105] *Perceval-Price v Department of Economic Development* [2000] NI 141 (Court of Appeal isolated and disapplied the words 'other than service of a person holding a statutory office' in s 1(9) of the Equal Pay Act (Northern Ireland) 1970 and art 82(2) of the Sex Discrimination (Northern Ireland) Order 1976, SI 1976/1042 (NI 15), for reasons of ensuring that the legislation complied with Art 141 (ex 119) EC).

[106] *Re Shields' Application* [2003] NI 161 (RUC Force Order, which had been made by the Chief Constable pursuant to s 19 of the Police (Northern Ireland) Act 1998 and which laid down criteria for promotion, was challenged as ultra vires for the reason that promotions were to be made in accordance with regulations made by the Secretary of State under the Police (Northern Ireland) Act 1998, s 25: held that the Order made by the Chief Constable did not conflict with the regulations made by the Secretary of State but rather supplemented them and that the legislation should be read as permitting the Secretary of State to lay down important ground rules which would then be supplemented by measures of the kind introduced by the Chief Constable).

[107] *Robinson v Secretary of State for Northern Ireland* [2002] NI 390 (House of Lords held that it had not been Parliament's intention to prevent the Northern Ireland Assembly from electing the First and Deputy First Ministers outside the six-week period specified for their election in the Northern Ireland Act 1998; and that, although the Act provided that the Secretary of State 'shall' call fresh Assembly elections in the event that the First and Deputy First Ministers were not elected within six weeks, the election of the Ministers outside that period was lawful and the Secretary of State had thereby also acted lawfully when proposing a delayed date for Assembly elections).

[108] *R v Secretary of State for the Home Department, ex p Leech (No 2)* ([1993] 4 All ER 539 (challenge to prison rules that permitted authorities to interfere with correspondence between prisoners and lawyers save where proceedings had already been initiated: held that the rules were ultra vires Prison Act 1952, s 47, as they impeded access to a lawyer for purposes of considering whether to bring proceedings and the Act did not provide for such interference either expressly or by necessary implication). Although, for some limits to the approach, see, eg, *R v Chief Constable of the RUC, ex p Begley* [1997] NI 278 (suspect had no common law fundamental right to have a solicitor present during police interviews; and the courts would not infer the right given Parliament's clear intention to exclude solicitors under the terms of Prevention of Terrorism (Temporary Provisions) Act 1989, s 14(1)).

[109] Human Rights Act 1998, s 3; and, eg, *Re King's Application* [2003] NI 43.

[110] Interpretation Act (Northern Ireland) 1954, s 38. And for the full range of statutory formulations and corresponding interpretive approaches see M Fordham, *Judicial Review Handbook*, 4th edn (Oxford, Hart Publishing, 2004) pp 745–59.

[111] *Ex p Lynch* [1980] NI 126, 133–4, quoting *Carltona v Commissioner of Works* [1943] 2 All ER 560, 564, Lord Greene MR; and *McEldowney v Forde* [1970] NI 11, 45, Lord Guest. On bad faith see [5.47]–[5.48].

entrusts a public authority with a decision-making power, the primary decision-making power rests with the authority and not with the courts.[112] In terms of the grounds for review, this may thus mean that the courts will rely upon the 'soft-edged' standard of review when a decision is taken to be one of 'policy' ([4.20]–[4.21]); and it may also lead the courts to conclude, given the context of a case, that not all of the grounds for review should be available and/or that restraint would be appropriate (see [4.16]–[4.17]). Under those circumstances, it may therefore be suggested that the decision-maker is taken to have an 'unfettered discretion',[113] although any understanding of power as unfettered is at the same time difficult to reconcile with the fundamental precept of the 'rule of law'.[114]

[4.24]   Permissive terms can, however, also be read more narrowly and the courts may, for instance, require that power is exercised reasonably and that all relevant considerations are taken into account.[115] Moreover, where fundamental rights are in issue (particularly absolute rights[116]), the common law and ECHR may subject an exercise of power to a test of 'anxious scrutiny' (the common law) and/or a test of proportionality (the ECHR).[117] In other circumstances, the courts may even read permissive terms as not importing discretion but rather as imposing a duty to act. Whether permissive terms will be read in this way will, of course, depend on context and, in particular, on whether the 'power' is to be exercised for the benefit of particular individuals and/or the wider public. As Earl Cairns LC stated in *Julius v Bishop of Oxford*:

> there may be something in the nature of the thing empowered to be done, something in the object for which it is to be done, something in the conditions in which it is to be done, something in the title of the person or persons for whose benefit the power is to be exercised, which may couple the power with a duty, and make it the duty of the person on whom the power is reposed, to exercise that power when called upon to do so.[118]

[4.25]   Recipients of statutory power may finally be under a number of common law duties in respect of the exercise/non-exercise of the power, and these duties continue to develop in the light of the ECHR (the recipient thus here retains discretion but must exercise it in the light of common law/ECHR obligations). Subject to context, these include:

---

[112] See *R v Secretary of State for the Home Department, ex p Brind* [1991] 1 AC 696, 757–8, Lord Ackner: 'Where Parliament has given to a minister or other person or body a discretion, the court's jurisdiction is limited, in the absence of a statutory right of appeal, to the supervision of the exercise of that discretionary power, so as to ensure that it has been exercised lawfully. It would be a wrongful usurpation of power by the judiciary to substitute its, the judicial view, on the merits and on that basis to quash the decision.' See further [1.03] and [1.05].

[113] See, eg, *Re Fulton's Application*, 1 September 2000, unreported, and *Re Corden's Application*, 29 September 2000, unreported.

[114] See *R v Tower Hamlets LBC, ex p Chetnik Developments Ltd* [1988] AC 858, 872, Lord Bridge: 'In a system based on the rule of law, unfettered governmental discretion is a contradiction in terms.'

[115] See *Secretary of State for Education and Science v Tameside MBC* [1977] AC 1014, 1047, Lord Wilberforce; and *R v Secretary of State for Trade and Industry, ex p Lonrho Plc* [1989] 1 WLR 525, 533, Lord Keith. On the different meanings of reasonableness see [6.05]–[6.11].

[116] On which see [1.21].

[117] See [6.10]–[6.11] (common law) and [6.18]–[6.28] (ECHR).

[118] (1880) 5 App Cas 214, 222, considered in, eg, *Re Croft's Application* [1997] NI 457, 466–7; *Johnston v Dept of Agriculture for Northern Ireland*, 7 December 1995, unreported; *Re Narain's Application*, 11 January 1991, unreported; and *City Brick and Terra Cotta Co Ltd v Belfast Corporation* [1958] NI 44, 76, Curran LJ.

the duty to consider whether to exercise the power[119]; the duty to act reasonably[120]; the duty to act in good faith[121]; the duty to act fairly[122]; the duty to act in the public interest[123]; the duty to avoid undue delay[124]; the duty to communicate a decision[125]; the duty to give reasons[126]; and the duty to act in a manner that is consistent with the purpose of the legislation[127] (which purpose may be apparent from the legislation or implied by judicial interpretation). This last duty entails not just that decision-makers understand the nature of the power and give effect to it (illegality as traditionally defined[128]) but also that they exercise the power for proper purposes.[129] Where a power is exercised for an improper purpose, this will be indicative of an abuse of power and/or an unreasonable use of the power. However, where the improper purpose is only one of several 'mixed purposes' and the true and dominant purpose is held to be lawful, the improper purpose may be regarded as incidental and the decision allowed to stand. The same 'dominant purpose' test may also apply where there are two purposes, one of which is lawful and the other not.[130]

Duties and Discretion

[4.26]   The existence of a statutory duty is typically signified by the use of mandatory language in a statute, for instance, the word 'shall'.[131] The basic distinction between a statutory power and a statutory duty lies in enforceability: while a statutory power need not be exercised should the recipient of the power decide not to exercise it (subject to arguments about its nature and context), a statutory duty must be performed.[132] Should a public authority therefore expressly refuse to discharge its duty and/or act in a manner that suggests non-compliance, an application for judicial review should typically seek an order of mandamus as the remedy most suited to ensuring that the decision-maker's obligations are met. An applicant may, depending on context, also seek damages for any loss they have suffered in consequence of the non-performance of the duty.[133]

[4.27]   Legislation can, however, also be read as including discretion as to how a duty is to be performed, and this may complicate the question of which—if, indeed, any—remedy is appropriate (on the converse circumstance where permissive terms may be read as imposing duties see [4.24]). Such an interpretation is most often given to legislation that

[119]   *R v Secretary of State for the Home Department, ex p Fire Brigades Union* [1995] 2 AC 513.
[120]   *Secretary of State for Education and Science v Tameside MBC* [1977] AC 1014, 1047, Lord Wilberforce.
[121]   *R (Hanna) v Ministry of Health and Local Government* [1966] NI 52, 58, Lowry J (citing *Board of Education v Rice* [1911] AC 179).
[122]   *R (Hanna) v Ministry of Health and Local Government* [1966] NI 52, 58, Lowry J (citing *Board of Education v Rice* [1911] AC 179). On the elements of fairness see ch 7.
[123]   *R v Tower Hamlets LBC, ex p Chetnik Devlopments* [1988] AC 858, 872, Lord Bridge.
[124]   *R v Secretary of State for the Home Department, ex p Phansopkar* [1976] QB 606.
[125]   *R (Anufrijeva) v Secretary of State for the Home Department* [2004] 1 AC 604.
[126]   *Re McCallion's Application* [2005] NICA 21; and [7.43]–[7.44].
[127]   See, eg, *Re De Brun and McGuinness's Application* [2001] NI 442.
[128]   *Council of Civil Service Unions v Minister for the Civil Service* [1985] AC 374, 408, Lord Diplock. See [5.01].
[129]   *Padfield v Minister of Agriculture, Fisheries and Food* [1968] AC 997; and see [5.44]–[5.46]
[130]   See, eg, *Re Kelly's Application* [2000] NI 103; and [5.45].
[131]   Interpretation Act (Northern Ireland) 1954, s 38; and see, eg, *Re Brownlee's Application* [1985] NI 339.
[132]   *R (G) v Barnet LBC* [2004] 2 AC 208, 219, para 12, Lord Nicholls.
[133]   On the remedies available on an application for judicial review see [3.72]–[3.80] and ch 8.

imposes obligations—sometimes called 'target duties'[134]—in relation to the provision of public services like policing, healthcare, housing, child protection, road safety, and so on.[135] While the use of mandatory language in such legislation reflects the social imperative of providing services to members of society, the courts are aware that public authorities may here have to make value judgements and that the courts should, for reasons of relative expertise, be slow to intervene in the decision-making process. This may be particularly so where a decision is concerned with spending priorities, as the courts accept that limited financial resources may mean that difficult discretionary choices must be taken in the performance of a statutory duty.[136] The courts may thus—though not always—accept that limited resources will result in a public authority reducing expenditure on services that it is under a duty to provide[137]; and they may on that basis decide either that the decision-maker has not acted unlawfully or, in the event that it has acted or will act unlawfully, grant a declaration in preference to an order of mandamus that may have the effect of dictating the financial priorities of the authority. Declarations may also be preferred in cases that are not centrally concerned with questions of resource allocation but in which the courts consider that an order of mandamus would nevertheless result in undue judicial interference in areas of decision-making better left to others.[138]

[4.28]   The courts may likewise be reluctant to make awards of damages where an individual argues that they have suffered loss as a result of discretionary choices made in the performance of a statutory duty.[139] For instance, where an action is framed as breach of statutory duty, existing case law indicates that the statutory duties in question may be read as owed not to specific individuals but rather to wider society.[140] This approach has

---

[134] See, eg, *Family Planning Association of Northern Ireland v Minister for Health, Social Services and Public Safety* [2005] NI 188, reading art 4 of the Health and Personal Social Services (Northern Ireland) Order 1972, SI 1972/1265 (NI 14), as imposing a target duty in respect of the provision of health services.

[135] See, eg, in respect of policing, *Re E's Application* [2004] NIQB 35, para 55, Kerr J: 'the various obligations imposed by [the Police (Northern Ireland) Act 2000] cannot be regarded as absolute in their terms . . . It is, of course, [an officer's]) general duty to fulfil the statutory obligations provided for and he may not refrain from doing so arbitrarily or capriciously. Where, however, as in this case, a judgment is made, in the interest of general public order throughout the community . . . it does not follow that breach of (the duty) is thereby automatically established.'

[136] See, eg, *R v Inner London Education Authority, ex p Ali* (1990) 2 Admin LR 822 (regarding the provision of educational facilities).

[137] Compare and contrast *R v Gloucestershire CC, ex p Barry* [1997] AC 584 (local authority that was assessing how to discharge its obligations to a chronically sick and disabled person was allowed to have regard to resource considerations when reaching its decision) and *R v East Sussex CC, ex p Tandy* [1998] AC 714 (authority that reduced the hours of home teaching provided for a child who suffered from ME could not, on the true construction of s 298 of the Education Act 1993, take into account resource considerations when assessing what was 'suitable education').

[138] See, eg, *Re McBride's Application (No 2)* [2003] NI 319 (Court of Appeal refusing to grant an order of mandamus in a case in which the Army Board had acted unlawfully in failing to discharge two soldiers who had been convicted of murder: while a declaration would issue, the mandatory order would be inappropriate as 'decisions on what is best for the Army and its soldiers are best left to the Army and it would be an unwise usurpation of power if the court were . . . to intervene by mandamus ([2003] NI 319, 366, para 52, McCollum LJ)).

[139] On the availability of damages as a remedy in judicial review see [8.21]–[8.29].

[140] See, eg, *X v Bedfordshire CC* [1995] 2 AC 633 (no private law duty owed to children under the Children and Young Persons Act 1969, the Child Care Act 1980, and the Children Act 1989); *O'Rourke v Camden LBC* [1998] AC 188 (no private law duty owed to the homeless under the Housing Act 1985); *Maye v Craigavon Borough Council* [1998] NI 103 (art 7(1) of the Litter (Northern Ireland) Order 1994, SI 1994/1896 (NI 10), which imposes a duty to keep roads free from litter, not imposed for the protection of a limited class of the public but rather for the benefit of the public at large); and *Metcalfe v Chief Constable of the RUC* [1995] NI 446 (exercise of DPP's powers under art 5(1) of the Prosecution of Offences (NI) Order 1972, SI 1972/538 (NI 1), could not give rise to a claim for damages because of 'compelling considerations rooted in the welfare of the whole community'). See further [8.26]–[8.27].

been particularly apparent in the context of social welfare schemes concerned with child abuse and housing, and the courts have emphasised that such legislative schemes are not intended to give rise to private law causes of action but that they instead sound in—and are thereby only actionable in—public law.[141] Moreover, where claims have been framed as negligence actions, the courts have here been reluctant to impose common law duties of care on public service providers, particularly where the exercise of discretion is said to involve matters of 'policy' (which are regarded as 'non-justiciable': see [4.15][142]). Although case law on negligence liability has become markedly more complex in recent years (particularly in child welfare cases),[143] the House of Lords has, in general, continued to emphasise that the interests of the wider public are better served where decision-makers are not made readily liable in damages.[144] Negligence actions that centre upon the exercise of discretion may therefore be struck out on the ground that the decision-maker does not owe a common law duty of care to the individual[145] (the point has added force where an action concerns the exercise/non-exercise of statutory powers as opposed to discretionary choices made in relation to statutory duties[146]). Claims may alternatively fail at the breach stage; that is, when the court considers the reasonableness of the decision-maker's actions/inactions.[147]

ERRORS OF LAW AND ERRORS OF FACT

[4.29]   Judicial review is concerned with the legality of decision-making processes and outcomes, not with their merits.[148] In constitutional terms, this distinction between legality and merits (or 'review' and 'appeal') is based on the understanding that it is not the function of the courts to ensure that a decision etc is objectively 'right', but rather that it is lawful. Questions of legality will, as such, ordinarily centre on whether the decision-maker has understood 'correctly the law that regulates his decision-making power and [given] effect to it',[149] and the courts have here developed an increasingly robust ultra vires doctrine under which any error of law made within a statutory framework by an inferior body or tribunal is, subject to very few exceptions, reviewable. However, of equal importance in terms of safeguarding the rule of law is the approach of the courts to errors of fact. Although the courts do not typically review for error of fact—such

---

[141]   *X v Bedfordshire CC* [1995] 2 AC 633 (child welfare legislation); and *O'Rourke v Camden LBC* [1998] AC 188 (homelessness legislation).

[142]   *Barrett v Enfield LBC* [2001] 2 AC 550.

[143]   See G Anthony, 'The Negligence Liability of Public Authorities: Was the Old Law the Right Law?' (2006) NILQ 409.

[144]   See [8.23]; and *Gorringe v Calderdale MBC* [2004] 1 WLR 1057 (highway authorities); *D v East Berkshire Community Health NHS Trust* (healthcare professionals who suspect parents of abusing their children) [2005] 2 AC 373; and *Brooks v Metropolitan Police Commissioner* [2005] 2 All ER 489 (police in their dealings with victims of crime).

[145]   See, eg, *D v East Berkshire Community Health NHS Trust* [2005] 2 AC 373; and *Brooks v Metropolitan Police Commissioner* [2005] 2 All ER 489.

[146]   Eg, *Stovin v Wise* [1996] AC 923; and *Gorringe v Calderdale MBC* [2004] 1 WLR 1057, 1067, para 32, Lord Hoffmann.

[147]   See *Barrett v Enfield LBC* [2001] 2 AC 550, 591, Lord Hutton.

[148]   *R v Secretary of State for Northern Ireland, ex p Finlay* [1983] 9 NIJB 1, 10, Hutton J; *Re Glor Na nGael's Application* [1991] NI 117, 129, Carswell J; and *Re Bow Street Mall's Application* [2006] NIQB 28, para 110 [sic], Girvan J.

[149]   *Council of Civil Service Unions v Minister for the Civil Service* [1985] AC 374, 408, Lord Diplock.

review is understood to have the potential to lead courts towards the constitutionally forbidden realm of an 'appeal'—it is accepted that some errors of fact should be regarded as a species of illegality (whether classified under that heading or under substantive review). The courts will thus review a decision: where there has been an error of precedent fact; where the decision-maker has failed to take into account all relevant considerations or has taken into account irrelevant considerations; where a decision has been reached on the basis of no evidence; and/or where there has been an error of material fact. The corresponding intensity of review will then depend on the context of the application for judicial review: while decisions taken in areas of wide discretion will prompt judicial restraint ([4.20]–[4.21]), decisions that have an impact on an individual's fundamental rights may be subject to 'anxious scrutiny'.[150]

Errors of Law

The *Anisminic* Principle

[**4.30**]   The authority that is most famously associated with the proposition that any error of law is judicially reviewable is *Anisminic Ltd v Foreign Compensation Commission*.[151] Prior to that case—which concerned the lawfulness of an administrative tribunal's determination about Anisminic Ltd's entitlement to compensation—the courts drew a distinction between errors of law that went to the jurisdiction of a decision-maker such as an inferior court or tribunal, and errors of law that were made within jurisdiction. Errors of law that went to jurisdiction had always been subject to review, as any error as to the nature of a decision-maker's power would, if unchecked, effectively allow the decision-maker to redraw the boundaries of its authority.[152] However, where an error of law was made within the decision-maker's jurisdiction, the approach of the courts was different and shaped by what was, in essence, a separation of powers argument. The courts here accepted that, where statute entrusted a body with a decision-making power, the decision-maker was entitled to make errors of law or of fact so long as those errors were made within their jurisdiction. The only exception to this rule was where there was an error of law on the face of the record, as the courts could in those circumstances intervene to quash decisions that were self evidently unlawful.[153]

[**4.31**]   Post-*Anisminic* any error of law is now regarded as going to jurisdiction, and the distinction between decisions within and without jurisdiction is redundant for the purposes of judicial review[154] (as too is 'error of law on the face of the record'[155]). Judicial review's central doctrine is, instead, the ultra vires doctrine which underpins most developments in judicial review (at least when proceedings concern the lawfulness

---

[150] See *R v Secretary of State for the Home Department, ex p Bugdaycay* [1987] AC 514, 531; and see [6.10]–[6.11].

[151] [1969] 2 AC 147.

[152] See, eg, *Re Doherty's Application* [1988] NI 14 (preconditions for the renewal of a licence under the Licensing Act (Northern Ireland) 1971 were not met and errors in respect of those preconditions went to jurisdiction).

[153] For consideration of error on the face of the record see *R v Secretary of State for Northern Ireland, ex p Quinn* [1988] 2 NIJB 10, 20, Carswell J.

[154] *R v Secretary of State for Northern Ireland, ex p Quinn* [1988] 2 NIJB 10, 20–21, Carswell J.

[155] *R v Hull University Visitor, ex p Page* [1993] AC 682, 701, Lord Browne-Wilkinson.

of decisions or other measures taken within the framework of statute[156]). This shift from jurisdiction to ultra vires has, among other things, also resulted in the law rejecting a distinction between errors of law that are 'void' and those that are merely 'voidable' (that is, made within jurisdiction). This is because the ultra vires doctrine entails that decision-makers must always be bound by the demands of legality (see [4.05]) and it is, in consequence, only when all of those demands are observed that a decision-maker 'is as much entitled to decide [a] question wrongly as it is to decide it rightly'.[157]

Courts of Law

[**4.32**]   One area of confusion in the post-*Anisminic* era has concerned the reviewability, for errors of law, of decisions of lower courts. While *Anisminic* was read as establishing that the jurisdictional distinction had been abolished in respect of the decisions of administrative tribunals and decision-makers, it was unclear whether it had also been abolished in respect of the decisions of lower courts such as coroner's courts, county courts, and magistrates' courts.[158] The confusion was caused in large part by influential dicta that suggested both that *Anisminic* was not intended to apply to lower courts[159] and that finality clauses in respect of the decisions of lower courts would limit judicial review to the previous jurisdictional approach[160] (although on the questionable constitutional value of finality clauses see [4.10]). While these dicta have never been formally rejected in subsequent case law, the greater weight of authority does, however, now indicate that decisions of lower courts are open to review on the basis of the extended ultra vires principle.[161] There have thus been cases concerning the decisions of coroner's courts,[162] county courts,[163] and magistrates' courts[164] in which the wider reading of the *Anisminic* principle has been either expressly or impliedly accepted.

---

[156]   On judicial review and non-statutory power see ch 2 and [4.06]–[4.08].

[157]   *Anisminic Ltd v Foreign Compensation Commission* [1969] 2 AC 147, 171, Lord Reid.

[158]   See, eg, *Re McColgan's Application* [1986] NI 370 (decision of a county court judge in a criminal cause); *Re J MCL's Application* [1986] NI 397 (decision of a county court judge in a civil matter); and *Re McLaughlin's Application*, 27 October 1989, unreported (decision of a county court judge in a civil matter).

[159]   *R v Belfast Recorder, ex p McNally* [1992] NI 217, 223*ff*, Lowry LCJ.

[160]   *Re A Company* [1981] AC 374, 382–3, Lord Diplock; and *R v Hull University Visitor, ex p Page* [1993] AC 682, 703, Lord Browne-Wilkinson.

[161]   See, eg, *Re Molloy's Application* [1998] NI 78, 86–7.

[162]   See, most famously, *R v Greater Manchester Coroner, ex p Tal* [1985] QB 67 (whether coroner had, among other things, erred in law in admitting hearsay evidence: application dismissed). And for instances of challenges to coroners' decisions in Northern Ireland see, eg *Re Northern Ireland Human Rights Commission's Application* [2002] NI 236 (whether coroner correct to rule that the Commission did not have the power to intervene in proceedings: application granted) and *Re Bradley's Application* [1995] NI 192 (whether coroner had erred in law by permitting the jury to reach a verdict that pointed towards a finding of justifiable homicide: application granted).

[163]   Eg, *Re PM's Application* [2007] NIQB 2 (whether a county court judge's order that documentation should be produced to a police officer was unlawful: application granted); *Re J's Application* [2004] NIQB 75 (challenge to judge's decision to grant a father direct, unsupervised access to his child: application dismissed); and *Re Fair Employment Commission for Northern Ireland's Application*, 30 November 1990, unreported (whether county court judge had, inter alia, acted unlawfully by failing to give sufficient reasons, pursuant to s 29(2) of the Fair Employment (Northern Ireland) Act 1976, for the finding that the Commission had not made out a case of discrimination: application granted).

[164]   *Neill v North Antrim Magistrates' Court* [1992] 4 All ER 846 (magistrate had erred in law in committing to trial on the basis of inadmissible evidence); *Re DPP's Application* [2007] NIQB 10 (whether a Youth Court's refusal to adjourn proceedings in an assault trial and its decision to dismiss all charges when the prosecution could not proceed should be quashed: application granted); *Re DPP's Application* [2007] NIQB 3 (whether a resident magistrate's refusal to adjourn proceedings at the request of the prosecution should be quashed for

[**4.33**]   This acceptance of *Anisminic* represents a further strengthening of the ultra vires doctrine,[165] although the corresponding case law has at the same time emphasised the need for caution when reviewing lower court decisions. The reason for this is simply that an absence of caution could result in the High Court being overwhelmed by applications for judicial review made by individuals who, certainly in the criminal context, would wish to 'put off the evil day'[166] (the so-called 'floodgates' argument). The House of Lords has thus emphasised that the High Court should grant leave to bring applications for judicial review in the criminal context only where the error of law is 'substantial' and might lead to 'demonstrable injustice' or might have 'substantial adverse consequences' for the defendant[167]; and case law on the review of decisions of coroner's courts has likewise emphasised that applications for judicial review will not automatically be granted merely because some error of law has been committed during an inquest.[168] The courts have, in similar vein, noted that judicial review is a discretionary remedy and that it will ordinarily not be available where the individual has an alternative remedy that provides a fuller and more effective means of recourse, for instance an appeal.[169]

[**4.34**]   One final point about lower courts is that statute may retain—and the higher courts recognise—the pre-*Anisminic* jurisdictional distinction for the purposes of damages actions against members of the judiciary. For instance, in *Neill v Wilson*[170] the issue was whether a resident magistrate could be sued for wrongful imprisonment by an individual who had been committed for trial in custody on the basis of inadmissible evidence. Under article 5 of the Magistrates' Courts (Northern Ireland) Order 1981[171] no action was to lie against a magistrate where an act was done 'with respect to any matter within his jurisdiction', and the High Court held that the admission of the evidence had here occurred within jurisdiction. Although the House of Lords had earlier quashed the committal on appeal in judicial review proceedings,[172] the High Court referred to dicta in other House of Lords judgments to the effect that the *Anisminic* principle did not

reasons of the resident magistrate's alleged failure to carry out a proper inquiry into the need for an adjournment: application granted); *Re Cunningham's Application* [2004] NI 328 (challenge to a resident magistrate's decision to remand the applicant in custody where the magistrate had failed to consider all arguments made in respect of the merit of continued detention: application granted); *Re Glen's Application* [2002] NIQB 61 (challenge to a resident magistrate's refusal to stay proceedings against the applicant where there had been a loss of evidence by the police: application dismissed); and *Re McFadden's Application* [2002] NI 183 (challenge to a resident magistrate's failure to give reasons for refusing to stay proceedings as contrary to Art 6 ECHR: application dismissed).

[165]   See *R v Bedwellty Justices, ex p Williams* [1997] AC 225, 232, Lord Cooke: '[O]ne can say . . . that the authorities now establish that the Queen's Bench Division of the High Court has normally in judicial review proceedings jurisdiction to quash a decision of an *inferior court*, tribunal or other statutory body for error of law, even though the error is neither apparent on the face of the record nor so serious as to deprive the body of jurisdiction in the original and narrow sense of power to enter on the inquiry and to make against persons subject to its jurisdiction the kind of decision in question' (emphasis added).

[166]   *Neill v North Antrim Magistrates' Court* [1992] 4 All ER 846, 857, Lord Mustill.

[167]   *Neill v North Antrim Magistrates' Court* [1992] 4 All ER 846, 857, Lord Mustill; and see also *R v Bedwellty Justices, ex p Williams* [1997] AC 225.

[168]   See, eg, *Re Bradley's Application* [1995] NI 192, 203, Carswell LJ, citing *R v Greater Manchester Coroner, ex p Tal* [1985] QB 67, 83.

[169]   *R v Bedwellty Justices, ex p Williams* [1997] AC 225, 235, Lord Cooke (although it was held in the instant case that judicial review was available). On alternative remedies and judicial review see [2.34]–[2.35].

[170]   [1999] NI 1.

[171]   SI 1981/1675 (NI 26).

[172]   *Neill v Northern Antrim Magistrates' Court* [1992] 4 All ER 846.

apply to the interpretation of legislation of the kind in issue.[173] It was thus only where acts were committed without jurisdiction that damages could sound,[174] and even then article 6 of the Magistrates' Courts (Northern Ireland) Order 1981 required proof of bad faith on the part of the magistrate.[175]

'Domestic' Decision-makers

[**4.35**]   The main exception to the *Anisiminic* principle is made when a decision-maker enjoys what may be termed a 'domestic' jurisdiction. 'Domestic' here denotes a set of rules, regulations, or arrangements that are internal to an institution or series of institutions and which are thereby distinct from the ordinary law of the land. While the courts will here review a decision to ensure that it is taken within jurisdiction in the pre-*Anisminic* meaning of that term,[176] the scope for review is thereafter limited, 'as the applicable law is not the common law . . . but a peculiar or domestic law of which the [decision-maker] is the sole judge . . . of which the courts have no cognisance'.[177] Examples of decision-makers with such jurisdiction include university visitors,[178] religious bodies,[179] and visitors to the Inns of Court.[180]

Errors of Fact

[**4.36**]   Courts are generally reluctant to become involved in assessing factual disputes on an application for judicial review, as the courts are centrally concerned with matters of legality that are typically understood to preclude the need for fact-finding.[181] Although the distinction between 'law' and 'fact' may not always be easy to make—for instance, are inferences drawn from established facts to be regarded as matters of law, matters of fact, or matters of mixed law and fact?[182]—the courts have emphasised that matters of fact are for the original decision-maker and that the courts should for that

---

[173] Namely *Re McC (A Minor)* [1985] AC 528, 546–7, Lord Bridge: 'I do not believe that the novel test of excessive jurisdiction which emerges from [*Anisminic*], however valuable it may be in ensuring that the supervisory jurisdiction of the superior courts over inferior tribunals is effective to secure compliance with the law and is not lightly to be ousted by statute, has any application whatever to the construction [of the governing legislation]' (here Magistrates' Courts Act (Northern Ireland) 1964, s 15).

[174] As in *Re McC (A Minor)* [1985] AC 528 (magistrates had power to try, convict, and sentence the respondent, but the power of sentence could be exercised only where the respondent had been informed of their right to legal aid; failure to give this information was thus in breach of a statutory condition precedent, and the magistrates had on the facts acted 'without jurisdiction or in excess of jurisdiction' within the meaning of the Magistrates' Courts Act (Northern Ireland) 1964, s 15).

[175] On bad faith see [5.47]–[5.48].

[176] *Re Perry's Application* [1997] NI 282 (challenge to a decision of the board of visitors of Queen's University of Belfast whereby it stated that it did not have jurisdiction to hear the applicant's complaint regarding a permanent ban on his employment in an academic post at the university: order of certiorari granted on appeal).

[177] *R v Hull University Visitor, ex p Page* [1993] AC 682, 700, Lord Browne-Wilkinson.

[178] *R v Hull University Visitor, ex p Page* [1993] AC 682.

[179] *R v Chief Rabbi, ex p Wachmann* [1992] 1 WLR 1036.

[180] *R v Visitors to the Inns of Court, ex p Calder* [1994] QB 1.

[181] *Re McGuigan's Application* [1994] NI 143.

[182] See further Lord Woolf, J Jowell, and A Le Sueur, *De Smith, Woolf, and Jowell's Principles of Judicial Review* (London, Sweet and Maxwell, 1999), pp 129–44.

reason be slow to intervene.[183] This approach, which is reflected in the traditionally narrow approach of the courts to discovery and cross-examination in review proceedings,[184] is of a more general importance, although it can be particularly pronounced where a matter is one of 'fact and degree'. A matter of degree is one upon which reasonable people may arrive at different conclusions given the same evidence and, as conclusions on such matters will often be reached by decision-makers who are more experienced on such matters than are judges, the courts accept that the decision-makers are better placed to make corresponding value judgements. So long as any final decision is not tainted by illegality, perversity, or procedural irregularity, it will thus stand.[185]

[**4.37**]   There are, however, four forms of error of fact that will attract judicial intervention, namely: error of precedent fact; relevancy; 'no evidence'; and error of material fact. The corresponding development of review for such errors has had an importance not just in terms of safeguarding common law understandings of the rule of law, but also in terms of ensuring that judicial review is compliant with various aspects of the ECHR.

Precedent Fact

[**4.38**]   An error of precedent fact is made when a decision-maker takes a decision in the absence of facts which must exist objectively before the decision maker has the power of decision under legislation (such facts were previously also described as 'jurisdictional',[186] although that term has fallen into disuse with the post-*Anisminic* demise of the jurisdictional approach to judicial review: see [4.30]–[4.31]). Review for error of precedent fact can, as such, be linked to the ground of illegality, as the courts are here enquiring whether the decision-maker has the power to make the decision that they have purported to make. The courts are thus not concerned with the decision-maker's evaluation of facts or the respective weight that has been given to a particular fact, but rather with the question whether the required facts exist so as to allow the decision-maker to exercise the power entrusted by the legislature. In the absence of the facts there can, in short, be no lawful exercise of the power.

[**4.39**]   Arguments about errors of precedent fact are relatively rare. However, where the issue arises in proceedings, the courts will scrutinise decisions closely as errors of precedent fact would, if unchecked, allow subordinate bodies effectively to assume power for themselves. In *Re Sherlock and Morris's Application*, Kerr J thus said that the court 'will exercise its own independent judgment where a precedent fact requires to be satisfied'[187];

---

[183] Eg, *Re O'Neill's Application* (1990) 3 NIJB 1, 29–30, Murray LJ, referring to Lord Brightman in *R v Hillingdon LBC, ex p Pulhofer* [1986] AC 484, 518: 'Where the existence or non-existence of a fact is left to the judgment and discretion of a public body and that fact involves a broad spectrum ranging from the obvious to the debatable to the just conceivable, it is the duty of the court to leave the decision of that fact to the public body to whom Parliament has entrusted the decision-making power save in a case where it is obvious that the public body, consciously or unconsciously, is acting perversely.'

[184] See [3.48]–[3.52] and [3.59]. But note too the more liberal approach heralded by *Tweed v Parades Commission for Northern Ireland* [2007] 1 AC 650.

[185] See *R v Barnet LBC, ex p Nilish Shah* [1983] 2 AC 309, 341, Lord Scarman: 'If [the decision-maker] gets the law right, or, as lawyers would put it, directs itself correctly in law, the question of fact . . . is for the authority, not the court, to decide. The merits of the application are for the [decision-maker] subject only to judicial review to ensure that the authority has proceeded according to the law.'

[186] For use of the term see, eg, *Re McManus' Application*, 4 May 1990, unreported.

[187] [1996] NIJB 80, 88, citing *R v Secretary of State ex p Onibiyo* [1996] 2 All ER 901, 912, Sir Thomas Bingham.

and in *Re Obidipe's Application*—which arose in the immigration context and where the precedent fact at issue was whether the applicant had illegally entered the UK—Girvan J suggested that the approach of the courts to precedent fact will be more demanding where fundamental rights are in issue.[188] While the court ultimately dismissed the application for judicial review, it thus emphasised that the decision-maker's reasonable belief that the applicant was an illegal entrant is not enough to establish the fact, which must instead be established with reference to the civil standard of proof. The court also stated that the standard of proof may be applied variably given the nature of the rights affected.[189]

Relevancy

[**4.40**]   Challenges to decisions on the basis of relevancy can be linked to either of the grounds of illegality or substantive review/unreasonableness.[190] Relevancy here refers to a situation where a decision-maker has failed to take into account all relevant considerations and/or to disregard irrelevant considerations when making the determination. Considerations for these purposes will ordinarily be identified expressly or impliedly in the statute that underpins the decision (illegality), although the courts will also intervene where there are 'matters so obviously material to a decision on a particular project that anything short of direct consideration of them . . . would not be in accordance with the intention of the Act'.[191] Challenges with reference to this latter kind of relevant consideration may thus sound in unreasonableness: the failure to take account of the considerations was so unreasonable that no reasonable authority could have acted in that way.[192]

[**4.41**]   The orthodox judicial approach to arguments of relevancy is one that (a) enquires whether all relevant considerations have been taken into account by the decision-maker and irrelevant ones ignored and, if so, (b) allows the decision to stand subject to arguments of unreasonableness, perversity, and so on.[193] The rationale for this approach is that it enables courts to avoid becoming involved in disputes about the respective weights given to relevant considerations, although it is an approach that is not without exception. For instance, the courts have long been willing to subject decisions that impact upon fundamental rights to a common law test of 'anxious scrutiny' where arguments of relevancy arise[194]; and the proportionality principle may also entail some modification of approach. The principle, which applies in Human Rights Act 1998 cases but which is of increasing importance in judicial review more generally,[195] requires that courts set a decision against

---

[188]   [2004] NIQB 77, considering *Khawaja v Secretary of State for the Home Department* [1984] 1 AC 74.

[189]   [2004] NIQB 77, para 7: 'It is not enough that the Immigration Officer reasonably believes that he is an illegal entrant if the evidence does not justify his belief. The appropriate standard of proof is the civil standard, the degree of probability being proportionate to the nature and gravity of the issue. In cases involving grave issues of liberty the degree of probability required would be high.' See also *Re Idris' Application* [2005] NIQB 74, para 7, Deeney J; and *Re Udu's Application* [2005] NIQB 81, para 11, Girvan J.

[190]   See *Re Friends of the Earth's Application* [2006] NIQB 48, para 18, Weatherup J.

[191]   *Re Duffy's Application* [2006] NICA 28(1), paras 13–14, Kerr LCJ, quoting *Creednz v Governor General* [1981] 1 NZLR 172, Cooke J, and *Re Findlay* [1985] AC 318, 333–4, Lord Scarman.

[192]   On unreasonableness see [6.05]–[6.11].

[193]   See further [5.40]–[5.43].

[194]   *R v Secretary of State for the Home Department, ex p Bugdaycay* [1987] AC 514.

[195]   On its status under the Human Rights Act 1998 see *R v Secretary of State for the Home Department, ex p Daly* [2001] 2 AC 532; and on its increasing influence in judicial review more generally see *Re McBride's Application* [2002] NIQB 29, and *Re McQuillan's Application* [2004] NIQB 50, para 38, Weatherup J. See further [6.18]–[6.28].

the interests affected by it and assess whether the decision-maker has struck the appropriate balance between the two.[196] Should the proportionality principle's influence on judicial review continue to grow, this would suggest that courts may have to ask not just whether all relevant considerations have been taken into account and so on, but also whether they have been reconciled in the balanced manner associated with proportionality review. However, to the extent that this perhaps posits increased judicial intervention, it may be that the scope for that intervention will be limited by judicial use of the 'discretionary area of judgment' doctrine that has been developed in tandem with the proportionality principle and which seeks to avoid undue judicial involvement in the decision-making process.[197]

'No Evidence'

[4.42] Decisions may also be challenged on the basis of the 'no evidence' rule.[198] This rule applies, at its highest, where a decision is unsupported by any evidence whatsoever, although it can also apply where it is argued that the existing evidence does not support the conclusion reached. A challenge of this latter kind would ordinarily be made on the ground of *Wednesbury* unreasonableness: that is, that the decision is so unreasonable that no reasonable authority that had cognisance of the evidence would have made the same decision.[199] Should a challenge be made with reference to the proportionality principle, this may, however, require the courts to lower the threshold for intervention, albeit subject to arguments about the 'discretionary area of judgment'.[200]

Error of Material Fact

[4.43] It is finally possible to challenge a decision as vitiated by an error of material fact. Such errors are made where there is 'misunderstanding or ignorance of an established and relevant fact' and/or where the decision-maker acts 'upon an incorrect basis of fact'.[201] The prospect of review for such error is sometimes taken as indicative of the increasingly expansive nature of judicial review,[202] although it is at the same time unclear quite how far it entails closer judicial involvement in disputed questions of fact. More expansive authorities have, for instance, suggested that there is now a 'wrong factual basis' doctrine in administrative law[203] and that judicial intervention is justified where

---

[196] *Re Conor's Application* [2005] NI 322, 329, para 27.

[197] For application of the doctrine see, eg, *Re Stewart's Application* [2003] NI 149, 159, para 26 (planning authorities enjoy a 'discretionary area of judgment' when setting the property rights of individuals against the wider public interests in permitting the appropriate development of property); and see further [6.25]–[6.26].

[198] See further W Wade and C Forsyth, *Administrative Law*, 9th edn (Oxford, Oxford University Press, 2004) pp 272–3.

[199] See [6.05]–[6.11].

[200] See [6.25]–[6.26].

[201] *Secretary of State for Education and Science v Tameside MBC* [1977] AC 1014, 1030, Lord Scarman, and 1047, Lord Wilberforce; and see, eg, *Re Treacy's Application* [2000] NI 330, 359.

[202] See *Re Department of the Environment's Application* [2005] NI 119, 134, para 39, Weatherup J: 'With the expanding scope of judicial review the modern approach to a case where it appeared to the applicant that there had been a breach of planning control might be to regard the decision to issue a notice in circumstances where there was no breach of planning control as liable to be set aside on the ground of material error of fact.'

[203] W Wade and C Forsyth, *Administrative Law*, 9th edn (Oxford, Oxford University Press, 2004) p 278, citing *R v Criminal Injuries Compensation Board ex p A* [1999] 2 WLR 974, and *R (Alconbury) v Secretary of State* [2003] 2 AC 295, 321, para 53, Lord Slynn.

the error is material to the decision and where it results in 'unfairness' to the applicant ('fairness' being said to be a matter of law).[204] However, a more orthodox approach regards error of material fact merely as an aspect of relevancy and holds that the courts should intervene only where the decision-maker has failed to take a material consideration into account.[205] Any scope for further judicial involvement is, from this perspective, limited to that set by *Wednesbury* unreasonableness or, depending on context, by the proportionality principle and the discretionary area of judgment doctrine.[206]

[**4.44**]   Notwithstanding this uncertainty about its implications, error of material fact has assumed a central—though not uncontested—position in case law regarding rights of access to independent and impartial tribunals under Article 6 ECHR.[207] Article 6 ECHR requires that individuals whose civil rights are in issue have access to courts or tribunals with 'full jurisdiction' in a matter,[208] and case law in Northern Ireland and in England and Wales has raised the question whether the High Court has such jurisdiction given the nature of the traditional grounds for review.[209] In holding that the High Court has had the requisite jurisdiction, the House of Lords and the Northern Ireland courts have emphasised that judicial review on ordinary grounds was sufficient for the purposes of Article 6 ECHR as it allows the courts to, among other things, review decisions for error of fact.[210] On the other hand, the cases in question were underwritten by considerations of the separation of powers,[211] and some subsequent case law has since distinguished the existing authorities when finding that Article 6 ECHR has been violated precisely because the error of fact doctrine does not enable the High Court to substitute its own findings of fact for those of the original decision-maker.[212] Error of material fact may therefore be poised for further—and necessary—development.

CONCLUSION

[**4.45**]   This chapter has introduced the grounds for judicial review. Five points can be made by way of summary:

i.   The grounds for review, which overlap with one another, are developed in the light of the common law and the demands of EU law and the ECHR. They are, in that sense, in a continuing state of evolution.

---

[204] This was the approach of the Court of Appeal in England and Wales in *E v Secretary of State for the Home Department*[2004] 2 WLR 1351 (immigration appeal tribunal erred by refusing to have regard to evidence which had not been before the tribunal at the time of the hearing but which had come to light before it made its decision).

[205] See, eg, *Re D's Application*, [2003] NIJB 49, 57–8, para 40, Coghlin J, citing, among others, *R (Thallon) v Department of the Environment* [1982] NI 26, 49.

[206] [6.25]–[6.26].

[207] See [7.72]–[7.74]

[208] *Bryan v UK* (1996) 21 EHRR 342.

[209] See *R (Alconbury) v Secretary of State for the Environment, Transport and the Regions* [2003] 2 AC 295; *Runa Begum v Tower Hamlets LBC* [2003] 2 AC 430; and *Re Foster's Application* [2004] NI 248.

[210] See *R (Alconbury) v Secretary of State for the Environment, Transport and the Regions* [2003] 2 AC 295, 320–22, paras 51–3, Lord Slynn; and *Re Foster's Application* [2004] NI 248, 261, para 47, Kerr J.

[211] See further [7.71], considering *R (Alconbury) v Secretary of State for the Environment, Transport and the Regions* [2003] 2 AC 295 and *Runa Begum v Tower Hamlets LBC* [2003] 2 AC 430.

[212] *Re Bothwell's Application* [2007] NIQB 25, para 21 ff; and *Tsfayo v UK*, App 60860/00, 14 November 2006.

ii. The common law places a particular emphasis on the 'rule of law' and the need to prevent the 'abuse of power' (see [4.04]–[4.09]). Developments in judicial review that relate to decisions taken within the framework of statute are thus underscored by an enhanced ultra vires doctrine that no longer distinguishes between errors of law that go to the jurisdiction of the decision-maker and those that are made within jurisdiction. Any error of law is, subject to only very few exceptions, open to challenge (see [4.30]–[4.35]).

iii. The grounds for review are, at the same time, context-sensitive. While the reach of the grounds has thus expanded, the courts will exhibit self-restraint depending on the nature of the dispute before them. Paradigm examples of cases in which restraint is considered appropriate are 'political' disputes and those that raise national security considerations (see [4.14]–[4.21]).

iv. The courts will also exhibit more or less restraint depending on the degree of discretion that a decision-maker has under statute. Although the extent of discretion is largely a function of judicial interpretation of the statute, the existence of a statutory 'power' will typically be taken to indicate that a decision-maker should be free lawfully to choose between different outcomes. Where a statute in turn imposes a 'duty', this will point more towards an obligation on the decision-maker to act in a particular way. The courts do, however, also accept that some statutory duties can import an element of discretion and they may for that reason be reluctant to interfere with decisions, acts, or failures to act (see [4.22]–[4.28]).

v.   Judicial review is concerned with the legality of decision-making processes and outcomes, not with their merits. While the courts will thus review decisions or other measures for errors of law, they have historically been more reluctant to review for error of fact. There are, however, some important exceptions to this rule, and these can be linked to a further strengthening of the 'rule of law'. The courts will thus review on the basis of 'precedent fact', 'relevancy', 'no evidence', and 'error of material fact'. Review for 'error of material fact' potentially also has a particular significance in respect of ensuring common law compliance with the demands of Article 6 ECHR (see [4.36]–[4.44]).

5

Illegality

INTRODUCTION

[5.01]   This chapter considers illegality as a ground for judicial review. Illegality has been defined to mean 'that the decision-maker must understand correctly the law that regulates his decision-making power and must give effect to it'.[1] At its most obvious, this ground thus entails that a decision or other measure may be challenged where it has no legal basis (for example, where the decision-maker did not have the power that it purported to have[2]); and it also means that a decision-maker's failure to act may be challenged when the decision-maker is under a statutory duty to act in a particular way.[3] Moreover, where a decision-maker has a statutory power and/or is entitled to make discretionary choices as to the performance of a statutory duty, it will act unlawfully if the power is exercised or the duty performed in a manner that is contrary to any one of a number of common law requirements. Decisions and other measures—which can here include primary Acts of the Westminster Parliament—may also be challenged on the ground that they are contrary to relevant provisions of EU law and/or the ECHR.

[5.02]   The chapter begins with a section that considers the importance of a number of 'constitutional statutes' that can found challenges not only to the decisions etc of public authorities, but also to Acts of the Westminster Parliament and of the Northern Ireland Assembly (viz, the European Communities Act 1972, the Human Rights Act 1998, and the Northern Ireland Act 1998). It next considers the core requirements of legality that apply to subordinate legislation; and it then outlines the range of related common law constraints that govern the exercise of discretion by statutory bodies, local authorities, government departments, and other 'public' authorities.[4] The conclusion summarises the main points in each section.

[5.03]   One further point by way of introduction is that the grounds for review—illegality, substantive review, and procedural impropriety—overlap with one another and should not be regarded as distinct.[5] This therefore means that some of the developments discussed in this chapter are also of relevance to the other grounds for review and could alternatively be characterised as matters of substantive review or procedural impropriety.

---

[1] *Council of Civil Service Unions v Minister for the Civil Service* [1985] AC 374, 408, Lord Diplock.

[2] See, eg, *Omagh District Council's Application* [2007] NIQB 61 (planning policy introduced by the Department of Regional Development deemed unlawful, as the Department had purported to act in an area that fell, as per the Planning (Northern Ireland) Order 1991, SI 1991/1220 (NI 11), within the responsibility of the Department of the Environment).

[3] On powers and duties see [4.22]–[4.28].

[4] On 'public authorities' see ch 2.

[5] See, eg, *Boddington v British Transport Police* [1999] 2 AC 143, 152, Lord Irvine LC.

The point is true not only in respect of the various common law requirements, but also of some of the requirements associated with the European Communities Act 1972 and the Human Rights Act 1998.

'CONSTITUTIONAL STATUTES' AND ILLEGALITY

[5.04]   The term 'constitutional statute' is used by the courts to identify those statutes that the common law regards as qualitatively different from, and superior to, other primary Acts of the Westminster Parliament.[6] The term was first used, at least within its present meaning,[7] to describe the European Communities Act 1972, which gives effect to EU law,[8] although it has since also been used to describe the Human Rights Act 1998[9] and the Northern Ireland Act 1998.[10] In practical terms, such higher order statutes are distinguishable from other Acts on the ground that constitutional statutes are not subject to the ordinary rules of implied repeal,[11] whereas other statutes are. Constitutional statutes can, instead, be repealed only where the Westminster Parliament uses 'express words in the later statute, or . . . words so specific that the inference of an actual determination to effect the result contended for [is] irresistible'.[12] This approach signifies that the Acts contain values and principles that the courts regard as of particular democratic importance because they (a) condition the legal relationship between citizen and State in some general, overarching manner and/or (b) enlarge or diminish the scope of fundamental constitutional rights.[13] By placing such statutes at one remove from the ordinary rules on implied repeal the courts have thus created an open category of statute[14] in which questions of illegality can assume an added constitutional significance.

[5.05]   The constitutional statutes of most importance to judicial review in Northern Ireland are the European Communities Act 1972, the Human Rights Act 1998, and the Northern Ireland Act 1998.[15] These Acts not only impose a series of obligations on a wide range of public authorities and decision-makers; they also permit the courts to review primary Acts of the Westminster Parliament and the Northern Ireland Assembly for compatibility with EU law and the ECHR (Acts of the Assembly can be challenged on other grounds too[16]: see [5.23]–[5.24]). While it is perhaps misleading to speak of the Westminster Parliament acting 'illegally' in this context—constitutional orthodoxy would hold that EU law and the ECHR bind Parliament only insofar as Parliament has

---

[6]   See [1.28]–[1.34].

[7]   See, eg, as an historical forerunner *Belfast Corporation v OD Cars* [1960] AC 490, 517, Viscount Simmonds, describing the Government of Ireland Act 1920 as a 'constitutional Act'.

[8]   See *Thoburn v Sunderland CC* [2003] QB 151. See too *Levi Strauss v Tesco Stores* [2000] EWHC 1556.

[9]   *Re Sinn Féin's Application* [2003] NIQB 27, para 31, Coghlin J.

[10]   *Robinson v Secretary of State for Northern Ireland* [2002] NI 390, 402, para [25], Lord Hoffmann; and, eg, *Re McComb's Application* [2003] NIQB 47.

[11]   Viz the rule that where two statutes conflict with one another, the latter statute is taken to have repealed impliedly the earlier one: see *Ellen Street Estates v Minister of Health* [1934] 1 KB 590, 597, Maugham LJ.

[12]   *Thoburn v Sunderland CC* [2003] QB 151, 187.

[13]   See *Thoburn v Sunderland CC* [2003] QB 151, 186, Laws LJ.

[14]   *Watkins v Home Office* [2006] 2 AC 395, 419, para 62, Lord Rodger.

[15]   Other examples include the Magna Carta, the Bill of Rights 1688, the Act of Union, the Reform Acts, the Scotland Act 1998, and the Government of Wales Act 1998: see *Thoburn v Sunderland CC* [2003] QB 151, 186, Laws LJ.

[16]   Northern Ireland Act 1998, s 6.

bound itself under the terms of the European Communities Act 1972 and the Human Rights Act 1998[17]—it is axiomatic that Acts of the Assembly (and its predecessors), or Orders in Council made when the Assembly has been suspended,[18] can be challenged on vires grounds. Important questions do, however, here remain about whether the Assembly should simply be regarded as the constitutional equivalent of other recipients of delegated power such as statutory bodies and local authorities (see [5.24]).

The European Communities Act 1972

[5.06]   The key constitutional provisions of the European Communities Act 1972 are sections 2 and 3. Section 2(1) thus provides for the direct effect of EU law in the UK domestic system[19]; section 2(2), as read with Schedule 2, enables Her Majesty by Order in Council and designated Ministers or departments (which may include Northern Ireland Ministers and departments[20]) by regulation to make provision for the purpose of implementing EU law[21]; and section 2(4) imposes an interpretive obligation whereby all past and future legislation is to be read and given effect subject to the provisions of the European Communities Act 1972.[22] Section 3 then gives effect to the case law of the ECJ by requiring UK courts to determine all matters of EU law in accordance with that case law and, in the event that the meaning of EU law is unclear or there are questions as to its validity, by referring the matter to the ECJ in accordance with the Article 234 EC reference procedure.[23]

[5.07]   It has long been accepted that the combined effect of these provisions is the ascription of supremacy to EU law when it conflicts with domestic legislation, whether primary or subordinate in form and whether enacted prior or subsequent to the European Communities Act 1972.[24] The point famously came to the fore in the *Factortame* case when the House of Lords, on having made a reference to the ECJ, granted an injunction to prevent the Secretary of State enforcing the terms of the

---

[17] See [4.09].

[18] Northern Ireland Act 2000, repealed by the Northern Ireland (St Andrews Agreement) Act 2006 and the Northern Ireland (St Andrews Agreement) Act 2007.

[19] 'All such rights, powers, liabilities, obligations, and restrictions from time to time created or arising by or under the Treaties, and all such remedies and procedures from time to time provided for by or under the Treaties, as in accordance with the Treaties are without further enactment to be given legal effect or used in the United Kingdom shall be recognised and available in law, and be enforced, allowed and followed accordingly; and the expression "enforceable Community right" and similar expressions shall be read as referring to one to which this subsection applies.'

[20] Section 2(5); and Northern Ireland Act 1998, Sch 12, paras 1–11.

[21] 'Subject to Schedule 2 to this Act, at any time after its passing Her Majesty may by Order in Council, and any designated minister or department may by regulations, make provision—(a) for the purpose of implementing any Community obligation of the United Kingdom, or enabling any such obligation to be implemented, or of enabling any rights enjoyed or to be enjoyed by the United Kingdom under or by virtue of the Treaty to be exercised.' Sch 2 provides that s 2(2) cannot be used to impose or increase taxation, to enact retrospective legislation, to sub-delegate legislative power, or to create criminal offences.

[22] '. . . any enactment passed or to be passed, other than one contained in this Part of this Act, shall be construed and have effect subject to the foregoing provisions of this section.'

[23] 'For the purposes of all legal proceedings any question as to the meaning or effect of any of the Treaties, or as to the validity, meaning or effect of any Community instrument, shall be treated as a question of law (and, if not referred to the European Court, be for determination as such in accordance with the principles laid down by and any relevant decision of the European Court).'

[24] *A v Chief Constable of West Yorkshire* [2005] 1 AC 51, 57, para 9, Lord Bingham.

Merchant Shipping Act 1988.[25] While it was initially unclear how such judicial dis-application of 'subsequent' primary legislation could be reconciled with the doctrine of parliamentary sovereignty,[26] the description of the 1972 Act as a constitutional statute that is no longer subject to the ordinary rules of implied repeal has since given a greater coherence to the relationship between EU law and UK domestic law. The current under-standing is, in short, that Parliament remains finally sovereign in the sense that it can leg-islate expressly to repeal all or part of the European Communities Act 1972 but that the courts will, in the absence of that express repeal, continue to give effect to the 1972 Act, which incorporates a variety of enforceable rights and obligations. The result is that EU law derives its supremacy in the UK system from the common law and it is on that basis that the courts can review primary legislation for compatibility with EU law and the European Communities Act 1972.[27]

[5.08]   The corollary of the ascription of supremacy to EU law is that all decisions taken in areas governed by EU law—whether of a public law or a private law nature—must accord with relevant provisions of the EC Treaty and related measures (typically Directives, Regulations, and Decisions[28]), together with the case law of the ECJ. The institutional competences of the EU have recently expanded to include the areas of, among others, security and foreign policy,[29] but it is in the areas associated with the internal market that EU law will be likely to be of most relevance in the domestic courts. The internal market is, at core, concerned with the free movement of capital, goods, per-sons, and services,[30] although the EU has related competence in the areas of agriculture,[31] competition,[32] State aid,[33] the environment,[34] equal pay,[35] health and safety,[36] and social policy[37] (among others).[38] EU law has therefore recently been used in Northern Ireland courts to challenge: aspects of planning policy[39]; nationality requirements that govern eligibility for employment in certain public service posts[40]; the refusal to grant a road service licence to an individual for the purpose of providing a bus service[41]; the levels of pay for part-time tribunal chairpersons[42]; the failure of the UK government to introduce

---

[25]   See, eg, *R v Secretary of State for Transport, ex p Factortame Ltd (No 2)* [1991] 1 AC 603.

[26]   See W Wade, 'Sovereignty—Revolution or Evolution?' (1996) 112 LQR 568.

[27]   See further M Elliott, 'Embracing "Constitutional"' Legislation: Towards Fundamental Law?' (2003) 54 NILQ 25; and [1.29].

[28]   On which see Art 249 EC.

[29]   See P Craig and G de Búrca, *EU Law: Text, Cases and Materials*, 4th edn (Oxford, Oxford University Press, 2008) ch 1.

[30]   Principally, Arts 56–8 EC (capital); Arts 23–5 and 28–31 EC (goods); Arts 39–41 and 43–8 EC (persons); and Arts 49–50 EC (services).

[31]   Arts 32–8 EC.

[32]   Arts 81–2 EC.

[33]   Arts 86–9 EC.

[34]   Arts 6 and 174 EC.

[35]   Art 141 EC.

[36]   Art 190 EC.

[37]   Art 137 EC.

[38]   See further G Anthony, *EC Law for Northern Ireland Practitioners* (Belfast, SLS Legal Publications, 1999).

[39]   *Re Friends of the Earth's Application* [2006] NIQB 48.

[40]   *Re O'Connor's Application* [2005] NIQB 11 (application dismissed); *Re O'Boyle's Application* [1999] NI 126 (application dismissed); and *Re Colgan's Application* [1996] NI 24 (application granted).

[41]   *Re McParland's Application* [2002] NI 292.

[42]   *Perceval-Price v Department of Economic Development* [2000] NI 141.

legislation to implement the Working Time Directive in Northern Ireland law[43]; and public health legislation that placed limits on meat production.[44]

[5.09]   Where an argument of illegality is made with reference to EU law, the High Court must determine the matter in the light of its obligations under Article 10 EC (the so-called 'loyalty' clause).[45] These include the obligation to interpret national law to be consistent with non-directly effective EU Directives that have not been implemented in domestic law (or have been implemented incorrectly)[46]; the requirement that national courts refer matters of EU law to the ECJ in the event that the national court is uncertain as to the meaning or validity of EU law[47]; the requirement that national courts award damages to individuals for a 'sufficiently serious' breach of their EU law rights by any of the legislative, executive, or judicial branches of the State[48]; and the requirement that national courts give effect to the general principles of EU law such as proportionality, equality, legitimate expectation, and fundamental rights standards found in, among others sources, the ECHR.[49] This last obligation provides one example of how the grounds for judicial review can overlap with one another (see [5.03]), as a decision or other measure may be challenged as disproportionate vis-à-vis EU law and, on that basis, as ultra vires the European Communities Act 1972.[50] This obligation is also of relevance to the idea of 'spill-over', as it is sometimes argued that general principles of EU law that are not a part of the common law should be developed by the courts in parallel domestic cases that do not involve points of EU law.[51]

[5.10]   National courts are finally required to ensure that there is effective protection of EU law rights that are raised on an application for judicial review.[52] This obligation

[43] *Re Burns' Application* [1999] NI 175. On the failure to implement Directives see too *Re Seaport Investments Ltd's Application* [2007] NIQB 62 (the Environmental Assessment of Plans and Programmes Regulations (NI) 2004 had not correctly implemented Directive 2001/42 EC in domestic law).

[44] *Re Eurostock's Application* [1999] NI 13.

[45] 'Member States shall take all appropriate measures, whether general or particular, to ensure fulfilment of the obligations arising out of this Treaty or resulting from action taken by the institutions of the Community. They shall facilitate the Community's tasks. They shall abstain from any measure which would jeopardise the attainment of the objectives of the Treaty.'

[46] Known as the 'indirect effect' doctrine: see Case 14/83, *Von Colson v Land Nordrhein-Westfalen* [1984] ECR 1891, and Case C-106/89 *Marleasing SA v La Commercial Internacional de Alimentacion SA* [1990] ECR I-4153. And for acceptance of the doctrine by the House of Lords see *Webb v EMO Air Cargo (UK) Ltd (No 2)* [1995] 4 All ER 577.

[47] Article 234 EC, European Communities Act 1972, s 3, and RSC Ord 114. But see also Case 283/81, *Srl CILFI and Lanificio di Guvardo SpA v Ministry of Health* [1982] ECR 3415.

[48] Known as the 'state liability' doctrine: see *Re Burns' Application* [1999] NI 175. The leading EU cases are Cases C-6/90, *Francovich and Bonifaci v Italy* [1991] ECR I-5357; Joined Cases C-46 & 48/93, *Brasserie du Pêcheur SA v Germany, R v Secretary of State for Transport, ex p Factortame Ltd* [1996] 1 ECR 1029; Joined Cases C-178–179 & 188–190/94, *Dillenkofer v Germany* [1996] 3 CMLR 469; and Case C-224/01, *Köbler v Austria* [2003] ECR I-10239. See further [8.36]–[8.38].

[49] On the general principles of law see T Tridimas, *The General Principles of EC Law*, 2nd edn (Oxford, Oxford University Press, 2006), and P Craig, *EU Administrative Law* (Oxford, Oxford University Press, 2006).

[50] See, on substantive review, ch 6.

[51] On 'spill-over' see [1.18]. For an example of the courts refusing to apply a general principle of EU law—here the proportionality principle—outside the context of a question of EU law see *Re O'Boyle's Application* [1999] NI 126. But on the place of proportionality in domestic law see now [6.12]–[6.28].

[52] See, eg, Case 33/76, *Rewe-Zentralfinanz eG and Rewe-Zentral AG v Landwirtschaftskammer für das Saarland* [1976] ECR 1989; Case 47/76, *Comet v Produktschap voor Siergewassen* [1976] ECR 2043; Case 158/80, *Rewe Handelsgesellschaft Nord mbH v Hauptzollamt Kiel* [1981] ECR 1805; Case C-213/89, *R v Secretary of State for Transport, ex p Factortame* [1990] ECR I-2433; Case 326/88, *Anklagemyndigheden v Hansen & Sons I/S* [1990] ECR I-2911; and Case C271/91, *Marshall v Southampton and South West Hampshire Area Health Authority (No 2)* [1993] ECR I-4367. And see, in the Northern Ireland courts, *Johnston v Chief Constable of the RUC* [1998] NI 188.

sounds both at the interim stage in proceedings and at the end of proceedings should arguments of illegality be established. The nature of this obligation and the corresponding case law are considered in chapters three and eight.[53]

The Human Rights Act 1998

[**5.11**]   The Human Rights Act 1998, in contrast to the European Communities Act 1972 (as interpreted by the courts), does not enable the courts to disapply primary Acts of the Westminster Parliament. The 1998 Act, which does not have retrospective effect,[54] instead safeguards primary legislation by permitting courts only to make declarations that primary legislation is incompatible with the ECHR[55] (declarations do not have any effect on the force or validity of the legislation in respect of which they are made[56]). The Act does, however, at the same time include a number of provisions that have raised fundamental questions about the role of the courts in judicial review proceedings. Prominent among these is section 2, which obliges courts to 'take into account' ECHR case law and related general principles of law. While it is accepted that the section does not thereby impose a blanket obligation to give effect to the ECHR in cases under the Act,[57] it has been emphasised that departures from ECHR case law should be exceptional and that the courts 'should follow any clear and constant jurisprudence' of the ECtHR.[58] This has resulted in the courts giving fuller effect to, among other things, the proportionality principle when assessing whether primary legislation is compatible with the ECHR and when reviewing the legality of the actions/inactions of 'public authorities'.[59] This principle in turn requires courts to enquire whether a decision-maker has struck the appropriate balance between a decision and the rights affected by it,[60] and this has taken the courts beyond their traditional role in judicial review proceedings.[61] The courts have thus had to reconcile this (potentially) more intrusive role with the need for (appropriate) judicial self-restraint.[62]

Primary Legislation

[**5.12**]   Primary legislation for the purposes of the Human Rights Act 1998 is defined in section 21 (it includes Acts of the Westminster Parliament and prerogative Orders in Council but does not include Acts of the devolved legislatures or Orders in Council made at times when the Assembly or its predecessors have been suspended). Where an application for judicial review challenges the compatibility of primary legislation with the

---

[53] See [3.45]–[3.46] and [3.77]–[3.78]; and [8.32]–[8.39].
[54] Sections 7 and 22; and, eg, *R (Hurst) v London Northern District Coroner* [2007] 2 WLR 726; *Jordan v Lord Chancellor* [2007] 2 WLR 754; and *In Re McKerr* [2004] 1 WLR 807. And see [1.32].
[55] Section 4(2).
[56] Section 4(6).
[57] See, eg, *R v Lyons* [2003] 1 AC 976, 996–7, para 46, Lord Hoffmann.
[58] *R (Alconbury) v Secretary of State for the Environment, Transport and the Regions* [2003] 2 AC 295, 313, para 26, Lord Slynn. See too *Kay v Lambeth LBC* [2006] 2 AC 465.
[59] Section 6; and on the meaning of 'public authority' see [2.22]–[2.25].
[60] *Re Matthew's Application* [2004] NIQB 9, para 26.
[61] See [6.18]–[6.28].
[62] On restraint, both more generally and in the context of the Human Rights Act 1998, see [4.14]–[4.21] and [6.25]–[6.26].

ECHR, the courts are required by section 3, 'so far as it is possible to do so', to interpret the legislation in a way that is compatible with the ECHR (the obligation applies to both primary and subordinate legislation 'whenever enacted'). In deciding whether a particular piece of primary legislation attracts the section 3 interpretive enjoinder, the courts will, however, first assess whether an applicant's ECHR rights are engaged and whether the legislation would breach those rights in the absence of a revised interpretive approach.[63] The issue of breach may, as such, raise questions about the appropriate limits to judicial consideration of the content of a statute, as legislation will often deal with matters of social policy or with the framework for the provision of public services.[64] Under these circumstances, the courts have noted that Parliament is primarily responsible for such legislative choices and that the courts should be slow to interfere with the choices of the democratically elected legislature.[65] While this emphasis on restraint will be moderated according to context and to the rights affected by legislation (absolute or qualified, and so on[66]), it is consonant with traditional understandings of the separation of powers, albeit as modified to the human rights context. The courts have therefore emphasised that Parliament will often be taken to enjoy a 'discretionary area of judgment' and that the courts may, when assessing the proportionality of a legislative scheme relative to an individual's rights, 'defer, on democratic grounds, to the considered opinion of the elected body . . . whose act . . . is said to be incompatible with the Convention'.[67]

[5.13]   Where the courts consider that legislation should be read in the light of section 3, this will require them to use a purposive and contextual interpretive technique.[68] The canon of interpretation in section 3 has been described as a 'strong adjuration',[69] and a court must try to achieve the harmonious interpretation of legislation relative to the ECHR, whether by reading words into or out of legislation,[70] by giving existing words a meaning that is deemed more suited to their human rights context,[71] or by departing from its own precedents[72]—though not those of a higher court[73]—where the previous interpretive approach would result in an incompatibility.[74] The boundaries of this obligation are, however, set by what is 'possible' and this has led to some disagreement as to what may legitimately be achieved.[75] Hence there are, on the one hand, dicta to the effect

---

[63] *Department for Social Development v MacGeagh* [2006] NI 125, 132, para 20, citing *R v DPP, ex p Kebeline* [2000] 2 AC 326, 373, Lord Cooke.

[64] See, eg, *R (Pro-life Alliance) v BBC* [2004] 1 AC 185 (regulation of broadcasting); and *Marcic v Thames Water Utility* [2004] 2 AC 42 (regulation of privatised water services).

[65] See, eg, *Wilson v First County Trust* [2004] 1 AC 816, 844, para 70, Lord Nicholls, and *R (Countryside Alliance) v Att-Gen* [2007] UKHL 52.

[66] See [1.21].

[67] *R v DPP, ex p Kebeline* [2000] 2 AC 326, 381, Lord Hope. On the discretionary area of judgment see further [6.25]–[6.26].

[68] On interpretive techniques see [1.25]–[1.27].

[69] See, eg, *Re McKay's Application* [2002] NI 307, 316, and *Department for Social Development v MacGeagh* [2006] NI 125, 132, para 20, citing *R v DPP, ex p Kebeline* [2000] 2 AC 326, 373, Lord Cooke.

[70] Eg, *Re King's Application* [2003] NI 43 (words read into art 11 of the Life Sentences (Northern Ireland) Order 2001, SI 2001/2564 (NI 2), to ensure compliance with Art 6 ECHR).

[71] Eg, *Ghaidan v Mendoza* [2004] 2 AC 557 (word 'spouse' read to include same-sex partners for the purposes of the Rent Act 1977, Sch 1, paras 2, 3(1)).

[72] Eg, *Ghaidan v Mendoza* [2004] 2 AC 557 (House of Lords declining to follow its earlier ruling in *Fitzpatrick v Sterling Housing Association* [2002] 1 AC 27).

[73] *Kay v Lambeth LBC* [2006] 2 AC 465.

[74] Eg, *Foyle, Carlingford and Irish Lights Commission v McGillion* [2002] NI 86 (Northern Ireland Court of Appeal departing from one if its own precedents).

[75] For a judicial survey of the relevant authorities see *Re ES's Application* [2007] NIQB 58, para 50ff, Gillen J.

that Parliament has chosen to give the courts an enhanced interpretive role[76] and that section 3 should thereby be used creatively so as to avoid a proliferation of declarations of incompatibility that would not have any legal effect on the legislation in question nor be binding on the parties to the proceedings.[77] On the other hand, there are strong dicta to caution against 'judicial interpretation' being allowed to become 'judicial legislation' as this would defeat the purpose of the Act.[78] The point here is simply that the Act is structured around the sovereignty of Parliament and that overactive interpretation could have the effect of negating legislation that Parliament has deliberated upon. From this perspective, the declaration of incompatibility would be preferred as the option better suited to the constitutional setting to the Act.

[**5.14**]   Should the High Court or the Court of Appeal be considering whether to make a declaration of incompatibility—it is only the High Court and Court of Appeal in Northern Ireland that can do so under the Human Rights Act 1998[79]—the court must give notice to the Crown in accordance with section 5 of the Act and the corresponding rules of court.[80] Should a declaration be made, the issue of incompatibility becomes one for Parliament, which may choose to repeal or amend the legislation or to leave it in force.[81] In the event that Parliament chooses to leave the legislation in force it remains sovereign and binding on those affected by it.

Subordinate Legislation

[**5.15**]   Subordinate legislation is defined in section 21 of the Act to include (most) Orders in Council[82]; Acts of the Northern Ireland Assembly and of the earlier Northern Ireland Parliament and Assembly; orders, rules, regulations, bye-laws, and other measures made under Acts of the Northern Ireland Assembly and its predecessors or Orders in Council applying only to Northern Ireland (most obviously those that have made under the Northern Ireland Acts 1974 and 2000 at times of the suspension of the Northern Ireland institutions); and orders, rules, regulations, bye-laws and other measures made under primary legislation.[83] Where proceedings give rise to the question whether subordinate legislation or a provision within it is compatible with the ECHR[84], the courts must here too attempt, 'so far as it is possible to do so', to interpret the legislation compatibly. However, should such interpretation not be possible, it is implicit that the courts can, subject to one important exception, strike down the subordinate leg-

---

[76] *Ghaidan v Mendoza* [2004] 2 AC 557, 570, para 26, Lord Nicholls.

[77] Section 5(6); and see, eg, *Department for Social Development v MacGeagh* [2005] [2006] NI 125, 132, para 20.

[78] *Re S* [2002] 2 AC 291, 313, para 39, Lord Nicholls.

[79] Human Rights Act 1998, s 4(5); and *Re McR's Application* [2003] NI 1 (Offences Against the Persons Act 1861, s 62 incompatible with Art 8 ECHR).

[80] RSC Ord 121, r 2; and see [3.22] and [8.48].

[81] Section 10 and Sch 2.

[82] The exceptions are (a) Prerogative Orders in Council, (b) those made under the Northern Ireland Act 1998, s 84(1) ('Her Majesty may by Order in Council make provision with respect to elections [but not the franchise] and boundaries in respect of district councils in Northern Ireland') and (c) those that amend an Act of a kind mentioned in the definition of primary legislation.

[83] Subject to an exception where the subordinate legislation operates to bring one or more provisions of the primary legislation into force or amends any primary legislation: s 21(1).

[84] As in, eg, *Re Toner's Application* [2007] NIQB 18 (whether, inter alia, art 4 of the Northern Ireland Assembly (Elections) Order 2001, SI 2001/2599, is compatible with Art 3, Protocol 1 ECHR: application dismissed).

islation or sever the offending provision[85] (see too the effect of section 6: [5.17]). This thus means that Acts of the Assembly and Orders in Council at times of suspension may be struck down under the Act,[86] notwithstanding the argument that Acts of the Assembly and Orders in Council are of a constitutionally different quality from other forms of 'subordinate' legislation (see [5.24]). A challenge to an Act of the Assembly (or Order) or a measure made under an Act (or Order) will also give rise to a 'devolution issue' as defined in Schedule 10 to the Northern Ireland Act 1998, which contains a number of related procedural obligations (see [5.23]).

[**5.16**]   The important exception to the power to strike down subordinate legislation is where that legislation has been 'made in the exercise of a power conferred by primary legislation' and 'the primary legislation concerned prevents removal of the incompatibility'.[87] Under these circumstances, and consistent with the Human Rights Act's emphasis on the sovereignty of Parliament, the courts may merely make a declaration that the subordinate legislation is incompatible with the ECHR.[88] Should the High Court or the Court of Appeal be considering whether to make such a declaration—it is only the High Court and Court of Appeal in Northern Ireland that can do so under the Human Rights Act 1998[89]—the court must give notice to the Crown in accordance with section 5 of the Act and the corresponding rules of court.[90] However, should a declaration in time be made, this will not 'affect the validity, continuing operation or enforcement of the provision in respect of which it is given' and neither is it 'binding on the parties to the proceedings in which it is made'.[91] The matter instead becomes one for Parliament, which may choose to modify or repeal the legislation in accordance with section 10 of, and Schedule 2 to, the Human Rights Act 1998.

Public Authorities

[**5.17**]   The key provision of the Human Rights Act 1998 as it applies to public authorities is section 6, which states: 'It is unlawful for a public authority to act in a way which is incompatible with a Convention right'.[92] 'Public authorities' for these purposes do not include 'either House of Parliament or a person exercising functions in connection with proceedings in Parliament', but they do include courts and tribunals, 'core' public authorities (local councils, statutory bodies, government departments,[93] the police, the health service, and so on), and 'any person certain of whose functions are functions of a public nature' (so-called 'mixed function' authorities).[94] Although the wording of the section has given rise to some difficulties in practice—there is continued uncertainty about how far it applies to privatised utilities and to some private bodies performing contracted-out government functions[95]—it has been said that the Act has the aim of ensuring that human

---

[85] See *Re ES's Application* [2007] NIQB 58, para 63, Gillen J.

[86] See too Northern Ireland Act 1998, s 6.

[87] Section 4(3)–(4).

[88] Section 4(4).

[89] Human Rights Act 1998, s 4(5).

[90] RSC Ord 121, r 3A; and see [3.22] and [8.48]

[91] Section 5(6).

[92] Section 6(1).

[93] See too Northern Ireland Act 1998, s 24.

[94] Section 6(3). On the terms 'core' and 'mixed function authorities' see [2.22].

[95] See [2.22]–[2.25]; and, most recently, *YL v Birmingham City Council* [2007] 3 WLR 112 (private care home providing accommodation for publicly funded residents under the terms of a contract with a local authority that had a statutory duty to make arrangements for accommodation was not a public authority for the purposes of the Act).

rights obligations have as wide a reach as possible in the modern administrative state.[96] Individuals who satisfy the Act's section 7 'victim' requirement[97] may therefore bring proceedings against a public authority where that authority has acted or proposes to act in a manner that is contrary to the ECHR (an 'act' for these purposes includes a failure to act,[98] and subordinate legislation too may be challenged under the section, albeit subject to the section 3 interpretive obligation: see [5.13] and [5.15]). Where an argument of actual or possible illegality is made out, a court may then 'grant such relief or remedy, or make such order, within its powers as it considers just and appropriate'.[99]

[5.18]   Where the legality of a public authority's act or failure to act is challenged in judicial review proceedings, the issue will be resolved, as per section 2 of the Human Rights Act 1998, on the basis of relevant ECHR jurisprudence (see [5.11]; although common law fundamental rights standards may also be relevant,[100] as too may case law from other common law jurisdictions[101]). Whether an argument of illegality can be made out will depend on judicial perception of the context of the case, in particular as is set by the nature of the rights involved. The provisions of the ECHR that are contained in Schedule 1 to the Human Rights Act 1998[102] are often subdivided into qualified rights and absolute rights,[103] and the judicial role on an application for judicial review can vary accordingly. For instance, where qualified rights are in issue there may be greater scope for judicial restraint as qualified rights can be subject to limitation on one or other of the grounds listed in the ECHR so long as those limitations are authorised by law and 'necessary in a democratic society' and are proportionate (restraint will typically take form in use of the 'discretionary area of judgment' doctrine in any proportionality enquiry[104]). However, where absolute rights are affected by a decision or other measure, the scope for judicial restraint should in theory be reduced as absolute rights—for example, the Article 2 ECHR right to life or the Article 3 ECHR prohibition of torture—cannot be subject to any limitation. Thus, even though there have been some references to the discretionary area of judgment doctrine in cases involving absolute rights,[105] judicial invigilation should here be at its highest. Such cases, in the language of the common law, call for 'anxious scrutiny'.[106]

---

[96] See the statements by the Home Secretary, June 1998, at *Hansard* 314 HC 406–14. And on the modern administrative State see P Leyland and G Anthony, *Textbook on Administrative Law*, 5th edn (Oxford, Oxford University Press, 2005) ch 3.

[97] See [3.67]–[3.70].

[98] Section 6(6). But note that it does not include 'a failure to (a) introduce in, or lay before, Parliament a proposal for legislation; or (b) make any primary legislation or remedial order'.

[99] Section 8(1). On remedies see [3.47] and [3.79]–[3.80], and [8.40]–[8.48].

[100] See [6.10]–[6.11].

[101] See [1.15].

[102] Viz Arts 2–12 and 14 ECHR, Arts 1–3 of Protocol 1, and Arts 1–2 of Protocol 6, as read with Arts 16–18 ECHR. In numerical order these are: the right to life (Art 2); the prohibition of torture, inhuman or degrading treatment (Art 3); the prohibition of slavery and forced labour (Art 4); the right to liberty and security (Art 5); the right to a fair trial (Art 6); no punishment without law (Art 7); the right to respect for private and family life (Art 8); freedom of thought, conscience, and religion (Art 9); freedom of expression (Art 10); freedom of association and assembly (Art 11); the right to marry (Art 12); the prohibition of discrimination (Art 14); restrictions on political activities of aliens (Art 16); the prohibition of abuse of rights (Art 17); limitation on the use of restrictions on rights (Art 18); the protection of property (Art 1, Protocol 1); the right to education (Art 2, Protocol 1); the right to free elections (Art 3, Protocol 1); abolition of the death penalty (Art 1, Protocol 6); and death penalty in time of war (Art 2, Protocol 6).

[103] Although see too the distinction between derogable and non-derogable rights at [1.21].

[104] On which see [6.25]–[6.26].

[105] See, eg, *Re A's Application* [2001] NI 335 and *Re E's Application* [2004] NIQB 35 and [2006] NICA 37.

[106] *R v Secretary of State for the Home Department, ex p Bugdaycay* [1987] AC 514, 531.

[5.19]   A related point of importance on public authorities concerns the consequences of their failure to give express consideration to rights under the Human Rights Act 1998 during the decision-making process. Although the Northern Ireland courts had previously held that such a failure would ordinarily render a decision unlawful because the authority could not have satisfied itself that its decision was ECHR-compliant,[107] the House of Lords has since established in a number of cases involving qualified rights that a failure to have regard for human rights considerations need not have that effect.[108] The central question on an application for judicial review is, instead, whether the final decision of the authority violates a right and, in the event that it does not, the Lords have held there is no anterior requirement that the process leading to the decision should have been informed by human rights considerations. However, while this might, at one level, appear to lessen the nature of the human rights burden placed upon decision-makers, a failure to consider rights during the decision-making process may still have implications for any subsequent role to be played by a reviewing court. Put shortly, in the event that a decision-maker does not give consideration to rights during the decision-making process, it may be that the court would have to subject to the final decision to close scrutiny to ensure that the decision-maker has struck the appropriate balance between all affected rights and that the decision is in that way compliant with the ECHR.[109] On the other hand, should the decision-maker give express consideration to the rights of the individual in a context in which it has been given a wide discretion, the courts may consider that it would be constitutionally appropriate to demonstrate a greater degree of restraint relative to the final choice made.[110] The courts, in other words, may again recognise that the decision at hand falls within the decision-maker's 'discretionary area of judgment'.[111]

[5.20]   It should finally be noted that public authorities have a defence to any argument of illegality under section 6 where, '(a) as the result of one or more provisions of primary legislation, the authority could not have acted differently; or (b) in the case of one or more provisions of, or made under, primary legislation which cannot be read or given effect in a way which is compatible with the Convention rights, the authority was acting so as to give effect to or enforce those provisions'.[112] It has since been explained that defence (a) is available where the effect of primary legislation is that the authority has no alternative other than to do what the legislation tells it to do and that the authority is, in that sense, under a duty to act in accordance with primary legislation of the sovereign Parliament (the relevant duty may be found in one provision in one statute, in several provisions in one statute, or in provisions contained in several statutes as read conjunctively; on primary legislation and the Act see [5.12]–[5.14]).[113] Defence (b) is then likewise founded on the doctrine of parliamentary sovereignty and applies where an authority has a discretion to give effect to or enforce provisions of or made under

---

[107] See, eg, *Re Connor's Application* [2005] NI 322 (authority failed to give express consideration to the applicant's rights under Art 8 ECHR) and *Re Misbehavin' Ltd's Application* [2006] NI 181 (authority failed to give consideration to the applicant's rights under Art 10 and Art 1, Protocol 1 ECHR).

[108] *Belfast City Council v Miss Behavin' Ltd* [2007] 1 WLR 1420 (Art 10 ECHR freedom of expression and Art 1, Protocol 1 property rights); and *R (SB) v Governors of Denbigh High School* [2007] 1 AC 1000 (Art 9 ECHR manifestations of religious belief).

[109] *Belfast City Council v Miss Behavin' Ltd* [2007] 1 WLR 1420, 1432, para 37, Baroness Hale.

[110] *Belfast City Council v Miss Behavin' Ltd* [2007] 1 WLR 1420, 1432, para 37, Baroness Hale.

[111] On which see [6.25]–[6.26].

[112] Section 6(2).

[113] *R (Hooper) v Secretary of State for Work and Pensions* [2006] 1 All ER 487, 512, para 71, Lord Hope.

primary legislation which cannot, as per section 3 of the Human Rights Act, be read compatibly with the ECHR (the source of the discretion may, again, be in one or more statutory provisions). Should the authority choose to exercise or not to exercise the power with the result that there is a 'breach' of an individual's rights, there will be no illegality as the action/inaction will have given effect to primary legislation that remains valid even where it has been made the subject of a declaration of incompatibility (see [5.14][114]). The defence in this way allows decision-makers to give effect to Parliament's intentions as,

> if the defence was not there the authority would have no alternative but to exercise its discretion in a way that was compatible with the Convention rights. The power would become a duty to act compatibly with the Convention, even if to do so was plainly in conflict with the intention of Parliament.[115]

The Northern Ireland Act 1998

[5.21] The Northern Ireland Act 1998, as amended,[116] has been described in the House of Lords as a 'constitution for Northern Ireland, framed to create a continuing form of government against the history of the territory and the principles' in the Belfast Agreement.[117] The Act, among other things, thus delimits the legislative powers of the Northern Ireland Assembly[118]; specifies how executive power in the Assembly is to be allocated and exercised (including in relation to the making of Statutory Rules)[119]; makes provision for elections to the Assembly[120]; creates, and delimits the powers of, the Northern Ireland Human Rights Commission (NIHRC) and the Equality Commission[121]; and imposes equality obligations on public authorities as defined in the Act.[122] These provisions of the Act have since given rise to a significant number of applications for judicial review, and there have been challenges to exercises of the Assembly's legislative powers,[123] to executive acts[124] and decisions,[125] to decisions of the Secretary of State for Northern Ireland,[126] and to the determinations of other public authorities.[127] While many

---

[114] And see [8.46]–[8.48].

[115] *R (Hooper) v Secretary of State for Work and Pensions* [2006] 1 All ER 487, 512, paras 72–3, Lord Hope.

[116] Northern Ireland (St Andrews Agreement) Act 2006, as read with the Northern Ireland (St Andrews Agreement) Act 2007.

[117] *Robinson v Secretary of State for Northern Ireland* [2002] NI 390, 402, para 25, Lord Hoffmann.

[118] Sections 5–15.

[119] Sections 16–30.

[120] Sections 31–5.

[121] Sections 68–72 (NIHRC); (see too the Justice and Security (Northern Ireland) Act 2007, ss 14–20); and ss 73–4 and Sch 8 (Equality Commission).

[122] Sections 75–6 and Sch 9.

[123] Eg, *Re Landlord's Association for Northern Ireland's Application* [2006] NI 16, challenging successfully the compatibility of the Housing (Northern Ireland) Order 2003 with the ECHR (the Order [SI 2003/412] had originally been introduced as a Bill in the Assembly and was carried over as an Order in Council under the Northern Ireland Act 2000).

[124] Eg, *Re McBride's Application* [2002] NIQB 64 (fishing regulations challenged as contrary to the ECHR: application dismissed).

[125] Eg, *Re De Brun and McGuiness's Application* [2001] NI 442 (challenge to the First Minister's refusal to nominate Sinn Féin Ministers to meetings of the North/South Ministerial Council: application granted).

[126] *Robinson v Secretary of State for Northern Ireland* [2002] NI 390 (challenge to, inter alia, Secretary of State's decision not to call fresh Assembly elections in the light of the Assembly's failure to elect a First and Deputy First Minister within the time-frame specified in s 16(8) of the Act: application dismissed).

[127] Eg, *Re Northern Ireland Human Rights Commission* [2002] NI 236 (challenge to a coroner's determination that the NIHRC did not have the power to apply to intervene in judicial proceedings: application granted).

of the cases have been decided on the basis of established judicial review principles, some have touched upon important questions about the nature of devolved power and whether the Assembly, when it is acting in its legislative capacity, is simply to be compared to any other recipient of delegated power.[128] Some cases have likewise raised questions about how far, if at all, the Act's 'constitutional' provisions on equality are enforceable by way of application for judicial review.[129]

[5.22]   Political difficulties between, in particular, October 2002 and May 2007 resulted in the periodic suspension of the Northern Ireland Assembly.[130] Under suspension, Northern Ireland legislation—that is, 'provision for any matter for which the 1998 Act authorises or requires provision to be made by Act of the Assembly'—was made by Order in Council under the Northern Ireland Act 2000.[131] Such Orders in Council are the constitutional equivalent of Acts of the Assembly, and they too may be challenged with reference to the terms of the Northern Ireland Act 1998[132] (although the suspension of the Assembly meant that some legislative procedures did not need to be adhered to during suspension[133]). Executive functions at times of suspension were, moreover, performed by Northern Ireland departments 'subject to the direction and control of the Secretary of State' for Northern Ireland (who was responsible for discharging the functions of the First and Deputy First Ministers),[134] and all such executive functions were governed by the relevant constraints on executive power in the Northern Ireland Act 1998. Suspension did not, however, affect the work of NIHRC or the Equality Commission, save insofar as the Commissions perform functions in relation to the Assembly.[135] The equality duties of public authorities also remained unaffected.

Acts of the Assembly/Orders in Council

[5.23]   The Northern Ireland Assembly has legislative competence in respect of 'transferred' matters under the Northern Ireland Act 1998, which are to be distinguished from 'reserved' and 'excepted' matters.[136] While the Assembly may legislate for transferred matters (subject to a provision that safeguards the sovereignty of Parliament[137]), it can legislate for reserved matters and excepted matters only with the consent of the Secretary

---

[128] See, eg, Re Northern Ireland Commissioner for Children and Young People's Application [2004] NIQB 40, para 15, Girvan J stating in the context of a challenge to a draft Order in Council: 'Although the legislation in the present case would be by way of Order in Council and thus technically subordinate, one must not lose sight of the fact that such subordinate legislation in Northern Ireland replaces primary legislation and to that extent differs from the more ordinary understood concept of delegated legislation.'

[129] Re Neill's Application [2006] NICA 5.

[130] Northern Ireland Act 2000; repealed by the Northern Ireland (St Andrews Agreement) Act 2006 and the Northern Ireland (St Andrews Agreement) Act 2007.

[131] Section 1; and para 1(1) of the Sch to the Act.

[132] Para 1(2) of the Sch to the Act.

[133] Re Neill's Application [2006] NICA 5 (requirement that the Secretary of State formally consent to Northern Ireland legislation in the reserved sphere (Northern Ireland Act 1998, s 8) not applicable at times of suspension when the Secretary of State's department was piloting legislation under the Northern Ireland Act 2000).

[134] Northern Ireland Act 2000, Sch, para 4.

[135] See, eg, Northern Ireland Act 1998, s 69(4) (NIHRC's power to advise the Assembly whether a Bill is compatible with the ECHR); and Northern Ireland Act 1998, Sch 9 (Commission's role in overseeing the enforcement of equality duties).

[136] 'Reserved' matters are those falling within a description specified in Sch 3 to the Act; and 'excepted' matters are those falling within a description specified in Sch 2.

[137] Section 5(6).

of State (the excepted matters must be 'ancillary to other provisions dealing . . . with reserved or transferred matters').[138] The corresponding limits to the Assembly's legislative powers are found in section 6 of the Northern Ireland Act 1998, which states that a provision of an Act will be outside the competence of the Assembly if:

(a) it would form part of the law of a country or territory other than Northern Ireland, or confer or remove functions exercisable otherwise than in or as regards Northern Ireland;

(b) it deals with an excepted matter and is not ancillary to other provisions (whether in the Act or previously enacted) dealing with reserved or transferred matters;

(c) it is incompatible with any of the Convention rights;

(d) it is incompatible with Community law;

(e) it discriminates against any person or class of person on the ground of religious belief or political opinion;

(f) it modifies an enactment in breach of section 7.[139]

Where an Act of the Assembly (or an Order in Council at time of suspension) is challenged under section 6 and the High Court considers that the challenge is not frivolous or vexatious,[140] the proceedings will give rise to a 'devolution issue' as defined in Schedule 10 to the Act.[141] Under those circumstances, the High Court must give notice of the issue to the Attorney-General, the Attorney-General for Northern Ireland, and the appropriate Northern Ireland Minister or department.[142]

[5.24]   The key constitutional question about illegality and Acts of the Assembly or Orders in Council is whether they are to be regarded merely as a form of subordinate legislation or whether they are a form of primary legislation demanding a modified judicial approach when their validity is challenged. On the one hand, use of the term 'subordinate legislation' might be justified by the fact that the power to legislate has been devolved by the Westminster Parliament which remains sovereign[143]; and there is, in addition, the fact that Acts or Orders are defined as subordinate legislation for the purposes of the Human Rights Act 1998 and may be deemed unlawful where they are incompatible with the ECHR and incapable of being interpreted in a manner that is ECHR-compliant (see [5.15]–[5.16]).[144] However, on the other hand it can be argued, certainly in relation to Acts of the Assembly, that these are primary legislative measures enacted by a democratically elected body that is accountable to its own locally defined political community[145]

---

[138] Section 8.

[139] 'Convention rights' are to be read in the light of the Human Rights Act (s 98); and s 7 lists entrenched enactments that, subject to s 7(2), may not be modified by Act of the Assembly or subordinate legislation (these are the European Communities Act 1972, the Human Rights Act 1998, and ss 43(1)–(6) and (8), s 67, ss 84–6, s 95(3) and (4), and s 98 of the Northern Ireland Act 1998 (s 7(2) permits modification of s 3(3) or (4) or s 11(1) of the European Communities Act 1972)).

[140] RSC Ord 120, r 2; and *Judicial Review: Practice Note 01/2006*, Part C.

[141] Sch 10, para 1: 'In this Schedule 'devolution issue' means (a) a question whether any provision of an Act of the Assembly is within the legislative competence of the Assembly . . . (d) any question arising under this Act about excepted or reserved matters'.

[142] Northern Ireland Act 1998, Sch 10, para 5; and RSC Ord 120, r 3. And see, eg, *Re Neill's Application* [2005] NIQB 66, para 11. See further [3.23]

[143] Northern Ireland Act 1998, s 5(6).

[144] See, eg, *Re Landlord's Association for Northern Ireland's Application* [2006] NI 16, challenging successfully the compatibility of the Housing (Northern Ireland) Order 2003 with the ECHR.

[145] See generally B Hadfield, 'The Foundations of Review, Devolved Power and Delegated Power' in C Forsyth (ed), *Judicial Review and the Constitution* (Oxford, Hart Publishing, 2000) p 193.

(the point is perhaps less forceful in respect of Orders in Council, as these were made when the elected body was suspended). While the close scrutiny and control of such measures vis-à-vis the ECHR and EU law may thus be justified with reference to the need for the UK to discharge its international obligations, different considerations may apply where it is argued that the provisions of an Act transgress the boundary between transferred matters and those that are reserved and excepted. Challenges of this kind ultimately centre on whether competences within a 'constitutional statute' should be given a narrow interpretation or one that is more expansive and facilitative of local legislative processes.[146] Some guidance on the appropriate approach may be found in Northern Ireland's previous experience with devolution under the terms of the Government of Ireland Act 1920, some of which would suggest that the latter approach is to be preferred.[147]

Statutory Rules

[5.25] Statutory Rules of Northern Ireland are subordinate legislation within the conventional meaning of that term, as they are made under Acts of the Assembly or Orders in Council at times of suspension[148] (they may also be made under section 2(2) of the European Communities Act 1972, Acts of the former Northern Ireland Parliament, Orders in Council made under the Northern Ireland (Temporary Provisions) Act 1972, Orders in Council made under the Northern Ireland Act 1974, and Acts of the Westminster Parliament whether specific to Northern Ireland or of UK-wide application). The Rules—which may be in the form of orders, rules, schemes, regulations, or bye-laws[149] and which are made by the authority named in the empowering legislation[150]—must conform with any procedural requirements specified in the Act or Order[151] and also with a range of common law constraints that apply to subordinate legislation more generally (see [5.31]–[5.37]).[152] Statutory Rules of Northern Ireland may also be challenged under section 24 of the Northern Ireland Act 1998, which provides, inter alia, that a Minister or Northern Ireland department has no power to make subordinate legislation so far as the legislation '(a) is incompatible with any of the Convention rights; (b) is incompatible with Community law; (c) discriminates against a person or class of person on the ground of religious belief or political opinion; . . . or

---

[146] See Northern Ireland Act 1998, s 83.

[147] See *Belfast Corporation v OD Cars* [1960] AC 490, 517–19, Viscount Simmonds; and *Gallagher v Lynn* [1938] NI 21 (Northern Ireland legislation is to be read in the light of a 'pith and substance' test whereby if, on a view of the statute as a whole, it is found that the substance of the legislation is within the express powers, then the legislation is not invalidated if incidentally it affects matters that are outside the authorised field). But compare *Hume v Londonderry Justices* [1972] NI 91 (Divisional Court adopting criticisms of the 'pith and substance' test when quashing convictions that had been secured on the basis of a statutory rule that had empowered members of HM forces to require three or more persons to disperse: Government of Ireland Act 1920, s 4(1)(3) made the armed forces of the Crown an excepted matter, and the statutory rule was without legal basis). For commentary see B Hadfield, *The Constitution of Northern Ireland* (Belfast, SLS Legal Publications, 1989) p 84 *ff*.

[148] Statutory Rules (Northern Ireland) Order 1979, art 4.

[149] Statutory Rules (Northern Ireland) Order 1979, art 4.

[150] See too Statutory Rules (Northern Ireland) Order 1979, Sch 2.

[151] Interpretation Act Northern Ireland 1954, s 41. But see too [7.18]–[7.21] on the distinction between mandatory and directory procedural requirements.

[152] And see, eg, *Re Cullen's Application* [2005] NIQB 9 (challenging, inter alia, the Game Preservation (Special Protection for Irish Hares) Order (Northern Ireland) 2003 made under s 7C(1) of the Game Preservation Act (Northern Ireland) 1928 Act: application dismissed).

(e) in the case of legislation, modifies an enactment in breach of section 7'.[153] These grounds for review correspond to several of those contained in section 6 and which provide the basis for challenges to Acts of the Assembly and they are thus consonant with basic rules on the hierarchy of laws: if Acts may be enacted only within certain parameters, the point is perforce true of subordinate legislation made under those Acts.

[5.26]   Where subordinate legislation is challenged under section 24 and the High Court considers that the challenge is not frivolous or vexatious,[154] the proceedings will give rise to a 'devolution issue' as defined in Schedule 10 to the Act.[155] Under those circumstances, as with challenges to Acts under section 6 of the Northern Ireland Act 1998 (see [5.23]), the High Court must give notice of the issue to the Attorney-General, the Attorney-General for Northern Ireland, and the appropriate Northern Ireland Minister or department.[156]

Public Authorities (including Northern Ireland Ministers and Departments)

[5.27]   Two provisions of the Northern Ireland Act 1998 are of particular relevance to the decisions or other measures of public authorities, which include Northern Ireland Ministers and departments but exclude the Assembly (on which see [5.23]–[5.24]). The first is section 24, which, in addition to providing for challenges to Statutory Rules (see [5.25]), states that a Minister or Northern Ireland department has no power to do any act that '(a) is incompatible with any of the Convention rights; (b) is incompatible with Community law; (c) discriminates against a person or class of person on the ground of religious belief or political opinion; (d) . . . aids or incites another person to discriminate against a person or class of person on that ground' (grounds (c) and (d) do not, however, apply in relation to any act which is unlawful by virtue of the the [Fair Employment and Treatment (Northern Ireland) Order 1998], or would be unlawful but for some exception made by virtue of [Part VIII of that Order][157]). Where an act or decision is challenged under section 24 and the High Court considers that the challenge is not frivolous or vexatious,[158] the proceedings will give rise to a 'devolution issue' as defined in Schedule 10 to the Act.[159] Under those circumstances, the High Court must give notice of the issue to the Attorney-General, the Attorney-General for Northern Ireland, and the appropriate Northern Ireland Minister or department.[160]

---

[153] Section 7 lists entrenched enactments that, subject to s 7(2), may not be modified by Act of the Assembly or subordinate legislation. These are the European Communities Act 1972, the Human Rights Act 1998, and ss 43(1)–(6) and (8), s 67, ss 84–6, s 95(3) and (4), and s 98 of the Northern Ireland Act 1998 (s 7(2) permits modification of s 3(3) or (4) or s 11(1) of the European Communities Act 1972).

[154] RSC Ord 120, r 2; and *Judicial Review: Practice Note 01/2006*, Part C.

[155] Sch 10, para 1: 'In this Schedule "devolution issue" means . . . (b) a question whether a purported or proposed exercise of a function by a Minister or Northern Ireland department is, or would be, invalid by reason of section 24'.

[156] Northern Ireland Act 1998, Sch 10, para 5; and RSC Ord 120, r 3. And see, eg, *Re McBride's Application* [2002] NIQB 64 (regulations challenged as contrary to Convention rights: application dismissed). See further [3.23].

[157] Northern Ireland Act 1998, s 24(2).

[158] RSC Ord 120, r 2; and *Judicial Review: Practice Note 01/2006*, Part C.

[159] Sch 10, para 1: 'In this Schedule "devolution issue" means . . . (b) a question whether a purported or proposed exercise of a function by a Minister or Northern Ireland department is, or would be, invalid by reason of section 24; (c) a question whether a Minister or Northern Ireland department has failed to comply with any of the Convention rights, any obligation under Community law or any order under section 27 so far as relating to such an obligation'. Section 27 is titled 'Quotas for purposes of international etc obligations'.

[160] Northern Ireland Act 1998, Sch 10, para 5; and RSC Ord 120, r 3. See further [3.23].

[5.28]   The second provision is section 75, as read with Schedule 9 to the Act. Section 75(1) states:

A public authority shall in carrying out its functions relating to Northern Ireland have due regard to the need to promote equality of opportunity—

(a) between persons of different religious belief, political opinion, racial group, age, marital status or sexual orientation;
(b) between men and women generally;
(c) between persons with a disability and persons without; and
(d) between persons with dependants and persons without.

Public authorities for these purposes are defined in section 75(3) to include a range of government departments, corporations, and other bodies listed in several other pieces of legislation[161] and 'any other person designated . . . by order made by the Secretary of State'. A public authority covered by the Act is obliged to make an equality scheme that will show how it proposes to fulfil the duties imposed by section 75,[162] and the scheme must be submitted to the Equality Commission for approval[163] (the Equality Commission must either approve the scheme or refer it to the Secretary of State, who must, in turn, either approve the scheme, require it to be revised, or make a scheme for the authority[164]). Should it be thought that an authority has thereafter failed to comply with its equality scheme, the Equality Commission may investigate a complaint 'made in writing by a person who claims to have been directly affected by the failure' or, alternatively, invoke its residual power to investigate where 'it believes that a public authority' is failing to abide by its obligations under its scheme.[165] In the event that the complaint or decision to investigate has been justified, the Equality Commission can seek to enforce the Act either by recommending that an authority take a particular course of action, by referring the matter to the Secretary of State, and by laying a report before the Assembly and Parliament (as appropriate).[166]

[5.29]   The significance of section 75 and Schedule 9 has since been considered by the Northern Ireland Court of Appeal in *Re Neill's Application*.[167] The application for judicial review here challenged the legality of the Anti-social Behaviour (Northern Ireland) Order 2004[168] on the ground that the Northern Ireland Office had failed to give effect to its equality scheme before deciding to lay a draft of the Order in Council before Parliament. The central issue for the Court of Appeal was whether judicial review was available for purposes of enforcing section 75 or whether breaches of the kind at issue were to be remedied under Schedule 9. In holding that judicial review was not available, the Court concluded that the instant case had given rise to 'precisely the type of situation

---

[161] Viz, Sch 2 to the Parliamentary Commissioner Act 1967; sch 2 to the Commissioner for Complaints (Northern Ireland) Order 1996; and Sch 2 to the Ombudsman (Northern Ireland) Order 1996.

[162] Sch 9, para 4.

[163] Sch 9, para 6.

[164] Sch 9, paras 6–7. But note that paras 6 and 7 do not apply to public authorities as defined with reference to Sch 2 to the Parliamentary Commissioner Act 1967, and that the procedure for agreeing schemes for these authorities is that contained in para 12 (ie the Secretary of State performs no role, and the Commission lays before Parliament and the Assembly a report of any breach of the authority's obligations).

[165] See, respectively, Sch 9, paras 10(2) and 11(1)(b). And for consideration of the relationship between the two provisions see *Re Neill's Application* [2005] NIQB 66, paras 45–6.

[166] Sch 9, paras 11–12.

[167] [2006] NICA 5.

[168] SI 2004/1998 (NI 12).

that the procedure under Schedule 9 [was] designed to deal with . . . [The Equality Commission] is given explicit powers to bring any failure on the part of the authority to the attention of Parliament and the Northern Ireland Assembly'.[169] Although the Court noted that judicial review may be available in some instances—it referred specifically to the possibility of substantive breaches of section 75 being brought before the courts—it held that the Northern Ireland Office's breach was procedural in form and subject to the sanctions contained in Schedule 9. The Schedule thus offered an alternative remedy that was essentially 'political' in form and to be distinguished from other 'legal' remedies under the Act, for instance the judicial power to award damages to individuals who are adversely affected by religious or political discrimination contrary to section 76.[170]

[5.30]   Public authorities are, in addition, bound to give effect to EU law and the ECHR. Where the authority is a Northern Ireland Minister or a government department the obligation is imposed specifically by section 24 of the Northern Ireland Act 1998 (see [5.27]); while the obligation in respect of other public authorities is contained in the European Communities Act 1972 and section 6 of the Human Rights Act 1998 (see [5.08] and [5.17]–[5.20][171]; although section 6 would apply to Ministers and departments too). The remaining statutory powers and duties of relevance to Northern Ireland public authorities are contained in Acts of the Assembly/Orders in Council, Acts of the Westminster Parliament, and various pieces of subordinate legislation. Changes in the nature of public power and the nature of service delivery do, however, mean that judicial review may also be available to challenge the decisions of some 'public' authorities whose power of decision does not in fact have a statutory underpinning.[172]

SUBORDINATE LEGISLATION AND ILLEGALITY

[5.31]   Subordinate legislation can be defined as 'an instrument made by a person or body (the delegate) under legislative powers conferred by Act (the enabling Act)'.[173] In terms of illegality, the basic rule is that subordinate legislation will be ultra vires the enabling Act if it does not comply with the terms of the Act as read, where appropriate, with the UK's constitutional statutes (on which see [5.04]–[5.30][174]). Subordinate legislation in Northern Ireland can, as such, be made at two constitutional levels and this can give rise to different considerations depending on the level at which the legislation has been made. For instance, where the legislation is made in the form of Statutory Rules under Acts of the Assembly, Orders in Council, and so on (see [5.25]–[5.26]), this will constitute subordinate legislation as conventionally understood and will be open to challenge on correspondingly conventional grounds (subordinate legislation can also take the form of, among other things, bye-laws made by local councils[175]). Where, in contrast, the 'subordinate' legislation is in the form of Acts of the Assembly or Orders in Council made

---

[169] [2006] NICA 5, para 27.
[170] On alternative remedies see [2.34]–[2.35].
[171] But see too [2.22]–[2.25] on the definitional problems associated with the term 'public authority' under s 6 of the Human Rights Act 1998.
[172] See generally ch 2.
[173] F Bennion, *Statutory Interpretation*, 4th edn (London, Butterworths, 2002) p 197.
[174] And [1.28]–[1.34].
[175] Local Government Act (Northern Ireland) 1972, ss 90–94.

under the Northern Ireland Act 1998 and Northern Ireland Act 2000 respectively, conventional grounds for challenge may be of less relevance.[176] While such measures may be quashed where they are incompatible with EU law and/or the ECHR (see [5.07]; [5.15]; and [5.23]), it has been argued that more general vires challenges should have to account for the fact that the legislative competence of the Assembly cannot simply be equated to statutory discretion given to administrative authorities. Under these circumstances, it has been suggested that the language of subordinate legislation is misplaced[177] (see [5.24]).

[5.32]   The conventional grounds for challenging the lawfulness of subordinate legislation such as Statutory Rules are largely the same as those that govern challenges to exercises of statutory discretion by administrative bodies.[178] Statutory Rules and administrative decisions can, for instance, both be challenged with reference to EU law (see [5.07]–[5.08]); and they may also be challenged as contrary to the ECHR under the Human Rights Act 1998 or, where appropriate, section 24 of the Northern Ireland Act 1998 (see [5.15] and [5.23]). Prior to the enactment of the Human Rights Act 1998, case law in England and Wales had established that it was also possible to challenge the legality of subordinate legislation, administrative decisions, and so on, with reference to common law fundamental rights standards.[179] While the case law on administrative decisions was certainly of relevance in Northern Ireland,[180] the decisions on subordinate legislation were arguably of less analogical value, at least in respect of Statutory Rules. This is because the case law in England and Wales held that subordinate instruments could interfere with an individual's common law fundamental rights only where the empowering Act of Parliament provided for such interference either in express terms or by necessary implication.[181] As Statutory Rules made prior to 1998 were largely made under Acts of the former Northern Ireland Parliament or Orders in Council, it was those Acts and Orders in Council that fell directly within the rule propounded in England and Wales as it was they, and not the Statutory Rules, that had been made under Acts of the Westminster Parliament (viz, the Government of Ireland Act 1920, the Northern Ireland (Temporary Provisions) Act 1972, and the Northern Ireland Act 1974).[182] The point is, however, now largely moot as issues of human rights compliance—whether in respect of Acts of the Assembly, Orders in Council, and/or Statutory Rules—will typically be governed by the Human Rights Act 1998 and the Northern Ireland Act 1998.

[176] See *Re Northern Ireland Commissioner for Children and Young People's Application* [2004] NIQB 40, para 15.

[177] See A McHarg, 'What is Delegated Legislation?' (2006) PL 539.

[178] See, eg, *Re McCann's Application* [2004] NIQB 47 (challenge to, inter alia, Legal Aid Criminal Proceedings (Costs) Rules (Northern Ireland) 2003, SR 2003/511: application dismissed). On discretion see [4.22]–[4.28].

[179] See further [6.10]–[6.11].

[180] See, eg, *Re T's Application* [2000] NI 516, 540*ff*; and *Re Austin's Application* [1998] NI 327, 337.

[181] Eg, *R v Secretary of State for the Home Department, ex p Leech* [1993] 4 All ER 539 (prison rules that permitted authorities to interfere with correspondence between prisoners and lawyers save where proceedings had been initiated ultra vires Prison Act 1952, s 47, as they impeded access to a lawyer for purposes of considering whether to bring proceedings); and *R v Lord Chancellor, ex p Witham* [1998] QB 575 (court fees that interfered with common law rights of access to court ultra vires Supreme Court Act 1981, s 130). But compare, eg, *R v Chief Constable of the RUC, ex p Begley* [1997] NI 278 (suspect had no common law fundamental right to have a solicitor present during police interviews; and the courts would not infer the right given Parliament's clear intention to exclude solicitors under the terms of Prevention of Terrorism (Temporary Provisions) Act 1989, s 14(1)).

[182] And see, eg, *Re McCullough's Application* [1997] NI 423 (art 65(b) of the Police and Criminal Evidence (NI) Order 1989, SI 1989/1341 (NI 12)—which empowered police officers to, among other things, photograph suspects—should not be given a narrow reading as it covered a wide range of activities carried out by officers in their dealings with suspects).

[5.33]   Statutory Rules may also be challenged where they are argued to have been made with reference to irrelevant considerations/in the absence of relevant considerations, for an improper purpose, and/or in bad faith (see [5.40]–[5.48]). It is, moreover, possible to challenge subordinate legislation on the ground that it is procedurally flawed, although there are limits to common law constraints in this context. For instance, while subordinate legislation may be challenged as having been made in breach of a statutory requirement to consult specified parties,[183] the common law will not in general impose a duty to consult in the absence of a statutory obligation[184] (a position which differs from that in respect of some administrative decisions[185]). The underlying rationale here is simply that a common law requirement to consult when making legislation would, given the numbers of people potentially affected by a measure, be unduly burdensome both for the relevant authority and for the courts should the failure to consult be challenged in judicial review proceedings. The only apparent exception to this rule is where an applicant can demonstrate that they had a legitimate expectation of consultation, for example as a result of pre-existing government practice or of a statement made to them.[186]

[5.34]   Unreasonableness too is a ground for challenging Statutory Rules.[187] Statutory Rules may, for instance, be vague and lacking in certainty and be challenged as unreasonable on that ground[188]; and their content may also be challenged as manifestly unfair or as having been made in defiance of logic.[189] Whether such arguments will prevail will, however, depend on the context of the dispute, the nature of the subordinate legislation in question, and judicial understanding of the appropriateness or otherwise of intervention.[190] For example, arguments that equate vagueness with unreasonableness have previously been rejected where the legislation in question has been introduced at times of emergency[191] (although such case law would now have to be read in the light of emergency case law under the Human Rights Act 1998[192]); and the courts have also held that they should be slow to interfere with subordinate legislation on grounds of unreasonableness where the legislation has a pronounced socio-economic policy element.[193] The courts have in similar vein emphasised that they will be slow to interfere with subordinate legislation that is subject to approval in Parliament, particularly when the point arises at pre-approval stage.[194]

---

[183]   See further [7.18]–[7.24].

[184]   *Re Northern Ireland Commissioner for Children and Young People's Application* [2004] NIQB 40, para 12, Girvan J, applying *Bates v Lord Hailsham* [1972] 3 All ER 1019.

[185]   See [7.32].

[186]   *Re General Consumer Council's Application* [2006] NIQB 86, para 36, Weatherup J. See too, by analogy, *Re Campbell's Application* [2005] NIQB 59, para 20, Kerr LCJ, rejecting the argument that there can be no common law duty to give reasons for a legislative choice where the choice is absent in any form of scrutiny other than that provided by way of judicial review. And see [7.27].

[187]   See [6.05]–[6.11].

[188]   Eg, *McEldowney v Forde* [1971] NI 11, 57*ff*, Lord Diplock.

[189]   Eg, *R v Secretary of State for the Environment, ex p Nottinghamshire CC* [1986] AC 240.

[190]   See [4.14]–[4.21].

[191]   *McEldowney v Forde* [1971] NI 11 (regulations that made it a criminal offence to belong to an organisation describing itself as a 'republican club' or 'any like organisation however described' held intra vires Civil Authorities (Special Powers) Act (Northern Ireland) 1922, s 1).

[192]   Eg, *A v Secretary of State for the Home Department* [2005] 2 AC 68 (measures introduced at times of an emergency threatening the life of the nation for the purposes of Art 15 ECHR must be proportionate).

[193]   Eg, *R v Secretary of State for the Environment, ex p Nottinghamshire CC* [1986] AC 240.

[194]   *Re Northern Ireland Commissioner for Children and Young People's Application* [2004] NIQB 40, para 15, Girvan J, citing *R v HM Treasury, ex p Smedley* [1985] 1 All ER 590.

[5.35]   There are three further points of importance about subordinate legislation. The first concerns the fora in which the legality of legislation can be challenged. Although a challenge may be made by way of application for judicial review,[195] authority has established that arguments of illegality can be also be made collaterally, that is, within other proceedings. Such collateral challenges will typically be made in criminal proceedings where an individual who has been charged with an offence under subordinate legislation argues in their defence that the legislation itself is unlawful[196] (collateral arguments may also be made in respect of decisions that preceded prosecution, that is, that the decisions were unlawful and that the prosecution is in that way flawed). While such challenges will generally not be permitted where the defendant had prior opportunity to challenge the legislation or decisions taken under it,[197] the position is different where the individual only becomes aware of legislation once charged with an offence. Under these circumstances, the criminal proceedings will provide the first chance to challenge the legislation, and the courts presume that Parliament did not intend to deprive the defendant of an opportunity to defend himself or herself in this way (the presumption can be rebutted by express language in statute).[198] Such openness to collateral challenges is perhaps also consonant with the courts' more general aversion to so-called 'satellite litigation', whereby individuals in (typically) criminal proceedings seek to stall ongoing criminal proceedings by raising a public law issue by way of a separate application for judicial review.[199]

[5.36]   The second point concerns the effect of a finding, on an application for judicial review, that subordinate legislation is unlawful. Legislation that is ultra vires is, in short, to be read as having never had legal effect.[200] Marched to its logical conclusion this means that anything done under the legislation is likewise without effect and that any individual affected by the legislation can rely upon the judgment of the court.[201] However, while this suggests that a finding of ultra vires could have a significant complicating impact, much will in fact depend on the remedy (if any) granted by the court. Even though the court may find that the legislation is unlawful, it may at the same time decline to grant a remedy whether for reason of the applicant's failure to observe a procedural requirement[202] or where it prefers to exercise its discretion to refuse relief.[203] A court may equally grant a declaration that legislation is unlawful but refuse to grant an order of certiorari that would have the effect of quashing it. Such legislation, while tainted by illegality, will in that way remain in force.[204]

---

[195]   As in, eg, *Re Neill's Application* [2006] NICA 5 (challenge to the lawfulness of the Anti-social Behaviour (Northern Ireland) Order 2004, SI 2004/1998 (NI 12): application dismissed).

[196]   See, eg, *Belfast Corporation v Daly* [1963] NI 78 (collateral challenge to the lawfulness of a bye-law in a criminal prosecution: challenge failed before the Court of Appeal in proceedings by way of case stated).

[197]   As in, eg, *R v Wicks* [1998] AC 92 (individual who was prosecuted for failing to comply with a planning enforcement notice could not challenge collaterally the lawfulness of the notice as the corresponding legislative framework contained an elaborate statutory code with detailed provisions regarding appeals).

[198]   *Boddington v British Transport Police* [1999] 2 AC 143.

[199]   See [2.36].

[200]   See [4.05].

[201]   *Hoffmann-La Roche & Co v Secretary of State for Trade and Industry* [1975] AC 295, 365, Lord Diplock.

[202]   On which see ch 3.

[203]   Se [3.81]–[3.87] and [8.08]–[8.09].

[204]   For the full range of possibilities see W Wade and C Forsyth, *Administrative Law*, 9th edn (Oxford, Oxford University Press, 2004) p 300*ff*. See further [8.14].

[5.37] The third point, which also goes to remedies, concerns severance. Where subordinate legislation is challenged and the court makes a finding of illegality in respect of one or more its provisions, it may be possible for the court to sever and quash those provisions while allowing the remainder of the legislation to remain in force.²⁰⁵ Whether this will be possible will very much depend on the structure of the legislation in question, and it may be that the 'good' cannot be separated from the 'bad' (through use of the so-called 'blue pencil test'²⁰⁶). However, where it is possible to sever, this can have the dual benefit of protecting an individual from an illegality while at the same time allowing significant parts of a legislative scheme to remain in place.²⁰⁷ The courts can in this way reconcile some of the competing imperatives of judicial review.²⁰⁸

DISCRETION AND ILLEGALITY

[5.38] Arguments of illegality in the vast majority of cases will centre on how a public authority has chosen to exercise its discretion, for example where it has made a decision and/or acted in a particular way, or made no decision and/or failed to act. Discretion—which denotes the ability lawfully to choose between different courses of action—is ordinarily synonymous with the existence of a statutory power, although it may also exist in a statutory duty and, more exceptionally in public law terms, in non-statutory power.²⁰⁹ Where discretion is granted by statute, arguments of illegality will focus on whether the decision-maker has acted in a manner that is consistent with the power that the legislature has delegated to them (the power may relate to, among other things, the making of subordinate legislation, the allocation of licences, the regulation of activities, the payment of grants, the workings of the social welfare system, and so on). While much will here depend on judicial interpretation of the statute and of the context to the dispute,²¹⁰ the justification for judicial intervention is the need to safeguard the intentions of the legislature and to ensure that the decision-maker does not rewrite its powers and duties by acting outside those intentions. Where, on the other hand, the discretion has a non-statutory source, the rationale for judicial intervention is different and focused more on considerations of the need to protect individuals in the face of exercises of de facto public power. The courts will thus intervene here when the issues raised are regarded as 'justiciable'²¹¹ or as having implications for the wider 'public interest'.²¹²

---

²⁰⁵ See, eg, *Re Christian Institute and Ors' Application* [2007] NIQB 66 (challenge to the lawfulness of the Equality Act (Sexual Orientation) Regulations (Northern Ireland) 2006, SR 2006/439, that had been made under s 82 of the Equality Act 2006: application granted only in respect of those provisions governing harassment, which were quashed).

²⁰⁶ On which see, eg, *Hume v Londonderry Justices* [1972] NI 91, 115.

²⁰⁷ See, eg, *Re Euro Stock's Application* [1999] NI 13 (challenge to public health legislation that had serious financial implications for the applicant—relevant provisions of the legislation quashed but remainder kept in force pending an Art 234 EC reference on its legality to the ECJ (the legislation was the Specified Risk Material Order (Northern Ireland) 1997, SR 1997/551)).

²⁰⁸ On which see [1.04]–[1.10].

²⁰⁹ On statutory powers, duties, and discretion see [4.22]–[4.28]; and on non-statutory power see ch 2 and [4.06]–[4.08].

²¹⁰ See [4.14]–[4.21].

²¹¹ See, in respect of the royal prerogative, [4.06]–[4.08]. But on justiciability see too [4.14]–[4.17].

²¹² See [2.14]–[2.17].

[**5.39**]　There are six principal ways to challenge the legality of exercises of discretion (some of which overlap both with each other and with the grounds of substantive review and procedural impropriety, and which may alternatively be considered under those headings). The first is with reference to the UK's 'constitutional statutes', viz the European Communities Act 1972, the Human Rights Act 1998, and the Northern Ireland Act 1998 (see [5.07]–[5.08], [5.17]–[5.20], and [5.27]–[5.30]). The remaining five—considered below—relate to the common law constraints of relevancy, propriety of purpose, bad faith, non-delegation of power, and non-fettering of discretion.

Relevancy

[**5.40**]　The relevancy doctrine requires, at its most basic, that exercises of discretion take into account all relevant considerations and ignore those that are irrelevant[213] (it can on this basis be regarded as a species of error of fact[214]). Considerations for these purposes will ordinarily be identified expressly or impliedly in the statute that delegates power to the decision-maker, although the courts will also intervene where there 'are matters so obviously material to a decision on a particular project that anything short of direct consideration of them . . . would not be in accordance with the intention of the Act'.[215] Whether a consideration is relevant is therefore a matter of law[216] to be determined through interpretation of the statute (or statutes) and, where appropriate, with reference to the wider context of the decision (considerations in statute may be read as obligatory or discretionary—those that are obligatory must be taken into account and those that are discretionary may be taken into account[217]). While the courts have recognised that it will sometimes be appropriate to exhibit restraint when decisions are challenged—for instance, where statute has given a decision-maker a wide discretion—they have emphasised that all exercises of discretion should still conform to the relevancy doctrine.[218] Relevancy thus acts as an important constraint on even the widest forms of discretion and, in that manner, safeguards the rule of law.[219]

[**5.41**]　Arguments of relevancy can arise in two main ways. The first is as outlined above: that is, where it is argued that a decision is vitiated by irrelevant considerations or has been taken in the absence of relevant considerations. Challenges of this kind impugn the decision as illegal in the sense that it is ultra vires the statute and/or unreasonable in the sense that no reasonable authority could have taken irrelevant considerations into account or failed to take account of relevant ones (the burden of establishing the point rests with the applicant,[220] although this task may be eased where a decision-maker is

---

[213] *Re Colgan's Application* [1996] NI 24, 43.

[214] See [4.38]–[4.39].

[215] *Re Duffy's Application* [2006] NICA 28(1), paras 13–14, Kerr LCJ, quoting *Creednz v Governor General* [1981] 1 NZLR 172, Cooke J, and *Re Findlay* [1985] AC 318, 333–4, Lord Scarman. See too *Re Friends of the Earth's Application* [2006] NIQB 48.

[216] *Re Wellworth Co's Application* [1996] NI 509, 527, quoting *Tesco Stores Ltd v Secretary of the State for the Environment* [1995] 2 All ER 636, 642, Lord Keith.

[217] *R (Hurst) v London Northern District Coroner* [2007] 2 WLR 726, 746, para 57, Lord Brown; and *Re Cullen's Application* [2005] NIQB 9, para 33.

[218] *Re Duffy's Application* [2006] NICA 28(1), para 12, Kerr LCJ.

[219] On the rule of law see [4.04]–[4.09].

[220] On the onus of proof see [3.24]–[3.26].

under a duty to give reasons and the reasons given are 'manifestly bad'[221]). Such arguments are commonplace in the case law, and successful arguments of relevancy have been made where: the Department of the Environment failed to consider objections to an application for planning permission[222]; the Department of the Environment took into account a previous, but void, purported grant of planning permission when granting a subsequent application for permission[223]; the Secretary of State for Northern Ireland failed to take account of the fact that there was a real and immediate threat to the life of the applicant when deciding to exclude the applicant from the Key Person Protection Scheme[224]; the Recorder of Belfast did not take account of the fact that the applicant for a licence had been released under legislation enacted to give effect to the Belfast Agreement[225]; the decision-maker failed to have regard to the (then) unincorporated ECHR when interfering with an individual's property rights[226]; the Water Service failed to have regard to requirements specified in legislation before granting permission for new connections to the sewerage system[227]; a local council did not address the question of the adequacy of available facilities when deciding whether a leisure centre should open on Sundays[228]; an appeals tribunal calculated a sum of money to be repaid by an individual partly with incorrect reference to the age of the individual[229]; and a tribunal failed to take into account a report that should have informed its deliberations.[230]

[5.42]   An applicant may also argue that a decision is unlawful even though the decision-maker has taken all relevant considerations into account and ignored irrelevant ones.[231] Challenges of this kind are essentially concerned with the merits of the decision and with the respective weight that the decision-maker has given to each consideration. The courts' historical approach in such cases emphasised that judicial review was generally not available[232] and that, where it was, it was limited to the standard set by *Wednesbury* unreasonableness, as the task of making a decision in the light of the considerations was that of the decision-maker.[233] However, while the *Wednesbury* approach remains important when fundamental rights are unaffected by a decision, it has not survived the requirement that the courts give effect to the proportionality principle in cases under the Human Rights Act 1998[234] (*Wednesbury* had, in any event, already been modified in some pre-Human Rights Act cases that engaged common law fundamental rights[235]). Although the

---

[221] *Re Thompson's Application* [2004] NIQB 62, para 7, Girvan J. On the duty to give reasons see [7.43]–[7.46].

[222] *Re Rowsome's Application* [2004] NI 82.

[223] *R (Thallon) v Department of the Environment* [1982] NI 26.

[224] *Re W's Application* [2004] NIQB 67; *Re Brolly's Application* [2004] NIQB 69; and *Re F's Application* [2005] NI 280. But compare *Re Meehan's Application* [2004] NIJB 53.

[225] *Re McComb's Application* [2003] NIQB 47. See further [1.34]

[226] *Cowan v Department of Enterprise, Trade and Industry* [2000] NI 122; cf *Belfast City Council v Miss Behavin' Ltd* [2007] 1 WLR 1420 (decision-makers not required to take human rights points into account in the decision-making process so long as their final decisions are consistent with the Human Rights Act 1998: see [5.19]).

[227] *Re Friends of the Earth's Application* [2006] NIQB 48.

[228] *Re O'Neill's Application* [1995] NI 274.

[229] *RA (DHSS) v Enniskillen Supplementary Benefits Appeals Tribunal* [1980] NI 95.

[230] *Re Jamison's Application*, 14 October 1996, unreported.

[231] *Re O'Connor's Application* [1991] NI 77, 88, Murray LJ.

[232] See, eg, in the planning context, *Re QUB's Application*, 9 April 1997, unreported; *Re Lisburn Consortium's Application*, 14 January 2000, unreported; and *Re Walsh's Application* 8 May 2000, unreported.

[233] *R v Secretary of State, ex p Henry*, 31 May 1994, unreported. On *Wednesbury* see [6.05]–[6.11].

[234] *R v Secretary of State for the Home Department, ex p Daly* [2001] 2 AC 532.

[235] See, eg, *R v Secretary of State for the Home Department, ex p Bugdaycay* [1987] AC 514.

courts have linked the proportionality principle to a 'discretionary area of judgment' doctrine that pursues judicial restraint in appropriate cases,[236] the principle potentially requires a reviewing court to assess whether the decision-maker has struck the correct balance between all relevant considerations.[237] The corresponding question for the courts in cases under the Human Rights Act 1998, therefore, is perhaps whether a particular decision should attract 'closer look' review (for example, where absolute rights are engaged) or whether a relevancy enquiry should be guided by the need to observe the decision-maker's area of judgment (for example, where qualified rights are in issue).[238]

[5.43]   One final point about relevancy concerns cases where irrelevant considerations have been taken into account but where those considerations have not been central to the final decision. Under those circumstances, there is authority to suggest that the final decision may be allowed to stand so long as the dominant considerations that guided the decision are lawful.[239] Whether the dominant considerations are lawful is, in turn, a matter that may be resolved with reference to the reasons for the decision (if any[240]) and the respondent's corresponding affidavit evidence. In the event that the dominant considerations are lawful or those that are unlawful are independent and capable of severance (see [5.37]), the decision may be deemed valid.

Purposes

[5.44]   Arguments about impropriety of purpose are made where 'a statutory power is given for purpose A and the donee of the power exercises it for purpose B'.[241] Such arguments, which may overlap with or be made instead of arguments of relevancy (that is, that the purpose pursued is an irrelevant consideration[242]; see [5.40]–[5.43]), fasten upon the need to give effect to the legislature's intention in enacting a particular statute. The corresponding purposes of a power will either be found in the express terms of the statute or read as implicit in the overall statutory scheme. Where a decision-maker acts beyond those express or implied purposes, he or she will thus have acted ultra vires the statute, and any decision or other measure may, for instance, be quashed as illegal. A decision or other measure may also, or alternatively, be characterised as *Wednesbury* unreasonable.[243]

[5.45]   Arguments about impropriety of purpose can, however, become more complex where it is contended that the decision-maker pursued a number of purposes and that the improper purpose was only one of those. Such 'mixed purpose' cases are resolved through use of the 'dominant purpose' test; that is, the test that enquires whether the dominant purpose behind a decision or other measure was lawful or unlawful. The

---

[236] See *R v DPP, ex p Kebeline* [2000] 2 AC 326, 381, Lord Hope. And see [6.25]–[6.26].

[237] *R v Secretary of State for the Home Department, ex p Daly* [2001] 2 AC 532, 547, Lord Steyn.

[238] Although note that the discretionary area of judgment doctrine has been invoked in some cases involving absolute rights: see, eg, *Re A's Application* [2001] NI 335 (Art 2 ECHR) and *Re E's Application* [2004] NIQB 35 (Art 3 ECHR). And see [6.25]–[6.26].

[239] *Re McKevitt's Application* [2004] NIQB 70, para 28.

[240] See [7.43]–[7.46].

[241] *Re Neeson's Application* [1986] NI 92, 101; and *Re McCann's Application*, 13 November 1992, unreported.

[242] See, eg, *Re Kelly's Application* [2000] NI 103; and *Re Hegan's Application*, unreported, available through Lexis.

[243] See [6.05]–[6.11].

central task for the court under such circumstances is: to identify the different purposes that informed a decision; to decide which of the purposes were within the power and which were not; and to decide whether those purposes that were within the power predominated. While it has been recognised that it may not always be easy to formulate or apply the test[244]—it has been suggested that the courts may instead ask whether irrelevant considerations had a substantial or material influence on the decision or other measure[245]—it is clear that the test is intended to ensure that decisions and so on do not automatically fall because they are part tainted by illegality.[246] There is thus some overlap here with the logic of severance and the understanding that the lawful elements of a decision or other measure should be distinguished from the unlawful with the result, where possible, that the decision is allowed to stand (see [5.37] and [5.43]).

[5.46] Case law on purposes—whether mixed or not—sometimes also refers to decisions as having been taken for a 'collateral', 'extraneous', or 'ulterior' purpose. While each of these terms can be read interchangeably with 'improper' insofar as they are all concerned with illegality, it has been suggested that the term 'improper' is different because it connotes moral impropriety and an intention to use a power unlawfully.[247] Whether the courts in fact use the term 'improper' for this reason is, however, unclear and there is no definitive judicial statement on the point. On the other hand, the fact that the terms 'collateral' and 'ulterior' have been preferred in some—though not all[248]— highly politicised disputes would suggest that the courts are anxious to avoid the use of terminology that may be taken to question the integrity of political decision-makers.[249] The term 'improper' has thus been used more readily in what may be regarded as less politically charged disputes, for instance those concerned with the administration of criminal justice[250] and disciplinary matters in the armed forces.[251]

---

[244] See *Re Kelly's Application* [2000] NI 103, 113, Carswell LCJ.

[245] *Re Kelly's Application* [2000] NI 103, 113, Carswell LCJ, citing W Wade and C Forsyth, *Administrative Law*, 7th edn (Oxford, Oxford University Press, 1994) p 439.

[246] For application of it see, eg, *Re French's Application* [1985] NI 310 (a council resolution to the effect that councillors could not participate in meetings until they had signed an anti-violence declaration was unlawful as its dominant purpose was not the improvement of security but the legally inadmissible purpose of excluding certain councillors); *Curran v MoD*, 11 March 1994, unreported (decision to transfer constables out of the jurisdiction was unlawful because dominant—and wrongful—purpose was punishment); and *Re Kelly's Application* [2000] NI 103 (regulations governing access to the legal profession in NI were lawful on account of their dominant purpose).

[247] See H Woolf, J Jowell, and AP Le Sueur, *De Smith, Woolf and Jowell's Principles of Judicial Review*, 4th edn (London, Sweet & Maxwell, 1999) p 196.

[248] Eg, *Re Downes' Application* [2006] NIQB 77 (court finding that the Secretary of State had exercised power for an improper political purpose—viz 'confidence building'—when appointing the Interim Victims' Commissioner)

[249] See, eg, *Re French's Application* [1985] NI 310 (a council resolution to the effect that councillors could not participate in meetings until they had signed an anti-violence declaration was unlawful as its dominant purpose was not the improvement of security but the ulterior purpose of excluding certain councillors); *Re Neeson's Application* [1986] NI 92 (council decision to delegate functions to committees was unlawful as it had been taken for the ulterior purpose of excluding Sinn Féin councillors from the work of the council); *Re De Brun and McGuinness' Application* [2001] NI 442 (First Minister's decision not to nominate Sinn Féin Ministers to meetings of the North/South Ministerial Council pursued a purpose that was collateral to the power being exercised). And see further, eg, *R v Secretary of State for Northern Ireland ex p Close and others*, 31 October 1986, unreported, and *R v Castlereagh Borough Council ex parte Morrow*, 13 February 1987, unreported (both challenging the lawfulness of council measures adopted in opposition to the Anglo-Irish Agreement).

[250] *Re Cunningham's Application* [2004] NI 328 (use of statutory powers for an improper purpose when bringing charges against a terror suspect).

[251] *Curran v MoD*, 11 March 1994, unreported (decision to transfer constables out of the jurisdiction was an improper use of the power contained in the Ministry of Defence regulations, as the power to transfer was not designed to be used, as here, for reasons of punishment).

Bad Faith

[5.47]   Exercises of discretion may also be deemed unlawful where it can be shown that the decision-maker has acted in 'bad faith'.[252] At its highest, bad faith will vitiate a decision where it is shown that the decision-maker has acted dishonestly, or taken action which he or she knew to be improper.[253] While there is clearly some potential for overlap here between bad faith and 'relevancy' and 'propriety of purpose' as means for challenging decisions (on which see [5.40]–[5.46]), bad faith is perhaps better viewed as distinct in the sense that the applicant has to show that the decision-maker intended to abuse their power, or was reckless as to whether they did so (this is certainly the understanding of the concept that infuses the tort of misfeasance in public office[254]). Bad faith therefore 'always involves a grave charge. It must not be treated as a synonym for an honest mistake'.[255]

[5.48]   Challenges based on bad faith are rare in the case law, undoubtedly because of the difficulties of making out the argument. Nevertheless, the heading remains as an important safeguard against the potential abuse of power, and it in that sense corresponds with other little-used headings such as actual bias.[256]

Delegation

[5.49]   Where statute gives a decision-maker a discretionary power, whether of a judicial, legislative, or administrative nature,[257] it is generally unlawful for the decision-maker to delegate that power of decision to another person or body[258] unless the statute itself expressly provides for such delegation.[259] This notion is sometimes expressed in the Latin maxim *delegatus non potest delegare*, which means that a body or person to whom power has been delegated by Parliament cannot itself delegate the power.[260] The principle of non-delegation does not, however, take form as a rule but rather as a presumption to the effect that the legislature intends that only the beneficiary of a statutory scheme may exercise the corresponding power. While the presumption is strong, it can nevertheless be rebutted where the courts find that there is something in the wider statutory scheme that permits of delegation. The courts, moreover, recognise that decision makers may have to take the advice of others or make use of agents or employees in the decision-making process, and the courts will here consider that the principle of non-delegation has not been offended where the beneficiary of the statutory scheme retains the final

---

[252] *Associated Provincial Picture Houses v Wednesbury Corporation* [1948] 1 KB 223, 228–9.
[253] For consideration see *Neill v Wilson* [1999] NI 1.
[254] *Three Rivers District Council v Bank of England (No 3)* [2003] 2 AC 1; and see [8.28]–[8.29].
[255] *Cannock Chase District Council v Kelly* [1978] 1 All ER 152, 156.
[256] On which see [7.61].
[257] *Re Adair's Application* [2003] NIQB 16, para 8.
[258] See, eg, *Re Bell's Application* [2000] NI 245 (Health and Social Services Board had unlawfully delegated to its Director of Pharmaceutical Services the power to determine whether a pharmacy should be allowed to relocate to different premises).
[259] Eg, Local Government Act (Northern Ireland) 1972, ss 18–19.
[260] For use of the term see, eg, *R v Law Society, ex p Maher*, 23 May 1986, unreported.

decision-making power[261] (although it may not always be easy to identify precisely the roles played by the recipients of power and those that assist them[262]). In the converse circumstance where the decision-maker regards itself as bound by the opinion of others, the courts will make a finding of unlawful delegation or, depending on how the argument is made, of an unlawful fettering of discretion[263] (on which see [5.52]–[5.54]).

[5.50]　There is one main exception to the principle of non-delegation, which has historically been made in respect of central government departments. Under the so-called *Carltona* doctrine,[264] the courts accept that it is legitimate for junior Ministers and governmental officials to take decisions in the name of a government Minister entrusted with a particular statutory power[265] (the exception now also applies to Ministers in the devolved Executives[266] but does not apply to local authorities and statutory bodies[267]; the principle may be displaced by a contrary intention in a statute[268]). The corresponding rationale for the exception is based largely on considerations of pragmatism, as the courts accept that it would not be practically possible for a Minister to apply his or her mind to each decision. However, the exception is also aligned to a constitutional justification that centres on the doctrine of ministerial responsibility and the understanding that Ministers are finally answerable to Parliament for each of the actions of their departments. Where officials act in the name of the Minister, it is therefore sometimes said that there is in fact no delegation of power as the junior Minister or official represents the 'alter ego' of the Minister.[269] Should a Minister in consequence choose for an important matter 'an official of such junior standing that he could not be expected competently to perform the work, the minister would have to answer for that in Parliament'.[270]

[5.51]　The workings and logic of the *Carltona* doctrine are not without criticism, and it has been argued that decisions and other measures that have implications for fundamental rights and freedoms should be taken personally by the relevant Minister.[271] It has also been queried whether the doctrine, which was formulated more than 60 years ago, is suited to the modern structures of government. The point here is simply that the proliferation of, among other things, Next Steps Agencies has resulted in the comprehensive redesign of public service delivery and of the corresponding relationship between central government and civil servants. Case law in England and Wales has, however, held that

---

[261] See, eg, *Re Adair's Application* [2003] NIQB 16 (Secretary of State had not unlawfully delegated to Sentence Review Commissioners his power to recall prisoners released on licence as he had retained the freedom to release a prisoner even where this would conflict with the advice of the Commissioners).

[262] See *Re North Down Borough Council's Application* [1986] NI 304, considering the relationship between a council and town clerk.

[263] *Lavender and Sons Ltd v Minister of Housing and Local Government* [1970] 1 WLR 1231, considered in *Re Meekatharra's Application*, 25 April 1995, unreported.

[264] *Carltona Ltd v Commissioner of Works* [1943] 2 All ER 560; and see, eg, *McKernan v Governor of HM Prison* [1983] NI 83.

[265] See, eg, *Re McCann's Application* [2004] NIQB 47, para 13, Girvan J, applying *Carltona* in the context of a challenge to subordinate legislation.

[266] *Beggs v Scottish Ministers* [2007] 1 WLR 455.

[267] *Re Bell's Application* [2000] NI 245.

[268] *Re Lockhart's Application* [2007] NIQB 35, para 34.

[269] *R v Secretary of State for the Home Department, ex p Oladehinde* [1991] 1 AC 254, 284, Sir John Donaldson. And see *Re Bell's Application* [2000] NI 245, 254, Girvan J.

[270] *Carltona Ltd v Commissioner of Works* [1943] 2 All ER 560, 563, Lord Greene MR.

[271] For judicial consideration of the point see *Re Henry's Application* [2004] NIQB 11, paras 37–8, Weatherup J. And for earlier case law see, eg, *McKernan v Governor of HM Prison Belfast* [1983] NI 83, and *R v Harper*, 1 May 1990, unreported.

Carltona remains of application in the context of Next Steps Agencies, although the courts have at the same time indicated that the matter may need to be decided on a case-by-case basis.[272]

Fettering of Discretion

[5.52]   It is a basic rule of administrative law that a public authority entrusted with discretion must retain for itself the option of exercising that discretion on a case-by-case basis. This rule against the 'fettering of discretion' is most frequently argued to be offended where a public authority adopts a policy to guide it in the exercise of its discretion,[273] for instance where it has to allocate a limited number of licences[274] or admit individuals to educational institutions[275] or to governmental schemes.[276] Although the courts have long recognised that it is legitimate for public authorities to formulate policies that are 'legally relevant to the exercise of (their) powers, consistent with the purpose of the enabling legislation, and not arbitrary, capricious or unjust',[277] they have at the same time emphasised that authorities must remain free to depart from their policies, or make exceptions to them, as the circumstances of individual cases require.[278] A public authority cannot therefore adopt a policy that (a) is so rigid that it in effect becomes a rule to be applied in any given case or (b) establishes an unacceptably high threshold for individual applicants to cross.[279] Should such a policy be adopted, the corresponding decisions of the authority may be challenged either on the ground that they are ultra vires the empowering statute (where relevant[280]) or, depending on circumstance, on the ground that the individual has not been given a fair hearing on the matter (procedural impropriety). This latter point corresponds to the requirement that decision-makers must not prejudge a matter or 'shut their ears'[281] to individual applications simply because the authority has in place a particular policy. However, where the decision-maker has granted the individual a hearing—whether as a result of a statutory or common law obligation to do so—it is thereafter free to apply its policy notwithstanding the

---

[272]   *R v Secretary of State for Social Services, ex p Sherwin* (1996) 32 BMLR 1.

[273]   For an alternative use of the term 'policy'—viz to denote essentially political questions—see [6.03].

[274]   *Re McBride's Application* [1997] NI 269, 273, Carswell LCJ.

[275]   *Re Bogues' Application* [1985] NI 218 (policy governing entry to secondary schools).

[276]   *Re Herdman's Application* [2003] NIQB 46 (access to the Key Person Protection Scheme).

[277]   *Re Herdman's Application* [2003] NIQB 46, para 19, quoting *Halsbury's Laws of England*, Vol 1 (1), para 32; and see, eg, *R (Rodgers) v Swindon NHS Primary Care Trust* [2006] 89 BMLR 211 (health authority policy of not providing herceptin® to patients in early stages of cancer unless they could demonstrate 'exceptional personal or clinical circumstances' whenever resources were available was irrational, as it was impossible to envisage what those 'exceptional' circumstances might be and the policy would amount, in practice, to a complete refusal of funding).

[278]   *British Oxygen Co Ltd v Ministry of Technology* [1971] AC 610; and, eg, *R v Secretary of State, ex p Doherty*, 1 March 1995, unreported; *Re Russell's Application* [1996] NI 310, 360, Hutton LCJ; *Re McBride's Application* [1997] NI 269, 273; *Re Blayney's Application* [2003] NIQB 51, para 16; and *Re Herdman's Application* [2003] NIQB 46, para 19.

[279]   *Re Herdman's Application* [2003] NIQB 46, para 20; and see, eg, *Re Scappaticci's Application* [2003] NIQB 56 (no over-rigid adherence to government policy where the government had refused in the instant case to confirm or deny whether the applicant had been a British Army agent).

[280]   See, in the non-statutory context, eg *Re W's Application* [1998] NI 219 (challenge to the Secretary of State's refusal to use the royal prerogative to make an *ex gratia* payment of compensation: application dismissed as the wider decision not to make more general provision for *ex gratia* payments would be undermined by the co-existence of a duty to consider the circumstances of individual cases).

[281]   The term is used in, eg, *Re Russell's Application* [1996] NI 310, 360, Hutton LCJ.

applicant's viewpoint. Any further challenge at that stage would thus centre on the reasonableness of the authority's decision and/or the related argument that the authority had failed to take the individual's representations into account[282] (see [5.40]–[5.43]). Should the individual's fundamental rights be affected by the outcome, a challenge may also be made on the ground that the decision lacks proportion[283] or has not been accompanied by sufficient reasons given the authority's obligations under the Human Rights Act 1998.[284]

[5.53]   Public authorities can also fetter their discretion in other ways. For instance, an authority may be said to have fettered its discretion where it has unlawfully delegated its power of decision to another person or body[285] (see [5.49]–[5.51]); and an authority may likewise fetter its discretion where it enters into a contractual arrangement that has the effect of limiting some of its statutory powers. Given that there may be a practical need for an authority to engage in a contractual relationship for purposes of performing some of its functions, the courts will not, however, automatically hold that a contract that has a limiting effect is void. The courts will, instead, enquire whether the contract is compatible with the relevant statutory scheme and, in the event that it is, will accept the corresponding limitation on statutory power.[286]

[5.54]   One further point about the rule against the fettering of discretion concerns the potential for a tension between that rule and the protection of substantive legitimate expectations. The doctrine of substantive legitimate expectation entails, at its strongest, that a public authority that has made a clear, unambiguous, and lawful representation to an individual that it will act in a particular manner cannot subsequently resile from the representation save where there is an overriding public interest justification for doing so.[287] Although the corresponding case law on the protection of substantive legitimate expectation is complex and overridden by considerations of the limits to the judicial role, it is predicated on the understanding that there will be circumstances in which individuals can prevent authorities from exercising their discretion in a particular manner. To the extent that the rule against the fettering of discretion thus seeks to ensure that authorities retain their power to make discretionary choices, the doctrine of substantive legitimate expectation has the clear potential to constrain those same choices.

CONCLUSION

[5.55]   There are five points that can be made by of way of conclusion on illegality as a ground for review:

i.   The ground of illegality requires that decision-makers understand correctly the law that regulates their decision-making power and that they give effect to the law

---

[282] *Re Bogues' Application* [1985] NI 218.

[283] On proportionality see [6.18]–[6.28].

[284] On the duty to give reasons generally and in the human rights context see [7.43]–[7.45].

[285] As was argued unsuccessfully in *Re Murphy's Application* [2004] NIQB 85 (applicant arguing that one government department had left a decision for which it had responsibility to another department, which had no responsibility in respect of the matter).

[286] See further HWR Wade and CF Forsyth, *Administrative Law*, 9th edn (Oxford, Oxford University Press, 2004) p 330*ff*.

[287] See *Re Neale's Application* [2005] NIQB 33; and [6.29]–[6.45].

accordingly. The law, for these purposes, is found not only in statute law, but also in the common law and in EU law and the law of the ECHR (as given effect by the European Communities Act 1972 and the Human Rights Act 1998).

ii. The ground of illegality is not always free-standing, and there can be an overlap in reasoning under the headings of illegality, substantive review, and procedural impropriety. There can also be an overlap when EU law and/or the ECHR are in issue.

iii. The common law recognises a category of 'constitutional statutes'. These statutes, which are not subject to the ordinary domestic rules on implied repeal, impose a range of obligations on public authorities and, in some instances, on the Northern Ireland Assembly and the Westminster Parliament (albeit subject to the argument that these are self-imposed obligations). The most important such statutes are the European Communities Act 1972, the Human Rights Act 1998, and the Northern Ireland Act 1998 (see [5.04]–[5.30]).

iv. Subordinate legislation can be challenged as contrary to one or other of the constitutional statutes, its parent statute (or related Acts), or the range of common law requirements on illegality. Where the challenge is made with reference to the constitutional statutes, it is important to note that the term 'subordinate legislation' does not have a constant meaning and that different considerations may arise depending on context (see [5.31]). Where the challenge is made with reference to the common law it is important to note that, while most of the requirements are of potential application, not all are (see [5.31]–[5.37]).

v. The range of common law requirements that govern the legality of decision-making may be sub-divided into the five headings of relevancy, purposes, bad faith, delegation, and fettering of discretion (see [5.38]–[5.54]). These headings apply most obviously when decisions or other measures are taken within a statutory framework. The requirements can, however, also found challenges to some exercises of non-statutory power.

6

Substantive Review:
Wednesbury, *Proportionality,*
Legitimate Expectation, Equality

INTRODUCTION

[**6.01**] This chapter considers the scope for substantive review of the discretionary choices of public decision-makers.[1] Substantive review here refers to those situations where courts grant remedies to applicants who have demonstrated that a decision or other measure is unlawful because it is, for instance, arbitrary, manifestly unjust, substantively unfair, disproportionate, lacking in reason, and/or constitutive of an abuse of power. In historical terms, courts in Northern Ireland have generally been reluctant to engage in substantive review because judicial review is concerned with the legality of a decision and not with its merits.[2] However, while the distinction between 'review' and 'appeal' remains of importance,[3] the courts have more recently developed new principles and doctrines (most notably proportionality and substantive legitimate expectation) that have the potential to result in 'closer look' review. This chapter thus identifies the key features of these doctrines and principles and how they can result in more intensive judicial scrutiny of discretionary choices. It also explains how the courts have sought to reconcile the emergence of the principles with concerns about the need for courts to observe the separation of powers doctrine.[4]

[**6.02**]   The chapter begins with a section on the significance of the *Wednesbury* unreasonableness/irrationality principle that has traditionally been synonymous with a restraint-based approach to substantive review. It next considers the importance of the proportionality principle that has long been of application in EU law cases and which has recently assumed an added prominence under the Human Rights Act 1998. There then follow two further sections that consider, respectively, the doctrines of legitimate expectation and equality/non-discrimination. The conclusion provides a summary of the various sections.

[**6.03**]   Two further points can be made by way of introduction. The first concerns the fact that statute will often give a decision-maker a greater or lesser degree of discretion

---

[1] On discretionary choices see [4.22]–[4.28].

[2] See [1.05]; and, eg, *R v Secretary of State for Northern Ireland, ex p Finlay* [1983] 9 NIJB 1, 10, Hutton J; *Re Glor Na nGael's Application* [1991] NI 117, 129, Carswell J; and *Re Bow Street Mall's Application* [2006] NIQB 28, para 110 [sic], Girvan J.

[3] *Re Duffy's Application* [2006] NICA 28, para 40, Kerr LCJ.

[4] On which see [1.03] and [1.05].

in a matter that comes within its competence (albeit that the extent of any discretion will depend upon judicial interpretation of the statute).[5] Although the rule is not absolute, courts will tend to be more deferential to substantive choices that are made in areas where the decision-maker has been given a wide discretion and/or where the courts regard the decision as essentially political in nature (the courts here often refer to 'policy' decisions).[6] The rationale for such restraint is founded on the separation of powers doctrine and the understanding that, as the legislature has given the power of decision to the recipient of the delegated power, the courts should not intervene unless the decision-maker has 'taken leave of their senses'[7] (substantive review), misunderstood the nature of their power (illegality[8]), or acted in breach of a procedural requirement (procedural impropriety[9]). Where, in contrast, the decision-maker has only a limited discretion the courts may be more inclined to grant a remedy in respect of any corresponding substantive choices precisely because the range of options open to the decision-maker is smaller. The potential for such intervention is perhaps most apparent where a power is exercised in a way that interferes with, or would interfere with, an individual's absolute rights at common law or under the Human Rights Act 1998 (see [6.10]–[6.11] and [6.18]–[6.26]).

[6.04]   The second point concerns the scope for substantive review of the legislative choices of the Westminster Parliament when rights under EU law and/or the ECHR are affected by those choices. Although the term 'substantive review' is ordinarily associated with challenges to the choices of administrative and other subordinate decision-makers, the European Communities Act 1972 and the Human Rights Act 1998 now provide for (qualified forms of) review of Acts of Parliament that can lead to disapplication of an Act in the EU context and a declaration of incompatibility in the context of the ECHR[10] (the position in respect of Acts of the Northern Ireland Assembly and Orders in Council made at times when the Assembly has been suspended is different as these may be quashed[11]). Where an Act of Parliament is challenged as incompatible with any of the provisions of EU law and/or the ECHR, courts are to resolve the dispute with reference to a range of general principles of European law that include the proportionality principle. This principle, which also applies when administrative acts and decisions are challenged as contrary to EU law or the ECHR, is understood to demand 'closer look' review as it requires courts to assess whether the legislature has struck the correct balance between the objectives that a legislative scheme pursues and the rights and interests that are affected by it.[12] However, while the courts accept that they should give effect to the principle when reviewing Acts of Parliament, they have at the same time emphasised that there may be a heightened need for self-restraint given that they are dealing with the preferences of a democratically elected legislature. Substantive review of legislative (and other) choices under the Human Rights Act 1998 has thus been aligned to a 'discretionary area of judgment' doctrine that seeks to limit the judicial role to that deemed constitu-

---

    [5] See [4.22].
    [6] *R v Secretary of State for the Environment, ex p Nottinghamshire CC* [1986] AC 240; and see [4.23]. But for an alternative use of the term 'policy'—viz in the context of the adoption of policies to guide exercises of discretion—see [5.52].
    [7] *R v Secretary of State for the Environment, ex p Nottinghamshire CC* [1986] AC 240, 247, Lord Scarman.
    [8] Ch 5.
    [9] Ch 7.
    [10] See, respectively, [5.07] and [5.14].
    [11] See [5.15] and [5.23]–[5.24]
    [12] *Re Matthews' Application* [2004] NIQB 9, para 26.

tionally appropriate (see [6.25]–[6.26]); and case law in the EU context has similarly emphasised that application of the proportionality principle may need to account for a decision-maker's 'margin of appreciation' (see [6.15]–[6.16]).

WEDNESBURY UNREASONABLENESS/IRRATIONALITY

[6.05]   Judicial restraint relative to the substantive choices of administrative and other subordinate decision-making bodies is most famously associated with *Wednesbury* unreasonableness. The *Wednesbury* principle, which takes its name from the seminal *Wednesbury Corporation* case,[13] entails that the courts should only interfere with discretionary choices that are taken beyond the very outer reaches of a decision-maker's power. Although it is now sometimes doubted whether the principle has any continuing relevance to administrative law (see [6.27]–[6.28]), its constitutional logic remains linked to the separation of powers doctrine and the understanding that judicial intervention in substantive choices is permissible solely where 'a decision is really virtually untenable as the decision of a sensible person'.[14] In the *Wednesbury* case, Lord Greene MR thus spoke of judicial intervention as justified where a decision is 'so unreasonable that no reasonable authority' could have taken it.[15] And in the *GCHQ* case, Lord Diplock equated the *Wednesbury* threshold to 'irrationality' and said that a decision must be 'so outrageous in its defiance of logic or of accepted moral standards that no sensible person who had applied his mind to the question to be decided could have arrived at it'.[16]

[6.06]   *Wednesbury* unreasonableness/irrationality (the terms are interchangeable) is, however, also a multi-faceted principle. For example, while the principle is typically associated with the above formulations that require absurdity or capriciousness, it also has an 'umbrella' meaning that is consonant with the overlapping nature of the grounds of review.[17] The principle has, moreover, long been applied in a context-sensitive way that provides for more or less intensive judicial scrutiny of decisions depending on the nature of the dispute at hand and of the interests affected.[18] Hence, where a case involves political questions that are regarded as ill suited to the judicial process, the *Wednesbury* threshold may rise. Where, on the other hand, a case is concerned with the protection of common law fundamental rights, the threshold for intervention may be lowered (although such cases would now come under the Human Rights Act 1998; see [6.18]–[6.28]).

Wednesbury Unreasonableness: Its 'Umbrella' and 'Substantive' Meanings

[6.07]   *Wednesbury* is used within its umbrella sense when it describes decisions that are unreasonable on grounds of relevancy, improper purpose, or bad faith.[19] Although these

---

[13] *Associated Provincial Picture Houses v Wednesbury Corporation* [1948] 1 KB 223.

[14] *Re McCartney's Application*, 23 December 1993, unreported, Carswell LJ.

[15] *Associated Provincial Picture Houses v Wednesbury Corporation* [1948] 1 KB 223, 233.

[16] *Council of Civil Service Unions v Minister for the Civil Service* [1985] AC 374, 408.

[17] *Boddington v British Transport Police* [1999] 2 AC 143, 152, Lord Irvine LC; and see [4.02] and [5.03].

[18] *Re McBride's Application (No 2)* [2003] NI 319, 345, para 52. And on the context-sensitive nature of the grounds for review see [4.14]–[4.21].

[19] *Associated Provincial Picture Houses v Wednesbury Corporation* [1948] 1 KB 223, 228–9, Lord Greene MR.

grounds can be examined under the heading of illegality,[20] they equally speak to the need for statutory power to be exercised reasonably within the more general meaning of that word. For instance, it cannot be said that a decision-maker who has exercised their power for an improper purpose has used the power reasonably; and neither can it be said that there is a reasonable exercise of power where the decision-maker takes irrelevant considerations into account or ignores relevant ones.[21] While arguments of purpose and/or relevancy may in turn be made with reference to 'substantive *Wednesbury*' where the purpose pursued is grossly improper (so as to amount to an abuse of power[22]) or where there is an egregious failure to take account of a relevant consideration, behaviour that is 'so unreasonable that no reasonable authority' could behave in that way is not necessary for 'umbrella *Wednesbury*'. A simple failure to observe statutory purposes and the requirements of relevancy will instead suffice, albeit as subject to counter-arguments about the lawfulness of the dominant purpose or consideration.[23]

[6.08]   Where a discretionary choice has been made in a manner consistent with underlying statutory purposes and/or the relevancy doctrine, it may alternatively be challenged within the substantive meaning of the *Wednesbury* principle. The argument that would be made here is, again, that the final substantive choice of the decision-maker is 'so unreasonable that no reasonable authority' could have made it. Although such arguments can sometimes be made out in practice,[24] it is much more usual for them to fail given the difficulties in convincing the court that a decision crosses the *Wednesbury* threshold.[25] Substantive *Wednesbury*, while applied in a context-sensitive manner (see [6.09]–[6.11]), is premised on the understanding that different decision-makers may lawfully arrive at different conclusions[26] and that the courts should therefore not ask what a reasonable decision-maker *would* do but rather what no reasonable decision-maker *could* do.[27] This is widely regarded as a demanding test to satisfy, and the courts have variously described it as 'notoriously high' and one that imposes a 'heavy burden' on applicants.[28] Yet, whatever the perceived difficulties associated with the test, it remains linked to the constitutional imperative of judicial self-restraint and the understanding

---

[20] *Re Friends of the Earth's Application* [2006] NIQB 48, para 18, Weatherup J; and see, respectively, [5.40]–[5.43]; [5.44]–[5.46]; and [5.47]–[5.48].

[21] *Re Harkin's Application* [2001] NIQB 6; and *Re Cullen's Application* [2005] NIQB 9, para 33, Weatherup J.

[22] *Re Croft's Application* [1997] NI 457, 491, Girvan J.

[23] On which see [5.43] and [5.45].

[24] *Re Skelly's Application* [2005] NICA 31 (a criminal injuries compensation adjudicator's decision not to refer a matter for an oral hearing was *Wednesbury* unreasonable as it was founded on the understanding that an oral hearing would not result in a decision that was different from that originally reached by the agency: the Court of Appeal considered that the only possible conclusion that the adjudicator could have reached was that a different decision from that of the agency could have been made); and *Re Interface Europe's Application*, 10 September 1998, unreported (the Department of the Environment's conclusion that a particular area of land would inevitably be included within the development limits of a statutory plan that was yet to be finalised was irrational).

[25] See, eg, *R v Secretary of State, ex p Henry*, 31 May 1994, unreported, Kerr J, stating that a decision that is *Wednesbury* unreasonable falls within an 'exceptional category of decision whose illogicality or utter irrationality demands that it be condemned as unsustainable on any acceptable basis'.

[26] *Re Neill's Application* [2005] NIQB 66, para 48, Girvan J.

[27] P Cane, *Administrative Law*, 4th edn (Oxford, Clarendon Press, 2004) p 250.

[28] See, respectively, *Re Croft's Application* [1997] NI 457, 471, MacDermott LJ (citing *R v Inland Revenue Commissioners, ex p Unilever plc* [1996] STC 681, 692, Sir Thomas Bingham MR), and *Re Adams' Application* 7 June 2000, unreported, Gillen J. See too, eg, *R v Secretary of State, ex p Oliver* 2 June 1995, unreported; and *Re Floyd's Application* [1997] NI 414, 420 (Carswell LCJ speaking of the 'depth' of irrationality needed).

that discretionary powers are to be exercised by those to whom they have been delegated. As Lord Ackner has said:

> Where Parliament has given to a minister or other person or body a discretion, the court's jurisdiction is limited, in the absence of a statutory right of appeal, to the supervision of the exercise of that discretionary power, so as to ensure that it has been exercised lawfully. It would be a wrongful usurpation of power by the judiciary to substitute its, the judicial view, on the merits and on that basis to quash the decision.[29]

Wednesbury Unreasonableness and Context Sensitivity

[6.09]   The restraint-based logic of substantive *Wednesbury* is at its most apparent when decision-makers are taken to have a wide discretion in a matter and/or where a decision is viewed as essentially political in character (see [6.03]). Here, the courts may link the context of the case to the making of 'policy' choices that are ill suited to the judicial process and conclude that the need for restraint is even more pronounced (the term 'policy' denotes a 'political' decision rather than an administrative policy that may guide an authority in the exercise of its discretion[30]). For instance, cases involving national security considerations have typically been taken to demand judicial self-restraint,[31] and so too have cases concerned with aspects of national or regional economic policy.[32] Although the courts have here stated that the political decision-making process does not lie wholly beyond judicial control,[33] they have noted that they should demonstrate full caution before intervening. Hence the courts sometimes refer in such cases to the related standard of 'soft-edged' review that entails 'that the court should in such circumstances be somewhat more ready than in some other cases to assume a higher degree of knowledge and expertise on the part of the decider'.[34]

[6.10]   On the other hand, the *Wednesbury* threshold can be lowered to provide for 'closer look' review where a case is concerned with an individual's common law fundamental rights. These are rights that the courts developed with particular vigour prior to the coming into force of the Human Rights Act 1998 and which include the right to life,[35] access to a court,[36] and freedom of expression.[37] Modification of *Wednesbury* here has usually been associated with the test of 'anxious scrutiny'[38] whereby the courts are more demanding of the justification for decisions that impact on an individual's fundamental

---

[29] *R v Home Secretary, ex p Brind* [1991] 1 AC 696, 757–8, Lord Ackner, cited in *Re Doherty's Application (No 2)* [1995] NI 144, 152.

[30] On the legality of which see [5.52].

[31] See, historically, *The Zamora* [1916] 2 AC 77, 107, Lord Parker; but for the modern law see [4.18]–[4.19].

[32] See, eg, *R v Secretary of State for the Environment, ex p Nottinghamshire CC* [1986] AC 240.

[33] See, eg, in respect of national security, *Secretary of State for the Home Department v Rehman* [2003] 1 AC 153, 187, para 31, Lord Steyn.

[34] *Re Williamson's Application* [2000] NI 281, 303. See further [4.20]–[4.21].

[35] *R v Secretary of State for the Home Department, ex p Bugdaycay* [1987] AC 514, 531, Lord Bridge. And see, eg, *R v Lord Saville, ex p A* [1999] 4 All ER 860 (Saville Tribunal had erred in holding that soldiers who had fired live rounds on Bloody Sunday should not be allowed to give evidence anonymously).

[36] *R v Lord Chancellor, ex p Witham* [1997] 2 All ER 779.

[37] *R v Secretary of State for the Home Department, ex p Brind* [1991] 1 AC 696, 748–9, Lord Bridge.

[38] *R v Secretary of State for the Home Department, ex p Bugdaycay* [1987] AC 514, 531, Lord Bridge. See further M Fordham and T de la Mare, 'Anxious Scrutiny, the Principle of Legality and the Human Rights Act' (2000) 5 JR 40.

rights at common law[39] (the courts will also be more exacting in their scrutiny of, for instance, matters of precedent fact[40]; related approaches to the interpretation of legislation may likewise seek to safeguard common law rights[41]). In terms of discretion, the corresponding rationale is simply that the range of options open to a reasonable decision-maker should be curtailed when its decision has, or would have, implications for, at one end of the spectrum, the right to life and, at the other end, freedom of expression. While some cases may still raise difficult questions as to the appropriate level of review—for instance, disputes about the allocation of medical resources and the common law right to life[42]—the courts will thus examine decisions that impact upon common law fundamental rights more closely and require a correspondingly fuller justification the greater the interference with the right.[43] It is in this way that the *Wednesbury* threshold moves downwards, making it easier for applicants to succeed.

[**6.11**]   Most cases concerning fundamental rights will now be heard under the Human Rights Act 1998, although parallel arguments may still be made with reference to common law fundamental rights.[44] This has led to the argument that there is no further need for the modified *Wednesbury* principle as the courts are required, under the Act, to give effect to the European proportionality principle that is said to demand a more structured and consistent standard of review than its *Wednesbury* comparator (see [6.27]). *Wednesbury* has, however, yet to 'receive its quietus'[45] and it can for that reason be said that the authorities on 'anxious scrutiny' remain of some relevance. Those same authorities are also of note insofar as they, together with the authorities on 'policy' choices ([6.09]), illustrate the more general point about the context-sensitive nature of *Wednesbury* and other common law principles.

PROPORTIONALITY

[**6.12**]   The proportionality principle that is applied in EU law cases and in cases under the Human Rights Act 1998 is, in contrast to *Wednesbury*, understood to require that courts engage more immediately in 'closer look' review (the principle can also lead the courts towards review of Acts of Parliament—see [6.04]). Although it has been emphasised that use of the principle does not entail a shift to merits review[46] and, moreover,

---

[39] See *Re Austin's Application* [1998] NI 327, 337, applying *R v Ministry of Defence, ex p Smith* [1996] QB 517, 554, Sir Thomas Bingham MR.

[40] *Re Obidipe's Application* [2004] NIQB 77, para 7, Girvan J, considering *Khawaja v Secretary of State for the Home Department* [1984] 1 AC 74. And see [4.39].

[41] *R v Secretary of State for the Home Department, ex p Simms* [2000] 2 AC 115; and *Raymond v Honey* [1983] 1 AC 1, 10, Lord Wilberforce (cited in *Pettigrew v NIO* [1990] NI 179, 182, Hutton J). But compare *R v Chief Constable of the RUC, ex p Begley* [1997] NI 278 and *Re Russell's Application* [1990] NI 188.

[42] See, eg, *R v Cambridge Area Health Authority, ex p Child B* [1995] 2 All ER 129 (child cancer patient was refused further treatment at public expense: held that the court should apply *Wednesbury* in its ordinary form as interference with matters of resource allocation would take the reviewing court beyond its constitutionally permitted role in review proceedings).

[43] *Re T's Application* [2000] NI 516, 540*ff*.

[44] Eg, *In Re Officer L* [2007] 1 WLR 2135 (inquiry's refusal to grant anonymity to witnesses challenged as contrary to Art 2 ECHR and the common law right to life: House of Lords remitted the application to the High Court to consider whether the decision *Wednesbury* unreasonable).

[45] *R v Home Secretary, ex p Daly* [2001] 2 AC 532, 549, Lord Cooke.

[46] *Re McBride's Application* [2002] NIQB 29, Kerr J, quoting *R v Secretary of State for the Home Department, ex p Daly* [2001] 2 AC 532, 548, Lord Steyn.

that the outcome of *Wednesbury* and proportionality enquiries will often be the same,[47] it is accepted that proportionality can demand a more intensive judicial scrutiny of substantive choices.[48] This is because a court, on a proportionality enquiry, must be satisfied 'first that the objective [of a choice] justifies interference [with an individual's rights or interests], secondly, that the steps taken are rationally connected to the objective and not arbitrary and, thirdly, that there is minimum interference with the rights affected'[49] (a court should always also strive to strike 'a fair balance between the rights of the individual [and] the interests of the community'[50]). This test thereby requires a court to ask not whether a decision or other measure is within the range of choices open to a reasonable decision-maker (as per *Wednesbury*) but rather whether the decision is the least intrusive in the circumstances and one that has struck a fair and appropriate balance between all affected interests.[51] The Court of Appeal has since emphasised that this is a role that the judiciary is 'well equipped' to perform[52] and decision-makers will therefore typically be required to give courts a fuller justification for decisions and other measures (something that can have implications for, among other things, the duty to give reasons[53]). Proportionality has, in the result, been distinguished from *Wednesbury* in Human Rights Act 1998 cases on the ground that its levels of scrutiny go further than those of even the modified *Wednesbury* test[54] (on which see [6.10]–[6.11]).

[6.13] The proportionality principle is, however, also applied on the understanding that, in law, 'context is everything'.[55] For instance, its use in EU law cases can differ from that in cases involving the ECHR given the respective obligations of the State under each body of law; and the manner of its use in cases involving rights under the ECHR can, in turn, vary according to the nature of the rights involved (viz 'absolute' rights and 'qualified' rights[56]). The courts also accept that use of the principle should take account of the separation of powers doctrine and the corresponding fact that the courts should not usurp the function of either the legislature or executive/administrative decision-makers. The courts have on this basis emphasised that the principle does not 'make judges into legislators'.[57] They have also stated that they must observe the decision-maker's 'margin of appreciation' in EU law cases and their 'discretionary area of judgment' in cases under the Human Rights Act 1998.[58]

---

[47] *R v Secretary of State for the Home Department, ex p Daly* [2001] 2 AC 532, 547, Lord Steyn.

[48] *Re Martin's Application* [2003] NI 78, 88, paras 27–8, Weatherup J.

[49] *Re Matthew's Application* [2004] NIQB 9, para 26. See too *Re Connor's Application* [2005] NI 322, 329, para 27.

[50] *R (Razgar) v Secretary of State for the Home Department* [2004] 2 AC 368, 390, para 20, Lord Bingham, and *Huang v Secretary of State for the Home Department* [2007] 2 AC 167, para 19, Lord Bingham.

[51] *Re Sinn Féin's Application* [2005] NI 412, 433, para 54, Weatherup J, citing *Stretch v UK* (2004) 38 EHRR 12, para 37.

[52] *Department of Social Development v MacGeagh* [2006] NI 125, 138, para 36.

[53] On which see [7.43]–[7.46].

[54] *Re Boyle's Application* [2005] NIQB 41, para 15, Weatherup J, citing *Smith and Grady v UK* (2000) 29 EHRR 493.

[55] See *Re ED's Application* [2003] NI 312, 317, para 22, Kerr J, citing *R v Secretary of State for the Home Department, ex p Daly* [2001] 2 AC 532, 548, Lord Steyn. See too *Re McBride's Application* [2002] NIQB 29.

[56] See [1.21].

[57] *Re P* [2006] NIFam 5, para 18, Gillen J.

[58] See, eg, *Re McParland's Application* [2002] NI 292, 299 (EU law); and *Re A's Application* [2001] NI 335, 342ff (Human Rights Act 1998). For a recent formulation that embraces all of the elements of the principle (closer look review; interests of society; separation of powers) see *Re Christian Institute & Ors' Application* [2007] NIQB 66, para 83, Weatherup J: 'the approach to proportionality requires consideration of: (1) The overarching need to balance the interests of society with those of individuals and groups; (2) The recognition

Proportionality and the European Communities Act 1972

[**6.14**]   The obligation to give effect to the proportionality principle in EU law cases is a corollary of the courts' more general obligation to accord supremacy to EU law in the light of the case law of the ECJ.[59] Proportionality is one of a number of general principles of law that govern the actions both of the EU institutions and of the Member States when acting within areas of EU competence,[60] and national courts must have recourse to the principle when reviewing national legislative and administrative acts for compliance with, for example, the free movement guarantees in the EC Treaty[61] (although the principle can arise in other ways too[62]). Where a national legislative or administrative authority has placed limitations on an individual's free movement guarantees, a reviewing court must thus enquire: (a) whether the objective of the limitation is found in the Treaty; (b) whether the measure adopted or decision taken was necessary to achieve the objective; and (c) whether the measure imposed an excessive burden on the individual vis-à-vis the objective of the measure or decision. In the event that the measure or decision is or may be found to be disproportionate, the individual is entitled to a remedy that will ensure effective protection of his or her EU law rights. Depending on circumstance, that remedy may take form in an award in damages.[63]

[**6.15**]   The scope for variable application of the principle in the EU context can be seen most clearly in respect of challenges to national legislative measures, whether of the Westminster Parliament or, at the devolved level, of the Northern Ireland Assembly. For instance, where an Act interferes with EU law's 'constitutional' rights of movement or of equal treatment under the EC Treaty,[64] a reviewing court should examine the measure closely given that the ECJ has long read the power of derogation—whether in the Treaty[65] or a Directive[66]—in narrow terms.[67] Although the ECJ has said that national

---

of the latitude that must be accorded to legislative and executive choices in relation to the balance of public and private interests; (3) The . . . objective being sufficiently important to justify limiting the fundamental right; (4) The measures designed to meet the . . . objective being rationally connected to it, that is, the measures must not be arbitrary, unfair or based on irrational considerations; (5) The need for proportionate means being used so as to impair the right or freedom no more than   necessary to accomplish the objective . . . The Court should consider whether the measures fall within a range of reasonable alternatives, rather than seeking to ascertain whether a lesser degree of interference is a possibility; (6) The need for proportionate effect in relation to the detrimental effects and the advantageous effects of the measures and the importance of the objective.' The wider formulation is restated in, *Re Tweed's Application* [2007] NIQB 69, para 56, Weatherup J.

[59]   European Communities Act 1972, s 3; and see [1.16]–[1.19] and [5.06]–[5.10].

[60]   See generally P Craig, *EU Administrative Law* (Oxford, Oxford University Press, 2006) chs 17 and 18.

[61]   See, eg, *Re O'Boyle's Application* [1999] NI 126, considering the relationship between proportionality and Art 39(4) (ex Art 48(4)) EC (designation of certain posts as public service posts that are only open to Member State nationals).

[62]   See P Craig, *EU Administrative Law* (Oxford, Oxford University Press, 2006) ch 18; and see, eg, *Cunningham v Milk Marketing Board for Northern Ireland*, 14 December 1990, unreported, considering proportionality in the context of the Common Agricultural Policy.

[63]   See [3.78] and [8.36]–[8.38]

[64]   See, eg, Case 240/83, *Procureur de la République v Association de Défense des Brûleurs Usagées* [1985] ECR 520, 531, describing the free movement of capital, goods, persons, and services as general principles of law that have constitutional force.

[65]   See, eg, Case 36/75, *Rutili v French Minister of the Interior* [1975] ECR 1219.

[66]   See, eg, Case C-328/91, *Secretary of State for Social Security v Thomas* [1993] ECR I-1247.

[67]   See generally P Craig and G de Búrca, *EU Law: Text, Cases and Materials*, 4th edn (Oxford, Oxford University Press, 2000) chs 18–24.

authorities may enjoy a 'margin of appreciation' in such matters[68]—UK courts have sometimes also identified the imperative of self-restraint when reviewing the preferences of the legislature[69]—the settled nature of large areas of EU law means that national legislative interference with them is generally to be permitted in only exceptional and closely controlled circumstances. Where, on the other hand, a national measure has been enacted for the purpose of implementing a Directive it may be that the proportionality principle will be applied in a less exacting manner (the national measure may here take the form of an Act or subordinate legislation introduced on the basis of section 2(2) of the European Communities Act 1972[70]). This is because Directives, while prescriptive as to the result to be achieved, leave to national authorities a choice of form and method vis-à-vis achieving that result.[71] Under those circumstances, and given the national authority's margin of appreciation, national courts may therefore consider that the legislative choice should be accepted so long as that choice is consistent with the final objective of the Directive.[72] This may be so even where the national court regards aspects of the choice as 'surprising' and 'undesirable'.[73]

[**6.16**] Executive and administrative decision-makers too may enjoy a margin of appreciation, although the courts have been careful to emphasise that the margin accorded here is less than that accorded to the legislature.[74] The corresponding rationale rests on domestic public law orthodoxy; that is, while the legislature enjoys a potentially wide margin of appreciation given that it is elected and entrusted with a law-making role, subordinate decision-makers enjoy a lesser margin because they are typically empowered to take decisions only within the framework established by an Act of Parliament. However, while this can in theory lead to a much more exacting proportionality enquiry into administrative choices, the courts have observed that there may be a need for some degree of deference where, for instance, executive or administrative decisions are taken on the basis of expert evidence[75] or in the face of resource considerations.[76] Under those circumstances, the mode of review— proportionality as moderated by the margin of appreciation—may be little different to that associated with *Wednesbury* unreasonableness[77] (see [6.05]–[6.11]).

[**6.17**]   One final point about the proportionality principle in the EU order concerns its centrality to the workings of other doctrines and general principles of EU law such as

---

[68] Eg, regarding measures adopted for purposes of public order or internal security; see Case C-265/95, *Commission v French Republic* [1997] ECR I-6959, 6999, para 33.

[69] *Re McBride's Application* [2002] NIQB 64, Weatherup J, stating that legislative choices must be 'manifestly inappropriate'; and *Stoke-On-Trent CC and Norwich CC v B & Q plc* [1991] Ch 48, 69, Hoffmann J.

[70] See [5.06].

[71] Art 249 EC.

[72] *Re McParland's Application* [2002] NI 292, 299, citing *R v Secretary of State for Trade and Industry, ex p Eastside Cheese Company* [1999] 3 CMLR 123.

[73] *Re McParland's Application* [2002] NI 292, 299.

[74] *R v Secretary of State, ex p Eastside Cheese Company* [1999] 3 CMLR 123, 145–6.

[75] *R v Secretary of State, ex p Eastside Cheese Company* [1999] 3 CMLR 123 (court affording a narrower margin of appreciation to the Secretary of State in an application that challenged the lawfulness of food safety measures adopted by the Secretary of State on the basis of expert evidence and in the face of an outbreak of E. coli).

[76] *R v Chief Constable of Sussex, ex p International Trader's Ferry Ltd* [1999] 2 AC 418 (Chief Constable's decision to limit, for reasons of finite resources, the policing of protests against the export of live animals not disproportionate).

[77] *R v Chief Constable of Sussex, ex p International Trader's Ferry Ltd* [1999] 2 AC 418, 439, Lord Slynn.

equality, legitimate expectation, and the precautionary principle. Each of these is linked to the proportionality principle in the sense that, where a decision-maker wishes to act in a way that will discriminate against an individual (equality), to resile from a previous representation or policy (legitimate expectation), or to adopt a particular preventative measure in the face of a risk (precaution), resulting the decision or other measure must be necessary and the least intrusive of the available options[78] (subject to related arguments about the scope of the decision-maker's discretion). While the corresponding body of ECJ case law on the interaction of these principles is of immediate application only when cases arise under the European Communities Act 1972,[79] the development of domestic doctrines of legitimate expectation and equality/non-discrimination has raised important questions about how far EU law's approach should be allowed to 'spill over' into domestic, non-EU law cases.[80] The argument, in short, is that a proportionality-based approach to legitimate expectation and equality is qualitatively superior to one centred on the traditional ground of *Wednesbury* review and that the proportionality approach is for that reason to be preferred. The argument has, moreover, since been part-acted upon in relation to legitimate expectation (see [6.38]–[6.40]), and there is, in the result, a more general debate about how far *Wednesbury* should be regarded as of continuing relevance to the wider body of domestic administrative law (see [6.27]–[6.28]).

Proportionality and the Human Rights Act 1998

[6.18]   The leading authority on the requirement that the courts give effect to the proportionality principle in cases under the Human Rights Act 1998—section 2 of which obliges the courts to 'take into account' the body of ECHR jurisprudence that includes the proportionality principle—is *R (Daly) v Secretary of State for the Home Department*.[81] Prior to that case, it had been suggested that it was not necessary to recognise proportionality as a free-standing ground for review in Human Rights Act 1998 cases as the principle could be subsumed within the variable standard of *Wednesbury* unreasonableness (on which see [6.09]–[6.11]).[82] However, while the House of Lords in *Daly* accepted that there is a significant degree of overlap between the *Wednesbury* and proportionality principles, it concluded that proportionality should be recognised as distinct because it can provide for a more intensive standard of review than *Wednesbury*.[83] Lord Steyn thus noted that 'proportionality may require the reviewing court to assess the balance which the decision-maker has struck, not merely whether it is within the range of rational and reasonable decisions'; and he likewise observed that proportionality 'may go further than the tradi-

---

[78] See P Craig, *EU Administrative Law* (Oxford, Oxford University Press, 2006) chs 15, 16, and 19.

[79] See [1.17] and [5.08]–[5.10].

[80] On 'spill-over' see [1.18].

[81] [2001] 2 AC 532. On the position of the principle prior to the Act—proportionality not a ground of review in domestic law and of application only in cases falling under the European Communities Act 1972—see *R v Secretary of State for the Home Department, ex p Brind* [1991] 1 AC 696, followed in, eg, *R v Secretary of State for Northern Ireland, ex p Crawford* 17 November 1994, unreported.

[82] See, eg, *R v Secretary of State for the Home Department, ex p Mahmood* [2001] 1 WLR 840. See too the consideration of authority in *Re Austin's Application* [1998] NI 327, 332*ff*.

[83] See too *R v Shayler* [2003] 1 AC 247, 272, *ff*, Lord Bingham; *Re Martin's Application* [2003] NI 78, 88, para 27 ff; *Re J's Application* [2004] NIQB 75; and *Re McDonnell; Re Lily's Application* [2004] NI 349, 364, para 40.

tional grounds of review inasmuch as it may require attention to be directed to the relative weight accorded to interests and considerations'.[84] His Lordship moreover added that proportionality and modified *Wednesbury* should not be regarded as co-equivalent because the ECtHR had previously held that modified *Wednesbury* was not necessarily apposite to the protection of human rights.[85]

[**6.19**]   *Daly* has had the effect of placing proportionality at the centre of cases under the Human Rights Act 1998, whether those cases are concerned with the legality of administrative decisions and acts, with the legality of subordinate legislation, or with the compatibility with the ECHR of primary and, more infrequently, subordinate legislation.[86] While this has in some instances led to closer scrutiny of decisions and other measures, the courts have emphasised that use of the principle should not be taken to herald a shift to 'merits review'. Use of the principle has therefore been linked to a 'discretionary area of judgment' doctrine that, while not the same as the ECtHR's 'margin of appreciation' doctrine (see [6.25]), imports some of its logic into the domestic constitutional context.

Proportionality in the ECHR and the 'Margin of Appreciation'

[**6.20**]   The proportionality principle is central to the workings of the ECHR, where it is alluded to in the text of various Articles and where it exists as a general principle of law.[87] The principle seeks to ensure that any State interference with a fundamental right is no more than is necessary in all the circumstances, and it applies most obviously when qualified rights such as privacy, manifestation of religious belief, expression, association, and property are in issue.[88] Here, the text of the ECHR requires that any interference with a right pursues one or more of the grounds for interference listed in the relevant Articles and that the interference is in accordance with the law and 'necessary in a democratic society'.[89] However, the application of the principle is not limited to disputes concerned with the classic qualified rights and it can be of relevance in other contexts too. For instance, use of force within the meaning of Article 2 ECHR's guarantee of the right to life must be no more than is 'absolutely necessary' in the circumstances (the State is here also required both to plan operations with a view to minimising force[90] and to conduct an effective investigation into any force which results in death[91]); and limitations on the right of access to a court under Article 6 ECHR, while acceptable where they

---

[84] [2001] 2 AC 532, 547. And on relevancy see [4.40]–[4.41] and [5.40]–[5.43].

[85] [2001] 2 AC 532, 547, citing *Smith and Grady v UK* (2000) 29 EHRR 493.

[86] Human Rights Act 1998, ss 3–6. Primary and subordinate legislation for the purposes of the Act are defined in s 21. On the Act see further [5.11]–[5.20].

[87] See generally J McBride, 'Proportionality and the European Convention on Human Rights' in E Ellis (ed) *The Principle of Proportionality in the Laws of Europe* (Oxford, Hart Publishing, 1999) p 23.

[88] Respectively, Arts 8, 9, 10, 11, and Art 1, Protocol 1 ECHR.

[89] See, in relation to privacy, religion, expression, and association, Arts 8(2), 9(2), 10(2), and 11(2), which refer to, inter alia, limitations in the interests of national security (Arts 8, 10, 11) and public safety (Arts 8, 9, 10, 11). Art 1(1), Protocol 1 in turn provides that property rights may be interfered with where such interference is 'in the public interest and subject to the conditions provided for by law and by the general principles of international law'. On qualified rights see [1.21].

[90] *McCann, Farrell and Savage v UK* (1996) 21 EHRR 97.

[91] *Jordan v UK* (2003) 37 EHRR 2; *Kelly v UK*, 4 May 2001; *McKerr v UK* (2002) 34 EHRR 20; *Shanaghan v UK*, 4 May 2001; *McShane v UK* (2002) 35 EHRR 23; *Finucane v UK* (2003) 37 EHRR 29; and *Reavey v UK*, 27 Nov 2007. And see, eg, *Re Mongan's Application* [2006] NIQB 82. But see too, on the non-retrospective effect of the Human Rights Act 1998 *In Re McKerr* [2004] 1 WLR 807, *R (Hurst) v London Northern District Coroner* [2007] 2 WLR 726, and *Jordan v Lord Chancellor* [2007] 2 WLR 754; and [1.32].

pursue a legitimate aim, must not be allowed to impair the very essence of the right.[92] Moreover, where a State wishes to invoke the Article 15 ECHR power of derogation from certain rights in the face of a 'public emergency threatening the life of the nation', the resulting measures adopted by the State must be must be 'strictly required' by the exigencies of the situation.[93] Discriminatory measures within the meaning of Article 14 ECHR will, in turn, be permitted only where they pursue a legitimate aim and strike an appropriate balance between the aim pursued and the rights affected.[94]

[6.21]   ECHR jurisprudence on the proportionality principle is, however, also linked to a 'margin of appreciation' doctrine.[95] This doctrine is premised on the understanding that national authorities will, 'by reason of their direct and continuous contact with the vital forces of their countries', sometimes be better placed than the ECtHR to determine which measures are necessary in, or suited to, the national context.[96] The doctrine is invoked most frequently where there is no uniform national approach to the issue before the ECtHR, as the ECtHR considers that its role here is not to impose a uniform standard on the Contracting Parties but rather to ensure that individual national systems do not fall beneath a minimum European standard. While the doctrine does not thereby entail that national measures should avoid scrutiny—the ECtHR has emphasised that the margin of appreciation goes 'hand in hand' with European supervision and that the extent of that supervision will be determined by the nature of the right in issue and the corresponding nature of State measures[97]—it does mean that the Strasbourg Court may exhibit a degree of restraint when it considers that there is a range of ECHR-compliant options open to the national authority. This may be so irrespective of whether the authority is legislative, executive/administrative, or judicial in form.[98]

[6.22]   In concrete terms, a national authority will most frequently to be taken to have a 'margin of appreciation' where its decision or other measure has an impact on qualified rights[99] (see [6.20]; a margin may also be accorded where, for instance, a State

---

[92] *Perez de Rada Cavanilles v Spain* (1998) 29 EHRR 109, 120, paras 44–5. And see, eg, *Re Bowden; Re JGS Services Ltd Application* [2004] NIQB 32 (one-month time-limit for purposes of challenging a vesting order was compliant with Art 6 ECHR).

[93] *A v Secretary of State for the Home Department* [2005] 2 AC 68 (but see too Lord Hoffmann's dissent at [2005] 2 AC 68, 129, para 86*ff*). Art 15 ECHR reads: '(1) In time of war or other public emergency threatening the life of the nation any High Contracting Party may take measures derogating from its obligations under this Convention to the extent strictly required by the exigencies of the situation, provided that such measures are not inconsistent with its other obligations under international law. (2) No derogation from Article 2, except in respect of deaths resulting from lawful acts of war, or from Articles 3, 4 (paragraph 1) and 7 shall be made under this provision.'

[94] *Gaygusuz v Austria* (1996) 23 EHRR 364; and, eg, *Re Parsons' Application* [2002] NI 378 (affirmed on appeal: [2004] NI 38). Art 14 ECHR reads: 'The enjoyment of the rights and freedoms set forth in this Convention shall be secured without discrimination on any ground such as sex, race, colour, language, religion, political or other opinion, national or social origin, association with a national minority, property, birth or other status.'

[95] See H Yourrow, *The Margin of Appreciation Doctrine in the Dynamics of European Human Rights Jurisprudence* (The Hague, Kluwer, 1996).

[96] *Buckley v UK* (1996) 23 EHRR 101, 129, para 75.

[97] *Handyside v UK* (1976) 1 EHRR 737, 754.

[98] *Handyside v UK* (1976) 1 EHRR 737, 754.

[99] See, eg, *Hatton v UK* (2003) 37 EHRR 611 (noise generated by night flights permitted under Art 8(2)); *Leyla Şahin v Turkey* (2007) 44 EHRR 5 (limitations on the wearing of religious garments in educational establishments permitted under Art 9(2)); and *Refah Partisi v Turkey* (2003) 37 EHRR 1 (decision to ban a political party that sought to undermine Turkey's secular constitutional settlement consistent with Art 11(2)).

enters an Article 15 ECHR derogation given its assessment that there is a 'public emergency threatening the life of the nation'[100]). Where, in contrast, a decision or other measure impacts upon an absolute right—typically the Article 2 right to life or the Article 3 prohibition of torture or inhuman or degrading treatment—the position can become more complex.[101] This is because the inviolable nature of absolute rights would suggest that a State should never be taken to have discretion on the question of how to observe such rights. However, while the 'no discretion' point may be incontrovertible where a case is concerned with the State's negative obligations (that is, its own obligation not to kill or torture), different considerations may apply in respect of its positive obligations (that is, where the State is under a duty to take steps actively to prevent one private party killing another private party, or subjecting another party to torture or inhuman or degrading treatment). Although the ECtHR adopts a strict approach to the State's positive obligation to ensure that there are effective criminal law provisions to deter offences against the person,[102] it is less demanding on the question of how the State should operationalise its resources—for instance, as relate to policing—for purposes of preventing the commission of an offence. Under these circumstances, the ECtHR has emphasised that the burden on States should not be 'impossible' to discharge and that the State should instead be expected to act 'reasonably' in the light of any threat to an individual.[103] The ECtHR, in this way, accepts that the State should have some discretion given 'the difficulties in policing modern societies, the unpredictability of human conduct and the operational choices which must be made in terms of priorities and resources'.[104]

The Standard of Review in Domestic Law

[6.23]   The corresponding body of case law on the application of the proportionality principle under the Human Rights Act 1998 proceeds on the understanding that the principle can, potentially, require 'closer look' review in any given case (see [6.12]–[6.13]). Whether a proportionality enquiry is required will depend, in the first instance, on whether rights under the ECHR are engaged by a decision or other measure, as decisions and so on that do not engage such rights will not fall under the Human Rights Act 1998 (although there would remain the notional prospect of a modified *Wednesbury* review where common law rights are engaged by administrative decisions or other measures: see [6.10]). However, where a decision both engages and interferes with rights under the ECHR,[105] the courts will ask whether the decision complies with the proportionality principle (if applicable). At its most simple, the principle will, again, require a court to ask: (a) whether the objective of the interference is sufficiently important to justify limiting a fundamental right; (b) whether the measures designed to meet that objective are rationally connected to it; and (c) whether the means used to impair the right are no more than

---

[100] See *A v Secretary of State for the Home Department* [2005] 2 AC 68, surveying all relevant ECtHR authorities.
[101] On absolute rights see [1.21].
[102] *Kiliç v Turkey* (2001) 33 EHRR 1357, 1398, para 62.
[103] *Osman v UK* (2000) 29 EHRR 245, 305–6, para 116.
[104] *Keenan v UK* (2001) 33 EHRR 913, 957, para 89.
[105] *R (SB) v Governors of Denbigh High School* [2007] 1 AC 1000.

are necessary to accomplish the objective.[106] Should the decision or other measure fail to satisfy one or more of these elements, the appropriate remedy should issue.[107]

[6.24]   Such application of the principle has had important implications for the nature and workings of judicial review, and the courts have made clear that they should not refrain from giving effect to it.[108] For instance, in terms of the judicial review procedure, the 'closer look' associated with the principle has led the courts to acknowledge that aspects of the procedure may need to be modified to enable the courts properly to conduct a proportionality enquiry.[109] The courts have likewise held that statutory requirements that would violate the ECHR for lack of proportion if read as mandatory should instead be read, if possible, as directory[110]; and they have also granted remedies to individuals in a significant number of cases. These have included applications where an Order in Council was disproportionate in its interference with property rights[111]; where the Northern Ireland Housing Executive had failed to take appropriate measures to evict a tenant who was intimidating other tenants contrary to Article 8 ECHR[112]; and where the application of prison policies was not consistent with the requirement of balance in Article 8 ECHR.[113] The courts have in similar vein been willing to grant a remedy—in the form of a declaration—where a disproportionate interference with a right has since ceased: while such matters are academic, they remain of public interest and deserving of a remedy.[114]

The 'Discretionary Area of Judgment'

[6.25]   The more intensive scrutiny associated with the principle has, however, been moderated by parallel use of a 'discretionary area of judgment' doctrine (alternatively referred to as the 'margin of discretion' or the 'deference or latitude' due to the decision-maker[115]). This doctrine imports the logic of the separation of powers into Human

---

[106] See *Re Martin's Application* [2003] NI 78, 84, para 16, citing *de Freitas v Permanent Secretary of Ministry of Agriculture* [1999] 1 AC 69, 80, Lord Clyde. See too, eg, *Re McKinney's Application* [2006] NICA 15, citing *R v Oakes* [1986] 1 SCR 103, 355: Canadian Supreme Court stating that, to satisfy the proportionality principle, '(1) [T]he measures adopted must be carefully designed to achieve the objective in question. They must not be arbitrary, unfair or based on irrational considerations. And they must be rationally connected to the objective. (2). [T]he means, even if rationally connected to the objective, should impair as little as possible the right or freedom in question. (3). [T]here must be proportionality between the effects of the measures which are responsible for limiting the Charter right or freedom, and the objective which has been identified as of sufficient importance.' And for a wider, and more recent, formulation see n 58 above, quoting *Re Christian Institute & Ors' Application* [2007] NIQB 66, para 83 and *Re Tweed's Application* [2007] NIQB 69, para 56.

[107] HRA 1998, ss 4 and 8; and see [3.79]–[3.80]; [5.11]–[5.20] and [8.40]–[8.48].

[108] *Department of Social Development v MacGeagh* [2006] NI 125, para 36.

[109] *Tweed v Parades Commission for Northern Ireland* [2007] 1 AC 650, concerning discovery; and see [3.53]–[3.54].

[110] *Foyle, Carlingford and Irish Lights Commission v McGillion* [2002] NI 86. On mandatory and directory requirements see [7.18]–[7.21].

[111] *Re Landlord's Association of Northern Ireland' Application* [2006] NI 16.

[112] *Re Donnelly's Application* [2003] NICA 55.

[113] *Martin v Northern Ireland Prison Service* [2006] NIQB 1 (policy of 'slopping out'); and *Re Mulhern's Application* [2004] NIQB 28 (anti-drugs policy as applied in the context of prisoner–lawyer relations).

[114] *Re TP's Application* [2005] NIQB 64. On the courts' more general approach to the availability of declarations in respect of academic matters see *Re McConnell's Application* [2000] NIJB 116, 119–20; and [8.17]–[8.18].

[115] *Tweed v Parades Commission for Northern Ireland* [2007] 1 AC 650, 673, para 55, Lord Brown. But note that the House of Lords has become increasingly sceptical about use of the term 'deference': see *Huang v Secretary of State for the Home Department* [2007] 2 AC 167, para 16, Lord Bingham. See further [4.17].

Rights Act 1998 case law by emphasising that, where a decision-maker is attempting to balance an individual's rights with those interests of wider society, the courts will 'recognise that there [may be] an area of judgment within which the judiciary [should] defer, on democratic grounds, to the considered opinion' of the decision-maker.[116] The doctrine thus pursues the constitutional imperative of judicial self-restraint and it seeks to prevent the shift to merits review that the proportionality principle was thought to have the potential to entail.[117] The doctrine is, moreover, 'home-grown' in the sense that the courts regard it as domestic in form and essentially distinct from the ECtHR's 'margin of appreciation' doctrine (on which see [6.20]–[6.22]).[118] Although the courts at the same time accept that 'it will be easier for such an area of judgment to be recognised where the Convention itself requires a balance to be struck, much less so where the right is stated in terms which are unqualified',[119] the corresponding body of case law on the domestic doctrine has identified a range of (sometimes conflicting) national constitutional considerations that might aid the courts when deciding whether restraint is required in any given case.[120] These include: whether the decision or other measure has been adopted by the legislature, a government Minister, or an unelected official (the legislature will, in general, be taken to enjoy a wider margin than a Minister, who will, in turn, enjoy a wider margin than the official)[121]; whether the decision or other measure is one that is more suited to resolution in the political context (for instance, a matter of economic policy or a question of national security)[122]; and whether the rights in question fall largely within the 'constitutional responsibility' of the courts (for example, the right to liberty, access to the courts, and so on).[123]

[6.26]   There has, inevitably, been some judicial disagreement about when it is appropriate to invoke the discretionary area of judgment doctrine, both in terms of the type of case that it is suited to[124] and in terms of when, in proceedings, the courts should exercise

---

[116] *R v DPP, ex p Kebeline* [2000] 2 AC 326, 381, Lord Hope.

[117] *Re Austin's Application* [1998] NI 327, 336–7, Coghlin J.

[118] *Re P's Application* [2006] NIFam 5, para 18, Gillen J.

[119] *R v DPP, ex p Kebeline* [2000] 2 AC 326, 381, Lord Hope.

[120] See *Re P* [2006] NI Fam 5, para 18*ff*, Gillen J, considering, among others, *R (Pro-life Alliance) v BBC* [2004] AC 185 and *International Transport Roth GmbH v Home Secretary* [2003] QB 728, 765ff, Laws LJ.

[121] See, eg, *Re A's Application* [2001] NI 335, 342*ff*, Kerr J (challenge to Chief Constable's decision not to reveal further information about the nature of a threat to the life of the applicant: application dismissed but with court stating that, as the decision under challenge had not been taken by an elected body, the degree of deference due to the decision was 'commensurately less'); *Re Gallagher's Application* [2003] NIQB 26, Kerr J (Sex Offenders Act 1997, s 1 challenged as incompatible with Art 8 ECHR: application dismissed because, at paras 20–21, 'In this context it is relevant that the scheme was introduced by a democratically elected Parliament . . . The task of deciding whether the measures are proportionate must be approached circumspectly, therefore, recognising that Parliament has determined what is required for the protection of the public from sex offenders'); and *Re McAuley's Application* [2004] NI 298, 310 (challenge to bail provisions in Terrorism Act 2000, s 67(2) as incompatible with Art 5 ECHR: application dismissed, the court quoting *Brown v Stott* [2003] 1 AC 681, 703, Lord Bingham: 'Judicial recognition and assertion of the human rights defined in the Convention is not a substitute for the processes of democratic government but a complement to them. While a national court does not accord the margin of appreciation recognised by the European court as a supranational court, it will give weight to the decisions of a representative legislature and a democratic government within the discretionary area of judgment accorded to those bodies').

[122] See *R (Alconbury Limited) v Secretary of State* [2003] 2 AC 327; and, eg, *Re Bow Street Mall's Application* [2006] NIQB 28, para 43, Girvan J.

[123] *Re P* [2006] NI Fam 5, para 18*ff*, Gillen J, considering, among others, *R (Pro-life Alliance) v BBC* [2004] AC 185, and *International Transport Roth GmbH v Home Secretary* [2003] QB 728, 765ff, Laws LJ.

[124] For a survey of some of the differing judicial opinions see *Department for Social Development v MacGeagh* [2006] NI 125, 136–8, paras 32–6, Kerr LCJ.

restraint.[125] The doctrine has, nevertheless, become central to the wider body of case law, and the courts have drawn upon it when holding: that the current approach to determining planning applications does not violate the Article 8 ECHR and Article 1, Protocol 1 rights of third parties[126]; that a prison policy that sought to regulate the risk of escape and which had been approved by a government minister was not contrary to Article 8 ECHR[127]; that bail provisions in the Terrorism Act 2000 were not incompatible with Article 5 ECHR[128]; and that provisions in the Sex Offenders Act 1997 dealing with the management of sex offenders are not incompatible with Article 8 ECHR.[129] It has also played an important role in cases concerned with absolute rights where it has been held that public decision-makers should be accorded a degree of discretion when discharging obligations that are positive, as opposed to negative, in form[130] (on the approach of the ECtHR in such cases see [6.22]).

Has Proportionality Displaced *Wednesbury*?

[6.27]   One final point of importance about the proportionality principle concerns it relationship with *Wednesbury* unreasonableness. Although *Wednesbury* has a long-standing domestic pedigree and is capable of adaptation depending on the context of a case (see [6.09]–[6.11]), it has been suggested that proportionality should now be allowed to displace *Wednesbury* in its entirety as a ground of review in domestic law. The argument made is simply that, as proportionality is now applied in preference to *Wednesbury* in EU law cases and in cases under the Human Rights Act 1998 (see [6.12]), it is 'unnecessary and confusing'[131] to retain *Wednesbury* in non-European law cases and that proportionality should be applied there too. The comparative strengths of proportionality are, in turn, said to lie in the fact that it can offer an equally robust template for judicial self-restraint—viz through parallel use of the discretionary area of judgment doctrine—and also in the fact that its analytical foundations are more structured than those of *Wednesbury* (through, for instance, the base requirement that decision-makers give reasons for their choices[132]). To put the point differently, it is argued that proportionality requires a more consistent method of reasoning on the part of both decision-makers and

---

[125] *Re Sinn Féin's Application* [2003] NIQB 27, paras 29–30, Coghlin J: 'it seems to me that considerable caution should be observed by the court when considering the stage at which and the extent to which resort should be had to such a concept in relation to the domestic application of Convention rights. One of the reasons frequently advanced for the need to observe a significant degree of "judicial deference" is the risk that the court may be tempted to substitute its own decision for that of the democratically elected legislature. However, in my opinion, an equal if not greater risk, is that an excessive degree of deference paid simply to the identity of the decision-maker may inhibit the court in the performance of its primary function under the Human Rights Act 1998 in determining whether an act of a public authority is lawful.'

[126] *Re Stewart's Application* [2003] NI 149, 159, para 26*ff*. See too *Re UK Waste Management's Application* [2002] NI 130, 142–3.

[127] *Re McCrory's Application* [2001] NIQB 19.

[128] *Re McAuley's Application* [2004] NI 298 (regarding Terrorism Act 2000, s 67(2)).

[129] *Re Gallagher's Application* [2003] NIQB 26.

[130] Eg, *Re A's Application* [2001] NI 335 (Art 2 challenge to Chief Constable's decision not to reveal further information about the nature of a threat to the applicant's life dismissed) and *Re E's Application* [2004] NIQB 35 and [2006] NICA 37 (no violation of the Arts 2 and 3 ECHR guarantees of private individuals who were threatened by protestors, as the operational choices of the police were reasonable in the circumstances).

[131] *R (Alconbury Limited) v Secretary of State for the Environment, Transport and the Regions* [2003] 2 AC 327, 321, para 51, Lord Slynn.

[132] See P Craig and S Schønberg, 'Legitimate Expectations After Coughlan' (2000) PL 684, 699.

the courts and that the wider body of domestic administrative law would benefit from its increased use.[133]

[6.28] Case law in Northern Ireland has since noted the debate about *Wednesbury*'s future, although no firm opinion has been voiced as to whether it should be 'consigned to history',[134] and it has been accepted that it is for the House of Lords to 'perform the burial rites'.[135] In the absence of *Wednesbury* receiving 'its quietus',[136] it is thus clear that it remains of relevance in cases that do not raise matters of European law[137] and that it may interact with other principles and doctrines in domestic administrative law (see, in relation to legitimate expectation and equality, [6.38]–[6.40] and [6.51]). Whether it will continue to be of relevance is, moreover, a question that is arguably of only limited practical importance as the High Court has noted that the judicial task in any given case is one of identifying the appropriate level of scrutiny irrespective of the principle applied.[138] On the other hand, it is undeniable that *Wednesbury* no longer occupies its formerly central position in administrative law and that it is now of diminishing significance. It may therefore be merely a matter of time before the principle is placed fully in abeyance.

LEGITIMATE EXPECTATION

[6.29] The doctrine of legitimate expectation is based on the understanding that there are some instances in which the law should prevent public authorities making discretionary choices that are contrary to an individual's expectation that the decision-maker will act in a particular manner.[139] Such expectations are typically recognised by the courts where a public authority has made a promise or a 'clear and unambiguous' representation to an individual,[140] although they may also be engendered by an authority's practices or policies (see [6.34]–[6.35]). In historical terms, the doctrine was limited to the recognition and protection of 'procedural legitimate expectations' (for example, of consultation in advance of a decision),[141] but it has since developed to include 'substantive legitimate expectations' that the courts protect by assessing whether a discretionary choice should be allowed to frustrate an individual's expectation of a particular outcome or benefit.[142] While the courts will not at the same time enforce an expectation where this would require an authority to act in breach of its statutory duties[143] (but see too [6.31]

---

[133] *R v Secretary of State for the Home Department, ex p Daly* [2001] 2 AC 532, 548–9, Lord Cooke; and see the seminal academic account in J Jowell and A Lester, 'Beyond *Wednesbury*: Substantive Principles of Administrative Law' (1987) PL 368.

[134] *Re McBride's Application* [2002] NIQB 29, Kerr J.

[135] *Re McQuillan's Application* [2004] NIQB 50, para 38, Weatherup J, citing *R (Association of British Civilian Internees) (Far East Region)) Foreign Secretary* [2003] 3 WLR 80, 92, para 35.

[136] *R v Secretary of State for the Home Department, ex p Daly* [2001] 2 AC 532, 549, Lord Cooke.

[137] *Re McBride's Application* [2002] NIQB 64, Weatherup J.

[138] *Re McBride's Application* [2002] NIQB 29, Kerr J; cited with approval in *Re McBride's Application (No 2)* [2003] NI 319, 345, para 52.

[139] S Schønberg, *Legitimate Expectations in Administrative Law* (Oxford, Oxford University Press, 2000).

[140] *Re Cullen's Application* [2005] NIQB 9, para 45, Weatherup J.

[141] See, eg, *Re Police Association of Northern Ireland's Application* [1990] NI 258, 271 ff; *Re Glor na nGael's Application* [1991] NI 117, 133; and *Re White's Application* [2000] NI 432, 444.

[142] *Re Treacy's Application* [2000] NI 330, 360 ff. For an earlier case see, eg, *Re O'Hare's Application* [1989] NI 77 (prisoner who had been punished by cellular confinement had a legitimate expectation that no further punishment would be imposed).

[143] *Re UK Waste Management's Application* [2002] NI 130, 142; *Re The Law Society of Northern Ireland* [2004] NIQB 48, para 49; and *Re Neale's Application* [2005] NIQB 33, para 34.

and [6.41]–[6.45]), they will enforce an expectation where they consider that the principles of 'fairness' and the 'rule of law' require protection of the individual.[144] For instance, it is well established that the principle of fairness has both a procedural and a substantive dimension,[145] and the courts have sought to use the principle to prevent the 'abuse of power' where individuals legitimately expect that decision-makers will follow a particular course of action.[146] This emphasis on preventing the abuse of power has, in turn, likewise informed judicial recourse to the rule of law principle and the understanding that there should be 'regularity, predictability and certainty in [the] government's dealing with the public'.[147] Although the rule of law may in other cases require that decision-makers do not fetter their discretion,[148] the courts have emphasised that there can be circumstances in which authorities should be bound by their prior representations about how they will exercise their discretion in the future. Any tension between the 'legitimate expectation' and 'fettering' doctrines is thus resolved with reference to the need for decision-makers to act with certainty and fairness towards individuals in given cases.

[6.30]   Where an individual has a substantive legitimate expectation the central question for the courts is how that expectation is to be protected. The traditional approach has been to limit substantive review to that associated with *Wednebsury* unreasonableness; that is, to permit judicial intervention only where the public authority's course of action is unreasonable within the umbrella sense of the *Wednesbury* principle or, alternatively, where it is so unreasonable that no reasonable authority could take it[149] (on *Wednesbury* see [6.05]–[6.11]). However, while the *Wednesbury* principle remains relevant in some cases, the courts have developed a further standard of review that can result in a more intensive review of discretionary choices (see [6.38]–[6.40]). This latter standard has been developed with reference to the language of 'fairness', 'balance', and 'abuse of power',[150] although it is, in reality, nothing other than a variant of the proportionality principle[151] (the case law has drawn in part on the ECJ's use of the proportionality principle when protecting legitimate expectations in EU law[152]). While there was, initially, some judicial opposition to the standard for reasons associated with the separation of powers doctrine,[153] it has now made the transition from 'heresy to orthodoxy' and is central to the case law.[154] Judicial use of the standard has therefore added to the more general debate about whether the proportionality principle should displace *Wednesbury* as the central principle of substantive review in domestic administrative law (on which see [6.27]–[6.28]). Its use has at the same time continued to raise questions

---

[144]   *Re Adams' Application*, 7 June 2000, unreported, Gillen J. On the rule of law see [4.04]–[4.09].

[145]   *R v Secretary of State for the Home Department, ex p Pierson* [1998] AC 539. On fairness and procedure see ch 7.

[146]   *R v North and East Devon Heath Authority, ex p Coughlan* [2000] 2 WLR 622, 645; and *Re Morrow and Campbell's Application* [2002] NIQB 4.

[147]   *Re Adams' Application*, 7 June 2000, unreported, Gillen J.

[148]   *R v Secretary of State for Transport, ex p Richmond upon Thames LBC* [1994] 1 WLR 74. On the rule against fettering discretion see [5.52]–[5.54].

[149]   *R v Secretary of State for the Home Department, ex p Hargreaves* [1997] 1 All ER 397, 412.

[150]   *Re Treacy's Application* [2000] NI 330, 362, considering *R v North and East Devon Heath Authority, ex p Coughlan* [2000] 2 WLR 622, 645.

[151]   *Nadarajah v Secretary of State for the Home Department* [2005] EWCA 1363.

[152]   See *Re Hampson's Application* [1998] NIJB 188, 193; and *R v Ministry of Agriculture, Fisheries and Food, ex p Hamble (Off-shore) Fisheries Ltd* [1995] 2 All ER 714, 724–8. And on legitimate expectations in EU law see P Craig, *EU Administrative Law* (Oxford, Oxford University Press, 2006) ch 16.

[153]   *R v Secretary of State for the Home Department, ex p Hargreaves* [1997] 1 All ER 397, 412.

[154]   *Re Hampson's Application* [1998] NIJB 188, 193, Girvan J.

about how far the more intensive standard of review can be reconciled with traditional understandings of the role of the courts.[155]

[**6.31**]   The clear majority of legitimate expectation cases will be concerned with public authority representations, practices, or policies that are lawful or intra vires the authority concerned (these may be described as 'lawfully created expectations': see [6.33]–[6.40]). In some cases, however, an individual may argue that they have an expectation arising from a representation that is ultra vires the authority or, alternatively, a representation that is intra vires the authority but which has been made by an unauthorised official (these may be termed 'unlawfully created expectations': see [6.41]–[6.45]). Cases of this kind raise difficult questions about how to reconcile the need for fairness with the constitutional demands of legality/the ultra vires doctrine[156] and, given the UK constitution's historical emphasis on legislative supremacy,[157] the courts have tended to prioritise the latter at the expense of the former. However, while the logic of the ultra vires doctrine remains very much to the fore of more recent case law,[158] judicial recognition that disputes should be resolved with reference to the legitimate expectation doctrine[159] now potentially requires a more elaborate process of judicial reasoning where an expectation is engendered by an unauthorised representation (any previous—and very limited—protection was achieved through use of the private law doctrine of estoppel[160]). The ECtHR's understanding that arguments of legality should not automatically trump the rights of individuals likewise has implications where an individual claims to have a legitimate expectation as a result of an ultra vires representation and where that expectation can be translated into a right under the ECHR[161] (see [6.43]).

[**6.32**]   It should finally be noted that legitimate expectation cases in which an authority has represented that it will act in a particular way are to be distinguished from cases in which an authority has already taken a lawful decision which it subsequently wishes to revoke. Cases of this latter kind are not concerned with statements and so on about what an authority will do but rather with the question whether an authority should be allowed to 'unmake' a decision that it has already taken. Where an individual has relied upon the decision, the demands of legal certainty would seem to entail that the decision should be regarded as irrevocable, as the individual's affairs will in that way remain unaffected by the authority's proposed change of mind.[162] However, to the extent that this accords with fairness, there is some contrary case law to suggest that an authority should be able to revoke a decision where the original decision was based upon a misunderstanding of fact which the authority has since become aware of.[163] On the other hand, this latter line of reasoning is apparently constrained by the need for the original decision to touch upon

---

[155] M Elliott, '*Coughlan*: Substantive Protection of Legitimate Expectations Revisited' (2000) 5 JR 27.

[156] See [4.04]–[4.05].

[157] See [1.12].

[158] *Re Clifford* [2004] NIQB 52, paras 23–4; and *Re Hughes' Application* [2004] NIQB 25, para 11.

[159] *R v East Sussex CC, ex p Reprotech (Pebsham) Ltd* [2003] 1 WLR 348, 358, paras 34–5, Lord Hoffmann, cited in eg, *Re Bowden; JGS Services Ltd; Re Scalene Investments Ltd* [2004] NIQB 32, para 54, and *Re SOS's Application* [2003] NIJB 252, 258, para 14.

[160] *Western Fish Products Ltd v Penwith DC* [1981] 2 All ER 204; applied in, eg, *R Bell & Co v DoE* [1982] NI 322.

[161] *Stretch v UK* (2004) 38 EHRR 12.

[162] *In Re 56 Denton Road, Twickenham* [1953] Ch 51.

[163] *Rootkin v Kent CC* [1981] 1 WLR 1186.

discretionary benefits rather than statutory rights. The capacity to revoke in such cases thus exists as one aspect of the rule against the fettering of discretion.[164]

Lawfully Created Expectations

When are they Recognised?

[6.33]   The question whether an individual has a legitimate expectation—and what is its content—is a question of law that is answered objectively and with reference to the full legal and factual context of a case.[165] In the first instance, the courts look to the actions of the public authority, as legitimate expectations can only 'be induced by the conduct of the decision-maker'.[166] Where that conduct takes the form of a representation—whether contained in one or more of: an individual statement; a circular; a report; or some other official document—this will provide the strongest foundation for judicial recognition of a legitimate expectation.[167] Although it can at the same time be difficult to establish that there has been a representation that sounds in law,[168] it is apparent that the courts will recognise an expectation as having been created where there has been a promise or a 'clear and unambiguous' representation to an individual, for instance a letter to the effect that the individual will be given a hearing or receive a particular benefit.[169] Under such circumstances, the courts accept that the specific and individualised nature of the representation can give the representation 'the character of a contract'[170] and that the need for 'regularity, predictability and certainty in [the] government's dealing with the public'[171] is at its most pronounced. While the character of a contract will, in turn, be lost where a statement is conditional,[172] where the statement does not constitute a final opinion,[173] or where the representation is made to a larger group of

---

[164] P Craig, *Administrative Law*, 5th edn (London, Sweet & Maxwell, 2004) p 662; and on the rule against the fettering of discretion see [5.52]–[5.54].

[165] *Re Hughes' Application* [2004] NIQB 25, para 11; and *Re Findlay* [1985] AC 318, 338.

[166] *Re Treacy's Application* [2000] NI 330, 364, Kerr J.

[167] *Re Cullen's Application* [2005] NIQB 9, para 45, Weatherup J.

[168] *Re Wright's Application* [2006] NIQB 90, para 52 (no clear representation that an inquiry to be held in the light of the Cory Report into controversial killings would comply with the corresponding recommendations of the report—although note that the judgment of the High Court was overturned, on other grounds, on appeal: [2007] NICA 24); *Re McAllister* [2006] NIQB 58, para 20 (no representation to a remand prisoner that he would be subject to a home leave scheme operated by the prison authorities as the home leave scheme did not apply to remand prisoners and it could not be assumed that remand prisoners would become sentenced prisoners); *R v Magill* [2006] NICC 13, para 52 (no evidence of a clear representation to the effect that criminal proceedings would be the subject of a committal hearing in the magistrates' court); *Re Mulhern's Application* [2004] NIQB 28, para 42 (consultation paper containing recommendations that were not subsequently adopted could not found an expectation); *Re Chan's Application* [1987] NI 13 (an internal staff instruction that was not addressed to the public could not found an expectation that an oral hearing would be given to an individual who was to be deported from the UK).

[169] *Re Cullen's Application* [2005] NIQB 9, para 45, Weatherup J.

[170] *Re Neale's Application* [2005] NIQB 33, para 34, citing *R v North and East Devon Heath Authority, ex p Coughlan* [2000] 2 WLR 622, 646, para 59. See too *Re UK Waste Management's Application* [2002] NI 130, 142.

[171] *Re Adams' Application*, 7 June 2000, unreported, Gillen J.

[172] *Re McFadden's Application* [2002] NI 183 (a criminal justice manager's letter to the applicant had not given an unconditional undertaking that the applicant would not be prosecuted as it had been made clear to the applicant that the direction of no prosecution was to be made on the basis of the evidence available).

[173] *Re Rowsome's Application* [2004] NI 82 (applicant could have no legitimate expectation that the respondent's preliminary opinion on a planning application would be the final opinion).

individuals and/or has implications for an innominate class of persons,[174] the courts are otherwise anxious to ensure that decision-makers do not 'act arbitrarily, capriciously or . . . abuse their powers'.[175] The case law has thus established that a clear and unambiguous representation to an individual can create a legitimate expectation even in the absence of detrimental reliance upon it[176] (although such reliance will, as a matter of fact, typically be present[177] and, where it is not, this may sound on whether the expectation should be protected—see [6.38]). The courts further accept that, where there is detrimental reliance, this need not always be monetary but may be moral in form.[178]

[6.34] Legitimate expectations may alternatively be grounded in the practices of a public authority.[179] For instance, an expectation of consultation may be engendered where an authority has previously consulted the affected individuals about decisions of the kind to be taken[180]; and a public authority cannot, without warning, change a long-standing practice that it is aware an individual has acted in the light of and derived a substantive benefit from.[181] In cases of this latter kind there will clearly be reliance on the practice, and the courts have held that it may amount to an abuse of power to allow the practice to be changed without giving the individual a corresponding opportunity to prepare for the change.[182] On the other hand, the fact that an individual has previously received a grant or a licence from an authority cannot, of itself, give rise to an expectation that a future application for a grant or licence will be successful.[183] While the position may be different where an authority has made a clear and unambiguous representation to the effect that a grant will be paid, the fact that there will often be more applications for grants/licences than there are resources available to meet them entails that one individual cannot have a legitimate expectation of success.[184] Individuals can, instead, expect only that their application for a grant or licence will be determined in a procedurally fair manner.[185]

[6.35] Where a public authority has adopted a policy to guide it in the exercise of its discretion an individual may argue that they have a corresponding expectation that the policy will be applied to their specific circumstances.[186] Such arguments may arise (a) where the authority decides to depart from its existing policy vis-à-vis the individual or (b) where the authority changes its policy and the individual considers that the previous policy should still be applied to them. In respect of (a), it appears that an individual

---

[174] *Re Wright's Application* [2006] NIQB 90, para 51 (applicant could not have a legitimate expectation arising from government announcement that an inquiry into a controversial killing would be held within certain terms of reference: while the announcement of the inquiry was of particular interest to the immediate relatives of the deceased, it was a matter of wider public interest and it would be straining language to describe the announcement as a promise to a small number of people). But see too n 168 above and [2007] NICA 24.

[175] *Re Morrow and Campbell's Application* [2002] NIQB 4, Coghlin J.

[176] *Re Neale's Application* [2005] NIQB 33, para 34.

[177] *R v Secretary of State for Education, ex p Begbie* [2000] 1 WLR 1115, 1124.

[178] *R (Bibi) v London Borough of Newham* [2002] 1 WLR 237, 246 para 31.

[179] *Re Wylie's Application* [2005] NI 359, 371, para 37, Weatherup J.

[180] *Council of Civil Service Unions v Minister for the Civil Service* [1985] AC 374.

[181] *R v Inland Revenue Commissioners, ex p Unilever* [1996] STC 681.

[182] *R v Inland Revenue Commissioners, ex p Unilever* [1996] STC 681.

[183] *Re West's Application* [2006] NIQB 39, para 20, Deeny J; and *Re Clifford's Application* [2004] NIQB 52, para 24, Weatherup J.

[184] *Re West's Application* [2006] NIQB 39, para 20, Deeny J.

[185] *Re West's Application* [2006] NIQB 39, para 20, Deeny J; and see, on procedural fairness, ch 7.

[186] On policies and discretion see [5.52].

may legitimately expect that their circumstances will be dealt with in accordance with the policy of the respondent[187]—there is authority in England and Wales to suggest that this may be so even where the applicant was unaware of the policy[188]—and that any departure from the policy must be reasoned and conform with the principle of equal treatment[189] (on which see [6.50]–[6.51]). Case law under (b) likewise suggests that an individual can have a legitimate expectation of a particular outcome in the light of the original policy but that the weight of the expectation will vary according to the context to the dispute. Hence, where the operation of the original policy was accompanied by a clear and unambiguous representation to the individual that the policy would be applied to them, the courts will recognise the expectation as having its greatest weight. Where, in contrast, there was no promise or representation, the expectation will be weaker and the corresponding judicial protection less exacting (see [6.38]–[6.40]).

[6.36]   One final point about recognition of legitimate expectations concerns unincorporated international treaties and conventions.[190] There have been several cases in which it has been argued that, where the government has signed and ratified an international instrument, this creates a substantive legitimate expectation that ministerial decisions will be taken in accordance with the State's obligations under the instrument.[191] The argument, which has been developed with reference to Australian authority and some related dicta in England and Wales,[192] has, however, failed for reasons of constitutional dualism. Although the courts accept that decision-makers and courts may look to international instruments for guidance when making decisions,[193] they have emphasised that such instruments can have no domestic legal effect in the absence of national legislation enacted for that purpose.[194] In terms of substantive legitimate expectations, the courts have thus held that expectations cannot be created on foot of unincorporated treaties and conventions as this would result in incorporation by the 'back door'.[195] The point has an added force where there is existing national legislation that prescribes precisely the opposite outcome to that argued for by the applicant.[196]

---

[187] *Re Wylie's Application* [2005] NI 359, 371, para 37.

[188] *R (Rashid) v Secretary of State for the Home Department* [2005] Imm AR 608 (applicant had a legitimate expectation that his application for asylum would be determined in accordance with Home Office policy notwithstanding that he was unaware of the policy at the time of the application—to permit otherwise would be to allow an abuse of power by the immigration authorities). For commentary see M Elliott, 'Legitimate Expectation, Consistency and Abuse of Power: the *Rashid* case' [2005] 10 JR 281.

[189] *Re Morrison's Application* [1998] NI 68, 75–6, Kerr J. See too, eg, *R v Secretary of State for the Home Deaprtment, ex p Urmaza* [1996] COD 479; and *R v Secretary of State for the Home Deaprtment, ex p Gangadeen* [1998] 1 FLR 762.

[190] On the more general role of unincorporated international law as a source of law see [1.23]–[1.24].

[191] See *Re McCallion's Application* [2005] NICA 21; *Re T's Application* [2000] NI 516; and *Re Phillips' Application*, 15 September 2000, unreported.

[192] Respectively *Minister for Immigration and Ethnic Affairs v Teoh* (1995) 128 ALR 353, 385; and, eg, *R v Secretary of State for the Home Deaprtment, ex p Ahmed & Patel* [1999] Imm AR 22, 36, and *R v Uxbridge Magistrates Court, ex p Adimi* [1999] 4 All ER 520, 535.

[193] *Re Adams' Application* [2001] NI 1, 24; and see *Re McCallion's Application* [2007] NIQB 76.

[194] *R v Home Secretary, ex p Brind* [1991] 1 AC 696 *R (Hurst) v London Northern District Coroner* [2007] 2 WLR 726.

[195] [2000] NI 516, 537, citing *Thomas v Baptiste* [2000] AC 1, PC.

[196] *Re McCallion's Application* [2005] NICA 21, para 24, rejecting arguments based on the UN Convention on the Rights of the Child in the light of the provisions of the Criminal Injuries (Compensation) (Northern Ireland) Order 1988, SI 1988/793 (NI 4).

How are they Protected?

[6.37]   The protection afforded to a legitimate expectation depends on the nature of the expectation at issue. For instance, where, as a result of a representation or a practice, the expectation is of consultation in advance of a decision, the court will require that there is an opportunity for consultation unless there is an overriding reason to deny the opportunity[197] (such as the interests of national security[198]). Cases of this kind have their origins in the common law rules of fairness,[199] and the courts delimit the corresponding standards of procedural fairness with reference to that considered reasonable in the circumstances.[200] Such protection is, in turn, unproblematic in constitutional terms as the courts are not concerned with the substantive outcome of the decision-making process but rather with how the outcome was reached. The courts, on this basis, have thus held that an asylum decision was unlawful because it was taken in breach of the applicants' expectation that they would be able to make representations on whether they should be returned to a third country[201]; and they have also found that a decision not to grant a licence to an applicant was unlawful because it was taken in breach of the applicant's procedural expectation of notice of adverse factors.[202] On the other hand, there have been cases where no remedy was granted in the face of insufficient consultation because the court was of the opinion, on the facts, that proper consultation would not have made a difference to the course of action that the applicants would have taken and that they had thereby suffered no significant unfairness.[203]

[6.38]   Where the legitimate expectation is substantive in form, the corresponding protection depends on whether the expectation is based upon, at one end of the scale, a clear and unambiguous representation to an individual or, at the other end, the mere existence of a policy. Where the expectation is based upon the former (or a practice that an individual has benefited from[204]) this will give rise to more intensive levels of judicial scrutiny as the courts may here '[(weigh] the requirements of fairness against any overriding interest relied upon'[205] by the authority when reaching its decision.[206] This

---

[197] *R v North and East Devon Heath Authority, ex p Coughlan* [2000] 2 WLR 622, 645, para 57.

[198] *Council of Civil Service Unions v Minister for the Civil Service* [1985] AC 374.

[199] *Southern Health and Social Services Board v Lemon*, 28 April 1995, unreported, Kelly LJ.

[200] See further [7.08]–[7.11].

[201] *Re Hove's Application* [2005] NIQB 24 (decision remitted to decision-maker pursuant to Judicature (Northern) Ireland Act 1978, s 21).

[202] *Re Cullen's Application* [2005] NIQB 9, para 46 (no remedy granted as the adverse factors were all capable of being addressed by the applicant in a later application for a licence). See too, eg, *Re Drummond's Application* [2006] NIQB 81 (decision vitiated by unfairness because it had been taken in breach of the individual's legitimate expectation that they would be able to make representations in advance of a decision whether to revoke their firearms licence).

[203] See, eg, *Re National Union of Public Employers and Confederation of Health Service Employees' Application* [1988] NI 255 (held that, although the applicant unions had a legitimate expectation of consultation in respect of hospital closures and the reorganisation of certain general medical services, they would not have addressed themselves to the merits or demerits of the proposals even if they had been furnished with fuller financial and staffing information).

[204] *R v North and East Devon Heath Authority, ex p Coughlan* [2000] 2 WLR 622, 645, para 57.

[205] *R v North and East Devon Heath Authority, ex p Coughlan* [2000] 2 WLR 622, 645, para 57.

[206] See, eg, *Re Neale's Application* [2005] NIQB 33 (retrospective application of a prison release policy to a small group of prisoners was unlawful as the prisoners had been given a clear and unambiguous representation that their release would be governed by a different policy and there was no overriding interest to justify the prison authorities resiling from that representation); and *Re Morrow and Campbell's Application* [2002] NIQB 4 (unlawful for the First and Deputy First Ministers not to circulate certain Executive Committee papers to Democratic Unionist Party (DUP) Ministers as there had been a representation that the DUP Ministers would receive the papers 'as of right').

approach, as with that associated with the proportionality principle, involves the courts in balancing competing interests for purposes of offsetting the 'abuse of power', and it thus takes judicial review far beyond the logic of orthodox *Wednesbury* unreasonableness (on which see [6.08]). Case law on the test has, however, at the same time established that the courts will employ it only where the representation in question is made to

> one or a few people giving the promise or representation the character of a contract . . . it is more likely to be held binding if made to a smaller number of people, on discrete facts, with no implications for an innominate class of persons.[207]

Case law has also established that, while reliance is not necessary for the purposes of recognising a legitimate expectation (see [6.33]), it will normally be required in order for an applicant to show that it would be unlawful to go back on a representation.[208] A court may finally consider that the public interest justification offered by the decision-maker should, in any event, trump the interests of the individual and that it would therefore not be unlawful to frustrate the expectation.[209]

[6.39]   Where the substantive legitimate expectation is based upon the mere existence of a policy which an authority has since changed, the approach of the courts is markedly different. Under these circumstances, the courts require only that a decision-maker bear in mind its previous policy 'giving it the weight it thinks right, but no more, before deciding whether to change course. Here the court is confined to reviewing the decision on *Wednesbury* grounds'.[210] The reason for this less intensive review lies in the fact that policies, in contrast to individualised representations, are of potential application to large sections of society (or even the public at large) and may be adopted in the light of, for instance, resource considerations and political priorities. Where an individual argues that they have a legitimate expectation of being treated in accordance with a prior policy and they cannot adduce evidence of a clear and unambiguous representation to that effect, the courts will therefore not depart from *Wednesbury* when assessing the lawfulness of the change in policy as to do so could involve them in matters that belong more immediately in the political realm (the point has been made in the context of, for instance, challenges to prison policies[211]). While this does not exclude the possibility of 'closer look' review where fundamental rights are in issue—*Wednesbury* can be applied in a modified manner, and proportionality will apply in cases under the Human Rights Act 1998—there is a more general presumption in favour of judicial self-restraint where changes in policy are in issue. Indeed, should those policies be concerned with matters

---

[207] *Re Neale's Application* [2005] NIQB 33, para 34, citing *R v North and East Devon Heath Authority, ex p Coughlan* [2000] 2 WLR 622, 646, para 59, and *R v Secretary of State for Education and Employment, ex p Begbie* [2000] 1 WLR 1115, 1130. But see too *R (Bancoult) v Secretary of State for Foreign and Commonwealth Affairs* [2007] EWCA 498 (Chagossians had a legitimate expectation, on foot of a promise made by the UK government in November 2000, that they would be at liberty one day to return to their homeland, and the subsequent frustration of that expectation by government was so unfair as to amount to an abuse of power).

[208] *Re Neale's Application* [2005] NIQB 33, para 34, citing *R (Bibi) v Newham LBC* [2002] 1 WLR 237, 246 para 29, Schiemann LJ.

[209] See, eg, *Re Halligan's Application* [2003] NIQB 42 (although applicant had no legitimate expectation on the facts of the case, arguments of public policy would have trumped her expectation that a named individual should never be permitted in the course of his lawful employment to be involved in awarding contracts tendered for by the applicant).

[210] *R v North and East Devon Heath Authority, ex p Coughlan* [2000] 2 WLR 622, 645, para 57. See too, eg, *Casey v Dept of Education for Northern Ireland*, 16 October 1996, unreported.

[211] See, eg, *Re Findlay* [1985] AC 318, 338, followed in, e.g., *Re Neill's Application* [2003] NIQB 50.

that are deemed contentious in a party political sense, the *Wednesbury* threshold may rise and take the form of 'soft-edged' review (on the context-sensitive nature of *Wednebsury* see [6.09]–[6.11]).

[6.40] The existence of different tests for the protection of substantive legitimate expectations depending on whether those expectations are engendered by representations or policies has not escaped criticism. The core of the criticism concerns the fact that the different types of cases are not 'hermetically sealed'[212] and that it might not always be easy to decide whether a case should be resolved with reference to *Wednesbury* or with reference to the more intensive standard of review[213] (for instance, at which stage does a representation made to a 'small' group of individuals become a representation with implications for an innominate class of persons? And does the judicial scrutiny of representations not entail some analysis of the reasons for a change in policy given that representations will typically be made in the light of policy?). While it is, at the same time, recognised that the courts should adopt a more or less demanding approach to review depending on whether the case has implications for a few individuals as opposed to many,[214] it has been said that the retention of two standards of review is both unnecessary and undesirable.[215] Given the point, the Court of Appeal in England and Wales has recently stated that the task for the courts in all legitimate expectation cases is to safeguard the 'requirement of good administration by which public bodies ought to deal straightforwardly and consistently with the public'.[216] Rejecting the need to place cases into different and potentially problematic categories, the Court thus considered that all cases should instead be resolved with reference to the question of what is proportionate in the circumstances of the dispute[217] (on the scope for variable application of the proportionality principle see [6.13]). The judgment would therefore appear to be one further example of the diminishing influence of *Wednesbury* unreasonableness (see [6.27]–[6.28]).

Unlawfully Created Expectations

[6.41] Arguments about 'unlawfully' created expectations arise where an individual seeks to enforce the terms of (a) a representation that has been made to them but which is ultra vires the authority or (b) a representation that is intra vires the authority but which has been made by an unauthorised official (that is, an official who purports to exercise a power that has not, or cannot, be delegated to him or her). Each instance raises difficult questions about how to reconcile the requirements of fairness with the doctrine

---

[212] *R v Secretary of State for Education and Employment, ex p Begbie* [2000] 1 WLR 1115, 1129, Laws LJ.

[213] See *Re De Brun and McGuinness's Application* [2001] NIQB 3, Kerr J: 'In order to decide into which, if any, of these categories a particular case falls, the circumstances in which the promise was made or the practice came into existence must be carefully examined.'

[214] *Re T's Application* [2000] NI 516, 535–6, quoting *R v Secretary of State for Education and Employment, ex p Begbie* [2000] 1 WLR 1115, 1129, Laws LJ

[215] P Craig and S Schønberg, 'Legitimate Expectations After Coughlan' (2000) PL 684.

[216] *Nadarajah v Home Secretary* [2005] EWCA 1363, para 68, Laws LJ. Although note the Court of Appeal in England and Wales has since also said that the *Coughlan* judgment that founded the category-based approach 'remains the benchmark of substantive legitimate expectation': *R (Bancoult) v Secretary of State for Foreign and Commonwealth Affairs* [2007] EWCA 498, para 73.

[217] *Nadarajah v Home Secretary* [2005] EWCA 1363, para 68*ff*.

of legislative supremacy that underlies the ultra vires doctrine, as recognition and protection of an expectation would effectively entail that the courts allow an authority to redraw the boundaries of its power (as with an ultra vires representation) or be bound by the determination of an individual who is not the lawful recipient of the power in question (as with an unauthorised representation that is intra vires the authority). Given the UK constitution's emphasis on legislative supremacy, the courts have historically limited the scope for protection of the individual by holding (a) that ultra vires representations cannot be binding and (b) that unauthorised representations that are intra vires the authority can be binding in only very narrow circumstances. However, while proposition (a) remains generally valid, it must now be read in the light of ECHR case law that holds that considerations of legality should not be allowed automatically to trump an individual's legitimate expectations where those expectations fall within the ECHR.[218] Proposition (b) should likewise be read in the light of the fact that ongoing development of the legitimate expectation doctrine[219] may require the courts to reason differently when deciding whether an unauthorised representation should be considered binding.

Representations that are Ultra Vires the Authority

[6.42]   The understanding that ultra vires representations cannot bind an authority rests upon UK constitutional orthodoxy and, in particular, the understanding that decision-makers may act only within the parameters of the powers that are granted to them, or the duties that are imposed upon them, by statute.[220] This position—which underlies illegality as a ground of review[221]—follows from the fact that a decision-making function will typically (though not exclusively[222]) be delegated to an authority under legislation enacted by the Westminster legislature or, alternatively, the Northern Ireland Assembly.[223] While the extent of any statutory power or duty will depend upon judicial interpretation of the statute,[224] the basic understanding is that a decision-maker may do only that which the legislature has authorised. Should an authority therefore state that it will do something that it cannot lawfully do, it will have made an ultra vires representation and one that is unenforceable in law. This thereby safeguards the doctrine of legislative supremacy, as any other outcome would entail that an authority had been able to redraw the parameters of its own power beyond those envisaged by the legislature.

[6.43]   Where an ultra vires representation is made in circumstances that fall outside the Human Rights Act 1998, it appears that the demands of legality will automatically trump any argued imperative of fairness to the individual.[225] However, where the representation is made in circumstances that fall under the Human Rights Act 1998, the issue becomes more complex given the ECtHR's understanding that considerations of legality should not automatically trump an individual's rights. The point is most readily associ-

---

[218] *Stretch v UK* (2004) 38 EHRR 12.
[219] *R v East Sussex CC, ex p Reprotech (Pebsham) Ltd* [2003] 1 WLR 348, 358, paras 34–5, Lord Hoffmann.
[220] On statutory powers and duties see [4.22]–[4.28].
[221] Ch 5.
[222] Ch 2.
[223] See [1.13] and [5.30].
[224] See [4.22].
[225] See, eg, *R (Bibi) v Newham London Borough Council* [2002] 1 WLR 237; and *Rowland v Environment Agency* [2004] 3 WLR 249.

ated with the ECtHR's judgment in *Stretch v UK*,[226] where the right at issue was a property right centred upon an (unlawful) expectation that the individual would have the benefit of a renewal of a lease. Although the ECtHR acknowledged the importance of arguments about legality and the rule of law, it stated that the question whether an individual's rights should be overridden must be answered on a case-by-case basis and in the light of the proportionality principle. While the domestic courts have not, in turn, yet acted on this understanding to the extent of holding that the demands of legality should yield to a right, they have suggested that public authorities should seek to exercise their powers benevolently where a previous representation has given rise to an expectation of a particular outcome.[227] It has since also been suggested that the benevolent exercise of power might take the form of an award of compensation to an individual who has suffered loss[228] and that, where such an award is not made, the individual might alternatively seek redress in an action for negligent misstatement.[229]

Unauthorised Representations that are Intra Vires the Authority

[6.44]   The limited scope for protecting individuals in the face of unauthorised representations that are intra vires the authority has similarly been justified with reference to the demands of legality, although the case law has also emphasised the importance of authorities being able to exercise their powers/perform their duties in the wider public interest. Protection of the individual here originally took form around the estoppel doctrine and the understanding that, when

> government officers, in their dealings with a subject, take on themselves to assume authority in a matter with which [the subject] is concerned, the subject is entitled to rely on their having the authority which they assume . . . and he ought not to suffer if [the officers] exceed it.[230]

While such use of the estoppel doctrine clearly pursued the interests of fairness to the individual, the greater weight of judicial opinion was nevertheless reluctant to allow a private law doctrine to be used to prevent authorities from exercising their powers and/or performing their statutory duties. This was not just because of the constitutional imperative of ensuring that lawful powers are exercised by those to whom they are entrusted, but also because it was thought that estoppel's private law origins left it ill suited to the resolution of disputes involving public interest questions of the kind that authorities are often required to address[231] (as in, for instance, planning cases). The courts thus sought to limit the reach of estoppel by holding that ostensible authority on the part of a public officer was not enough to activate the doctrine and that there had to be some further evidence justifying the individual's belief that the authority would be bound by the officer's representation.[232]

---

[226] (2004) 38 EHRR 12. See too, eg, *Pine Valley Developments Ltd v Ireland* (1991) 14 EHRR 319.

[227] *Rowland v Environment Agency* [2004] 3 WLR 249, 300, para 153*ff*, Mance LJ.

[228] J Beatson, M Matthews, and M Elliott, *Administrative Law: Text and Materials*, 3rd edn (Oxford, Oxford University Press, 2005) p 219.

[229] W Wade and CF Forsyth, *Administrative Law*, 9th edn (Oxford, Oxford University Press, 2004) p 341.

[230] *Howell v Falmouth Boat Construction Co Ltd* [1950] 2 KB 16, 26, Denning LJ.

[231] *Western Fish Products Ltd v Penwith District Council* [1981] 2 All ER 204.

[232] *Western Fish Products Ltd v Penwith District Council* [1981] 2 All ER 204, 220–21; applied in, eg, *R Bell & Co v DoE* [1982] NI 322. The courts also accepted that the doctrine might play a role in the specific circumstance where an authority waived a procedural requirement relating to an application made to it, whereby the authority could be estopped from relying on the lack of formality: see *Western Fish Products Ltd v Penwith District Council* [1981] 2 All ER 204, considered in, eg, *Re Thompson's Application* [1985] NI 170.

[**6.45**]   Given these reservations about the estoppel doctrine, in particular concerning the public interest, the courts have since stated that disputes about representations should instead be resolved with reference to the legitimate expectation doctrine.[233] This therefore means, at the level of recognising legitimate expectations, that an individual can argue that an unauthorised representation should bind an authority, albeit that the individual will still be required to adduce further evidence to support their belief that the officer in question was empowered to make the representation.[234] Should the courts, in turn, accept that an individual has a legitimate expectation, they must then consider how to protect the expectation, and it is here that the differences between the estoppel and legitimate expectation doctrines become apparent. While the doctrine of estoppel focuses on the interests of the two parties directly affected by a dispute, the legitimate expectation doctrine has evolved in the light of the need to reconcile individual interests with those of the wider public (see [6.38]–[6.39]). In assessing whether an unauthorised representation should be allowed to bind the authority, the courts will thus consider whether there would be merit, given the overall context to the case, in preventing the authority from exercising its powers/performing its duties in the public interest. The courts will here also give consideration to the related demands of the rule of law, although any corresponding arguments may have a variable force depending on whether the case falls within or outwith the Human Rights Act 1998 (see [6.43]).

EQUALITY

[**6.46**]   The principle of equality exists as one aspect of substantive review and is premised on the understanding that public decision-makers should treat like situations alike and different situations differently, unless there is good reason for them not to do so.[235] At common law, the principle gives rise to a basic tension between, on the one hand, the judicial desire to safeguard substantive fairness towards individuals and, on the other hand, the need for courts to avoid undue interference with lawful discretionary choices. For instance, substantive fairness is typically taken to be ensured where there is consistency in administrative decision-making and an absence of abuse of power in the form of discriminatory decisions that may frustrate equality of opportunity. However, to the extent that this is consonant with judicial review's emphasis on protection of the individual, it also raises familiar questions about how the courts should reconcile that protection with the rudiments of the separation of powers doctrine.[236] Decision-makers will, in short, frequently make decisions within a framework of statutory powers that denote a wide discretion to choose between different lawful outcomes in any individual

---

[233]   *R v East Sussex CC, ex p Reprotech (Pebsham) Ltd* [2002] 1 WLR 348, 358, paras 34–5, Lord Hoffmann; cited in eg, *Re Bowden; JGS Services Ltd; Re Scalene Investments Ltd* [2004] NIQB 32, para 54, and *Re SOS's Application* [2003] NIJB 252, 258, para 14.

[234]   See, eg, *Re Clifford* [2004] NIQB 52, paras 23–4 (applicant argued that he had a legitimate expectation of receiving a grant because of a contested statement made to him by an official: held there was no expectation as the applicant knew or ought to have known that determinations in relation to grant aid would not be matters for council officers but would be matters for determination by the council or a committee of the council); and *Re Hughes' Application* [2004] NIQB 25, para 11 (applicant could have no expectation of being transferred to a different prison as the statement relied upon had been made by a prison officer who was not authorised to make determinations of the kind at issue).

[235]   *Re Coroner for South Down's Application* [2004] NIQB 86, para 33, Weatherup J.

[236]   On the purposes of judicial review and corresponding constitutional tensions see [1.04]–[1.10].

circumstance.[237] Should a decision subsequently be challenged as contrary to the requirement of equal treatment, a court must thus identify the appropriate threshold for judicial intervention in a dispute about whether two cases are the same and whether they should be treated as such. A court, in other words, must decide whether common law review is to be guided by a presumption in favour of self-restraint of the kind synonymous with the *Wednesbury* principle, or whether a decision can legitimately be subject to 'closer look' review of the kind associated with the proportionality principle (on *Wednesbury* see [6.05]–[6.11]; and on proportionality see [6.12]–[6.28]).

[6.47]   Outside the common law, the principle of equality also takes form in a number of statutory provisions that pursue the elimination of unlawful discrimination.[238] The significance of some of these is returned to below ([6.52]–[6.53]), but two points of overarching importance for the workings of judicial review can be made here. The first is that, where a statute provides for an effective alternative remedy, the courts will require an individual to exhaust that remedy notwithstanding that the matter in question is one of public law. Although the requirement is not at the same time regarded as absolute, the courts have emphasised that a statutory scheme should ordinarily be used, as this is consonant with the doctrine of legislative supremacy. The courts have also emphasised that statute may, in any event, provide for superior procedures and remedies given the nature of the dispute.[239]

[6.48]   The second point concerns the intensity of review in situations that are not governed by statutory remedies and which may therefore give rise to judicial review proceedings. Should those review proceedings come under, most notably, the European Communities Act 1972 and/or the Human Rights Act 1998, the courts are obliged to give effect to the proportionality principle that exists as a general principle of EU law and which also informs the Article 14 ECHR non-discrimination case law of the ECtHR. While this may suggest that 'closer look' review will be inevitable, judicial perception of the context of a case may nevertheless result in review that is characterised by a greater or lesser degree of self-restraint. However, rather than use the language of *Wednesbury* in such instances, the courts may invoke the 'margin of appreciation' doctrine in EU law cases, and the 'discretionary area of judgment' doctrine in cases under the Human Rights Act 1998 (see [6.15]–[6.16] and [6.25]–[6.26] respectively).

[6.49]   It should finally be noted that the principle of equality has long also been used in a formal, as opposed to a substantive, sense in UK constitutional law. The formal sense is associated with the Diceyan conception of the rule of law; that is, the understanding that all persons, whether public or private, should be equally subject to the ordinary law of the land. The corresponding formalism in turn follows from the outworkings of Dicey's related doctrine of legislative supremacy, which entails that the Westminster Parliament can enact discriminatory legislation that will be applied equally to all those affected by it and irrespective of any argument of the need for substantive equality among different groups in society.[240] However, while it remains theoretically and practically possible for the Westminster Parliament to enact such discriminatory legislation, judicial

---

[237] On statutory powers see [4.22]–[4.25].

[238] See S Fredman, *Discrimination Law* (Oxford, Clarendon Press, 2002).

[239] See [2.34]–[2.35]; and, eg, *Re Neill's Application* [2006] NICA 5, and *Re Kirkpatrick's Application* [2004] NIJB 15.

[240] See J Jowell, 'Is Equality a Constitutional Principle?' (1994) 2 CLP 1.

acceptance of that legislation is now moderated by the substantive equality demands of EU law and the ECHR, as read with the European Communities Act 1972 and the Human Rights Act 1998, respectively. Acts of Parliament that are contrary to EU law's equality requirements can thus be disapplied by the courts (save where there are words that repudiate EU law either expressly or by 'irresistible' implication)[241]; and legislation that cannot be read in a manner that is compatible with the ECHR may be the subject of a declaration of incompatibility pursuant to section 4 of the Human Rights Act 1998.[242]

Common Law Equality

[6.50]   The relative strength of any argument founded upon the common law principle of equality will depend on whether a decision-maker has (a) chosen not to resolve a matter before it in the light of its existing policy on such matters or (b) made a discretionary choice in an area that is not, in fact, covered by any policy. In scenario (a) arguments about equality may be at their most persuasive precisely because policies are meant to engender certainty and consistency in the decision-making process.[243] Should an authority depart from its existing policy in a particular case, the affected individual may therefore argue that they had a legitimate expectation of being treated in accordance with the policy[244] and that the frustration of that expectation must be justified (on legitimate expectations see [6.29]–[6.45]). Where, in contrast, a dispute falls under scenario (b), it may be more difficult to make out the argument that the equality principle is engaged. This is because decisions here may be taken on the basis of a wide discretion that involves the authority in making value judgments about whether two discrete matters are, in fact, the same and to be treated as such.[245] Judicial acceptance of arguments about the need for equality in such circumstances could thus result in the courts becoming involved in matters that are, on a separation of powers analysis, matters for the authority.

[6.51]   The corresponding threshold for judicial intervention in substantive equality disputes that do not involve EU law and/or the ECHR remains *Wednesbury* unreasonableness.[246] The leading authority on the point is *Re McCallion's Application*,[247] which concerned challenges to various decisions taken by the Secretary of State in the administration of the criminal injuries compensation scheme. In finding that there had been a

---

[241] See *Thoburn v Sunderland CC* [2003] QB 151, considered at [1.29] and [5.04]–[5.07]; and see, eg, *R v Secretary of State for Transport, ex p Factortame Ltd (No 2)* [1991] 1 AC 603 (Merchant Shipping Act 1988 disapplied for reasons of, inter alia, discrimination on grounds of nationality); and *R v Secretary of State for Employment, ex p Equal Opportunities Commission* [1995] 1 AC 1 (Employment Protection Consolidation Act 1978 discriminated against women; although note that the remedy here was a declaration).

[242] See, eg, *A v Secretary of State for the Home Department* [2005] 2 AC 68 (Anti-terrorism, Crime and Security Act 2001, s 23, incompatible with ECHR for reasons of, inter alia, discrimination on the grounds of nationality in respect of the Art 5 ECHR right to liberty); and for a case in which the courts interpreted apparently discriminatory provisions in a manner that was compatible with the ECHR see *Ghaidan v Mendoza* [2004] 2 AC 557 (word 'spouse' read to include same-sex partners for the purposes of the Rent Act 1977, Sch 1, paras 2, 3(1)).

[243] *Re Morrison's Application* [1998] NI 68, 76.

[244] *Re Wylie's Application* [2005] NI 359, 371, para 37.

[245] *Re Morrison's Application* [1998] NI 68, 76.

[246] See *Re McCallion's Application* [2005] NICA 21; *Re Coroner for South Down's Application* [2004] NIQB 86, para 33, Weatherup J; *Re Croft's Application* [1997] NI 457, 491; and *Re Spence's Application*, 28 May 1993, unreported, McCollum J.

[247] [2005] NICA 21.

breach of the requirement of equal treatment insofar as the Secretary of State had failed to enquire whether there were grounds for distinguishing between two cases that were prima facie the same, the Court of Appeal stated that the equality principle is best analysed as part of the 'irrationality equation'. This clearly links the common law principle of equality to a presumption in favour of judicial self-restraint, and an applicant who relies upon the principle must be able to establish that the decision under challenge is unreasonable within either the umbrella or substantive meanings of *Wednesbury* (on which see [6.05]–[6.08]). Any scope for 'closer look' review would, on this basis, appear to be limited to judicial use of modified *Wednesbury* and/or the emergence of proportionality as the dominant common law principle for substantive review (see [6.09]–[6.11] and [6.27]–[6.28]). However, even if proportionality was to displace *Wednesbury* within the common law, judicial awareness of the need for self-restraint would remain and likely take the form of the discretionary area of judgment doctrine that is presently used in case law under the Human Rights Act 1998 (see [6.25]–[6.26]).

Statute Law and Equality

[6.52]   There are many legislative schemes that have been enacted for the reason of preventing discrimination and/or facilitating equality of opportunity for specific groups in society.[248] Some of these schemes have been introduced to give domestic effect to aspects of EU law (on which see [6.14]–[6.17][249]), while others have been introduced in the face of discrimination that is a UK-wide problem[250] or, in some instances, more particular to Northern Ireland.[251] Other schemes have likewise sought to address the problem of under-representation in some areas of public service by providing for positive discrimination.[252]

[6.53]   The key question in respect of legislation is whether it, or some related scheme, provides for remedies in the event of discrimination, as the courts will generally require an individual to avail himself or herself of those remedies in preference to judicial review proceedings (see [6.47]). For instance, in *Re Neill's Application*[253] the legality of the Anti-social Behaviour (Northern Ireland) Order 2004 was challenged on the ground that it had been made in breach of the Northern Ireland Office's equality obligations under the Northern Ireland Act 1998.[254] The central issue for the Court of Appeal was whether judicial review was available for purposes of enforcing the obligations or whether breaches of the kind at issue were to be remedied under the Northern Ireland Act 1998. While the Court of Appeal noted that judicial review may be available in some instances, it considered that the case before it gave rise to precisely the type of situation that the Act was designed to remedy.[255] Judicial review was therefore not available.

---

[248] See S Fredman, *Discrimination Law* (Oxford, Clarendon Press, 2002).

[249] And [1.16]–[1.19] and [5.06]–[5.10].

[250] Eg, race discrimination. See, in England and Wales, and Scotland, the Race Relations Act 1976, as amended; and, in Northern Ireland, the Race Relations (Northern Ireland) Order 1997, SI 1997/869 (N16), as amended. See too the Equality Act 2006.

[251] Eg, religious and political discrimination: see the Fair Employment and Treatment (Northern Ireland) Order 1998, SI 1998/3162. (N121).

[252] Eg, Police (Northern Ireland) Act 2000, ss 46–7.

[253] [2006] NICA 5.

[254] Northern Ireland Act 1998, s 75 and Sch 9. See further [5.28]–[5.29].

[255] [2006] NICA 5, para 27.

EU Law and Equality

[6.54]   The principle of equality exists at a number of levels in EU law. First, it exists in various Articles of the EC Treaty, which have effect in UK law under the terms of the European Communities Act 1972[256] and which may be enforced in domestic courts where they satisfy the EU law requirements for direct effect.[257] For instance, the Treaty contains a general prohibition on direct discrimination on grounds of nationality[258] that is further developed in Articles on the free movement of capital, goods, persons, and services (discrimination here—whether direct or indirect—may be justified only where it pursues a legitimate objective and conforms to the proportionality principle[259]). Discrimination in the workplace on grounds of gender too is generally prohibited by the Treaty,[260] which also provides that the EU institutions may take appropriate action to combat discrimination based on sex, racial or ethnic origin, religion or belief, disability, age, or sexual orientation.[261] Moreover, should the EC and related Treaties eventually be reorganised in the manner envisaged in the ongoing process of reform in the EU, this will give legal force to the equality chapter of the Charter of Fundamental Rights of the European Union (albeit that it appears that the Charter will not be binding in the UK[262]). This chapter not only reaffirms the EU's competence in respect of sex, race, ethnicity, and so on, but also contains provisions on, among others, children's rights and the rights of the elderly. However, given that the process of reform in the EU remains incomplete, the Charter of Fundamental Rights remains non-binding for the present and can, in consequence, be of only analogical force in proceedings.[263]

[6.55]   The equality principle can be found, secondly, in a range of EU legislative acts. These acts will have been adopted on the basis of Treaty Articles and, where the acts are in the form of Directives, the UK must adopt measures that will fully implement the Directives in national law[264] (measures may include Acts of Parliament[265] or regulations made under section 2(2) of the European Communities Act 1972[266]). In the event that a Directive is not fully implemented in domestic law an individual can invoke the provisions of a directly effective Directive in proceedings.[267] In the converse circumstance that a Directive has been fully implemented in domestic law, any corresponding role for judicial review will then depend on whether a dispute sounds in public law and, if so, on whether the wider statutory framework that gives effect to the Directive provides for a

---

[256]   On which see [1.16]–[1.19] and [5.06]–[5.10].
[257]   Case 26/62, *Van Gend en Loos v Nederlandse Aministratie der Belastingen* [1963] ECR 1, 13.
[258]   Art 12 EC.
[259]   See, eg, Arts 39, 43, and 49 EC (re: free movement of workers, freedom of establishment, and freedom to provide services, respectively); and C Barnard, *EU Substantive Law: The Four Freedoms* (Oxford, Oxford University Press, 2004).
[260]   Art 141 EC.
[261]   Art 13 EC.
[262]   See [1.19].
[263]   See, eg, *A and others v East Sussex CC* [2003] All ER (D) 233 at [73] (Munby J).
[264]   Art 249 EC.
[265]   E.g., the Sex Discrimination Act 1975, as amended, which gives effect to, *inter alia*, the Equal Treatment Directive (Dir 76/207/EEC OJ L 39/40). Note that the Act does not apply to Northern Ireland, where the Directive instead has effect under Sex Discrimination (NI) Order 1976 (SI 1976/1042), as amended.
[266]   Eg, the Race Relations Order (Amendment) Regulations (Northern Ireland) 2003, SR 341/2003, giving effect to Directive 2000/43, [2000] OJ L189/22 (the 'race' Directive). On s 2(2) see [5.06].
[267]   Case 41/74, *Van Duyn v Home Office* [1974] ECR 1337.

system of remedies.[268] If it does provide for a system of remedies, the courts will typically require that an individual exhaust that in preference to judicial review (see [6.47]).

[6.56] Equality finally exists as a general principle of EU law.[269] This means that, where a national decision-maker is making a decision within the realm of EU law (for example, in the context of the workings of the common fisheries policy[270]), it must treat like cases alike unless there is an objective justification for not doing so.[271] This is true not just where the decision in question has an impact on an individual from another Member State (the Treaty would in any event here require equality of treatment), but also where a decision is taken 'within' a Member State and absent any cross-national impact.[272] Moreover, should an authority treat differently two cases that are prima facie the same, it must be able to justify its choice with reference to a legitimate objective and in the light of the proportionality principle.[273] This may therefore involve UK courts in 'closer look' review, although the intensity of review may at the same time be moderated by use of EU law's margin of appreciation doctrine (see [6.14]–[6.16]).

Article 14 ECHR and the Prohibition of Discrimination

[6.57] Article 14 ECHR states that

> the enjoyment of the rights and freedoms set forth in this Convention shall be secured without discrimination on any ground such as sex, race, colour, language, religion, political or other opinion, national or social origin, association with a national minority, property, birth or other status.

Although the Article does not thereby enshrine a free-standing prohibition of discrimination[274] (viz its reference to 'the enjoyment of the rights and freedoms in the Convention'[275]), the case law of the ECtHR has established that there need not be a breach of one of the other rights and freedoms for there to be a breach of Article 14 ECHR.[276] It is, instead, sufficient for the decision or other measure under challenge to come 'within the ambit' of one of the other Articles, at which stage a court may determine whether there has been a violation of Article 14 ECHR.[277] While the domestic courts have since observed that it can be difficult to determine whether a matter actually

---

[268] *Perceval-Price v Department of Economic Development* [2000] NI 141; and *Re Coroner for South Down's Application* [2004] NIQB 86, para 25, Weatherup J.

[269] See P Craig, *EU Administrative Law* (Oxford, Oxford University Press, 2006) ch 15.

[270] *Re James' Application* [2005] NIQB 38 (applicant challenging successfully a decision to refuse him a decommissioning grant for his vessel within a scheme operated by the Department of Rural Development, as the decision did not accord with EU law's principle of equality).

[271] Cases 117/76 & 16/77, *Ruckdeschel v Hauptzollamt Hambourg-St Annen* [1977] ECR 1753, 1811.

[272] See, eg, *Re James' Application* [2005] NIQB 38.

[273] *R v Ministry of Agriculture Fisheries and Food, ex p First City Trading* [1995] EuLR 195, 219.

[274] See, eg, *Re Emerson's Application* [2006] NIQB 4, paras 10 ff.

[275] Cf Protocol 12 ECHR, not yet ratified by the UK government: '1. The enjoyment of any right set forth by law shall be secured without discrimination on any ground such as sex, race, colour, language, religion, political or other opinion, national or social origin, association with a national minority, property, birth or other status. 2. No one shall be discriminated against by any public authority on any ground such as those mentioned in paragraph 1.'

[276] Eg, *Abdulaziz, Cabales and Balkandali v UK* (1985) 7 EHRR 471.

[277] Eg, *Van der Mussele v Belgium* (1984) 6 EHRR 163, 178, para 43; *Department of Social Development v MacGeagh* [2006] NI 125, 142, para 54; and *Re Murdock's Application* [2003] NIQB 24, para 21.

falls 'within the ambit' of another Article,[278] it has been argued that the term should be given a wide reading so that Article 14 ECHR may be engaged.[279] Article 14 ECHR can, in that way, be given fuller effect.

[6.58]   Where an applicant argues that he or she has been discriminated against contrary to Article 14 ECHR as read with one of the other rights and freedoms, he or she must be able to identify a comparator who has, or would have, been treated more favourably.[280] The reviewing court must at that stage decide whether the comparison made is valid and, if it is, whether the less favourable treatment of the applicant can be justified.[281] Justification here requires the public authority to identify a legitimate objective that the less favourable treatment pursues and to satisfy the court that the treatment is proportionate in all the circumstances.[282] Should the court conclude that no legitimate objective has been pursued and/or that there has been a lack of proportion, a violation of Article 14 ECHR will be made out and a remedy should be granted.[283] On the other hand, the courts will also take account of the overall context to a dispute and may exercise restraint in the face of the decision-maker's choice. Under those circumstances, they will thus emphasise that the impugned decision or other measure falls within the decision-maker's 'discretionary area of judgment' (see [6.25]–[6.26]).

[6.59]   It should finally be noted that, while it is clear that Article 14 ECHR prohibits direct discrimination, it is less clear whether it similarly prohibits indirect discrimination[284] (viz discrimination caused by measures that are neutral on their face but which have a negative impact on particular groups). While there have thus been cases in which the Northern Ireland courts have been willing to assume that the Article does cover indirect discrimination,[285] the fact that the Article 14 ECHR point did not succeed may mean that the corresponding dicta are of only limited weight.

---

[278] Eg, *Re McDonnell and Lilly's Application* [2004] NI 349, 357, para 26; and *Ghaidan v Godin-Mendoza* [2004] 2 AC 557, 566, paras 10–11, Lord Nicholls.

[279] *Fallon-McGuigan v The Belfast Education and Library Board* [2005] NIQB 60, para 11.

[280] *Re Carson's Application* [2005] NIQB 80, Weatherup J, considering *Wandsworth LBC v Michalak* [2002] 4 All ER 436.

[281] *Larkos v Cyprus* (2000) 30 EHRR 597, 608, para 29; and, eg, *Re Landlord's Association for Northern Ireland's Application* [2006] NI 16, para 55.

[282] See, eg, *Re Parsons' Application* [2002] NI 378 (Protestant applicant challenged the lawfulness of the 50/50 recruitment quota for the Police Service of Northern Ireland, as legislated for in Police (Northern Ireland) Act 2000, ss 46–7: held that the quota was lawful because (1) it pursued the legitimate objective of making the police service more representative, ie by increasing Catholic representation, and (2) it was proportionate as its workings were to be reviewed every 3 years); and *Re McKay's Application* [2002] NI 307 (although members of the security forces were not treated more favourably when charged with a scheduled offence, differential treatment would not have violated Art 14 ECHR as there was clearly a legitimate aim in keeping members of the security forces apart from other prisoners).

[283] Human Rights Act 1998, s 8; and see, eg, *Re Landlord's Association for Northern Ireland's Application* [2006] NI 16 (discriminatory housing regulations not justified and therefore contrary to Art 14 ECHR).

[284] For some of the leading ECtHR case law see, eg, *Thlimmenos v Greece* [2000] 31 EHRR 411; *DH v Czech Republic* [2006] ECHR 113; and *Zarb Adami v Malta* [2006] ECHR 637.

[285] *Re Anderson's Application* [2001] NI 454. And see, in England and Wales, *R (Wilson) v Wychavon Council* [2007] EWCA Civ 52.

CONCLUSION

[**6.60**]   There are five points that can be made about the ground of substantive review:

i.   Substantive review has historically been synonymous with judicial self-restraint. This has meant that the courts have sought to avoid 'merits' review and have emphasised that judicial review is concerned solely with the legality of a decision. However, while the courts still point to the need for restraint, the emergence of new doctrines and principles has increased the potential for 'closer look' review. This is notably true of the doctrine of legitimate expectation and the proportionality principle.

ii. Self-restraint takes form most readily in the principle of *Wednesbury* unreasonableness. While it has at the same time been doubted how far this principle is of continuing relevance to administrative law, it is still referred to by the courts in cases outside the European Communities Act 1972 and the Human Rights Act 1998 (under which Acts the courts are obliged to give effect to the proportionality principle). It thus remains as an important principle, albeit as one of diminishing influence (see [6.05]–[6.11] and [6.27]–[6.28]).

iii. The proportionality principle can involve the courts in 'closer look' review in any case in which the principle applies. However, the courts are also aware of the need for self-restraint when using the principle, and they have linked its emergence to a 'margin of appreciation' doctrine in cases under the European Communities Act 1972 and a 'discretionary area of judgment' doctrine in cases under the Human Rights Act 1998. Use of these doctrines is at its most pronounced when the legislative choices of the Westminster Parliament are at issue in proceedings (see [6.12]–[6.28]).

iv. The doctrine of legitimate expectation has evolved to involve the courts (potentially) in 'closer look' review of discretionary choices. Such review will be apparent where a public authority has made a clear and unambiguous representation to an individual that the authority will act in particular way. On the other hand, the courts acknowledge that they should not seek to substitute their opinions on a substantive matter for those of the original decision-maker. Closer look review will therefore occur only where the representation in question is made to 'one or a few people giving the promise or representation the character of a contract'. Even then, the decision-maker may be able to resile from the representation for reasons of public interest (see [6.33]–[6.40]).

v.   The principle of equality exists in the common law, in EU law (in the Treaties, and related acts, and as a general principle), and in Article 14 ECHR. Where proceedings are governed by the common law principle of equality, the test for judicial intervention remains that set by *Wednesbury* unreasonableness. Where arguments are made under the European Communities Act 1972 and/or the Human Rights Act 1998, this can involve the courts in the 'closer look' review associated with the proportionality principle. Such closer look review may, however, be moderated by judicial reliance on the margin of appreciation and discretionary area of judgment doctrines in cases under the 1972 and 1998 Acts respectively (see [6.15]–[6.16] and [6.25]–[6.26]).

7

Procedural Impropriety

INTRODUCTION

[**7.01**]   This chapter examines procedural impropriety as a ground for judicial review. Decisions and acts may be challenged on this ground where the decision-maker has: (a) failed to observe procedural requirements that are laid down in the legislation that grants its power of decision;[1] (b) failed to observe the common law rules of fairness (viz the 'right to a hearing' and the 'rule against bias');[2] or (c) failed to act in accordance with the minimum procedural guarantees contained in Article 6 ECHR (other Articles of the ECHR may also impose obligations).[3] The judicial approach to arguments made with reference to these overlapping categories is heavily dependent on the legal and factual context to any given dispute, and questions can arise about how to interpret a particular legislative provision, about the relationship between legislation and the common law, about the content of the common law requirements of fairness relative to an individual's specific circumstances, and about whether Article 6 ECHR is engaged in a dispute. The corresponding case law has emphasised that the demands of procedural propriety are not 'engraved on tablets of stone'[4] and that the development and application of the law should remain context-sensitive and open to adaptation.[5] This chapter thus identifies the interpretive approaches and general principles that guide the courts when deciding whether a decision is tainted by procedural impropriety and, if so, what remedy (if any) should issue.[6] It also considers the nature of the overlap between the various categories of impropriety and, in particular, how Article 6 ECHR (among others) informs developments in the common law.

[**7.02**]   The chapter begins with a definitional section that notes the purposes of the ground of procedural impropriety and which then maps the relationship between statute law and the common law; outlines the reach of the common law rules of fairness; and identifies when Article 6 ECHR is engaged by decision-making processes. There next follow three sections that consider, in turn, judicial approaches to procedural requirements in statute, the right to a hearing, and the rule against bias (consideration of the ECHR is integrated into each of these sections). The conclusion provides a summary of the central points made.

---

[1] *Council of Civil Service Unions v Minister for the Civil Service* [1985] AC 374, 411, Lord Diplock.
[2] *Council of Civil Service Unions v Minister for the Civil Service* [1985] AC 374, 411, Lord Diplock.
[3] Human Rights Act 1998, s 6.
[4] *Lloyd v McMahon* [1987] 1 AC 625, 702, Lord Bridge.
[5] See, eg, *Re Tiernan's Application* [2003] NIQB 60, para 8; *Re McBurney's Application* [2004] NIQB 37, para 9; and *Re Henry's Application* [2004] NIQB 11, para 22.
[6] On remedies see further [3.72]–[3.87] and ch 8.

[7.03]   One final point by way of introduction concerns the chapter's use of the term 'fairness', as opposed to the term 'natural justice', which has, at least historically, been synonymous with the common law right to a hearing (*audi alteram partem*) and the rule against bias (*nemo judex in causa sua*). The term 'fairness' is preferred simply because case law has increasingly used it to describe the obligations that can be imposed on a wide-range of decision-makers that includes the judicial and the administrative. Although the content of the rules of 'fairness' will often be no different from that of 'natural justice' (the terms are in that sense interchangeable), the word 'justice' arguably corresponds more to a time when the common law rules were taken to apply only to judicial decision-makers or those decision-makers who were making determinations about an individual's rights.[7] The law has, however, since moved far beyond distinctions between judicial and other decision-makers, and the duty to act fairly[8] now potentially applies whenever '(anyone) decides anything'[9] (see [7.08]). The chapter thus uses the term 'fairness' merely because it reflects better the fact that the common law rules may be of application notwithstanding the nature of the decision-maker or the decision at hand. It is, however, ultimately only a label that is, in terms of content, essentially indistinguishable from natural justice.

SOME DEFINITIONAL POINTS

[7.04]   The ground of procedural impropriety performs a number of functions in terms of moderating the relationship between decision-makers and individuals. In the first instance, it performs a basic democratic function in the sense of requiring that those who will be affected by a decision are able to participate in the decision-making process through, for instance, the making of representations at a hearing. While the extent of any participation will be determined by the overall context to the decision (see [7.10]–[7.11]), the requirement that individuals be given a hearing is consonant with the understanding that the power of decision should not be exercised arbitrarily and absent any consideration of the opinions of those to be affected by it (the ground for review thus here plays 'an instrumental role in promoting just decisions'[10]). This presumption against arbitrariness is, moreover, complemented by procedural impropriety's emphasis on transparency in, and accountability for, the exercise of power. For instance, transparency may be facilitated both by the initial hearing and by a subsequent duty to give reasons for a decision; and accountability may be ensured where those reasons provide the basis for an appeal or, in the absence of an alternative remedy, an application for judicial review (on reasons see [7.25]–[7.29] and [7.43]–[7.46]).[11] Each of the values of non-arbitrariness, transparency, and accountability likewise informs the requirement that a decision-maker should not be self-interested in the decision to be taken: were it to be otherwise, the hearing may not be fair, the reasons misleading, and the corresponding scope for accountability limited.

---

[7] See generally P Craig, *Administrative Law*, 5th edn (London, Sweet & Maxwell, 2004) ch 13.

[8] *R (Governors of Campbell College) v Department of Education* [1982] NI 123, 131.

[9] *Board of Education v Rice* [1911] AC 179, 182, Lord Loreburn, cited in, eg, *R v Secretary of State, ex p Gilmore*, 10 April 1987, unreported. Although for consideration of the application of the rules in the specific fields of licensing, discipline, trade unions, immigration, employment, academia, planning, and sport see M Supperstone, J Goudie, and P Walker, *Judicial Review* (London, LexisNexis, Butterworths, 2005) p 336*ff*.

[10] *Raji v General Medical Council* [2003] 1 WLR 1052, 1058, para 13, Lord Steyn.

[11] On judicial review and alternative remedies see further [2.34]–[2.35].

[7.05]   The values of non-arbitrariness, transparency, and accountability take form to a greater or lesser extent in statute law, the common law, and/or Article 6 ECHR, and the relevant authorities and principles of law are considered below ([7.17]–[7.78]). There are, however, three definitional points that underlie those authorities and principles and which are of a more general importance to the workings of procedural impropriety as a ground for review. These concern: the relationship between statute law and the common law; the reach—and the context-sensitive nature—of common law fairness; and the scope of Article 6 ECHR.

The Relationship between Statute Law and the Common Law

[7.06]   Legislation that delegates a power of decision to a subordinate body will often contain a range of procedural requirements or safeguards and, where a decision-maker fails to act in a manner that is consistent with those, any corresponding decision may be deemed ultra vires (see [7.17]–[7.21]). In constitutional terms, this is consonant with the doctrine of legislative supremacy and the understanding that decision-makers must observe the parameters of legislation that entrusts them with a particular decision-making function.[12] However, even where the decision-maker has acted in a manner that is consistent with statutory requirements, it does not necessarily follow that a corresponding decision is procedurally sound.[13] This is because the courts have long held that the question whether there has been procedural fairness is a question of law for the courts, which may use the common law to imply 'so much and no more . . . by way of additional procedural safeguards as will ensure the attainment of fairness'.[14] Such use of the common law will be particularly apparent when an individual's rights or interests are affected by a decision and, even though the courts will not prescribe the additional procedures to be followed by the decision-maker, they will assess whether the procedures adopted are fair in all the circumstances[15] (the courts thus accept that it is for the decision-maker to decide on the form of procedures beyond those specified in statute, albeit that affected parties may have a common law right to make submissions as to the procedure to be adopted[16]). The courts in this way fill any gaps that may be left in legislation by viewing fairness as a wider common law precept rather than one to be defined by statute.

[7.07]   The fact that the common law can supplement legislative schemes should not, however, be taken to mean that use of the concept of fairness challenges the UK constitution's emphasis on legislative supremacy. Thus, although the courts have stated that they will scrutinise the fairness of wider decision-making processes closely,[17] they do so on the presumption that Parliament implicitly requires that decisions be made in accordance with the demands of common law fairness.[18] One corollary of this is that

---

[12] See further ch 5.

[13] *Re Price's Application* [1986] NI 390, 393, Kelly LJ.

[14] *Lloyd v McMahon* [1987] AC 625, 702, Lord Bridge, quoted in, eg, *Re Tiernan's Application* [2003] NIQB 60, para 8; *Re McBurney's Application* [2004] NIQB 37, para 9; *Re Henry's Application* [2004] NIQB 11, para 22; *Re Gordon's Application* [2006] NIQB 63, para 17.

[15] *Re McCabe Ltd's Application* [2003] NIQB 77, para 25.

[16] *Re Bothwell's Application* [2007] NIQB 25, para 8.

[17] *R v Panel on Take-overs and Mergers, ex p Guinness plc* [1990] 1 QB 146.

[18] *Re Quigley's Application* [1997] NI 202, 210, considering *R v Secretary of State for the Home Dept, ex p Doody* [1994] 1 AC 531, 560, Lord Mustill. And see *R v Secretary of State for the Home Department, ex p Pierson* [1998] AC 539, 573–4, Lord Browne-Wilkinson.

Parliament may legislate, either expressly or by necessary implication, to place common law guarantees in abeyance[19] (although there would remain the prospect of a declaration of incompatibility with the ECHR should the legislation also impact upon Article 6 ECHR's procedural guarantees[20]). Some case law has in similar vein held that, where legislation lays down an exhaustive procedural code, it may be neither necessary nor legitimate for the courts to imply further safeguards.[21]

The Reach of Common Law Fairness

'Rights', 'Interests', and 'Legitimate Expectations'

[**7.08**]   The common law rules of fairness—alternatively termed the rules of 'natural justice' (see [7.03])—have a broad reach and apply most obviously when a decision-making process has implications for an individual's 'rights' or 'interests'. Although rights and interests can be difficult to define and/or distinguish,[22] it is accepted that the common law rules can apply where a decision is to be taken in respect of something to which the individual is legally, though not absolutely, entitled (for instance, property[23] or liberty[24]) or in respect of something which the individual has been given and upon which he or she depends (for instance, a licence for an economic activity[25] or a contract of employment that has since given rise to disciplinary proceedings[26]). This approach to the reach of the rules is more recent in design, as the law previously fastened upon distinctions that tended to limit the application of the rules to 'judicial' determinations in respect of 'rights', as opposed to 'administrative' determinations in respect of 'interests' (or 'privileges').[27] However, the law has now moved beyond such distinctions[28] and it is accepted that the rules are of potential application whenever '(anyone) decides anything'.[29] Decision-makers are, with only very few exceptions, thus under a general common law duty to act fairly[30] (for an exception see [7.11] and [7.50] on prosecution decisions taken by the Public Prosecution Service).

[**7.09**]   The rules of fairness can also apply in cases where an individual has no recognised right or interest but where the court considers that the individual has a legitimate expectation of fair treatment (a so-called 'procedural legitimate expectation'). In this context, the application of the rules of fairness follows not from the fact of something that the individual has (such as a property right or a licence) but rather from the judicial

---

[19] *R v Secretary of State for the Home Department, ex p Pierson* [1998] AC 539, 573–4, Lord Browne-Wilkinson.

[20] See [5.14]; and [8.46]–[8.48].

[21] See, eg, *Furnell v Whangarei High School's Board* [1973] AC 660; and *R v Secretary of State for the Environment, ex p Hammersmith and Fulham LBC* [1991] 1 AC 521.

[22] P Craig, *Administrative Law*, 5th edn (London, Sweet & Maxwell, 2004) p 414.

[23] *Cooper v Wandsworth Board of Works* (1863) 14 CBNS 180.

[24] *In Re McClean* [2005] UKHL 46.

[25] *McInnes v Onslow Fane* [1978] 3 All ER 211, 218.

[26] *Re Glasgow's Application* [2004] NIQB 34.

[27] See P Craig, *Administrative Law*, 5th edn (London, Sweet & Maxwell, 2004) ch 13.

[28] The move is typically attributed to the House of Lords ruling in *Ridge v Baldwin* [1964] AC 40.

[29] *Board of Education v Rice* [1911] AC 179, 182, Lord Loreburn, cited in, eg, *R v Secretary of State, ex p Gilmore*, 10 April 1987, unreported.

[30] *R (Governors of Campbell College) v Department of Education* [1982] NI 123, 131.

desire to control decision-making with reference to the values of consistency and the rule of law.[31] For instance, an individual may argue that they have a procedural legitimate expectation as a result of prior governmental practice[32] or of a government statement to the effect that the individual would be consulted in advance of a decision being taken[33] (practices and statements may, depending on context, also give rise to 'substantive legitimate expectations'[34]: see [7.12]–[7.13]). While an expectation will not thereby enjoy immediate legitimacy—the question of legitimacy is to be determined objectively and with reference to the full legal and factual context of a case[35]—the courts are anxious to ensure that government is held to the highest standards of 'regularity, predictability and certainty in (its) dealing with the public'.[36] Hence where an individual has, for example, a legitimate expectation of consultation in advance of a decision, the courts will require that there is an opportunity for consultation unless there is an overriding reason to deny the opportunity[37] (such as the interests of national security[38]). They will here also require that the process of consultation is adequate, albeit that the question of what is adequate will depend on context (see [7.10] and [7.32]).

Fairness as a Context-dependent Requirement

[7.10] The application of the common law rules is, however, moderated by the context of any decision and the demands of fairness may vary accordingly. The point is perhaps most famously associated with Lord Bridge's statement that

> what the requirements of fairness demand when any body, domestic, administrative, or judicial, has to make a decision which will affect the rights of individuals depends on the character of the decision-making body, the kind of decision it has to make and the statutory or other framework in which it operates.[39]

Where the courts consider that the circumstances of a decision demand that procedural protection should be at its highest—for instance, where a licence for an economic activity is to be revoked[40]—an individual may thus expect to benefit from the full range of safeguards associated with a fair hearing (see [7.30]–[7.48]). However, where an individual is seeking the renewal of their licence, or where they are applying for a licence for the first time, the demands of fairness may lessen.[41] In other cases, the courts may even consider that, while procedural protections would ordinarily be desirable, the circumstances surrounding the decision override the demands of fairness. Typical examples here

---

[31] See [6.29].

[32] *Council of Civil Service Unions v Minister for the Civil Service* [1985] AC 374.

[33] Eg, *Re Hove's Application* [2005] NIQB 24 (applicants for asylum had a legitimate expectation that they would be allowed to make representations before a decision whether to return them to a third country was taken).

[34] On which see [6.29]–[6.45].

[35] *Re Hughes' Application* [2004] NIQB 25, para 11; and *Re Findlay* [1985] AC 318, 338.

[36] *Re Adams' Application*, 7 June 2000, unreported, Gillen J.

[37] *R v North and East Devon Heath Authority, ex p Coughlan* [2000] 2 WLR 622, 645, para 57.

[38] *Council of Civil Service Unions v Minister for the Civil Service* [1985] AC 374.

[39] *Lloyd v McMahon* [1987] AC 625, 702, quoted in, eg, *Re Gordon's Application* [2006] NIQB 63, para 17; *Re Cullen's Application* [2005] NIQB 9, para 46; and *Re Tiernan's Application* [2003] NIQB 60, para 8.

[40] *Re Sayer's Application*, 23 December 1992, unreported, citing *McInnes v Onslow Fane* [1978] 3 All ER 211, 218.

[41] *Re Sayer's Application*, 23 December 1992, unreported, citing *McInnes v Onslow Fane* [1978] 3 All ER 211, 218.

would include decisions taken in respect of counter-terrorism[42] and national security more generally[43] (see [7.49]–[7.52]).

[**7.11**]　A related issue is whether the demands of fairness need to be met at each and every stage of a decision-making process, or whether it is only the overall process that needs to be fair. This issue can arise in two main ways: first, where an individual argues that they have not been party to a preliminary determination that will inform a final decision in respect of him or her; and, second, where a decision has been taken in apparent breach of the rules of fairness but where the individual has an alternative right of appeal. The common law's starting point here is that decision-makers should seek to observe the demands of fairness at all stages but that, where it is not possible to do so, the overall process should be fair.[44] In respect of preliminary determinations, there is thus authority to the effect that, where the determination concerns the question whether to, for instance, initiate criminal proceedings against an individual, there is no right to a hearing at that stage as the individual can question all evidence and so on at trial[45] (the courts have, in any event, also said that the rules of fairness should not apply to prosecution decisions given the complex nature of the statutory function performed by the Public Prosecution Service[46]; although prosecution decisions can at the same time be embraced by the Human Rights Act 1998 and procedural obligations can flow from that source, for example, in respect of the giving of reasons—see [7.50]). The corresponding approach where there is a right of appeal then depends on the nature of the appeal and whether it might 'cure' the original defect (the so-called 'curative' principle). Hence where there is a full right of appeal, it is more likely that this will be able to cure the original defect, and an individual would therefore ordinarily be required to exhaust that effective alternative remedy rather than raise the matter by way of an application for judicial review (should review proceedings be brought the High Court may decide, in its discretion, not to grant a remedy[47]). However, where the appeal is limited to a point of law, it may be that the absence of fairness during the original decision-making process cannot be remedied by that alternative means. Under those circumstances, the High Court may therefore quash the original decision on an application for judicial review and require that it be retaken in the light of the demands of fairness (on the role of the curative principle see further [7.47]; and see too [7.48] on the significance of the related concept of 'composite' compliance with Article 6 ECHR).

Procedural and Substantive Fairness

[**7.12**]　It should finally be noted that common law fairness now has both a procedural and a substantive dimension[48] and that a remedy may issue both where there has been a

---

[42] *Re Shuker's Application* [2004] NI 367 (Attorney-General's decision not to 'de-schedule' certain offences under the Terrorism Act 2000 not open to review for failure to comply with the requirements of procedural fairness).

[43] *Council of Civil Service Unions v Minister for the Civil Service* [1985] AC 374 (government's failure to consult unions in advance of a change in employment conditions justified for reasons of national security).

[44] *In Re McClean* [2005] UKHL 46, para 34, Lord Bingham; and *Re Gallagher's Application* [2007]NIQB 37, para 9.

[45] *Wiseman v Borneman* [1971] AC 297.

[46] See *Re Boyle's Application* [2006] NICA 16; and *Re Adams' Application* [2001] NI 1.

[47] *Re Burke's Application*, 9 March 1994, unreported, applying *Calvin v Carr* [1980] AC 574. On effective alternative remedies see [2.34]–[2.35].

[48] *R v Secretary of State for the Home Department, ex p Pierson* [1998] AC 539, 589, Lord Steyn.

breach of procedure and/or where the final decision is substantively unfair. The clearest manifestation of this change has been in relation to legitimate expectations (see [7.09]), as the courts now accept that an individual may have an enforceable expectation of, for instance, consultation in advance of a decision being taken (procedural fairness), as well as an expectation that the decision will be consistent with an outcome that the individual expected given an earlier representation made to them (substantive fairness).[49] While the courts are at the same time less likely to intervene to protect substantive expectations where the representation has 'implications for an innominate class of persons',[50] they will intervene where the representation has been made to 'one or a few people giving the promise or representation the character of a contract'[51] (subject to the counter-argument that there is a public interest justification for frustrating the expectation[52]). The objective here is thus to safeguard the rule of law and to prevent the 'abuse of power'.[53]

[**7.13**]   This shift towards review for substantive fairness has attracted criticism because it is thought to have the potential to challenge the separation of powers doctrine that has long defined the workings of the grounds for judicial review.[54] Comparable criticisms have not, in contrast, generally been made in respect of developments in procedural fairness precisely because the courts are here concerned with the question of how a decision has been reached rather than with whether the decision is substantively justified. On the other hand, it can be said that matters of procedure and substance may not always or easily be disentangled, and that a 'procedural' development may have 'substantive' implications. The point can perhaps best be seen in respect of a common law duty to give reasons: while the duty may be described as a facet of the right to a hearing (see [7.43]–[7.46]), any reasons given may subsequently be used to found an application for judicial review that centres on arguments of relevancy, unreasonableness, lack of proportion, abuse of power, and so on.[55]

The Scope of Article 6 ECHR

[**7.14**]   Article 6 ECHR's procedural guarantees are central to the workings of the ECHR, and there is a large body of case law on the form that protection of the individual should take[56] (see [7.30]–[7.78]). The first paragraph of the Article reads:

> In the determination of his civil rights and obligations or of any criminal charge against him, everyone is entitled to a fair and public hearing within a reasonable time by an independent and impartial tribunal established by law.[57]

---

[49] See [6.29]–[6.45].

[50] *Re Neale's Application* [2005] NIQB 33, para 34, citing *R v Secretary of State for Education and Employment, ex p Begbie* [2000] 1 WLR 1115, 1130.

[51] *Re Neale's Application* [2005] NIQB 33, para 34, citing *R v North and East Devon Heath Authority, ex p Coughlan* [2000] 2 WLR 622, 646, para 59.

[52] See, eg, *Re Halligan's Application* [2003] NIQB 42, para 40.

[53] *R v North and East Devon Heath Authority, ex p Coughlan* [2000] 2 WLR 622, 645; and *Re Morrow and Campbell's Application* [2002] NIQB 4.

[54] See [1.03] and [1.05]; and ch 6.

[55] See further chs 5 and 6.

[56] See A Lester and D Pannick (eds), *Human Rights Law and Practice*, 2nd edn (London, Lexis Nexis Butterworths, 2004) p 203 ff.

[57] The full text of Art 6(1) reads: 'In the determination of his civil rights and obligations or of any criminal charge against him, everyone is entitled to a fair and public hearing within a reasonable time by an independent and impartial tribunal established by law. Judgment shall be pronounced publicly but the press and the

For the purposes of a clear majority of judicial review cases, the key term in the Article is 'civil rights'. This term, which has an autonomous Convention meaning,[58] has historically been associated with the concept of private law rights as is used in civil law systems,[59] with Article 6 ECHR applying where there is a 'dispute' (or 'contestation') about those rights.[60] This historical reference point has, in turn, given rise to considerable difficulty in the international and domestic case law, as it is not always clear whether administrative determinations are embraced by Article 6 ECHR[61] (it has been suggested that public law rights are covered only where they are of a personal and economic nature and are not contingent upon a large measure of official discretion[62]). In recent years, the ECtHR has, however, tended to adopt a broad approach to the interpretation of the term, and 'civil rights' have been taken to be engaged in disputes involving land use,[63] monetary claims against public authorities,[64] licences (whether applied for or to be revoked),[65] social security benefits,[66] and disciplinary proceedings.[67] On the other hand, Article 6(1) has not been taken as engaged in the context of immigration and deportation decisions[68] or in the context of some public sector employment disputes.[69] The Northern Ireland courts have similarly held that civil rights have not been engaged by decisions about whether a trial should take place before a jury[70]; by adjudications concerning alleged offences against prison discipline[71]; by a decision to refuse to grant an individual a firearms licence[72]; by a decision to exclude an individual from the Key Person Protection Scheme[73]; by a refusal to make a discretionary award of compensation to an individual under the terms of the Criminal Injuries (Compensation) (Northern Ireland) Order 1988[74]; and by a decision to withhold payments of public monies to political parties associated with paramilitary organisations.[75]

[7.15]   One consequence of the origins of, and the interpretation given to, 'civil rights' is that the procedural guarantees in Article 6 ECHR do not have as a broad a reach as the

public may be excluded from all or part of the trial in the interests of morals, public order or national security in a democratic society, where the interests of juveniles or the protection of the private life of the parties so require, or to the extent strictly necessary in the opinion of the court in special circumstances where publicity would prejudice the interests of justice.'

[58] *Engel v Netherlands* (1979–80) 1 EHRR 647; and, eg, *Re Shuker's Application* [2004] NI 367, 378, para 34.
[59] *Re Brolly's Application* [2004] NIQB 69, para 20.
[60] See *H v Belgium* (1988) 10 EHRR 339, 346, para 40; and, eg, *Re Belfast Telegraph Ltd's Application* [2001] NI 178. But see too *Le Compte, Van Leuwen and De Meyere v Belgium* (1982) 4 EHRR 1, 16, para 45 (ECtHR stating that word 'contestation' should not be construed technically); and *Moreira de Azevedo v Portugal* (1991) 13 EHRR 721, 737, para 66 (ECtHR doubting whether the requirement of a contestation/dispute is necessary).
[61] See P Craig, 'The Human Rights Act, Article 6 and Procedural Rights' (2003) PL 753.
[62] *Re Brown's Application* [2003] NIJB 168, 173, para 11, citing *Runa Begum v Tower Hamlets LBC* [2003] 2 AC 430, 465, para 112, Lord Walker.
[63] Eg, *Ringeisen v Austria* (1979–80) 1 EHRR 455; and *Skarby v Sweden* (1990) 13 EHRR 90.
[64] *Editions Periscope v France* (1992) 14 EHRR 597.
[65] See, respectively, *Benthem v Netherlands* (1986) 8 EHRR 1, and *Pudas v Sweden* (1988) 10 EHRR 380.
[66] *Mennitto v Italy* (2002) 34 EHRR 48.
[67] *Le Compte, Van Leuven and De Meyere v Belgium* (1982) 4 EHRR 1.
[68] *Maaouia v France* (2001) 33 EHRR 42.
[69] *Pellegrin v France* (2001) 31 EHRR 651.
[70] *Re Shuker's Application* [2004] NI 367.
[71] *Re McMillan's Application* [2002] NI 175.
[72] *Re Brown's Application* [2003] NIJB 168.
[73] *Re Brolly's Application* [2004] NIQB 69.
[74] *Re Creighton's Application* [2001] NIJB 210.
[75] *Re Sinn Féin's Application* [2005] NI 412.

common law rules of fairness[76] (on which see [7.08]–[7.13]). The Article has, however, still had a significant impact on those common law rules, which have been modified to absorb the elements of the ECHR (see, for instance, [7.59] on the test for apparent bias). Article 6 ECHR has, moreover, raised important questions about the intensity of judicial review that is required where an individual challenges a determination in respect of their 'civil rights'. This is because the Article requires that individuals have access to 'an independent and impartial tribunal' that has 'full jurisdiction' in the matter before it.[77] Questions have thus arisen about how far the High Court can be said to have full jurisdiction on an application for judicial review when the judicial review procedure has historically fastened upon a 'review, not appeal' distinction.[78] The corresponding answers given, to date, have focused on the understanding that 'full jurisdiction' is a con-text-dependent requirement and that it may not be necessary for a reviewing court to hear a full appeal in all cases.[79] The courts have also emphasised that, although judicial review does not consider the merits of a decision, there remains a wide range of argu-ments that might be made even within the traditional grounds for review.[80] On the other hand, it is now also recognised that judicial review may not be sufficient in some cases precisely because the courts cannot, among other things, reach their own conclusions on disputed questions of fact or substitute their decisions for those of the original decision-maker[81] (see [7.69]–[7.74]).

[**7.16**]   Article 6 ECHR also applies in respect of 'criminal charges', where its text spec-ifies a number of minimum guarantees for the individual.[82] While these will obviously be of more immediate relevance in criminal proceedings, the Article's guarantees in the criminal context have influenced those applicable in the civil and may thereby be of ana-logical value in many applications for judicial review.[83] Issues about criminal charges have, moreover, arisen in some applications for judicial review, albeit that the number of cases is small. These include cases in which the courts were asked to decide whether the decision to revoke a prisoner's early release licence was a determination in respect of a criminal charge (it was not)[84] and in which a challenge was made to a magistrate's refusal

[76] See, eg, *Re Glasgow's Application* [2004] NIQB 34 (disciplinary proceedings against a police officer not governed by Art 6 ECHR but covered by the common law rules of fairness).

[77] *Bryan v UK* (1995) 21 EHRR 342.

[78] See [1.05]; and ch 6.

[79] *R (Alconbury) v Secretary of State for the Environment, Transport and the Regions* [2003] 2 AC 295, 330, para 87, Lord Hoffmann; *Re Foster's Application* [2004] NI 248, 261, para 46, Kerr J; *Re Brown's Application* [2003] NIJB 168, 174–5, paras 14–16; and *Re McQuillan's Application* [2004] NIQB 50, paras 36–7, Weatherup J.

[80] *Runa Begum v Tower Hamlets LBC* [2003] 2 AC 430, 439, para 7, Lord Bingham, quoted in *Re Foster's Application* [2004] NI 248, 261, para 47, Kerr J.

[81] *Re Bothwell's Application* [2007] NIQB 25, para 21ff; and *Tsfayo v UK*, App 60860/00, 14 November 2006.

[82] These are: '(2) Everyone charged with a criminal offence shall be presumed innocent until proved guilty according to law. (3) Everyone charged with a criminal offence has the following minimum rights: (a) to be informed promptly, in a language which he understands and in detail, of the nature and cause of the accusation against him; (b) to have adequate time and facilities for the preparation of his defence; (c) to defend himself in person or through legal assistance of his own choosing or, if he has not sufficient means to pay for legal assist-ance, to be given it free when the interests of justice so require; (d) to examine or have examined witnesses against him and to obtain the attendance and examination of witnesses on his behalf under the same conditions as witnesses against him; (e) to have the free assistance of an interpreter if he cannot understand or speak the language used in court.' And see, eg, *Re C and Ors' Application* [2007] NIQB 101.

[83] On the two limbs of Art 6 ECHR see A Lester and D Pannick (eds), *Human Rights Law and Practice*, 2nd edn (London, Lexis Nexis Butterworths, 2004) p 203ff.

[84] *Re Adair's Application* [2003] NIQB 16.

to adjourn a trial in order to allow the defendant to be represented by his counsel of choice.[85]

PROCEDURAL REQUIREMENTS AND STATUTE

[7.17]   Legislation that delegates a power of decision to a subordinate body will often contain a range of procedural provisions that seek to ensure transparency in, and accountability for, exercises of the power of decision ([7.04]; such provisions will also pursue fairness towards those to be affected by a decision, although the question whether the demands of fairness are met is ultimately one for the courts—see [7.06]). Where a decision-maker fails to act in accordance with a statutory provision, the issue for the courts is whether the legislature intended that any corresponding decision should thereby be unlawful. This, in turn, reduces to an exercise in statutory interpretation in which 'the paramount objective is to ascertain the intention of the legislature in enacting the provision under consideration'.[86] In seeking to identify that intention, the courts have said that 'it is necessary to have regard to the use of mandatory or directory language within the provision, to establish the purpose for the use of such language and to determine from the context of the provision and other aids to interpretation what consequence should flow from any breach'.[87] Depending on context, this may also lead the courts to ask whether substantial compliance with a particular provision is sufficient or whether precise compliance is required given the overall legislative objective.

Ascertaining Legislative Intent

[7.18]   The starting point when deciding whether a decision should be deemed unlawful for reason of failure to observe a statutory provision is whether the provision is 'mandatory' or 'directory'. Although the classification of provisions with reference to these categories is no longer regarded as definitive of the matter,[88] non-observance of a mandatory requirement is more likely to be taken to constitute an illegality than is a failure to observe a directory requirement (although a failure to observe either can, in any given case, still constitute an illegality). Mandatory provisions for these purposes are typically signified by the use of words like 'shall',[89] which can be read as imposing a duty to act in a particular way rather than conferring a discretionary power[90] (directory provisions, in contrast, will give the decision-maker a discretion on whether to observe a particular procedure). Where the legislature has used the mandatory term, this is thus indicative of the importance to be attached to the corresponding procedural requirement

---

[85]   *Re Doherty's Application* [2002] NI 11 (held that, while the Art 6 right to choose counsel is not absolute, it should not be lightly overruled. The magistrate should therefore have evaluated why the defendant wished to be represented by a particular counsel and, on that basis, have decided whether an adjournment was justified).

[86]   See *Re ED's Application* [2003] NI 312, 316, para 11, citing *Re Robinson's Application* [2002] NI 206, 214, Carswell LCJ. And see further, eg, *Wallace v Quinn* [2004] NI 164, 170–71, paras 10–12.

[87]   *Re McCready's Application* [2006] NIQB 60, para 14, Morgan J.

[88]   See eg, *Wallace v Quinn* [2004] NI 164, 170–71, paras 10–12. See too *Re Bowden; JGS Services Ltd; Re Scalene Investments Ltd* [2004] NIQB 32, para 31.

[89]   Interpretation Act (Northern Ireland) 1954, s 38; and *Re ED's Application* [2003] NI 312, 316, para 12.

[90]   On powers, duties, and discretion see [4.22]–[4.28].

that the decision-maker is to observe. Should the decision-maker fail to observe the requirement, the courts may decide that the decision should fall precisely because the decision-maker has failed to 'understand correctly the law that regulates his decision-making power and [to] give effect to it'.[91]

[**7.19**]   The rule regarding mandatory provisions is not, however, absolute, and the courts may give such provisions a more flexible reading in the light of the legislature's presumed intentions. For instance, the courts may read a provision as both mandatory and directory; that is, mandatory as to substantial compliance but directory as to precise compliance.[92] The idea of substantial compliance is one that can shield decision-makers from findings of illegality insofar as the courts will not allow matters of mere technicality to trump a decision and to cause 'unjust and unintended consequences'[93] where the decision has been taken in a manner that is compliant overall with the legislative scheme.[94] On the other hand, the need for substantial compliance can have the opposite implication for decision-makers where there is only formal adherence to a requirement during the decision-making process. Under these circumstances, merely formal adherence could serve to defeat the purpose of the requirement, as the decision-maker may be able to sidestep the legislation's actual objective. Hence where statute imposes, for example, a duty of consultation or a duty to give reasons for a decision, the consultation held must be adequate and the reasons given meaningful within their statutory context (see [7.22]–[7.29]). Failing this, the decision may be deemed unlawful.

[**7.20**]   The courts may also give a provision a less strict interpretation 'if the effect of adopting a mandatory construction would be substantial public inconvenience'.[95] This approach is justified with reference to notions of 'public policy', although the courts at the same time attribute their decision to the legislature's intentions. In *Robinson v Secretary of State for Northern Ireland*[96] the courts thus held that it had not been Parliament's intention to prevent the Northern Ireland Assembly electing the First and Deputy First Ministers outside the six-week period specified for their election in the Northern Ireland Act 1998.[97] Although the Act provided that the Secretary of State 'shall' call fresh Assembly elections in the event that the First and Deputy First Ministers were not so elected,[98] the courts considered that the election of the Ministers outside that period was lawful and that the Secretary of State had thereby also acted lawfully when proposing a delayed date for Assembly elections. This was because, in 'public policy' terms, the 1998 Act was to be viewed as a 'constitution' for Northern Ireland[99] that Parliament had intended to have every opportunity to function. A rigid reading of the time-limit within the legislation would have had precisely the opposite effect.

---

[91] *Council of Civil Service Unions v Minister for the Civil Service* [1985] AC 374, 408; and see ch 5.

[92] *Re ED's Application* [2003] NI 312, 316, para 13, quoting W Wade and CF Forsyth, *Administrative Law*, 8th edn (Oxford, Oxford University Press, 2000) p 228.

[93] *R v Immigration Appeal Tribunal, ex p Jeyeanthan* [1999] 3 All ER 231, 238–9, Lord Woolf CJ.

[94] See, eg, *Re McCready's Application for Leave* [2006] NIQB 60 (breach of the rules governing early release of prisoners had been technical only and did not detract from the overall lawfulness of the process vis-à-vis the applicant).

[95] *Re ED's Application* [2003] NI 312, 316, para 12.

[96] [2002] NI 390.

[97] Section 16(8).

[98] Section 32(3).

[99] [2002] NI 390, 402, para 25, Lord Hoffmann; and see [1.33]–[1.34].

[7.21]   It should finally be noted that legislation that has implications for an individual's rights under the ECHR falls to be interpreted in accordance with section 3 of the Human Rights Act 1998.[100] Should a 'mandatory' provision thereby have implications that would not be ECHR-compliant, it should, 'so far as it is possible to do so', be read as 'directory' if that would ensure ECHR compatibility.[101] Such arguments may arise where, for example, rules of court specify in their original terms that certain procedures must be adhered to, absent which adherence an appeal cannot be heard. Whether review proceedings would be the appropriate forum for raising the issue would, however, depend on context, as the question may instead be raised as a preliminary matter before the court that may hear the appeal.[102]

Consultation

[7.22]   Legislation will often provide that a decision or other measure be made in the light of consultation with parties to be affected by the decision or measure (the common law too may impose a duty to consult: see [7.32]). Such provisions are consonant with the idea of public participation in decision-making processes (see [7.04]), and a failure to consult may, depending on statutory language and context, mean that a decision is unlawful. The question of who should be consulted will, in turn, depend on the statute, as the relevant legislation may either specify that certain groups should be consulted[103] or, instead, require that the decision-maker consult 'persons appearing to be representative' of those to be affected.[104] Where the legislation is of the former kind and an individual who has not been specified in the legislation claims that he or she should have been consulted, the courts may simply hold that the legislature did not intend that the applicant be consulted.[105] Where, in contrast, the legislation leaves it to the decision-maker to identify consultees, an aggrieved individual may challenge the failure to consult them on the ground of *Wednesbury* unreasonableness.[106] The individual may alternatively claim that they had a legitimate expectation of consultation as a result of prior practice and that the expectation had been unlawfully frustrated.[107]

---

[100] See [5.12]–[5.13].

[101] *Foyle, Carlingford and Irish Lights Commission v McGillion* [2002] NI 86.

[102] *Foyle, Carlingford and Irish Lights Commission v McGillion* [2002] NI 86 (appellant in a forfeiture case failed to serve a copy of the case stated to the respondent within 14 days of the case being dispatched by the clerk of petty sessions to the applicant, as was required by art 146(9) of the Magistrates' Courts (Northern Ireland) Order 1981, SI 1981/1675 (NI 26), and it fell to be determined as a preliminary point whether the consequence of that failure was that the appeal could not be entertained by the court).

[103] As in, eg, *Re Police Association for Northern Ireland's Application* [1990] NI 258 (Secretary of State required by s 34(2) of the Police Act (Northern Ireland) 1970 to consult the Police Association before making regulations concerning remuneration).

[104] Eg, the Local Government (Best Value) Act (Northern Ireland) 2002, s 1: '(1) A council shall make arrangements for continuous improvement in the way in which its functions are exercised, having regard to a combination of economy, efficiency, and effectiveness. (2) For the purpose of deciding how to carry out its duty under subsection (1), a council shall consult persons appearing to the council to be representative of (a) persons liable to pay rates in respect of hereditaments in the district of the council; (b) persons who use or are likely to use services provided by the council; and (c) persons appearing to the council to have an interest in the district of the council.'

[105] *Bates v Lord Hailsham* [1972] 3 All ER 1019.

[106] On *Wednesbury* see [6.05]–[6.11].

[107] *Re General Consumer Council* [2006] NIQB 86.

[7.23]   The nature of the consultation that is required thereafter depends on context, 'as the demands of fair consultation procedures will vary from case to case and will depend on the factors involved'.[108] Of course, where there is a requirement to consult and no consultation at all occurs, the fact of non-compliance will be self-evident and the court must ascertain whether the legislature thereby intended that the decision or other measure should be deemed unlawful (see [7.18]–[7.21]). However, more difficult is the situation where consultation does in fact occur but where it is claimed that the consultation was inadequate. Under these circumstances, the court must decide with reference to an objective test rather than one centred on *Wednesbury* unreasonableness whether the consultation met a minimum threshold of adequacy. That objective test is structured around four principal limbs of enquiry, namely: (1) whether the consultation occurred at a time when proposals were still at a formative stage; (2) whether the consultee was given adequate information on which to respond; (3) whether the consultee was given adequate time in which to respond; and (4) whether the decision-maker considered conscientiously the response to consultation.[109] Should the court find that one or more of these limbs have not been satisfied it may hold that the decision is unlawful for lack of adequate consultation, so long as the finding of illegality is at one with legislative intent. On the other hand, the court may decline to grant a remedy where it is of the opinion, on the facts, that proper consultation would not have made a difference to the course of action that the applicants would have taken and that they had thereby suffered no significant unfairness.[110] Neither will a court accede to arguments about procedural impropriety where the applicant did not respond to a genuine invitation to offer an opinion: 'Were it otherwise organisations with a right to be consulted could, in effect, veto the making of any (decision) by simply failing to respond to the invitation.'[111]

[7.24]   Where legislation is silent on the issue of consultation, the common law may instead require consultation where an individual or group has, for instance, a procedural legitimate expectation ([7.09]; such consultation must likewise be adequate within the meaning of the four-limb test—see [7.23]—and, in the event that it is not, the decision may be deemed unlawful). However, an important distinction for these purposes is that between administrative decisions and decisions made in respect of the form and content of draft subordinate legislation. While the legitimate expectation doctrine has long been used to found a common law right to consultation in respect of administrative decisions,[112] the courts have historically held that the common law should not impose a requirement of consultation in respect of subordinate legislation where the legislature has chosen not to do so.[113] The rationale for this approach has centred on (a) the fact that

---

[108] *Re Law Society of Northern Ireland's Application* [2004] NIQB 48, para 62.

[109] *Re Law Society of Northern Ireland's Application* [2004] NIQB 48, para 62; and *Re Buick's Application*, 3 June 1999, unreported, Coghlin J, citing *R v Brent London Borough Council ex p Gunning* [1986] 84 LGR 168, 189.

[110] See, eg, *Re National Union of Public Employers and Confederation of Health Service Employee's Application* [1988] NI 255 (held that, although the applicant unions had a legitimate expectation of consultation in respect of hospital closures and the reorganisation of certain general medical services, they would not have addressed themselves to the merits or demerits of the proposals, even if they had been furnished with fuller financial and staffing information).

[111] *Agricultural, Horticultural & Forestry Industry Training Board v Aylesbury Mushrooms Ltd* [1972] 1 All ER 280, 284, Donaldson J, quoted in *R v Northern Health and Social Services Board, ex p Larne Borough Council* [1988] 5 NIJB 90, 93–4.

[112] *Council of Civil Service Unions v Minister for the Civil Service* [1985] AC 374.

[113] *Bates v Lord Hailsham* [1972] 3 All ER 1019.

there is parliamentary control of such choices and that additional judicial control is thereby unnecessary and (b) the fact that the range of individuals who may be affected by legislation could be so diverse as to render consultation unworkable. However, while some recent case law has endorsed the traditional approach in respect of subordinate legislation,[114] other case law has since recognised that some contexts can give rise to an enforceable expectation of consultation in respect of subordinate legislation.[115] The common law's concern for certainty and consistency in public decision-making has thus apparently eclipsed one of orthodoxy's established rules.

Reasons

[7.25]   Statute may also require that a decision-maker give reasons for its decision. Such an obligation is said to engender transparency and public confidence in the decision-making process by, among other things, concentrating the mind of the decision-maker, demonstrating to the recipient that this has been so, showing that the issues have been conscientiously addressed, and/or alerting the recipient to a justiciable flaw in the process.[116] Reasons, which should be prepared by the decision-maker itself,[117] must therefore be 'adequate and intelligible',[118] although much will, at the same time, depend

> upon the particular circumstances and the statutory context in which the duty to give reasons arises . . . in many cases very few sentences should suffice to give such explanation as [is] appropriate to the particular situation.[119]

Should the decision-maker, in time, fail to give any reasons whatever or give reasons that do not satisfy the minimum threshold of adequacy, the courts must ascertain whether the legislature intended that the decision should thereby be deemed unlawful (see [7.18]–[7.21]). In the event that such intention is attributed to the legislature, the courts will be likely to quash the decision and require that it be retaken. However, where the courts consider that illegality need not necessarily follow the absence of reasons, they may instead order that reasons be given in the light of the statutory duty. Under

---

[114] *Re Northern Ireland Commissioner for Children and Young People's Application* [2004] NIQB 40, para 12, Girvan J.

[115] *Re General Consumer Council's Application* [2006] NIQB 86 (applicant had a legitimate expectation of consultation in advance of the laying before Parliament of a draft Order in Council because: (a) a programme of consultation with the applicant was announced in advance of the process; (b) the applicant was regarded as a key party to, and a major stakeholder in, the process; (c) the applicant had a special statutory position in relation to consumer issues and thus a particular statutory interest in the matters which were the subject matter of the draft Order; and (d) the applicant had a special position in the new legislative scheme set up by the draft Order as a guardian of the consumer interest). Cf *Re Christian Institute and Ors' Application* [2007] NIQB 66, paras 13–18 (applicants—who were challenging the lawfulness of equality regulations—had no legitimate expectation of consultation because there was no established practice of consultation and neither were there any special circumstances that could have created an obligation in public law to consult any of the applicants (the point was, however, rendered moot, as the respondent had engaged in consultation and the applicants were able to show that there had been inadequate consultation in respect of some of the provisions)).

[116] *Re Jordan's Application* [2003] NICA 30, para 15, Carswell LCJ, citing *R v Higher Education Authority, ex p Institute of Dental Surgery* [1994] 1 WLR 242, 256–7, Sedley J. See too *Stefan v General Medical Council* [1999] 1 WLR 1293, 1300, Lord Clyde.

[117] *Re KD* [2005] NICA 51, para 41.

[118] *Re Fair Employment Commission for Northern Ireland's Application*, 30 November 1990, unreported, citing *R v Mental Health Tribunal, ex p Pickering* [1986] 1 All ER 99, 102, Forbes J.

[119] *Re Adams' Application*, 7 June 2000, unreported, citing *Stefan v General Medical Council* [1999] 1 WLR 1293, 1304, Lord Clyde.

those circumstances, the duty will be observed although there will remain the possibility that the reasons will reveal further grounds for challenging the decision.

[7.26]   One related issue that features in the case law is the question of how far a public authority can add to its original reasons in the context of judicial review proceedings. This is essentially a matter concerned with the admissibility of evidence, and the starting position is that 'affidavits may supplement or explain [but] they may not contradict or provide an *ex post facto* rationalisation for the decision'.[120] Much will, however, again depend on the statutory context of the decision, and the basic position can become more complex given the nature of the duty. For instance, where there is a duty to give reasons as part of the notification of the decision to the parties, the courts will normally regard the provision of adequate reasons at the time of the decision as a condition of the decision's validity[121] (fuller explanation of the reasons would therefore not be possible). Where, in contrast, adequate reasons are not regarded as a condition of the decision's validity the courts may be willing to accept delayed reasons,[122] albeit that they will be cautious about doing so. In such cases, the courts will thus enquire whether the late reasons are consistent with the earlier ones, whether they appear to be genuine, and whether they amount to an *ex post facto* rationalisation of the decision. In the event that the delayed reasons are found to be inadmissible, the courts must decide whether the legislature intended that the decision should thereby be deemed unlawful[123] (see [7.18]–[7.21]).

[7.27]   Where statute does not impose a duty to give reasons, common law fairness may instead require that reasons be given (however, there is still no general duty to give reasons at common law: see [7.43]). For instance, the common law has long considered that good practice requires that magistrates give reasons for their decisions (although there is no concomitant legal duty[124]), and it has recently developed a duty both in respect of an increasingly wide range of administrative decisions[125] and in respect of some subordinate legislative choices.[126] Although the courts have traditionally refused to impose procedural obligations upon the legislative process because of, among other things, parliamentary controls[127] (but see now, regarding consultation, [7.24]), there are some forms of subordinate legislation that can be made without any parliamentary scrutiny beyond the initial scrutiny of primary legislation that delegates the power to make subordinate legislation.[128] In those circumstances—viz where the legislative choice is absent 'some form of scrutiny other than that provided by way of judicial review'—it has thus been held that the common law may impose a duty to give reasons so as to ensure that minimum levels of transparency and scrutiny are observed.[129] However, the courts have at the same time

---

[120]   *Re Harkins' Application* [2001] NIQB 6. See too *Re Bates' Application* [2004] NIQB 84, para 30; and *Re Windsor Securities' Application* [2006] NI 168, 176, para 21, considering *R v Westminster City Council, ex p Ermakov* [1996] 2 All ER 302.

[121]   *Lothian and Borders Police & Ors v Gemmell* [2005] CSOH 32, 70, Lord Reed.

[122]   See, eg, *Re Anglin's Application*, 29 August 1996, unreported (High Court accepted that the National Appeal Panel's duty to give reasons for its decision in respect of a pharmacist's application to relocate his premises had been satisfied by subsequent averments in affidavit evidence).

[123]   See *R (Nash) v Chelsea College of Art and Design* [2001] EWHC 538, para 34; and *Lothian and Borders Police & Ors v Gemmell* [2005] CSOH 32, 70, Lord Reed.

[124]   See *Re Allen's Application* [1998] NI 46; and *Re McFadden's Application* [2002] NI 183.

[125]   Eg, *Re McCallion's Application* [2005] NICA 21.

[126]   *Re Campbell and Ors' Application* [2005] NIQB 59, para 20, Kerr LCJ.

[127]   *Bates v Lord Hailsham* [1972] 3 All ER 1019.

[128]   Eg, the County Court (Amendment No 2) Rules (Northern Ireland) 2002, SR 2002/412.

[129]   *Re Campbell and Ors' Application* [2005] NIQB 59, para 20, Kerr LCJ.

said that it is likely that the common law reason-giving obligation that can apply to administrative decision-making cannot be 'imported wholesale into the legislative domain'.[130] The nature of reasons expected in the legislative context may therefore be different from that in the administrative and judicial contexts.

[7.28]   The ECHR too may require that reasons be given in the event that statute is silent (although the fact that the obligation here has it origins in the Human Rights Act 1998 may mean that it is in that sense attributable to legislative intent; on reasons and the ECHR see further [7.45]). For instance, it is now accepted that Article 6 ECHR requires magistrates to give reasons where they refuse an application to stay proceedings, albeit that the reasons need not be extensive.[131] An obligation can in similar vein arise under Article 2 ECHR,[132] where the ECtHR has identified a particular need for transparency when decisions are taken in the context of ongoing investigations into controversial deaths.[133] Articles 3 and 8 ECHR can, moreover, require that reasons be given where, for example, a patient in a mental health facility is to be administered treatment contrary to his or her stated wishes.[134]

[7.29]   Reasons may also be required under EU law as read with the European Communities Act 1972, for instance where a decision interferes with rights of free movement under the EC Treaty. In those circumstances, the general principles of EU law require that reasons be given so that the affected individuals can determine whether there are grounds for challenging the interference with their rights.[135] The duty here is also consonant with EU law's more general emphasis on transparency in decision-making processes at both the national and supranational levels.[136]

THE RIGHT TO A HEARING

[7.30]   The common law right to a hearing is centuries old and has historically sought to ensure that individuals who will be affected by a decision are able to make informed representations to the decision-maker in advance of the decision being taken.[137] The right corresponds, at its highest, with a constitutional right of access to a court[138] and, more generally, with the right to have a decision taken in the absence of actual or apparent bias on the part of the decision-maker (on the rule against bias see [7.58]–[7.78]; the common law here typically requires that 'he who hears should decide', albeit that the requirement may be modified in the light of, for instance, the *Carltona* doctrine[139]).

---

[130] *Re Campbell and Ors' Application* [2005] NIQB 59, para 22, Kerr LCJ.

[131] *Re McFadden's Application* [2002] NI 183.

[132] See *Re Kincaid's Application* [2007] NIQB 26 (application for judicial review brought by an individual who had been shot by another private party and who wished to be given fuller reasons for the decision not to prosecute that party: application dismissed).

[133] *Jordan v UK* (2003) 37 EHRR 2, para 124, criticising the failure of the Director of Public Prosecutions (DPP) to give reasons for a 'no prosecution' decision in respect of the use of lethal force by police officers; and on the current approach of the DPP (now the Public Prosecution Service—PPS) see http://www.ppsni.gov.uk/site/default.asp.

[134] *R (Wooder) v Feggetter* [2003] QB 219.

[135] Case 222/86, *UNECTEF v Heylens* [1987] ECR 4097.

[136] See further P Craig, *EU Administrative Law* (Oxford, Oxford University Press, 2006) pp 381–4.

[137] *Baggs Case* (1615) 11 Co Rep 93b.

[138] *R v Lord Chancellor, ex p Witham* [1998] QB 575.

[139] On which see [5.50]–[5.51].

Today, the right is of potential application in a wide range of circumstances, as the courts accept that the right to be heard may follow where an individual has a right or an interest that will be affected by a decision, or where the individual has a legitimate expectation of fair treatment. The common law right is, moreover, increasingly subject to the influence of Article 6 ECHR, which likewise corresponds with a right of access to a court[140] and which applies when a decision is to be taken in respect of, most obviously for the purposes of judicial review, an individual's 'civil rights'. While the interpretation given to 'civil rights' in ECHR case law at the same time means that Article 6 ECHR may not be of application in as many cases as the common law (see [7.15]), the Article has nevertheless raised significant questions about whether to adapt aspects of the common law right. Questions have likewise arisen about the nature of the common law rule against bias, which complements the right to a fair hearing (see [7.59] and [7.69]–[7.74]).

[**7.31**]   In terms of the content of the right to a hearing, the common law and Article 6 ECHR can each impose obligations before a decision is taken (for instance, notification of the issue to be addressed), during the hearing itself (as to the type of hearing, evidence, and so on), and after a decision has been reached (for example, reasons) (see [7.35]–[7.48]). The particulars of the common law right in any given case will, however, depend on context, and the levels of protection for an individual may vary according to the right, interest, or expectation affected (see [7.10]). Where an initial decision is reached in apparent breach of the applicable common law requirements and/or Article 6 ECHR, this may—but need not necessarily—mean that the decision is unlawful as it may be possible for the defect in the original decision to be 'cured' on appeal (under the common law: see [7.47]) or through 'composite' compliance with Article 6 ECHR (that is, where the individual has a right of recourse to a court or tribunal that is independent, impartial, and so on: see [7.48]). Moreover, even where a decision has been taken in breach of the common law requirements and cannot be cured on appeal, the court on an application for judicial review may in its discretion decline to grant a remedy (see [7.54]–[7.56]); and there may be other cases in which the courts accept that procedural protections should be placed in abeyance (for instance, in 'urgent' cases or where decisions are to be taken in respect of counter-terrorism or in the interests of national security more generally: see [7.49]–[7.52]). The guarantees in Article 6 ECHR similarly are not regarded as absolute, although the ECtHR does require that any limitation on them pursues a legitimate aim and does not impair the very essence of the right.[141]

[**7.32**]   There are two further points of overarching importance about the right to a hearing. The first is that, while the common law typically uses the language of 'a right to a hearing', it may in other instances use the language of 'consultation' (for example, where the courts consider that the individual has a legitimate expectation of fair treatment[142]). What consultation will require in any given case will, again, be a function of context 'as the demands of fair consultation procedures will vary from case to case and will depend on the factors involved'.[143] The courts do, however, require that any consultation satisfies an objective minimum test of adequacy that is structured around four limbs of

[140] *Golder v UK* (1975) 1 EHRR 524.

[141] *Perez de Rada Cavanilles v Spain* (1998) 29 EHRR 109, 120, paras 44–5.

[142] Eg, *Council of Civil Service Unions v Minister for the Civil Service* [1985] AC 374; *Re National Union of Public Employers and Confederation of Health Service Employee's Application* [1988] NI 255; and *Re General Consumer Council's Application* [2006] NIQB 86.

[143] *Re Law Society of Northern Ireland's Application* [2004] NIQB 48, para 62.

enquiry (see [7.23]). In the event that one or more of the limbs has not been satisfied and the respondent has been unable to justify the absence of consultation[144] (for example with reference to national security concerns[145]), a court may hold that the impugned decision is unlawful. On the other hand, the court may decline to grant a remedy where it is of the opinion, on the facts, that proper consultation would not have made a difference to the course of action that the applicants would have taken and that they had thereby suffered no significant unfairness.[146]

[7.33]   The second point concerns the need for decisions to be taken within a reasonable time.[147] This corresponds with a more general common law duty to avoid undue delay in the exercise of statutory powers or the performance of a statutory duty,[148] although it has a particular meaning in the context of the common law rules of fairness. The point here is that, as a decision will often have significant implications for an individual's rights or interests, a hearing should be held, and a resulting decision reached, within a time-frame that is fair and reasonable. While the question of what is reasonable will depend on matters such as the complexity of the issue to be resolved, the underlying objective is to ensure that the decision-making process does not interfere unduly with the individual's rights or interests. Common law fairness in this way includes a promptitude requirement that is likewise present in the text of Article 6 ECHR ('everyone is entitled to a fair and public hearing within a reasonable time'; and see [7.40]).

The (Variable) Content of the Right to a Hearing

[7.34]   The content of the right to a hearing, both at common law and under Article 6 ECHR, can be examined with reference to five complementary headings. These are: (1) Notification; (2) The Nature of the Hearing and Evidence; (3) Representation; (4) Reasons; and (5) Appeals and Rehearings.

Notification

[7.35]   It is a 'fundamental principle'[149] of the common law that an individual who may be adversely affected by a decision is given advance notification of the central issue which the decision-maker must address. The underlying justification is simply that: 'If the right to be heard is to be a real right which is worth anything, it must carry with it a right in the accused man to know the case which is to be made against him.'[150] While the

---

[144]   *R v North and East Devon Heath Authority, ex p Coughlan* [2000] 2 WLR 622, 645, para 57.

[145]   *Council of Civil Service Unions v Minister for the Civil Service* [1985] AC 374.

[146]   See, eg, *Re National Union of Public Employers and Confederation of Health Service Employees' Application* [1988] NI 255 (held that, although the applicant unions had a legitimate expectation of consultation in respect of hospital closures and the reorganisation of certain general medical services, they would not have addressed themselves to the merits or demerits of the proposals, even if they had been furnished with fuller financial and staffing information).

[147]   See, eg, *R v Lambeth LBC, ex p Crookes* (1997) 29 HLR 28 (delay in determining applications for housing benefit was inordinate and constituted a procedural impropriety).

[148]   See [4.25]; and, eg, *R v Home Secretary, ex p Phansopkar* [1976] QB 606.

[149]   *Re A & Ors Application* [2007] NIQB 30, para 40, Gillen J.

[150]   *Kanda v Government of the Federation of Malaysia* [1962] AC 322, 337, Lord Denning; cited in, eg, *Re A & Ors Application* [2007] NIQB 30, para 32; *Re Dallas' Application* [1996] NI 276, 298; and *R (Snaith) v The Ulster Polytechnic* [1981] NI 28, 42.

language of 'accused' and a 'case being made against' is perhaps more evocative of, for instance, criminal or disciplinary proceedings, the idea of notification is also germane to administrative decision-making processes that may have implications for an individual's rights (such as property rights) or interests (such as a licence). The need for notification can, in other instances, be founded upon a legitimate expectation of a fair hearing.[151]

[7.36]   The corollary of the right to notification is the opportunity to respond, as 'procedural fairness requires that a party has the right to know the case against him and the right to respond to that case'.[152] The right to respond, in turn, requires disclosure of material facts to the party affected[153] and adequate time to prepare a response[154] (the right to respond need not necessarily include the right of the party to cross-examine witnesses,[155] although such a right may exist within the nature of the hearing: see [7.39]) While the presumption in favour of disclosure can at the same time be subject to arguments of public interest immunity or of the need to maintain confidence/protect witnesses[156]—urgent cases too may have implications for the 'adequate time' requirement (see [7.51])—the common law here seeks to 'facilitate participation and involvement in the decision making process' and to 'accommodate the strong impulse for practical justice'.[157] It is therefore likely that there will be breach of the rules of common law fairness where the procedure adopted by the decision-maker prejudices the individual 'to the extent that his opportunity to participate effectively is seriously handicapped, certainly if it is in effect stultified'.[158]

[7.37]   The right to notification and to respond are likewise found in Article 6 ECHR's guarantees in respect of civil rights. The starting point here is the ECtHR's 'equality of arms' principle, which entails 'that each party must be afforded a reasonable opportunity to present his case under conditions that do not place him at a substantial disadvantage vis-à-vis his opponent'.[159] Where a decision is to be made in respect of an individual's 'civil rights' (see [7.14]), the equality of arms principle can thus impose a duty to disclose documents to individuals, albeit that disclosure may be limited where there is good cause for doing so.[160] The case law of the ECtHR has similarly established that the principle can require by implication that the individual should have adequate time to prepare his

---

[151]   *Re Cullen's Application* [2005] NIQB 9 (applicant had a legitimate expectation of notice of adverse factors relevant to his application for a licence: however, no remedy granted in the case as the adverse factors were all capable of being addressed by the applicant in a later application for a licence).

[152]   *Re McBurney's Application* [2004] NIQB 37, para 14, Weatherup J. See too, eg, *Re Henry's Application* [2004] NIQB 11, para 23, Weatherup J; and *Re McCabe Ltd's Application* [2003] NIQB 77, para 24, Weatherup J.

[153]   *Re McCabe Ltd's Application* [2003] NIQB 77, para 24.

[154]   *Re North Down Borough Council's Application* [1986] NI 304, 322.

[155]   *Re McCabe Ltd's Application* [2003] NIQB 77, para 24.

[156]   *Re A & Ors Application* [2007] NIQB 30, para 41, Gillen J; and, eg, *In Re McClean* [2005] UKHL 46 (use of the special advocate procedure acceptable when sentence review commissioners were considering whether the revoke the licence of a prisoner released early under the Northern Ireland [Sentences] Act 1998). On public interest immunity see [3.55].

[157]   *Re A & Ors Application* [2007] NIQB 30, paras 40 and 41, Gillen J.

[158]   *Re North Down Borough Council's Application* [1986] NI 304, 322, citing *R v Thames Magistrates Court, ex p Polemis* [1974] 2 All ER 1219, 1223, Lord Widgery CJ. And see, eg, *Re Thompson's Application* [2007] NIQB 8 (decision to deselect the applicant from a prison resettlement unit quashed because of the failure to observe the applicant's right to know and to respond) and *Re Drummond's Application* [2006] NIQB 81 (decision to revoke the applicant's firearms licence quashed as it had been taken in breach of the applicant's legitimate expectation that he would be able to make representations in advance of the decision).

[159]   *De Haes and Gijsels v Belgium* (1998) 25 EHRR 1, 57, para 53.

[160]   Eg, *McGinley and Egan v UK* (1999) 27 EHRR 1, 41, para 86.

or her case[161] (Article 6(3) ECHR contains an express requirement to that effect in the context of criminal proceedings).

The Nature of the Hearing and Evidence

[7.38]   The nature of the hearing that is required by the common law in any case will depend on the context that is set by the individual's right, interest, or expectation, and by the corresponding nature of the decision to be taken. At its highest, the full protection of the individual would require that there is an oral hearing at which the individual is both present and able fully to participate in although it is also open to an individual to decline the offer of a hearing). However, there is at the same time no 'fixed requirement for an oral hearing in all cases'[162] and it may be that written submissions will suffice where, for instance, an individual is making an application for the first time for a licence for an economic activity.[163] On the other hand, the common law may impose an obligation to grant an oral hearing in the very different circumstances where a prisoner who has been released early from prison on licence resists recall to prison for an alleged breach of the terms of the licence.[164] While the right to an oral hearing here is not absolute—the decision-maker is also tasked with protecting society from the risk of re-offending—the courts have emphasised that an oral hearing is to be preferred even in cases where there is no dispute as to primary facts. This is because facts not in dispute might still be open to explanation or mitigation, or because they might lose some of their significance in the light of other new facts. It is also because an oral hearing can bolster a prisoner's right of response ([7.36]) in the sense that it may otherwise be difficult for the prisoner to know which points are troubling the decision-maker and to address those points effectively.[165]

[7.39]   The common law rules of fairness do not, however, require that the strict rules of evidence have to be followed during a hearing (for instance, a decision-maker 'may take into account any material which, as a matter of reason, has some probative value'[166]); and neither do they necessarily require that there is an opportunity to test evidence through the cross-examination of witnesses.[167] Nevertheless, the overall procedure adopted during the hearing must be fair, and the more adversarial the hearing, the more will be expected by way of procedural safeguards. At its most rigorous, the common law may therefore require that:

> Where there is an oral hearing, a tribunal must . . . consider all relevant evidence submitted, inform the parties of the evidence taken into account, allow witnesses to be questioned and allow comment on the whole case . . . a [tribunal] should not rely on points not argued or private enquires made.[168]

[7.40]   Article 6 ECHR's guarantees in respect of civil rights likewise emphasise the importance of oral hearings at which the individual is able to participate, albeit that there

---

[161] *Albert and Le Compte v Belgium* (1983) 5 EHRR 533, 546, para 39.

[162] *Re Thompson's Application* [2007] NIQB 8, para 27.

[163] *Re Sayer's Application*, 23 December 1992, unreported, citing *McInnes v Onslow Fane* [1978] 3 All ER 211, 218.

[164] *R (Smith and West) v Parole Board* [2005] 1 All ER 755.

[165] *R (Smith and West) v Parole Board* [2005] 1 All ER 755.

[166] *R v Deputy Industrial Injuries Commissioner, ex p Moore* [1965] 1 QB 456, 487, Diplock LJ, quoted in *Re Devine's Application* [1990] 9 NIJB 96, 113–14.

[167] *Re Tiernan's Application* [2003] NIQB 60, para 9.

[168] *Re J's Application* [2004] NIQB 75, para 15, Gillen J.

is a stronger presumption in favour of such hearings in civil disputes where the dispute is centred upon, for example, the conduct of the individual[169] (other Articles may also require hearings, for instance Article 5 ECHR in the context of prisoner release disputes[170]). This emphasis on oral hearings corresponds not only with the 'equality of arms' principle (see [7.37]) but also with Article 6 ECHR's textual requirement that an individual be afforded a 'fair and public hearing'. While the rules of evidence are, in turn, a matter for the national system, those rules must accord with the ECHR's conception of what is fair in all the circumstances,[171] and this may require that there is an opportunity for cross-examination of witnesses even in civil disputes.[172] Article 6 ECHR also requires that the hearing is held within a 'reasonable time' given the nature of dispute, viz the complexity of the issues, nature of the individual's interests, and so on[173] (on the common law requirement that hearings be held within a reasonable time see [7.33]).

Representation

[**7.41**]   The common law does not prescribe a right to be legally represented in all cases but regards the matter as at the discretion of the decision-maker. That discretion is, however, to be exercised in the light of the so-called '*Tarrant* criteria',[174] and these, as with all aspects of the rules of fairness, are context-sensitive. Under the criteria, decision-makers should thus consider: the seriousness of the decision to be taken; whether any points of law are likely to arise; whether the individual will be able to present his or her own case; whether there may be procedural difficulties; the need for reasonable speed in reaching a decision; and the need for fairness as between the individual and other parties to the dispute.[175] Those same criteria are also to be considered where an application is made to the decision-maker by a party who wishes to attend the hearing as the friend or adviser of the individual to be affected by the decision.

[7.42]   Where an individual's civil rights within the meaning of Article 6 ECHR are engaged by a decision there is similarly no automatic entitlement to representation[176] (the position is different in respect of criminal charges[177]). The ECHR is, however, premised on the need for rights to be effectively protected, and representation will therefore be deemed necessary for purposes of protecting the right to a hearing where, among other things, a dispute is legally and factually complex. Legal and factual complexity can, moreover, have implications for entitlement to legal aid in civil proceedings before domestic tribunals, as the ECtHR has held that legal aid may be necessary in complex cases to ensure that those individuals who are unable to afford legal representation are

---

[169]   *Muyldermans v Belgium* (1993) 15 EHRR 204.

[170]   *R (Smith and West) v Parole Board* [2005] 1 All ER 755.

[171]   *Miailhe v France (No 2)* (1997) 23 EHRR 491, 511, para 43.

[172]   *X v Austria*, App 5362/72, 42 CD 145 (1972).

[173]   See, eg, *H v UK* (1988) 10 EHRR 95, 111, para 86 (period of 31 months to decide whether a mother should have access to her child in the care of the authorities unreasonable).

[174]   *R v Secretary of State for the Home Department, ex p Tarrant* [1985] QB 251.

[175]   See further, eg, *Re Byer's Application* [2004] NIQB 23, para 9, *Re McMillan's Application* [2002] NI 175, 177; *Re Morgan's Application* [2002] NIQB 1; and *Re Quinn's Application* [1988] 2 NIJB 10, 35–7.

[176]   *Webb v UK* (1984) 6 EHRR 120, 123 ff, Eur Comm.

[177]   Art 6(3)(c) reads: 'Everyone charged with a criminal offence has the following human rights: (c) to defend himself in person or through legal assistance of his own choosing or, if he has not sufficient means to pay for legal assistance, to be given it free when the interests of justice so require.'; and see, eg, *Re C and Ors' Application* [2007] NIQB 101.

able to present their cases properly and satisfactorily[178] (legal aid outside the human rights context is solely a matter for statute). On the other hand, the domestic courts have stated that the requirement publicly to fund civil proceedings will occur only 'exceptionally' and 'where it is impossible as a matter of practicality for a litigant to have access to the courts . . . where a matter of fundamental importance is at stake'.[179] The courts have likewise said that the scope for the individual to encounter difficulty should in any event be limited given the decision-maker's obligation 'to ensure that the [individual's] lay status is not exploited by [his or her] opponents'.[180]

Reasons

[**7.43**]   Reasons perform a number of important functions in administrative law (see [7.25]) and, cast in terms of the right to a fair hearing, they can allow the individual to determine whether the decision-maker has taken account of the arguments made by the individual and, if not, whether to challenge the decision. Where statute does not impose a duty to give reasons (see [7.25]–[7.29]), it falls to the common law to resolve whether a duty should be imposed in respect of a particular decision (reasons given under the common law must, as with those given under statute, be 'adequate and intelligible'[181] within their context;[182] they must also be prepared by the decision-maker itself[183]). Historically, the common law has not imposed a general duty to give reasons, largely because of the burden that it was thought this might place upon decision-makers (viz, it may 'demand an appearance of unanimity where there is diversity; call for the articulation of sometimes inexpressible value judgments; and offer an invitation to the captious to comb the reasons for previously unsuspected grounds of challenge'[184]; for the arguments in favour of a duty see [7.25]). However, while there is still no general duty to give reasons,[185] the common law has more recently developed so as to impose duties in a wide range of circumstances in which fairness is taken to demand that reasons be given.[186] This development of the law has been most pronounced in respect of administrative decisions, although a duty has also been imposed in respect of subordinate legislative choices that have been made in the absence of 'some form of scrutiny other than that provided by way of judicial review'[187] (see [7.27]). The common law has also moderated its position in respect of magistrates' courts as, to the extent that magistrates are still not under a legal duty, the courts have said that best practice requires that even a short statement of reasons be given for decisions[188] (reasons will in any event be required under Article 6 ECHR where a final determination has been made[189]: see [7.45]).

---

[178] *Airey v Ireland* (1979) 2 EHRR 305, 314–15, para 24.
[179] *Re Lynch's Application* [2002] NIQB 35.
[180] *Re Lynch's Application* [2002] NIQB 35.
[181] *Re Fair Employment Commission for Northern Ireland's Application*, 30 November 1990, unreported, citing *R v Mental Health Tribunal, ex p Pickering* [1986] 1 All ER 99, 102, Forbes J.
[182] *Re Adams' Application*, 7 June 2000, unreported.
[183] *Re KD* [2005] NICA 51, para 41.
[184] *Re Ferris' Application* 6 April 2000, unreported, citing *R v Higher Education Funding Council, ex p Institute of Dental Surgery* [1994] 1 All ER 651, 665, Sedley J.
[185] *Re Starritt's Application* [2005] NICA 48, para 27; *Re McCallion's Application* [2005] NICA 21, para 27; *Re Frazer's Application* [2005] NI 280, 289, para 17; and *Re Cummins' Application* [2002] NIQB 33.
[186] For judicial recognition of the point see, eg, *Re Kavanagh's Application* [1997] NI 368, 381; and *Re Tucker's Application* [1995] NI 14, 26.
[187] *Re Campbell and Ors' Application* [2005] NIQB 59, para 20, Kerr LCJ.
[188] *Re Allen's Application* [1998] NI 46.
[189] *Re McFadden's Application* [2002] NI 183; and *Re Glenn's Application* [2002] NIQB 61, para 30.

[7.44]   The leading statement of the law relating to administrative decision-makers is *Re McCallion's Application*.[190] In that case, the Northern Ireland Court of Appeal adopted a number of key points that had been distilled by the Divisional Court in England and Wales in *R v Ministry of Defence, ex p Murray*.[191] The most important of those, in more general terms, is that there is a perceptible trend towards an insistence on greater openness and transparency in the making of administrative decisions. However, the Court at the same time accepted that there is no general duty to give reasons and that it is for the applicant who claims that reasons should be given to show that the procedure of not giving reasons is unfair. In assessing whether there has been unfairness, courts should then consider, among other things: whether there is a right of appeal (the absence of which may be a factor in deciding that reasons should be given); the nature of the individual's interest that is affected by the decision (that is, the more important the interest the more likely it is that reasons will be required); and the corresponding function performed by the decision-maker. A court should also consider whether there are public interest considerations that militate against the giving of reasons; and neither should reasons be required if the procedures of the particular decision-maker would be frustrated by the imposition of such a requirement.

[7.45]   Article 6 ECHR likewise imposes a duty to give reasons for decisions that affect civil and criminal rights, notwithstanding that the obligation is not imposed in express terms. The justification for the obligation is, again, the need for fairness and to enable an individual to decide whether to challenge a decision (reasons, to this end, should be sufficient to aid the individual in understanding the essence of the decision[192]). A duty to give reasons can, moreover, be imposed by other Articles that are either procedural in form or which append adjectival elements to a substantive guarantee. Hence Article 5 ECHR contains an express requirement that an individual who is arrested is informed promptly, in a language which he or she understands, of the reasons for his or her arrest and of any charge against him or her; and Article 2 ECHR can require that reasons be given,[193] as the ECtHR has identified a particular need for transparency when decisions are taken in the context of ongoing investigations into controversial deaths.[194] Articles 3 and 8 ECHR can likewise require that reasons be given, for example, where a patient in a mental health facility is to be administered treatment contrary to his or her stated wishes.[195]

[7.46]   It should finally be noted that a duty to give reasons can arise under EU law, for instance where a decision interferes with rights of free movement under the EC Treaty. In those circumstances, the general principles of EU law require that reasons be given so

---

[190]   [2005] NICA 21, para 27.
[191]   [1998] COD 134, considering *R v Civil Service Appeal Board, ex p Cunningham* [1991] 4 All ER 310; *R v Secretary of State for the Home Department, ex p Doody* [1994] 1 AC 531; and *R v Higher Education Funding Council, ex p Institute of Dental Surgery* [1994] 1 All ER 651.
[192]   *Helle v Finland* (1998) 26 EHRR 159.
[193]   See *Re Kincaid's Application* [2007] NIQB 26 (application for judicial review brought by an individual who had been shot by another private party and who wished to be given fuller reasons for the decision not to prosecute that party: application dismissed).
[194]   *Jordan v UK* (2003) 37 EHRR 2, para 124, criticising the failure of the Director of Public Prosecutions (DPP) to give reasons for a 'no prosecution' decision in respect of the use of lethal force by police officers; and on the current approach of the DPP (now the Public Prosecution Service—PPS) see http://www.ppsni.gov.uk/site/default.asp.
[195]   *R (Wooder) v Feggetter* [2003] QB 219.

that the affected individuals can determine whether there are grounds for challenging the interference with their rights.[196] The duty here is also consonant with EU law's more general emphasis on transparency in decision-making processes at both the national and supranational levels.[197]

Appeals and Rehearings

[**7.47**]   Where a decision is reached in apparent breach of the common law's fair hearing requirements and/or the equivalent aspects of Article 6 ECHR, this may, but need not necessarily, mean that the decision is unlawful. Much will here depend on whether there is a remedy by way of an appeal and whether that remedy can cure the defects in the original decision-making process (the so-called 'curative' principle).[198] A cure, for the purposes of the common law, is more likely to be achieved where the individual has a full right of appeal against the decision, as the appellate body will be able to rehear all issues and substitute its decision accordingly (that 'effective alternative' remedy should therefore ordinarily be used in preference to judicial review; if review proceedings are brought the High Court may in its discretion decline to grant a remedy[199]). However, where an appeal is only partial, it may be that the original defect cannot be cured by that remedy and that the decision thereby remains tainted by impropriety. Under those circumstances, an application for judicial review may thus be appropriate and the High Court may, for instance, quash the decision and require that it be retaken. On the other hand, there may be cases where the High Court declines to grant a remedy because it is of the opinion, on the facts, that the impropriety had no bearing on the final decision and that a new decision would be no different to that under challenge.[200]

[**7.48**]   Article 6 ECHR likewise accepts that a defect in the original decision-making process which affects civil rights can be remedied on appeal or by an application for judicial review where the body hearing the issue has 'full jurisdiction' in the matter that comes before it[201] (the so-called 'composite' approach to compliance). A cure for these purposes will be achieved most readily where there is a full right of appeal, as the appellate body will be able to rehear all the issues and substitute its own decision for that of the original decision-maker. However, the ECtHR has at the same time held that the question of what constitutes 'full jurisdiction' depends on the context and that it may, in some circumstances, be sufficient for an individual to have an appeal on a point of law or a remedy by way of an application for judicial review. The significance of this point as relates to judicial review in Human Rights Act 1998 cases is considered at [7.69]–[7.74].

---

[196]   Case 222/86, *UNECTEF v Heylens* [1987] ECR 4097.

[197]   See further P Craig, *EU Administrative Law* (Oxford, Oxford University Press, 2006) pp 381–4.

[198]   *Re Gallagher's Application* [2007] NIQB 37, para 9.

[199]   *Re Burke's Application*, 9 March 1994, unreported, applying *Calvin v Carr* [1980] AC 574; and on effective alternative remedies see [2.34]–[2.35].

[200]   *R (McPherson) v Ministry of Education* [1980] NI 115.

[201]   *Bryan v UK* (1995) 21 EHRR 342; and see, eg *Re McFadden's Application* [2002] NI 183 (magistrate's failure to state reasons for refusing to stay proceedings 'cured' by application for judicial review, ie the reasons at that stage became apparent and the applicant was able to challenge the decision before the trial).

When is the Right to a Hearing Modified and/or Excluded?

[**7.49**]   Although the right to a hearing is regarded as a fundamental precept of both the common law and the ECHR, there are some (very limited) circumstances in which it is accepted that the rules do not apply or, to the extent that they do, that they should apply in only a modified form. The clearest example at common law is where a decision is taken in the interests of national security, as it has long been accepted that national security concerns can trump the right to be heard or, depending on context, to consultation.[202] While the courts will not at the same time accept unquestioningly a governmental assertion that national security issues underpinned a decision,[203] they do acknowledge that the role of the courts in protecting the individual must here account for wider security concerns.[204] The point can be seen in the analogous case of *Re Shuker's Application*,[205] where the applicant challenged the decision of the Attorney-General not to 'de-schedule' certain offences under the Terrorism Act 2000. In dismissing the application for judicial review, the High Court held that, while the Attorney-General's decision was justiciable, it was not reviewable on the basis that it failed to comply with the requirements of procedural fairness. This was because the court considered that the decision had involved the evaluation of material that was of a sensitive nature and that disclosure in such circumstances would have been against the public interest. The court also considered that Parliament had entrusted the decision-making power to the Attorney-General, and judicial restraint was for that reason appropriate. Judicial review would therefore lie only where there was, for instance, bad faith on the part of the decision-maker.[206]

[**7.50**]   The common law also considers that prosecutorial decisions of the Public Prosecution Service are not governed by the rules of fairness (see too [7.11] for the more general position in respect of preliminary determinations). The rationale here lies in the nature of the 'complex and almost unique' function performed by the office, which

> is not that of an adjudicator between two parties . . . the [Public Prosecution Service] has to consider and weigh a number of disparate and at times even competing interests e.g. the general public interest at any particular time, the interest of the putative accused, the victim, the supplier of information such as an informant, the various disinterested and interested witnesses.[207]

The corresponding case law on the application or otherwise of the rules of fairness has generally centred on whether there is a common law duty to give reasons for decisions not to prosecute and, in holding that no duty arises, the courts have held that there is no anterior duty to observe the rules of fairness such as would found a more specific duty to give reasons.[208] A common law challenge to the failure to give reasons can therefore succeed only where it can be established either that extant prosecution policy on reasons is

---

[202] *Council of Civil Service Unions v Minister for the Civil Service* [1985] AC 374.

[203] See [4.18]–[4.19].

[204] See, eg, in England and Wales *R v Secretary of State for the Home Department, ex p Cheblak* [1991] 1 WLR 890 (immigrant who was the subject of a deportation order for reasons of national security not entitled to full particulars of the case against him or to legal representation); and *R v Secretary of State for the Home Departmen, ex p Hosenball* [1977] 3 All ER 452 (Secretary of State was justified in not giving reasons to an individual who had been made the subject of a deportation order).

[205] [2004] NI 367.

[206] [2004] NI 367, 377, para 27. See also, eg, *R v DPP, ex p Kebeline* [2000] 2 AC 326; and *Re Kincaid's Application* [2007] NIQB 26, para 19*ff*. And on bad faith see [5.47]–[5.48].

[207] *Re Boyle's Application* [2006] NICA 16, para 33; and see too *Re Adams' Application* [2001] NI 1.

[208] *Re Adams' Application* [2001] NI 1.

irrational or, alternatively, where a particular decision is irrational in the light of that extant policy.[209] On the other hand, a duty to give reasons can arise in cases under the Human Rights Act 1998, for instance where a prosecution decision is taken to fall within the ambit of the Article 2 ECHR right to life.[210]

[7.51]   The common law also recognises that there may no right to a hearing for reasons of practicality, for instance where an urgent decision is to be taken in order to protect public health.[211] Case law on this point would, however, suggest that such modes of decision-making will be acceptable in only truly exceptional circumstances, and it would also appear that the common law will typically require that it is possible for the individual to have a hearing at a later stage[212] (on the 'curative' principle see [7.47]). In other instances, arguments of practicality may mean that it is not possible to grant a hearing to all affected parties and that the demands of the common law should lessen accordingly. An example here is in respect of the form and content of subordinate legislation as the common law has, in the absence of primary legislation specifying that certain individuals should be consulted, historically declined to intervene for lack of a hearing or of consultation.[213] Some more recent case law has, however, started to develop exceptions to this common law rule, for instance where an applicant is able to demonstrate that he or she had a legitimate expectation of consultation[214] (see [7.24]).

[7.52]   Case law under Article 6 ECHR likewise accepts that its procedural guarantees are not absolute and that they need not always be observed (for instance, where there are arguments of national security). The ECtHR does, however, require that any limitation upon the right to a fair hearing pursues a legitimate aim and does not impair the very essence of the right.[215] This requires that the lawfulness of any limitation be assessed with reference to the proportionality principle.[216]

Breach of the Right to a Hearing: Remedies and Waiver

[7.53]   Where a decision is reached in breach of the right to a hearing this will mean that the decision is unlawful.[217] Under such circumstances, the High Court on an application for judicial review will thus typically grant a remedy to the affected individual, for instance by quashing the original decision and requiring that it be retaken in the light of the demands of fairness.

[7.54]   The remedies available in judicial review are, however, discretionary[218] and the courts may refuse a remedy for one of three main reasons (the position may be more com-

---

[209]   *Re Boyle's Application* [2006] NICA 16, paras 40–45.

[210]   *Jordan v UK* (2003) 37 EHRR 2, para 124. On the current policy of the PPS see http://www.ppsni. gov.uk/site/default.asp.

[211]   *R v Davey* [1899] 2 QB 301 (person with an infectious disease removed to hospital).

[212]   See further M Supperstone, J Goudie, and P Walker, *Judicial Review* (London, LexisNexis, Butterworths, 2005) p 298ff.

[213]   *Bates v Lord Hailsham* [1972] 3 All ER 1019; and, eg, *Re Northern Ireland Commissioner for Children and Young People's Application* [2004] NIQB 40, para 12, Girvan J.

[214]   *Re General Consumer Council's Application* [2006] NIQB 86, para 36.

[215]   *Perez de Rada Cavanilles v Spain* (1998) 29 EHRR 109, 120, paras 44–5.

[216]   On which principle see [6.18]–[6.28]; and see, eg, *Tinnelly & McElduff v UK* [1998] 27 EHRR 249 and *Devenney v UK* [2002] 35 EHRR 24.

[217]   *Ridge v Baldwin* [1964] AC 40; and *R v Secretary of State for the Home Departmen, ex p Al Medhawi* [1990] 1 AC 876, 898, Lord Bridge.

[218]   See [3.81]–[3.87]; and [8.08]–[8.09].

plex when a case is brought under the European Communities Act 1972 and/or the Human Rights Act 1998[219]). The first is where an applicant has not exhausted an effective alternative remedy that could have cured the defect in the original decision-making process (see [7.47]—it might, as a matter of logic, even be argued that there has not yet been an illegality here). However, the question whether a defect could be cured by an appeal must be answered with reference to the nature of the remedy, for instance whether there is a full right of appeal or whether any appeal is limited to a point of law.[220] Where the right of appeal is in the latter form it may be that the appellate body could not have cured the defect and that the original decision would remain tainted by illegality. In that circumstance, an application for judicial review would be appropriate and relief may not be refused for reasons of an alternative remedy.[221]

[7.55]   The second reason concerns the conduct of the applicant. Applicants are expected to behave with candour and integrity during proceedings[222] and, should they fail to do so, they may be considered undeserving of a remedy notwithstanding a breach of their right to a hearing.[223] On the other hand, there is case law to suggest that the applicant may be considered undeserving only where he or she had some intention to mislead the court, or to misuse its process. The courts may not in the result censure an applicant for a simple, and largely inconsequential, oversight.[224]

[7.56]   The third possible reason for refusing a remedy concerns arguments of utility.[225] Such arguments may prevail where the courts consider that, even if the decision were to be taken again and in accordance with the correct procedures, the final decision would be no different to that under challenge. Rather than 'beat the air' in such circumstances,[226] the courts may therefore simply decline to make an order.[227] A court may

---

[219] See [8.39] (for European Communities Act 1972 and EU law) and [8.42] (for Human Rights Act 1998 and ECHR).

[220] *Re Burke's Application*, 9 March 1994, unreported, applying *Calvin v Carr* [1980] AC 574.

[221] On alternative remedies see [2.34]–[2.35].

[222] *Re D's Application* [2003] NI 295.

[223] *Re O'Neill's Application* [1990] 3 NIJB 1 (although the decision under challenge was deemed lawful, the court would, in any event, have been inclined to refuse a remedy because the applicant had both misled the Housing Executive as to the relevant facts and attempted to mislead the court as to those facts).

[224] *Re Equal Opportunity Commission's Application* [1988] NI 278 (court rejecting the argument that a remedy should be refused to the applicant because of its failure to raise, in earlier proceedings, the points that were argued in the present application: while the overlap in points might have been foreseen by counsel, the failure to raise the points earlier did not call for serious criticism given the context of the first hearing).

[225] See further [3.82] and citations therein.

[226] *R (McPherson) v Ministry of Education* [1980] NI 115, 121, Lord MacDermott.

[227] See, eg, *Re Wylie's Application* [2005] NI 359 (the court was satisfied that, even though there had been procedural shortcomings in respect of the decision not to grant the applicant a boat owner's licence, any representations made by the applicant would not have affected the outcome); and *R (Campbell College) v Department of Education* [1982] NI 123 (no benefit could arise from quashing the department's decision in respect of the school's proposed admission policy as, in the circumstances of the case, a reconsideration of the proposal in accordance with proper legal principles would inevitably have led to the same result). But compare, eg, *R (Snaith) v The Ulster Polytechnic* [1981] NI 28 (where the rules of fairness are breached by persons acting as judge in their own cause then certiorari should ordinarily issue, notwithstanding that a properly constituted body would probably have come to the same decision or would do so in the future); *R (Smyth) v Coroner for County Antrim* [1980] NI 123 (the court has power to issue certiorari where the rules governing a coroner's inquest are broken notwithstanding that it is arguable that no benefit would accrue—it is important in the interests of both the next of kin and the public more generally that a verdict is reached by considered and regular inquiry); and *R (Hennessy) v Department of the Environment* [1980] NI 109 (while the court may refuse to exercise its discretion to quash a decision vitiated by procedural unfairness where the result would be of no consequence, it must be a very rare case where on a failure to give a hearing on an appeal the applicant would not be entitled to review by way of certiorari).

likewise decline to grant a remedy where it is of the opinion, on the facts, that proper consultation would not have made a difference to the course of action that the applicants would have taken and that they had thereby suffered no significant unfairness[228]; and it may in other instances consider that the judgment of the court itself is sufficient relief, given the context of the case, and that there is no further need for a formal remedy.[229]

[7.57]   A respondent in judicial review proceedings may finally argue that the applicant had waived his or her procedural rights in advance of the impugned decision being taken (waiver is possible both at common law and under Article 6 ECHR[230]). Waiver, for these purposes, must be 'clear and unequivocal, and made with full knowledge of all the facts relevant to the decision whether to waive or not'.[231] Such knowledge is in turn said to be contingent upon disclosure of relevant factors and 'of the grounds upon which the complaint . . . might be made'.[232] Should the applicant thereafter wish to raise an objection, he or she must do so in a timely manner and not 'blow hot and cold; he cannot approbate and then reprobate; he cannot have it both ways'.[233] In the event that there is no objection and it can be said that there was 'an obvious and freely given election . . . not to proceed with [any] challenge' the courts may thus accept the argument of waiver, albeit that there may be countervailing arguments of 'public interest, where some greater public concern arises'.[234]

THE RULE AGAINST BIAS

[7.58]   The rule against bias entails, at its most basic, that a decision-maker should not be judge in his or her own cause (*nemo judex in causa sua*), irrespective of whether he or she is named as a party to the dispute. The rule, which can apply to decision-makers acting in either a judicial or an administrative capacity,[235] in this way complements the right to a hearing, as it could not be expected that a hearing would be fair if the decision-maker had an interest in the outcome of a dispute beyond an interest in the administration of justice between the parties.[236] In terms of the values that underlie the common law rules of fairness (as well as procedural requirements in statute—see [7.04]), the rule against bias thus seeks to eliminate arbitrariness in decision-making by requiring those who are,

---

[228] See, eg, *Re National Union of Public Employers and Confederation of Health Service Employees' Application* [1988] NI 255 (held that, although the applicant unions had a legitimate expectation of consultation in respect of hospital closures and the reorganisation of certain general medical services, they would not have addressed themselves to the merits or demerits of the proposals, even if they had been furnished with fuller financial and staffing information).

[229] *Re McCabe Ltd's Application* [2003] NIQB 77 (High Court considered that no need to interfere with the decision of the Industrial Court as the respective rights of the parties had in effect been declared in the judgment).

[230] *Millar v Dickson (Procurator Fiscal, Elgin)* [2002] 1 WLR 1615.

[231] *Re Glasgow's Application* [2006] NIQB 42, para 12, Weatherup J, citing *Locabail (UK) Ltd v Bayfield Properties Ltd* [2000] 1 All ER 65, 73, para 15, Lord Bingham.

[232] *Re Glasgow's Application* [2006] NIQB 42, para 13.

[233] *Corrigan v Irish Land Commission* [1977] IR 317, 326, Henchy J.

[234] *Re Glasgow's Application* [2006] NIQB 42, para 13.

[235] *R v Secretary of State for the Environment ex p Kirkstall Valley Campaign Ltd* [1996] 3 All ER 304, 323, Sedley J, cited in, eg, *Re Buick's Application*, 3 June 1999, unreported.

[236] *Re McCaffrey's Application* [2001] 378, 382, quoting de Smith, Woolf and Jowell, *Principles of Judicial Review*, 5th edn (London, Sweet & Maxwell, 1999) p 413.

or who may appear to be, partial to recuse themselves or 'step aside'. While the common law at the same time recognises that the rule should be of variable application depending on the nature of the decision-maker and any corresponding interest ([7.10])—it is also possible for an individual to waive his or her objection to any perceived bias (7.77])—the overall objective of the rule is the attainment of transparency in decision-making processes and the safeguarding of 'public confidence'[237] in those processes. The rule against bias in this way has both an internal and external dynamic: internal as concerns the interests of the individual affected by the decision; and external as concerns the public perception of the manner in which that decision is reached.

[7.59]   The corresponding body of case law identifies two types of bias, namely 'actual' and 'apparent' bias.[238] Each of these is examined more fully below ([7.61]–[7.68]), although one point of more general importance concerns the test for apparent bias. Until recently, the test was that laid down by the House of Lords in *R v Gough*[239] whereby the reviewing court would determine, with reference to the information available to it, whether there was a 'real danger of bias' on the part of the decision-maker. The test was not, at the same time, formulated in terms of the 'reasonable man', both because the court itself was taken to personify the reasonable man and because it was thought that the court would have available to it evidence that may not be available to the ordinary observer. However, this court-centred approach was criticised in other common law jurisdictions for the reason that it placed insufficient emphasis on public perception of the issue under challenge,[240] and it was thought in the UK that it may be incompatible with Article 6 ECHR's approach to bias[241] (viz to ask whether there was an objective risk of bias in the light of the circumstances identified by the court[242]). The House of Lords in *Porter v Magill* thus adopted a new test that requires a reviewing court, once it has ascertained all the circumstances that have a bearing on the suggestion of bias, to ask 'whether the fair-minded and informed observer, having considered the facts, would conclude that there was a real possibility' of bias.[243] The modern test is, in the result, more closely aligned with the approach to apparent bias both in other common law systems and in the ECHR.[244]

[7.60]   One further point about the impact of Article 6 ECHR on bias concerns the requirement that determinations about an individual's 'civil rights and obligations' be made by an 'independent and impartial tribunal established by law' (on 'civil rights' see [7.14]–[7.16]). This requirement has raised important questions about the workings of judicial review, as determinations about civil rights in the field of administration may often be taken by decision-makers who are neither 'independent' of the executive nor

---

[237] *Re O'Connor and Broderick's Application* [2006] NI 114, 121, para 18.

[238] See, eg, *Re Cullen's Application* [2005] NIQB 9, para 18.

[239] [1993] AC 646.

[240] See, eg, in Australia *Webb v R* (1994) 18 CLR 41.

[241] *Re Medicaments and Related Classes of Goods (No 2)* [2001] 1 WLR 700.

[242] *Piersack v Belgium* (1983) 5 EHRR 169, 179–80.

[243] [2002] 2 AC 357, 494, paras 102–3, Lord Hope. See too the HL judgments in *Lawal v Northern Spirit Ltd* [2004] 1 All ER 187, and *Davidson v Scottish Ministers* [2004] HRLR 34; and for consideration and application of *Porter* in the NI courts see, eg, *Re W & M* [2006] NI Fam 6; *Re O'Connor & Broderick's Application* [2006] NI 114; *Re Starritt's Application* [2005] NICA 48; *Re Cullen's Application* [2005] NIQB 9; *Re Moore's Application* [2004] NIQB 49; *Re Sheridan's Application* [2004] NIQB 4; *Re Foster's Application* [2004] NI 248; *Re Halligan's Application* [2003] NIQB 42.

[244] *Re Bothwell's Application* [2007] NIQB 25, para 15.

'impartial' (for instance, Ministers who are giving effect to central or devolved government policy, or local authority officers who may be conducting a review of a decision taken by the same authority; on the common law approach to impartiality in such cases see [7.67]–[7.68]). Under such circumstances, Article 6 ECHR is not automatically violated so long as the affected individual has a means of recourse to an independent and impartial tribunal that has 'full jurisdiction' in the matter in question.[245] In terms of the workings of judicial review, questions have thus arisen about whether the High Court can be said to have full jurisdiction when the judicial review procedure has historically fastened upon a 'review, not appeal' distinction that precludes judicial assessment of the merits of a decision.[246] The answers given, to date, have focused on the understanding that 'full jurisdiction' is a context-dependent requirement and that it may not be necessary for a reviewing court to hear a full appeal in all cases.[247] The courts have also emphasised that, although judicial review does not consider the merits of a decision, there remains a wide range of arguments that might be made even within the parameters of the traditional grounds for review.[248] On the other hand, it is now also recognised that judicial review may not be sufficient in some cases precisely because the courts cannot, among other things, reach their own conclusions on disputed questions of fact or substitute their decisions for those of the original decision-maker[249] (see [7.69]–[7.74]).

Actual Bias

[**7.61**] Actual bias is taken to exist where the decision-maker is 'either (1) influenced by partiality or prejudice in reaching the decision, or (2) actually prejudiced in favour of or against a party'.[250] Whether a decision is vitiated by such bias is a question of fact, and the courts have said that a claim of actual bias will succeed only 'when supported by the clearest evidence'.[251] The courts have, moreover, said that a claim of actual bias is 'an extremely serious allegation'[252] and it is therefore clear that any claim should not be made lightly (there have been very few in the case law[253]). Nevertheless, the ground remains an important, if little-used, safeguard against the potential abuse of power and it in that sense corresponds with other little-used headings such as bad faith.[254]

---

[245] *Bryan v UK* (1995) 21 EHRR 342.

[246] See [1.05]; and ch 6.

[247] *R (Alconbury) v Secretary of State for the Environment, Transport and the Regions* [2003] 2 AC 295, 330, para 87, Lord Hoffmann; *Re Foster's Application* [2004] NI 248, 261, para 46, Kerr J; *Re Brown's Application* [2003] NIJB 168, 174–5, paras 14–16; and *Re McQuillan's Application* [2004] NIQB 50, paras 36–7, Weatherup J.

[248] *Runa Begum v Tower Hamlets LBC* [2003] 2 AC 430, 439, para 7, Lord Bingham, quoted in *Re Foster's Application* [2004] NI 248, 261, para 47, Kerr J.

[249] *Re Bothwell's Application* [2007] NIQB 25, para 21ff; and *Tsfayo v UK*, App 60860/00, 14 November 2006.

[250] *Re Cullen's Application* [2005] NIQB 9, para 18, Weatherup J, citing *Re Medicaments and Related Classes of Goods (No 2)* [2001] 1 WLR 700, 711, para 38, Lord Phillips MR.

[251] *Re Foster's Application* [2004] NI 248, 265, para 66, Kerr J; and see too *Re Treacy's Application* [2000] NI 330, 353.

[252] *Re Foster's Application* [2004] NI 248, 265, para 66, Kerr J.

[253] See, eg, *Re Cullen's Application* [2005] NIQB 9 (applicant arguing unsuccessfully that the decision to refuse him a licence for hare coursing was tainted by actual bias, viz the relevant Minister had well-known anti-coursing views and had previously been an employee of the League Against Cruel Sports).

[254] On which see [5.47]–[5.48].

Apparent Bias

[7.62] The test for apparent bias is centred on the question whether 'the fair-minded and informed observer, having considered the facts, would conclude that there was a real possibility' of bias[255] (see [7.59]). In some instances, the test is applied on the basis of a presumption that the nature of the decision-maker's interest in the matter before it is such that the common law requires automatic disqualification from the decision-making process. However, in many other cases there is no automatic requirement of disqualification, and the issue will fall to be determined with reference to context. Here, the reviewing court must first ascertain all the circumstances that have a bearing on the suggestion of bias and, on that basis, decide whether the fair-minded and informed observer would conclude that there was a real possibility of bias.[256] This emphasis on context is all-important, as the courts accept that the rule against bias should be applied variably and in the light of the nature of the decision-maker and its corresponding interests. On the other hand, the courts have emphasised that they will not allow old distinctions in the law—for instance, as between judicial and administrative decision-makers (see [7.08])—to limit the reach of the rule.[257] The modern starting point is thus that context is key but that 'anyone (who) decides anything'[258] must do so fairly.

Automatic Disqualification: 'Pecuniary Interests' and 'Parties to the Dispute'

[7.63] The first, and most obvious, circumstance under which the common law requires the automatic disqualification of a decision-maker for reasons of apparent bias is where the decision-maker has a direct financial interest in the outcome of the dispute before it.[259] The rationale here is simply that, where there is such an interest, it can be presumed conclusively that any fair-minded and informed observer would consider that there was a real possibility of bias. While the presumption is, in turn, subject to a *de minimis* exception[260] and thus weakened where the relevant interest is 'remote and contingent'[261]—there is also the possibility of waiver of an objection—the common law's basic approach is to exclude decision-makers with financial interests in the dispute. Decision-makers are likewise excluded where the interest is proprietary.

[7.64] The same presumption applies where the decision-maker is a party to the dispute. At its broadest, an individual decision-maker (typically a judge) may be held to be a party where he or she is a member of an organisation that is one of the parties to the

---

[255] *Porter v Magill* [2002] 2 AC 357, 494, paras 102–3, Lord Hope. See too the HL judgments in *Lawal v Northern Spirit Ltd* [2004] 1 All ER 187, and *Davidson v Scottish Ministers* [2004] HRLR 34; and for consideration and application of *Porter* in the NI courts see, eg, *Re W & M* [2006] NI Fam 6; *Re O'Connor & Broderick's Application* [2006] NI 114; *Re Starritt's Application* [2005] NICA 48; *Re Cullen's Application* [2005] NIQB 9; *Re Moore's Application* [2004] NIQB 49; *Re Sheridan's Application* [2004] NIQB 4; *Re Foster's Application* [2004] NI 248; *Re Halligan's Application* [2003] NIQB 42.

[256] *Porter v Magill* [2002] 2 AC 357, 494, para 102, Lord Hope.

[257] *R v Secretary of State for the Environment ex p Kirkstall Valley Campaign Limited* [1996] 3 All ER 304, 323, Sedley J.

[258] *Board of Education v Rice* [1911] AC 179, 182, Lord Loreburn, cited in, eg, *R v Secretary of State, ex p Gilmore*, 10 April 1987, unreported.

[259] *Dimes v Grand Junction Canal* (1852) 3 HL Cas 759.

[260] *Locabail (UK) Ltd v Bayfield Properties* [2001] 1 All ER 65, 71, para 10.

[261] *R v Manchester, Sheffield and Licolnshire Rly Co* (1867) LR 2 QB 336, 339, Mellor J.

proceedings, or where he or she has a close institutional link to the party/organisation.[262] However, there is also authority to suggest that simple membership is not enough to justify automatic disqualification and that the decision-maker must have been actively involved in the institution of the proceedings in question.[263] In the event that the decision-maker is merely a member of an organisation it may therefore be that the issue of bias can no longer be resolved on the basis of the presumption.

Other Forms of Disqualifying Bias

[**7.65**]   Where a claim for automatic disqualification is rejected or is not made the reviewing court must, as per *Porter v Magill* ([7.59]), ascertain all the circumstances that have a bearing on the suggestion of bias. Depending on the context, this may require the court to draw inferences from any gaps or inconsistencies in evidence before it and, in that light, to ask whether the fair-minded and informed observer would conclude that there was a real possibility of bias.[264] The corresponding assessment of bias should be 'objective'[265] and account for the understanding that the 'indispensable requirement of public confidence in the administration of justice requires higher standards today than the case even a decade ago'.[266] This is thus consonant with the concern, expressed in *Porter v Magill*, that the legal process should be seen to link the resolution of disputes about bias to public perception of those same disputes. The fair-minded and informed observer is, in consequence, expected to adopt a balanced approach and not to be 'wholly uncritical' of legal culture.[267]

[**7.66**]   Given the context-driven nature of the rule against apparent bias, there are many different circumstances that have given rise to disqualification in practice.[268] Some recent examples in Northern Ireland include cases where: the decision-maker had formed a concluding view of a matter in advance of hearing the applicant's representations on the matter;[269] where the decision-maker in disciplinary proceedings had liaised with legal

---

[262]   See, most famously, *R v Bow Street Metropolitan Stipendiary Magistrate, ex p Pinochet Ugarte (No 3)* [2000] 1 AC 147 (House of Lords decision to extradite General Pinochet to Spain to face charges in respect of human rights violations had to be retaken as one of the judges—Lord Hoffmann—was an unpaid director and chairman of Amnesty International Charity Ltd; this charity, in turn, was controlled by Amnesty International, which had intervened in the case before the House of Lords).

[263]   *Meerabux v Attorney-General of Belize* [2005] 2 AC 513.

[264]   Eg, *Re Moore's Application* [2004] NIQB 49, para 13*ff.*

[265]   *Re Moore's Application* [2004] NIQB 49, para 22.

[266]   *Lawal v Northern Spirit Ltd* [2004] 1 All ER 187, 196, para 22, Lord Steyn, quoted in *Re O'Connor's and Broderick's Application* [2006] NI 114, 121, para 16.

[267]   *Lawal v Northern Spirit Ltd* [2004] 1 All ER 187, 196, para 22, Lord Steyn.

[268]   See M Fordham, *Judicial Review Handbook*, 4th edn (Oxford, Hart Publishing, 2004) p 1047 ff.

[269]   *Re McCaffery's Application* [2001] NI 378 (judge who was to hear multiple claims for damages arising from a bus accident had indicated on the basis of the evidence before him in the first three cases that he would not be inclined to award damages in the remaining cases where the plaintiffs were claiming for neck and back injuries but where there was no medical predisposition to such injuries). But contrast *Re TB*, 17 May 2002, unreported (Gillen J declining to disqualify himself from a hearing in a family law matter involving parties who had also been party to a previous dispute heard by the judge and in which he had been critical of one of the parties: legal and factual differences in the two disputes meant that *McCaffery's* could be distinguished). And see too *Re Treacy and Macdonald's Application*, 6 January 2000, unreported (Kerr J declining to disqualify himself from hearing an application for judicial review which challenged the lawfulness of the declaration of office taken by Queen's Counsel: judge rejected the argument that he had formed a concluding view in favour of the retention of the declaration).

advisers who were also advising the party that had brought the proceedings;[270] and where the decision-maker had performed intermingled functions in the sense of initiating an application to discharge the applicant and then authorising the subsequent discharge.[271] The appearance of bias has also been found in circumstances where the decision-maker had direct contact with a representative of a party to the dispute and where the corresponding explanation given to the court was confused and contradictory.[272]

Politics, Policy, and Bias

[**7.67**]   Cases concerning the rule against bias have historically centred on whether a particular judge should be disqualified from hearing a case, or whether a disciplinary tribunal has been properly constituted. A related issue is how far the rule against bias applies to political decision-makers and decision-making officials within public authorities. To take the example of political decision-makers, a Minister or local councillor may have previously voiced a particular political opinion on a matter and then subsequently be required to make a decision, within the framework of statute, in respect of that same matter.[273] Under those circumstances, the potential for the decision-maker to be guided by his or her earlier viewpoints is self-evident and the question is whether the decision should be regarded as vitiated by bias. That same question may arise where officials in a public authority have adopted a more general policy to guide them when making decisions in respect of matters of the kind before them.

[**7.68**]   The basic response to the question is that elected representatives and officials in public authorities are under a duty to act fairly[274] but that the manner of application of the rules of fairness will depend on context.[275] The common law has thus long recognised that the decisions of Ministers and locally elected representatives may legitimately be predisposed towards a particular outcome[276]; and it has also accepted that officials in public authorities may adopt policies to guide them in the exercise of their discretion. The common law does, however, at the same time require that political and administrative decision-makers give full consideration to any matter that comes before them.[277]

---

[270] *Re O'Connor's and Broderick's Application* [2006] NI 114 (a police disciplinary panel hearing proceedings brought in the name of and on the authority of the Chief Constable obtained legal advice from the head of legal services to the Police Service: the head of legal services was also legal adviser to the Chief Constable). But see too *Re Glasgow's Application* [2006] NIQB 42 (officer who was subject to disciplinary proceedings alleged bias in the light of the finding in *Re O'Connor's and Broderick's Application*: held on the facts that the applicant had waived his objection).

[271] *Re BW's Application* [2004] NIQB 39 (argument of apparent bias made out as the General Officer Commanding in Northern Ireland had initiated the application to discharge the applicant from the armed forces and then authorised the discharge; upheld on appeal, NICA, unreported).

[272] *Re Moore's Application* [2004] NIQB 49 (explanation offered for contact between a Planning Appeals Commissioner and a representative of the Department of the Environment was insufficient for the purposes of the fair-minded and informed observer test, ie it had been confirmed to the court that the contact had concerned the contest between the parties and there were unresolved questions about precisely what had been discussed).

[273] See, eg, *Re Cullen's Application* [2005] NIQB 9 (Minister with well-known anti-coursing views was required to determine, among other things, whether a licence for hare coursing should be granted).

[274] *R v Secretary of State for the Environment, ex p Kirkstall Valley Campaign Limited* [1996] 3 All ER 304, 323, Sedley J, cited in, eg, *Re Buick's Application*, 3 June 1999, unreported.

[275] *R v Amber Valley DC, ex p Jackson* [1985] 1 WLR 298.

[276] See, eg, *Re Northern Ireland Commissioner for Children and Young People's Application* [2004] NIQB 40, para 17.

[277] *R v Secretary of State for the Environment, ex p Kirkstall Valley Campaign Limited* [1996] 3 All ER 304.

Failure to do so in the sense of pre-determining the matter could amount to an unlawful fettering of discretion.[278]

Article 6 ECHR: 'Bias', 'Independent and Impartial Tribunals', and 'Full Jurisdiction'

[7.69]   The requirement that determinations about an individual's civil rights and obligations be made by an independent and impartial tribunal established by law is central to Article 6 ECHR's guarantee of the right to a fair hearing (on which see [7.14]–[7.16]). In terms of identifying bias (in the language of the common law) or an absence of impartiality (in the language of Article 6 ECHR), the ECtHR uses a test that is both subjective and objective in form.[279] The subjective part of the test corresponds with the actual bias element of the common law rule ([7.61]) and enquires into the personal convictions of the decision-maker in a particular dispute (the burden of establishing subjective bias is a heavy one and the decision-maker is presumed to be impartial until otherwise is shown[280]). The objective part of the test, which has since supplanted the old common law approach to apparent bias (see [7.62]), in turn centres on the question whether a legitimate doubt as to the impartiality of the tribunal can be 'objectively justified'.[281] The underlying rationale here is of the need for justice not only to be done but to be seen to be done[282] and, in making its enquiry, the ECtHR will thus consider whether the decision-maker offered guarantees sufficient for the purposes of excluding doubts as to impartiality[283] or whether there are ascertainable facts that allow doubts to remain.[284]

[7.70]   Article 6 ECHR's requirements of independence and impartiality were originally intended to apply to courts or tribunals that are making determinations about civil, or private, law rights and obligations (the word 'independent' in the text of the Article has thus historically denoted the need for the judicial decision-maker to be independent of the executive; independence may be lost if, for example, the decision-maker does not have security of tenure[285]). Where the decision-maker in question is acting in a judicial capacity and a lack of impartiality is established he or she must therefore stand aside. However, more complex is the position where the decision-maker is not a judge but is, for instance, a government Minister or an administrator who is making a decision within the framework of statute (Article 6 ECHR is now taken to apply to such 'public' law determinations where they have implications for an individual's personal and/or economic interests and are not contingent upon a large measure of official discretion[286]: see [7.14]). In such circumstances, the decision-maker may be neither independent of the executive/administration nor impartial, for instance where a Minister is giving effect to government policy,[287] or where a local authority officer is conducting an internal review

---

[278] On which see [5.52]–[5.54].

[279] See *Re Bothwell's Application* [2007] NIQB 25, para 14.

[280] *Hauschildt v Denmark* (1990) 12 EHRR 266, 279, para 47.

[281] *Ferrantelli and Santangelo v Italy* (1997) 23 EHRR 288, 310, para 58.

[282] See generally *Delcourt v Begium* (1979–80) 1 EHRR 355.

[283] *Piersack v Belgium* (1983) 5 EHRR 169, 179, para 30.

[284] *Hauschildt v Denmark* (1990) 12 EHRR 266, 279, para 48.

[285] *Re Bothwell's Application* [2007] NIQB 25.

[286] *Re Brown's Application* [2003] NIJB 168, 173, para 11, citing *Runa Begum v Tower Hamlets LBC* [2003] 2 AC 430, 465, para 112, Lord Walker.

[287] As in, eg, *R (Alconbury) v Secretary of State for the Environment, Transport and the Regions* [2003] 2 AC 295 (planning policy).

of a decision of the authority.[288] While such decision-making processes may not thereby be compliant with Article 6 ECHR, the ECtHR has held that there is no violation of Article 6 ECHR so long as the affected individual can have subsequent recourse to an independent and impartial tribunal that has 'full jurisdiction' in the matter before it.[289] This 'composite'[290] approach to compliance thus recognises the undesirability of subjecting administrative decision-making processes to the totality of Article 6 ECHR's judicial model of decision-making,[291] although the requirement that any subsequent tribunal should have 'full jurisdiction' has raised difficult questions about whether judicial review is sufficient for the purposes of Article 6 ECHR. This is because the traditional grounds for review—viz illegality, *Wednesbury* unreasonableness, and procedural impropriety— have been structured around a 'review, not appeal' distinction that has sought to preclude judicial assessment of the merits of a decision under challenge.[292] The corresponding query, therefore, is whether the High Court can be said to have the requisite jurisdiction when it cannot, among other things, substitute its own decision for that of the original decision-maker.

[7.71] The corresponding domestic case law in this area is complex and continues to evolve.[293] However, there are three main points that may be distilled from the existing authorities. The first is that the concept of 'full jurisdiction' is context-dependent and does not always require that a court or tribunal is able to substitute its decision for that of the original decision-maker (factors to be taken into account include 'the subject-matter of the decision appealed against, the manner in which that decision was arrived at and the content of the dispute, including the desired and actual grounds of appeal'[294]). In *Alconbury* the House of Lords thus held, for reasons associated with the separation of powers doctrine,[295] that the traditional grounds for judicial review were sufficient where a Minister who was responsible for planning policy made determinations in respect of individual planning applications. Although the Minister clearly was not impartial, the House of Lords considered that judicial restraint of the kind associated with the traditional grounds was appropriate both because Parliament had entrusted the Minister with a particular policy-making function that was accompanied by detailed procedural rules and because the Minister was thereafter answerable to Parliament for the manner in which he performed the function.[296] And in *Runa Begum* the House of Lords likewise held that the traditional grounds were sufficient in a social welfare case centred on a factual dispute about the suitability of housing that had been offered to the individual.[297] The individual had here argued that the grounds were insufficient precisely because they did not enable the court to substitute its finding of fact for that of a local authority

---

[288] As in, eg, *Runa Begum v Tower Hamlets LBC* [2003] 2 AC 430 (reviewing a decision to allocate housing to an individual).

[289] *Bryan v UK* (1996) 21 EHRR 342.

[290] See J Maurici and S Blackmore, 'Focus on Article 6' (2007) JR 56.

[291] See *Re Foster's Application* [2004] NI 248, 257, para 39*ff*, Kerr J.

[292] See [1.05]; and ch 6.

[293] See J Howell, '*Alconbury* Crumbles' (2007) JR 9.

[294] *Bryan v UK* (1996) 21 EHRR 342, 360, para 45, considered in, eg, *R (Alconbury) v Secretary of State for the Environment, Transport and the Regions* [2003] 2 AC 295.

[295] On which see [1.03].

[296] See, eg, [2003] 2 AC 295, 344, para 141, Lord Clyde: once 'it is recognised that there should be a national planning policy under a central supervision, it is consistent with democratic principle that the responsibility for that work should lie on the shoulders of a minister responsible to Parliament'.

[297] *Runa Begum v Tower Hamlets LBC* [2003] 2 AC 430.

official who had been deputed to conduct a review of the authority's original decision. However, in holding that Article 6 ECHR did not require an independent fact-finder in the case, the House of Lords emphasised that 'the question is whether, consistently with the rule of law and constitutional propriety, the relevant decision-making powers may be entrusted to administrators'.[298] Situating the case within its welfare context the House of Lords thus concluded that it was perfectly legitimate for the legislature to entrust decisions of the kind at hand to administrators with specialist expertise in the area, as they would be required to reach their decisions in accordance with particular procedures and their decisions would thereafter be subject to review on the traditional grounds. This, it was held, would avoid an over-judicialisation of the workings of the welfare state and, by analogy, other regulatory areas such as those concerned with licensing and planning.[299] In contrast, a more involved role for the courts was envisaged where decisions had implications for the private rights of individuals or where they were concerned with alleged breaches of the criminal law.

[**7.72**]   The second point is that the courts in Article 6 ECHR cases have emphasised that 'the spectrum of challenge by way of judicial review is not inconsiderable' and that '[t]he breadth of challenge available . . . must go some considerable way to assuage concerns about the protection of such rights as may arise under [Article 6]'.[300] The significance of this understanding is that, even though judicial review may not permit of an appeal on the merits, there remains a wide range of arguments that may be made even within the parameters of the traditional grounds for review. In *Runa Begum* Lord Bingham thus said that the traditional grounds allow the courts 'not only to quash a decision . . . if it is held to be vitiated by legal misdirection or procedural impropriety or bias or irrationality or bad faith but also if there is no evidence to support factual findings made or they are plainly untenable or if the decision-maker is shown to have misunderstood or been ignorant of an established and relevant fact'.[301] While this perhaps begs the question of the degree of elasticity in the error of fact doctrine[302] (see [7.73])—there are also well-worn criticisms of irrationality as a ground for review[303]—his Lordship's comments are indicative of the potential scope for judicial intervention. Indeed, it might be said that the scope for intervention may be drawn even more broadly where other rights are affected by a decision, as the courts may here apply the proportionality principle.[304] On the other hand, the wider body of case law on the proportionality principle has highlighted a judicial concern to avoid being drawn towards forbidden merits review and there is, in consequence, a parallel 'discretionary area of judgment' doctrine that emphasises the need for restraint in many cases.[305]

[**7.73**]   The third point is that there are now some cases in which the courts accept that judicial review is not able to ensure composite compliance with Article 6 ECHR; that is,

---

[298] [2003] 2 AC 430, 454, para 59, Lord Hoffmann.

[299] See too *Re Foster's Application* [2004] NI 248, 261, para 45.

[300] *Re Foster's Application* [2004] NI 248, 261, para 47, Kerr J.

[301] *Runa Begum v Tower Hamlets LBC* [2003] 2 AC 430, 439, para 7, Lord Bingham, quoted in *Re Foster's Application* [2004] NI 248, 261, para 47, Kerr J.

[302] On which see [4.43]–[4.44].

[303] See [6.27]–[6.28].

[304] *R Secretary of State for the Home Department, ex p Daly* [2001] 2 AC 532; and *Runa Begum v Tower Hamlets LBC* [2003] 2 AC 430, 451, para 49, Lord Hoffmann.

[305] See [6.25]–[6.26].

cases that are taken to fall outside the reasoning in *Alconbury* and *Runa Begum*. The origin of these cases is the ECtHR's judgment in *Tsfayo v UK*,[306] which arose out of a local authority housing benefit review board's decision that the individual had not shown good cause for a delay in making a claim for welfare entitlements (the review board was comprised of three councillors from the local authority and was therefore neither independent nor impartial). In finding that there had been a violation of Article 6 ECHR, the ECtHR drew a distinction between cases involving disputed questions of fact that 'required a measure of professional knowledge or experience and the exercise of administrative discretion pursuant to wider policy aims' (as in *Alconbury* and *Runa Begum*) and those, such as the instant case, in which the decision-maker 'was deciding a simple question of fact, namely whether there was "good cause" for the applicant's delay in making a claim'.[307] In cases of this latter kind, the ECtHR considered that a reviewing court should be able to substitute its findings for those of the original decision-maker as

> no specialist expertise [is] required to determine this issue . . . [Nor] . . . can the factual findings in the present case be said to be merely incidental to the reaching of broader judgments of policy or expediency which it was for the democratically accountable authority to take.[308]

However, the ECtHR noted that there had been no possibility of such review in the instant case as the domestic error of fact doctrine does not extend so far as to permit the High Court to substitute its own findings of fact for those of the original decision-maker.[309] There was, in the result, no composite compliance with Article 6 ECHR.

[7.74]   *Tsfayo* has since been considered in *Re Bothwell's Application*.[310] The issue here was whether the High Court had full jurisdiction in an application for judicial review in which a farmer whose cattle had been compulsorily destroyed sought to challenge the award of compensation made to him by the Department of Agriculture and Regional Development. The award had initially been challenged before an Appeals Panel that had among its members a representative of the Department, and the High Court had to decide whether judicial review could ensure composite compliance with Article 6 ECHR. In holding that it could not, the High Court said that 'judicial review does not extend to consideration of the merits of a decision but rather deals with challenges based on legality, procedural fairness and rationality [and] it is unsuited to the resolution of such disputes as to individual valuations'.[311] Notwithstanding that it might be argued that the determinations of the Appeal Panel had involved disputed questions of fact requiring expert knowledge, the High Court thus held that Article 6 ECHR was violated.

Exceptions to the Rule against Bias: Statute, Necessity, and Waiver

[7.75]   Although the rule against bias is regarded as a fundamental precept of both the common law and the ECHR, there are some limited circumstances in which it is accepted that the rule will not apply. For instance, primary legislation may be read as expending

---

[306] App 60860/00, 14 November 2006. See too, eg, *Kingsley v UK* (2002) 35 EHRR 177.
[307] App 60860/00, 14 November 2006, para 45.
[308] App 60860/00, 14 November 2006, para 45.
[309] On the different aspects of the error of fact doctrine see [4.36]–[4.44].
[310] [2007] NIQB 25. And see, in England and Wales, eg, *R (Wright) v Home Secretary* [2007] EWCA Civ 999.
[311] [2007] NIQB 25, para 24.

with the rule,[312] and the common law, on a traditional constitutional understanding, will here cede to the superior force of statute.[313] On the other hand, much will depend on how the statute is interpreted by the courts, as the common law has long held that fundamental rights at common law can only be interfered with through the use of express terms or by way of necessary implication.[314] Moreover, should the legislation have implications for an individual's rights under Article 6 ECHR, this will require that it be read, 'so far as it is possible to do so', in a manner that is consistent with the international guarantee.[315] In the event that the legislation cannot be read as ECHR-compatible, a declaration of incompatibility should be made.[316]

[7.76]   The common law also recognises that the rule against bias may not apply for reasons of necessity, for instance where no other qualified person is available to hear a dispute. Such arguments are most likely to arise in the context of judicial decision-making, where the common law may accept that the rule against bias should yield to the need to prevent a failure of justice (although it might be argued that this line of reasoning is a *non sequitur*). However, the common law will at the same time accede to such arguments only where the circumstances are truly exceptional.[317]

[7.77]   It is also possible for objections based on bias to be waived by the affected party (waiver is possible both at common law and under Article 6 ECHR[318]). The governing principles here are the same as those that apply to waiver of the right to a hearing (see [7.57]).

Breach of the Rule against Bias: Remedies

[7.78]   Where a decision is reached in breach of the rule against bias this will mean that the decision is unlawful.[319] Under such circumstances, the High Court on an application for judicial review will thus typically grant a remedy to the affected individual, for instance by quashing the original decision and requiring that it be retaken in the light of the demands of fairness. However, the remedies available in judicial review are discretionary and the High Court may refuse a remedy where, for instance, the applicant has not exhausted alternative remedies or where the applicant has acted without candour and integrity. A remedy may also be refused for reasons of utility, viz where the court considers that a retaken decision would be no different from that under challenge (on the discretionary nature of the remedies see further [7.54]–[7.56]).

---

[312] See, eg, *R (Bennion) v Chief Constable of Merseyside Police* [2002] ICR 136.

[313] See [1.14].

[314] *R v Secretary of State for the Home Department, ex p Simms* [2000] 2 AC 115; and *Raymond v Honey* [1983] 1 AC 1, 10, Lord Wilberforce.

[315] Human Rights Act 1998, s 3.

[316] Human Rights Act 1998, s 4; and see [5.14] and [8.46]–[8.48].

[317] See further M Supperstone, J Goudie, and P Walker, *Judicial Review* (London, LexisNexis, Butterworths, 2005) pp 380–81.

[318] *Millar v Dickson (Procurator Fiscal, Elgin)* [2002] 1 WLR 1615.

[319] *Ridge v Baldwin* [1964] AC 40; and *R v Secretary of State for the Home Department, ex p Al Medhawi* [1990] 1 AC 876, 898, Lord Bridge.

CONCLUSION

[7.79]   This chapter has examined procedural impropriety as a ground for review. Five points can be made by way of summary.

i.   Procedural impropriety is the ground for review that is concerned with fairness in decision-making processes. Corresponding procedural requirements can be found in three sources, namely statute law, the common law, and (most obviously) Article 6 ECHR.

ii. Where a decision-maker fails to observe a procedural requirement that is contained in statute, the courts must ascertain whether the legislature intended that any resulting decision should be deemed unlawful. In seeking to identify that intention, the courts have said that 'it is necessary to have regard to the use of mandatory or directory language within the provision, to establish the purpose for the use of such language and to determine from the context of the provision and other aids to interpretation what consequence should flow from any breach'.[320] The courts may also ask whether substantial compliance with a particular provision is sufficient or whether precise compliance is required given the overall legislative objective; and they may further consider whether public policy would best be served by finding that a decision is unlawful (see [7.18]–[7.21]).

iii. The common law rules of fairness—viz 'the right to a hearing' and 'the rule against bias'—exist in addition to any procedural requirements in statute, and a decision that complies with statute may still be deemed unlawful for failure to observe the common law rules ([7.06]). The question whether the common law rules have been breached will, however, depend on context, as the requirements of fairness vary from case to case and in light of the interests involved ([7.10]–[7.11]). At the same time, the reach of the common law rules has been greatly expanded in recent years, and they are of potential application whenever '[anyone] decides anything'.[321] An individual can, moreover, expect the protection of the common law where he or she has a right or interest that is affected by a decision, or where he or she has a legitimate expectation of fair treatment ([7.08]–[7.09]). On the other hand, there may be some instances where the common law rules may be placed in abeyance, for instance where a decision is underlain by national security considerations.

iv. Article 6 ECHR contains a range of procedural requirements that apply, most obviously for the purposes of judicial review, whenever a decision is to be taken in respect of an individual's 'civil rights' ([7.14]–[7.16]; the Article also applies to 'criminal charges'). The meaning given to 'civil rights'—they have historically been regarded as private law rights as understood within the civilian legal tradition—does, however, entail that Article 6 ECHR does not have as a broad a reach as the common law rules of fairness. Nevertheless, the Article has still had a significant impact on the common law rules, and the rule against bias in particular has been modified to absorb the demands of the ECHR ([7.59]).

---

[320] *Re McCready's Application* [2006] NIQB 60, para 14, Morgan J.
[321] *Board of Education v Rice* [1911] AC 179, 182, Lord Loreburn, cited in, eg, *R v Secretary of State, ex p Gilmore*, 10 April 1987, unreported.

v. Where a decision is taken in breach of the common law rules of fairness this may, but need not necessarily, mean that the decision is unlawful. Much will depend on whether the individual has, for instance, a right of appeal and whether the appellate body can cure the defect in the original decision-making process (the so-called 'curative' principle: see [7.47]). A failure to observe Article 6 ECHR during the original decision-making process likewise need not mean that the corresponding decision is unlawful, that is, if the individual can have recourse to an 'independent and impartial tribunal' that has 'full jurisdiction' in the matter before it (so-called 'composite' compliance). 'Full jurisdiction', in turn, is a context-dependent requirement, and the courts have emphasised that judicial review on ordinary grounds will often be sufficient for the purposes of Article 6 ECHR. Case law on the point does, however, continue to evolve and it may now be doubted whether judicial review is suited to the demands of Article 6 ECHR in all cases (see [7.69]–[7.74]).

8

Remedies

INTRODUCTION

[8.01]   This chapter considers the remedies that are available when an applicant has made out one or more of the grounds for judicial review.[1] The remedies, for these purposes, are found in sections 18–25 of the Judicature (Northern Ireland) Act 1978 and RSC Order 53, rules 1 and 7, as read with, where appropriate, the European Communities Act 1972 and the Human Rights Act 1998. The starting point in respect of the remedies is that they do not enable the High Court to substitute its decision for that of the original decision maker (viz the 'review, not appeal' distinction[2]; but see too [8.15]); and it is also well established that the remedies are discretionary and that the courts may refuse to grant relief for a wide range of reasons.[3] At the same time, it is equally well established that cases under the European Communities Act 1972 and the Human Rights Act 1998 must be resolved in accordance with the remedies regimes of the ECJ and ECtHR, respectively,[4] and that this can require amendment of pre-existing domestic principle and practice.[5] Judicial review proceedings under the Human Rights Act 1998 must likewise have regard for the particular remedies contained within that Act, most notably its provision for 'declarations of incompatibility' in the event that primary and (more exceptionally) subordinate legislation cannot be read in a manner that is compatible with the ECHR.[6]

[8.02]   The chapter begins with a section that outlines the origins, and discretionary nature, of the remedies that are now found in the Judicature (Northern Ireland) Act 1978 and RSC Order 53, rules 1 and 7. There then follow three sections that examine: (1) the specific remedies available under the Judicature (Northern Ireland) Act 1978 and RSC Order 53; (2) the remedies requirements of EU law as have effect under the European Communities Act 1972; and (3) the remedies regime of the Human Rights Act 1998. The conclusion provides a summary of the key points made.

---

[1]   On interim remedies see [3.42]–[3.47].

[2]   See [1.05]; and ch 6.

[3]   Sir T Bingham, 'Should Public Law Remedies be Discretionary?' (1991) PL 64.

[4]   European Communities Act 1972, s 3, and Human Rights Act 1998, ss 2 and 8.

[5]   *R v Secretary of State for Transport, ex p Factortame Ltd (No 2)* [1991] 1 AC 603; and *M v Home Office* [1994] 1 AC 377 (injunctions becoming available against Ministers of the Crown in, respectively, proceedings under the European Communities Act 1972 and purely domestic cases).

[6]   Sections 3–5.

THE ORIGINS, AND DISCRETIONARY NATURE, OF THE REMEDIES

Origins

[8.03]   The five principal remedies available under the Judicature (Northern Ireland) Act 1978 and RSC Order 53 are an order of mandamus, an order of certiorari, an order of prohibition, a declaration, and an injunction[7] (on the other remedies, including damages, see [8.10]–[8.31]). Of these, the first three are known as the 'prerogative' orders (formerly writs), which term denotes the historical fact that they were issued by the Crown. The orders as such performed a centralising function in the State, as they enabled the Crown to exercise control both over courts and over local and non-royal decision-makers (the remedies in time became judicialised as individuals increasingly sought redress in the King's Court rather than from the King himself).[8] Declarations and injunctions, in contrast, have their origins in equity, and this historically entailed that they were more flexible than the common law prerogative orders. In other words, while the prerogative orders were to develop in the light of highly technical distinctions that could render it difficult for individuals to gain access to them,[9] declarations and injunctions were originally unconstrained by strict rules of precedent and were defined more by equity's emphasis on flexibility in the face of injustice.[10] On the other hand, a judicial aversion towards solely declaratory relief meant that use of the declaration remained under-developed in public law cases, at least until the legislature intervened to encourage such relief.[11]

[8.04]   The effect of the Judicature (Northern Ireland) Act 1978 is to consolidate all of the remedies within one procedure; that is, it provides that the same procedural requirements should be observed irrespective of the type and number of prerogative orders sought and irrespective of whether a declaration and/or injunction is also sought or is sought in the alternative.[12] Case law under the Act has, in turn, coincided with a common law-led expansion of judicial review to include an increasingly wide range of decisions, whether sourced in statute,[13] the royal prerogative,[14] or other forms of non-statutory power[15] (excluding most forms of contractual relationship[16]). That period of expansion has also been characterised by a related rejection of historical distinctions that structured the grounds for review around the differences between, most notably, judicial and administrative decision-makers.[17] Each of the remedies in the Judicature (Northern

---

[7]   Section 18; and RSC Ord 53, r 1.

[8]   See generally, H Woolf, J Jowell, and AP Le Sueur, *De Smith, Woolf, and Jowell Principles of Judicial Review*, 5th edn (London, Sweet & Maxwell, 1999) ch 13.

[9]   See, eg, *R (Diamond and Fleming) v Warnock* [1946] NI 171 (the sister and Member of Parliament of a hunger-striker did not have standing to obtain an order of mandamus to compel the Home Secretary to release the prisoner).

[10]   J Martin, *Hanbury & Martin: Modern Equity*, 17th edn (London, Sweet & Maxwell, 2005) p 32*ff*.

[11]   See further H Woolf, J Jowell, and AP Le Sueur, *De Smith, Woolf, and Jowell Principles of Judicial Review*, 5th edn (London, Sweet & Maxwell, 1999) ch 13. The relevant statutory provision is now the Judicature (Northern Ireland) Act 1978, s 23.

[12]   *R v Secretary of State for Employment, ex p Equal Opportunities Commission* [1995] 1 AC 1.

[13]   See [2.07].

[14]   See [4.06]–[4.08].

[15]   See [2.10]–[2.27].

[16]   See, eg, *Re TSI (Ireland) Ltd's Application* [2005] NIQB 87; and [2.10]–[2.13].

[17]   See, in respect of procedural impropriety as a ground for review, [7.08].

Ireland) Act 1978 and RSC Order 53, rules 1 and 7 is thus now potentially available in respect of any decision of a subordinate decision-maker[18] that sounds in public law and in respect of which there is no effective alternative remedy.[19]

The Position of the Crown and its Ministers

[8.05]   Because the prerogative orders were historically issued by the Crown ([8.03]) it was axiomatic that they could not issue *against* the Crown, as that would have amounted to the constitutional incongruity of the Sovereign commanding itself to do something. However, while it remains the position that remedies cannot issue against the Queen in Her personal capacity (the Sovereign is not subject to legal process[20]), it is well established that the prerogative orders and/or declarations and injunctions can be granted in respect of the decisions, acts, and failures to act of Ministers of the Crown. This is the result of the House of Lords seminal judgment in *M v Home Office*,[21] which centred on the question whether interim and final injunctions could issue against Ministers of the Crown in judicial review proceedings notwithstanding that section 21 of the Crown Proceedings Act 1947 prohibits such relief in civil proceedings.[22] Holding that section 21 did not apply to the instant case because judicial review proceedings are not 'civil', the House of Lords noted not just that injunctions were already available in proceedings under the European Communities Act 1972 and that it was desirable that they should be available in 'domestic' cases too[23] (and see [8.35]); it also emphasised that declarations and the prerogative orders can be granted against Ministers of the Crown and that injunctions should be also be available given that the legislative reform of the judicial review procedure had been intended to consolidate the remedies. A Minister of the Crown acting in his or her official capacity may, in the result, be subject to any or all of the prerogative orders and/or declarations and injunctions. In contrast, where the remedy sought is damages for the commission of a tort, the Crown Proceedings Act 1947 provides that the Crown is here vicariously liable for the actions of its 'officer'[24] (on the principal torts see [8.22]–[8.29]).

[8.06]   There are two further points about the position of the Crown and its Ministers. The first is that there are some statutory provisions which require that the Crown be given notice of matters arising in proceedings. The most important of these for the purposes of remedies is section 5 of the Human Rights Act 1998, which provides that the Crown is entitled to notice in accordance with rules of court where a court is considering whether to make a declaration of incompatibility (see [8.46]–[8.48]). Where such notice is given, a Minister of the Crown (or a person nominated by him or her), a Northern Ireland Minister, and/or a Northern Ireland department is entitled, on giving notice in accordance with rules of court, to be joined as a party to the proceedings[25] (the

---

18   But not in respect of the High Court itself: see *Re Weir & Higgins' Application* [1988] NII 338, 351.
19   See ch 2.
20   See *M v Home Office* [1994] 1 AC 377.
21   [1994] 1 AC 377.
22   See, eg, *Burke v Patterson* [1986] NI 1.
23   [1994] 1 AC 377, 422, Lord Woolf. On such 'spill-over' of EU principle and practice see [1.18].
24   Crown Proceedings Act 1947, s 38(2).
25   Human Rights Act 1998, s 5(2).

corresponding rules of court are found in RSC Order 121). The Attorney-General and appropriate Northern Ireland Ministers and departments are likewise to be given notice where judicial review proceedings give rise to a 'devolution issue', which may include the question whether legislation enacted by the Northern Ireland Assembly is compatible with the ECHR.[26]

[8.07]   The second point concerns the position of Northern Ireland Ministers. Although Northern Ireland Ministers may, as respects transferred matters, exercise 'the prerogative and other executive powers of Her Majesty in relation to Northern Ireland',[27] it would appear that they are not to be regarded as Ministers of the Crown. This can be deduced both from the fact that various statutes use the term 'Northern Ireland Minister' as distinct from the term 'Minister of the Crown',[28] and also from the manner in which Northern Ireland Ministers and Ministers of the Crown are appointed (that is, Northern Ireland Ministers are appointed with reference to the terms of the Northern Ireland Act 1998,[29] while Ministers of the Crown are appointed by the Crown in accordance with constitutional convention). The point is, however, largely unremarkable in terms of remedies, as Northern Ireland Ministers and Ministers of the Crown may equally be subject to any of the prerogative orders and/or declarations and injunctions (see [8.05]).

Their Discretionary Nature

[8.08]   The prerogative orders and equitable remedies have always been discretionary in the sense that they did not, and still do not, issue automatically where an argument of illegality and so on was, or is, made out.[30] The historical approach of the courts instead depended on the context to a given case and the motivation and actions of the individual, and these remain as guiding considerations in the modern case law[31] (although different considerations may apply in cases under the European Communities Act 1972 and/or the Human Rights Act 1998: see [8.39] and [8.42]). For instance, the courts today may decline to grant a remedy where the applicant has not exhausted alternative remedies,[32] where the illegality is a technical irregularity that has caused the applicant no substantial wrong or a miscarriage of justice,[33] where the applicant has failed to bring proceedings within the requisite time-frame,[34] or where the applicant has acted without candour and

---

[26] See further [3.23] and [5.23].

[27] Northern Ireland Act 1998, s 23(2). Those matters that are transferred can be identified with reference to Schs 2 and 3 to the Act, which govern, respectively, excepted and reserved matters. On transferred matters see further [5.23].

[28] Eg, Northern Ireland Act 1998, s 27; and Human Rights Act 1998, s 5(2).

[29] Viz, ss 16–21, as amended by the Northern Ireland (St Andrews Agreement) Act 2006, s 8.

[30] See P Craig, *Administrative Law*, 4th edn (London, Sweet & Maxwell, 2003) ch 22.

[31] See further [3.81]–[3.87].

[32] *Re Kirkpatrick's Application* [2004] NIJB 15 (arguments about religious discrimination could be dealt with more effectively by the Fair Employment Tribunal).

[33] Judicature (Northern Ireland) Act 1978, s 18(5); and, eg, *Re Gribben's Application* [1987] NI 129 (failure to read aloud written statements that had been adduced in evidence in a case where the applicant had been convicted of failure to provide a specimen of blood or urine contrary to art 144 of the Road Traffic (Northern Ireland) Order 1981, SI 1981/154 (NI 1), had not, in the context, given rise to any unfairness and no remedy would issue).

[34] *Re Shearer's Application* [1993] NIJB 12, and *Re McCabe's Application* [1994] NIJB 27; the corresponding time-frame is 'promptly and in any event within three months' (RSC Ord 53, r 4(1)). On delay see further [3.27]–[3.29].

integrity.[35] A remedy may, in 'exceptional circumstances',[36] also be refused for reasons of utility, for example where there has been insufficient consultation but where the court is of the opinion that proper consultation would not have made a difference to the course of action that the applicants would have taken, and that they had thereby suffered no significant unfairness.[37]

[8.09]   The courts may also decline to grant a *particular* remedy in a given case because of the wider ramifications that the grant of the remedy might have. The point here is that an application for judicial review may frequently seek more than one of the remedies but that the court may consider that the grant of one specific remedy would be constitutionally inappropriate in the circumstances. The point can perhaps best be seen in relation to an order of mandamus, as this remedy has the effect of compelling a decision-maker to perform a public—usually a statutory—duty (see [8.11]–[8.12]). Should the performance of that duty involve discretionary choices[38] in respect of, for instance, resource allocation, the courts may consider that an order of mandamus should not issue as it may have the effect of dictating a resource choice in circumstances that could have implications for other parties not before the court (for instance, other NHS patients[39] or other applicants for a licence for an economic activity[40]). Rather than issue a remedy that would strain the logic of the separation of powers doctrine[41] insofar as it would involve the court in making a choice better left to others, a court may thus prefer to make a declaration in respect of the rights and obligations of the parties[42] (on declarations see [8.17]–[8.18]). A court may alternatively decline to grant any formal remedy for the reason that the judgment of the court itself has in effect declared the respective rights of the parties.[43]

THE JUDICATURE (NORTHERN IRELAND) ACT 1978 AND RSC ORDER 53

[8.10]   The range of remedies available under the Judicature (Northern Ireland) Act 1978 and RSC Order 53, rules 1 and 7 can be subdivided under three headings. These are: the prerogative orders, declarations and injunctions; damages; and remedies in respect of 'the holding of public office' and 'sentences in criminal cases'.

---

[35] *Re O'Neill's Application* [1990] 3 NIJB 1.

[36] *Re Hove's Application* [2005] NIQB 24, para 22; and *Re Zhanje's Application* [2007] NIQB 14.

[37] See, eg, *Re National Union of Public Employers and Confederation of Health Service Employees' Application* [1988] NI 255 (held that, although the applicant unions had a legitimate expectation of consultation in respect of hospital closures and the reorganisation of certain general medical services, they would not have addressed themselves to the merits or demerits of the proposals, even if they had been furnished with fuller financial and staffing information).

[38] On 'duties' and 'discretion' see [4.26]–[4.28].

[39] *R v Cambridge Area Health Authority, ex p Child B* [1995] 1 All ER 129.

[40] *Re Kirkpatrick's Application* [2004] NIJB 15, 23, para 36.

[41] On which see [1.03] and [1.05]; and ch 6.

[42] See, eg, *R (Bibi) v Newham London Borough Council* [2002] 1 WLR 237 (declaration issued in case where the applicants had established that they had a legitimate expectation of permanent housing).

[43] *Re McCabe Ltd's Application* [2003] NIQB 77 (although note that an order of mandamus was not sought in this case).

The Prerogative Orders, Declarations, and Injunctions

Mandamus

[8.11]   The order of mandamus is a coercive remedy and, where it is granted, it has the effect of requiring the decision-maker to perform a public—usually a statutory—duty. The coercive nature of the order in turn entails that a failure to comply with it may be a contempt of court (at least where the order included a time-limit for compliance[44]) and that the respondent may be punished by means of, for instance, a fine.[45] In earlier case law, it was thought that the individual who wished to obtain the remedy should first have to demand that the authority perform the duty and that proceedings could follow only where the authority refused to do so.[46] However, the so-called 'demand and refusal' requirement has featured less prominently in the modern case law, and its relevance may for that reason be doubted. On the other hand, it might be said that an element of 'demand and refusal' inheres in the Pre-action Protocol whereby potential applicants are expected to raise the contested issues in correspondence with the respondent in an attempt to avoid litigation.[47]

[8.12]   Grants of mandamus are rare in the case law and they tend to be issued where there is only one course of action lawfully open to the decision maker.[48] Where a duty entails the exercise of discretion on the part of the decision-maker the courts will therefore typically consider that an order of mandamus would be inappropriate. Although the extent of any discretion is, at the same time, a matter for judicial interpretation of the relevant statute,[49] the courts consider that the existence of discretion militates against mandamus as a remedy. The corresponding rationale is of the need to observe the constitutional limits to the judicial role (see [8.09]), as it is perceived that an order of mandamus could result in the courts dictating how a particular choice should be made.[50] The judicial concern for restraint will thus be at its highest where proceedings relate to 'target duties' in respect of public services like policing, healthcare, housing, child

---

[44]   RSC Ord 42, rr 4 and 5; and RSC Ord 45, r 4.

[45]   See, eg, *Re Cook's Application (No 2)* [1986] NI 283 (Belfast City Council fined for contempt of court for failing to hold meetings to carry out the business and functions of the council in accordance with an order of the court).

[46]   For a judicial survey see *The State (Modern Homes (Ireland) Ltd v Dublin Corp* [1953] IR 202, 213–16.

[47]   *Re Cunningham's Application* [2005] NIJB 224; and see [3.14]–[3.16].

[48]   Eg, *Re Zhanje's Application* [2007] NIQB 14 (Home Secretary ordered to allow an asylum seeker to re-enter the UK should she request to do so for the purposes of processing a human rights claim); *Re UK Waste Management Ltd's Application*, 22 January 1999, unreported (order of mandamus issued to compel planning authorities to make a final decision in the light of its earlier Notice of Opinion); *Re Cook's Application* [1986] NI 242 (order of mandamus granted to compel Belfast City Council to hold meetings in accordance with its duty to do so under the Local Government Act (Northern Ireland) 1972); and *Re Brownlee's Application* [1985] NI 339 (order of mandamus granted to compel an education board to make arrangements for the provision of transport to school for the applicant's son in accordance with its duty under art 41 of the Education and Libraries (Northern Ireland) Order 1972, SI 1972/1263 (NI 12)).

[49]   On 'duties' and 'discretion' see [4.26]–[4.28].

[50]   See, eg, *Re McBride's Application (No 2)* [2003] NI 319 (Court of Appeal refusing to grant an order of mandamus in a case in which the Army Board had acted unlawfully in failing to discharge two soldiers who had been convicted of murder: while a declaration would issue, the mandatory order would be inappropriate as 'decisions on what is best for the Army and its soldiers are best left to the Army and it would be an unwise usurpation of power if the court were . . . to intervene by mandamus' ([2003] NI 319, 366, para 52, McCollum LJ)).

protection, and road safety[51]: while the imposition of duties here reflects the social imperative of providing services to members of society, the courts are aware that decision–makers may have to make value judgments and that the courts should, for reasons of relative expertise, be slow to intervene in the decision-making process.[52]

Certiorari

[**8.13**]   Certiorari serves to quash a decision or other measure and, where it is granted, the decision or other measure in respect of which it is granted is regarded as having never had legal effect[53] (the remedy is coercive and a failure to observe it may be regarded as a contempt of court[54]). The remedy has its historical origins in the context of the control of inferior courts,[55] but it is now potentially available in respect of any decision of a subordinate decision-maker that sounds in public law and in respect of which there is no effective alternative remedy.[56] Where a decision or other measure has been the subject of an order of certiorari, the decision-maker is at liberty to retake the decision, but it must do so in accordance with the judgment of the court that quashed the original determination. The requirement that it do so may even be formalised by the simultaneous grant of an order of prohibition, the effect of which would be to prevent the decision-maker acting in the manner that has already been deemed unlawful (see [8.16]).

[**8.14**]   The remedy of certiorari is not without difficulty, precisely because it renders the decision or other measure in respect of which it is made as having been without any legal effect. For instance, in some cases the challenged decision or other measure may not be wholly unlawful and it might be doubted whether it is thereby necessary to quash the full decision; and complex questions may also arise when the remedy is sought in circumstances in which other decisions or acts have since been taken on the basis of the impugned decision. In both of these instances there can be a tension between, on the one hand, the need to uphold the rule of law[57] and, on the other, the need to safeguard the administration from the practical difficulties that may follow from quashing a partially lawful decision or quashing a measure that has formed the basis for a range of other decisions. In such cases, the courts have thus indicated that there may be scope to use the remedy flexibly or, more exceptionally where there is an illegality, to decline to grant it in favour of a declaration as to the decision or other measure's legal validity.[58] Hence,

---

[51]   See, eg, *Family Planning Association of Northern Ireland v Minister for Health, Social Services and Public Safety* [2005] NI 188, reading art 4 of the Health and Personal Social Services (Northern Ireland) Order 1972, SI 1972/1265 (NI 14), as imposing a target duty in respect of the provision of health services.

[52]   See, in respect of policing, eg, *Re E's Application* [2004] NIQB 35, para 55, Kerr J: 'the various obligations imposed by [the Police (Northern Ireland) Act 2000] cannot be regarded as absolute in their terms . . . It is, of course, [an officer's] general duty to fulfil the statutory obligations provided for and he may not refrain from doing so arbitrarily or capriciously. Where, however, as in this case, a judgment is made, in the interest of general public order throughout the community . . . it does not follow that breach of [the duty] is thereby automatically established.'

[53]   *Boddington v British Transport Police* [1999] 2 AC 143, 154.

[54]   *M v Home Office* [1994] 1 AC 377.

[55]   See the analysis in *R v Belfast Recorder, ex p McNally* [1992] NI 217, 223ff, Lowry LCJ.

[56]   See ch 2.

[57]   On which see [4.04]–[4.05].

[58]   See, eg, *Re Downes' Application* [2007] NIQB 1 (although the court had found that the appointment of the Interim Victims Commission was unlawful, it made a declaration in preference to granting an order of certiorari, as there were arguments of public interest in favour of allowing the Commissioner—who had been wholly blameless in the appointment process—to continue her work in advancing the interests of victims). See

where a decision is partially unlawful it has been suggested that the courts might be able to sever and quash only the offending part of the decision, albeit that the ability to do so will be contingent upon the unaffected part of the decision remaining coherent.[59] And in respect of a decision or other measure that has since provided the basis for a range of other decisions, a declaration might again be granted as this would have the advantage of leaving the impugned and related measures in force while at the same time bringing the need for modification to the attention of the decision-maker. Such an approach might be particularly apposite where subordinate legislation is challenged as ultra vires.[60]

[8.15]   Section 21 of Judicature (Northern Ireland) Act 1978 and RSC Order 53, rule 9(4) also provide for flexibility where the relief sought is certiorari and where the court is satisfied that there are grounds for quashing the decision. Here, it is provided that the court

> may, instead of quashing the decision, remit the matter to the lower deciding authority concerned, with a direction to reconsider it and reach a decision in accordance with the ruling of the court or may reverse or vary the decision of the lower deciding authority.

The power of remittal has typically been used in cases involving lower court decisions,[61] although there have also been cases in which decisions have been remitted to administrative decision-makers.[62] In contrast, the power to reverse or vary a decision has been used very infrequently.[63] This is undoubtedly because the provision empowers the High Court to substitute its decision for that of the original decision-maker and that regular such use of the provision would strain the 'review, not appeal' distinction that defines judicial review.[64]

Prohibition

[8.16]   An order of prohibition serves to restrain a respondent from acting in a way that is, or would be, unlawful. The nature of the remedy means that it may be requested in

---

too *Re Omagh District Council's Application* [2007] NIQB 61 (court declining to grant an order of certiorari that would quash an unlawful planning policy because of the adverse public consequences that could ensue: in the circumstances, a declaration was appropriate).

[59]   See *R (DHSS) v National Insurance Commissioners* [1980] 8 NIJB 9, Hutton J. And see too, in relation to subordinate legislation, *Re Christian Institute and Ors' Application* [2007] NIQB 66 (challenge to the lawfulness of the Equality Act (Sexual Orientation) Regulations (Northern Ireland) 2006, SR 2006/439, that had been made under s 82 of the Equality Act 2006: application granted only in respect of those provisions governing harassment, which were quashed).

[60]   See [5.36].

[61]   See, eg., *Re McLean's Application*, 25 November 1994, unreported (decision in respect of a bookmaker's licence remitted to resident magistrate); *Re Murphy's Application* [1991] 7 NIJB 97 (decision in respect of costs remitted to Recorder's Court); and *R (Att-Gen) v Belfast Justices* [1981] NI 208 (convictions of shoplifters who had given false names remitted to the magistrates' court so that it could, if satisfied that the offenders were the persons who were convicted, amend the convictions by substituting their real names).

[62]   Eg, *Re Zhanje's Application* [2007] NIQB 14 (decision to certify a human rights claim as unfounded for the purposes of para 5(4) of Sch 3 to the Asylum and Immigration (Treatment of Claimants etc) Act 2004 remitted to the Home Secretary); and *Re Ward's Application*, 4 June 1993, unreported (decision in respect of payment from the Social Fund remitted to Social Fund Inspector). See too, in the context of prison discipline, *Re Beattie's Application* [2007] NIQB 51 (finding of a breach of the prison rules remitted to the governor for reconsideration, as the evidence relied upon was insufficient to prove the charge); and *Re McCafferty's Application* [2007] NIQB 17 (decision to award 14 days' cellular confinement to prisoner remitted to governor to retake in the light of the fact that the prisoner had already had 14 days of restricted association).

[63]   See, eg, *Re McAuley's Application* [1992] 4 NIJB 1 (High Court granted legal aid to the applicant because it considered that the magistrate had failed to have regard to a relevant consideration when declining to do so).

[64]   On which see [1.05] and ch 6.

tandem with certiorari as, to the extent that certiorari quashes an illegal decision or other measure (see [8.13]), prohibition can issue to prevent the respondent making the same decision in the future. Prohibition is, moreover, now regarded as indistinguishable from an order of mandamus and an injunction,[65] as all three remedies can require a respondent to do, or not to do, anything in relation to the issues before the court. The remedy is also coercive and a failure to observe it may thus be regarded as a contempt of court.[66]

Declaration

[**8.17**]   A declaration is an inherently flexible remedy that takes form as a judicial statement of the legal position in a dispute and/or of the rights and obligations of the parties to the proceedings. The remedy can be at its most flexible when it is granted on its own (which possibility is expressly provided for by section 23 of the Judicature (Northern Ireland) Act 1978[67]), as the court can here make clear its view on a question of law without, for instance, granting an order of mandamus that would require the decision-maker to act in accordance with that view (on which see [8.11]). In contrast to the other remedies, the declaration is non-coercive and a failure to act in accordance with it will not give rise to a question of contempt of court.[68] On the other hand, a declaration to the effect that a decision-maker has acted or would act illegally should prompt the decision-maker to modify its position. In the event that the decision-maker continues to act contrary to the established legal position a further coercive remedy may thus be sought, albeit that the question whether it should be granted will depend upon the intention of the court that first granted the declaration.[69]

[**8.18**]   A declaration 'must serve some useful purpose',[70] and the courts are generally reluctant to grant the remedy where the matter between the parties has since become academic (in the sense that it is no longer live) or where the issues raised are speculative and where the judgment of the court would be in the form of advice.[71] However, a court will not at the same time reject an application for a declaration outright in such circumstances; that is, the court may grant a declaration where the remedy may still have a wider relevance. Hence, where a dispute between the parties has since become academic the court may grant a declaration where the issues raised are of public importance and

---

[65]   *M v Home Office* [1994] 1 AC 377, 415, Lord Woolf.

[66]   *M v Home Office* [1994] 1 AC 377.

[67]   '(1) No action or other proceeding shall be open to objection on the ground that a merely declaratory judgment or order is sought thereby. (2) The High Court may make binding declarations of right in any action or other proceeding whether or not any consequential relief is or could be claimed therein.'

[68]   For judicial consideration of the nature of the remedy see *Belfast West Power Ltd v Belfast Harbour Commissioners* [1998] NI 112, 120–22, Girvan J.

[69]   *Re McBride's Application* [2005] NIQB 54 (applicant who had previously been granted by the Court of Appeal a declaration that two soldiers were being unlawfully retained in the armed services sought, among other remedies, an order of mandamus to compel their discharge: held that no further remedy should be granted as the Court of Appeal had expressly considered whether to grant coercive remedies and had decided that they would be inappropriate).

[70]   *Re D's Application* [2003] NIJB 49, 59, para 49, Coghlin J, cited with approval in CA ([2003] NI 295, 305, para 24).

[71]   See, eg, *Re McCabe's Application* [2007] NICA 35 (Court of Appeal exercising its discretion not to make declarations in circumstances where a prisoner's rights under Arts 5(4) and 6(1) ECHR had been violated but where he would nevertheless have remained in prison: declarations here would have been 'valueless').

likely to arise again.[72] The power to issue a declaration in the converse circumstance where no issue has yet arisen and where the point at issue is thereby speculative is contained in section 23(3) of the Judicature (Northern Ireland) Act 1978, which reads: 'Notwithstanding that the events on which a right depends may not have occurred, the High Court may in its discretion make a binding declaration of right if it is satisfied that: (a) the question for decision involves a point of general public importance or that it would in the circumstances be unjust or inconvenient to withhold the declaration; and (b) the interests of persons not parties to the proceedings would not be unjustly prejudiced by the declaration'.[73]

Injunction

[**8.19**]   An injunction is an order that requires a party to proceedings either to act or not to act in a particular way (it may thus be mandatory or prohibitory in form). The remedy is coercive,[74] may issue at any time in proceedings,[75] and may be interim or final. Interim injunctions are granted in accordance with the 'balance of convenience' test that originated in private law[76] but which is applied in a modified form in public law proceedings.[77] Final injunctions, in turn, issue only where the grounds for review have been made out and where the court considers in its discretion that the remedy should be granted. Where granted, a final injunction is definitive of the rights of the parties and a subsequent failure to act in accordance with it may be regarded as a contempt of court.[78] This contempt principle also applies where the respondent is a Minister of the Crown[79] (see [8.05]).

[**8.20**]   Because injunctions may be mandatory or prohibitory they are now regarded as essentially indistinguishable from mandamus and prohibition.[80] However, it has also been suggested that the private law origins of the remedy render it ill suited to some circumstances and that one of the other remedies should be sought. The example given is where an individual wishes to compel a public authority to carry out its statutory duties but where the legislation in question cannot be interpreted as giving the individual

---

[72]   See *R v Secretary of State for the Home Department, ex p Salem* [1999] 1 AC 45. For cases in which a point of general interest has been taken to arise see, eg, *Re ES's Application* [2007] NIQB 58 (challenge to art 64 of the Children (Northern Ireland) Order 1995, SI 1995/755 (NI 2), as incompatible with Arts 6 and 8 ECHR allowed to proceed notwithstanding that the applicant was no longer affected by the provision in question: application granted); *Re E's Application* [2003] NIQB 39, [2004] NIQB 35 and [2006] NICA 37 (challenge to the mode of policing at the 'Holy Cross' dispute—which had since ended—allowed because of the matters of general interest involved); and *Re McBurney's Application* [2004] NIQB 37 (patient in a mental health facility who was awaiting a tribunal decision whether to discharge her brought proceedings in respect of an earlier decision not to discharge: held that while the earlier dispute was now academic the corresponding application raised questions of general interest about the involvement of a lay representative in the decision-making process); and for a case in which the court concluded that there was no point of general interest see, eg, *Re Nicholson's Application* [2003] NIQB 30 (application in respect of a prison adjudication dismissed as academic, as the prisoner had since been released and it was unlikely that the resolution of the issues in the application would provide guidance to the Prison Service in future cases).
[73]   For judicial consideration see, eg, *Re McConnell's Application* [2000] NIJB 116, 119–20.
[74]   *M v Home Office* [1994] 1 AC 377.
[75]   Judicature (Northern Ireland) Act 1978, s 91(1)(b).
[76]   *American Cyanamid Co v Ethicon Ltd* [1975] AC 396.
[77]   *Re Eurostock's Application* [1999] NI 13; and see [3.43].
[78]   *M v Home Office* [1994] 1 AC 377.
[79]   *M v Home Office* [1994] 1 AC 377.
[80]   *M v Home Office* [1994] 1 AC 377, 415, Lord Woolf.

a private right of action for a breach of the duty. Under those circumstances, it has been suggested that the applicant should instead seek an order of mandamus.[81]

Damages

[8.21]   Damages claims are very infrequent in applications for judicial review primarily because of the rule that an ultra vires act per se does not give rise to liability.[82] Damages, as per section 20 of the Judicature (Northern Ireland) Act 1978 and RSC Order 53, rule 7, are instead available only where the court is satisfied that the illegality would also have been actionable in private law[83] (most usually in tort). Although specific statutes may at the same time make provision for damages in the event of a wrong[84]—it is also possible to receive ex gratia payments of compensation where the Commissioner for Complaints has made a finding of maladministration[85]—damages thus remain as an exceptional remedy in the public law context. Their exceptional nature is also a consequence of a highly restrictive body of House of Lords case law on liability in respect of the performance of statutory duties and/or the exercise of statutory powers.[86]

[8.22]   The principal torts that may be used to found a claim for damages in respect of the exercise of statutory powers and/or the performance of statutory duties are negligence, breach of statutory duty, and misfeasance in public office.[87] Damages claims may also be made under the European Communities Act 1972 and the Human Rights Act 1998, where the courts are required to give effect to the damages case law of the ECJ and ECtHR, respectively (on which see [8.36]–[8.38] and [8.43]–[8.45]).

Negligence

[8.23]   A claim in negligence requires the plaintiff (applicant) to establish that the defendant (respondent) owed him or her a common law duty of care; that the defendant breached that duty of care; and that the breach of the duty of care caused the loss

---

[81]   See H Woolf, J Jowell and AP Le Sueur, *De Smith, Woolf, and Jowell Principles of Judicial Review*, 4th edn (London, Sweet & Maxwell, 1999) pp 596–7, and authorities therein.

[82]   *R (Quark Fishing) v Secretary of State for Foreign and Commonwealth Affairs* [2003] EWHC 1743, para 14.

[83]   Section 20 reads: 'In proceedings on an application for judicial review the High Court may, in lieu of or in addition to any other relief, award damages to an applicant, if: (a) he has, in accordance with rules of court, joined with his application a claim for damages arising from any matter to which the application relates; and (b) the court is satisfied that, if such claim had been made in a separate action begun by the applicant at the time of making his application, he would have been entitled to such damages.' RSC Ord 53, r 7 is in substantially the same terms.

[84]   Eg, Criminal Justice Act 1988, s 133, considered in *In Re McFarland* [2004] NI 380 and, eg, Re Boyle's Application [2007] NIQB 88.

[85]   See M Amos, 'The Parliamentary Commissioner for Administration, redress and damages for wrongful administrative action' (2000) PL 21; and the Commissioner for Complaints (Northern Ireland) Order 1996, SI 1996/1297 (NI7).

[86]   See G Anthony, 'The Negligence Liability of Public Authorities: Was the Old Law the Right Law?' (2006) 57 NILQ 409.

[87]   For consideration of other causes of action including, eg nuisance, see W Wade and CF Forsyth, *Administrative Law*, 9th edn (Oxford, Oxford University Press, 2004) ch 20. And for the application of ordinary tort principles in proceedings where no issue arose in relation to statutory powers or duties see *Ward v Chief Constable of the RUC* [2000] NI 543 (police sued in trespass to the person for use of excessive force).

complained of.[88] In the public law context, claims in negligence may arise when the plaintiff claims to have suffered loss from the manner in which a particular public service has, or has not, been provided to him or her. However, while there are a number of well-established scenarios that can give rise to public authority liability in negligence (the obvious example is medical negligence[89]), the courts have been more generally reluctant to impose liability on public service providers in novel situations. In broad terms, this has been justified with reference to the valid public policy concern that increased liability would strain already limited resources in a way that would diminish the overall quality of the service provided to wider society.[90] But there have been other more specific doctrinal considerations too, particularly where the provision of the public service entails the exercise of statutory discretion. Under these circumstances, the courts have emphasised that policy choices are 'non-justiciable' and that there can therefore be no liability in respect of such decisions.[91] In the event that the litigant is unable to separate 'policy' choices from 'other' choices that may be actionable,[92] there can be no cause of action.

[8.24]   The restrictive case law of the courts has tended to centre on the duty of care element.[93] At common law, a duty of care is owed where: (1) the defendant should foresee that his or her act or omission will harm the plaintiff; (2) there is a sufficient relationship of proximity between the parties; and (3) it is fair, just, and reasonable to impose a duty of care.[94] Although the House of Lords has recently held that duties of care have been owed in some novel situations—for instance, to children with special educational needs[95] and children who have been abused while in the care of local authorities[96]—the greater trend within the case law has been to hold that public service providers do not owe duties of care outside of established duty of care situations. In procedural terms, this has often led to claims for damages being struck out at a preliminary stage for the reason that they disclose no reasonable cause of action.[97] Indeed, while the courts were temporarily less inclined to strike out proceedings because of a concern about Article 6 ECHR rights of access to a court,[98] it is now accepted that Article 6 ECHR is not engaged by the question of whether a duty of care is owed to an individual in any given case.[99] The House of Lords has, in consequence, since held that negligence actions against the police (in respect

[88] J Murphy, *Street on Torts*, 12th edn (Oxford, Oxford University Press, 2007) chs 2–5.

[89] *Chester v Ashfar* [2005] 1 AC 134.

[90] See in respect of policing, eg, *Hill v Chief Constable of West Yorkshire* [1989] AC 53, 63, Lord Keith; *Brooks v Metropolitan Police Commissioner* [2005] 2 All ER 489, 504, para 30, Lord Steyn; and *Metcalfe v Chief Constable of the RUC* [1995] NI 446 .

[91] *Barrett v Enfield LBC* [2001] 2 AC 550; and on 'non-justiciability' see [4.14]–[4.17].

[92] A distinction that has long been criticised: see, eg, *Stovin v Wise* [1996] AC 923, 951, Lord Hoffmann.

[93] For a survey of some of the authorities see *McKnight v Department of Regional Development* [2005] NIQB 15, para 18*ff*; and *Maye v Craigavon Borough Council* [1998] NI 103.

[94] *Caparo Industries Plc v Dickman* [1990] 2 AC 605. And see, eg, *Robinson v Department of the Environment* [1989] NI 372 (duty of care owed to plaintiff who had suffered injury as a result of an inspector's failure to identify defects in a car's brake system as the statutory power which the Department's inspectors were alleged to have exercised negligently was specifically directed to safeguarding the section of the public to which the plaintiffs belonged from the particular danger which resulted).

[95] *Phelps v Hillingdon LBC* [2001] 2 AC 619.

[96] *Barrett v Enfield LBC* [2001] 2 AC 550.

[97] RSC Ord 18, r 19; and see *O'Dwyer v Chief Constable of the RUC* [1997] NI 403; and *Neill v Wilson* [1999] NI 1.

[98] *Barrett v Enfield LBC* [2001] 2 AC 550, 558–60, Lord Browne-Wilkinson, considering *Osman v UK* (2000) 29 EHRR 245.

[99] *Z v UK* (2002) 34 EHRR 97, 135, para 91*ff*.

of their treatment of a victim of crime[100]) and healthcare workers (who had made erroneous accusations that parents had abused their children[101]) had correctly been struck out; and it has likewise held that proceedings against a highway authority that ended in a finding of liability should have been struck out rather than being allowed to proceed to trial.[102]

[8.25] The restrictive approach can also be apparent in cases where a duty of care is owed, as the courts may alternatively limit liability with reference to the breach element. The starting point in breach cases is the question of what is reasonable in all the circumstances,[103] and it has been suggested that the courts should display caution when considering whether a public authority has acted reasonably when exercising its statutory discretion. Although the courts are at the same time mindful of the need to avoid resolving tort law issues on the basis of public law precepts,[104] it has been said that there will be 'room for differences of opinion as to the best course to adopt in a difficult field and that the discretion is to be exercised by the authority . . . and not by the court'.[105] Such language is, in turn, evocative of that of *Wednesbury* unreasonableness,[106] and a court that is considering whether a public authority has fallen beneath the objective standard of care must thus 'be satisfied that the conduct complained of went beyond mere errors of judgment in the exercise of discretion and constituted conduct which can be regarded as negligent'.[107]

Breach of Statutory Duty

[8.26] An action for breach of statutory duty is similar in structure to an action in negligence, although the duty here originates from the statute rather than the common law (the tort again requires breach and causation; whether fault is a pre-requisite for breach is a matter for interpretation of the statute).[108] While it will in some instances be clear from the literal terms of a statute that a public authority owes a duty to an individual[109] (the dispute would then be resolved with reference to the breach and causation elements), the question whether a statutory duty is actionable can become more complex where claims are made in respect of the performance or non-performance of 'target duties' (on which see [8.12]). Here, the courts have typically held that the nature of the duties is such that they are not owed to any one individual but rather to wider society and that they can, for that reason, sound only in public law.[110] Individuals, in the result, are not able to

---

[100] *Brooks v Metropolitan Police Commissioner* [2005] 2 All ER 489.

[101] *D v East Berkshire Community Health NHS Trust* [2005] 2 AC 373.

[102] *Gorringe v Calderdale MBC* [2004] 1 WLR 1057.

[103] *Bolam v Friern Hospital Management Committee* [1957] 1 WLR 582.

[104] *Gorringe v Calderdale MBC* [2004] 1 WLR 1057, 1060, Lord Steyn.

[105] *Barrett v Enfield LBC* [2001] 2 AC 550, 591, Lord Hutton.

[106] See [6.05]–[6.11].

[107] *Barrett v Enfield LBC* [2001] 2 AC 550, 591, Lord Hutton. And for an instance of a case failing on the breach element see, in the education context, *Carty v Croydon LBC* [2005] 2 All ER 517. Cf *Devon CC v Clarke* [2005] ELR 375.

[108] See J Murphy, *Street on Torts*, 12th edn (Oxford, Oxford University Press, 2007) ch 20.

[109] Eg, Roads (Northern Ireland) Order 1993, SI 1993/3160 (NI 15), art 8(1); and *Madden v DOE* [2003] NI 123.

[110] *X v Bedfordshire CC* [1995] 2 AC 633 (no private law duty owed to children under the Children and Young Persons Act 1969, the Child Care Act 1980, and the Children Act 1989); *O'Rourke v Camden LBC* [1998] AC 188 (no private law duty owed to the homeless under the Housing Act 1985); *Maye v Craigavon Borough Council* [1998] NI 103 (art 7(1) of the Litter (Northern Ireland) Order 1994, SI 1994/1896) (NI 10), which imposes a duty to keep roads free from litter, not imposed for the protection of a limited class of the public but

make damages claims in respect of such duties and can challenge decisions or other measures only with reference to the public law grounds for review.[111]

[8.27]   The approach of the courts may be equally restrictive even where a duty is owed to an individual. For instance, in *Cullen v Chief Constable of the RUC*[112] the plaintiff had been arrested on suspicion of involvement with terrorism but he claimed that he had been denied access to his lawyer in breach of the duty to ensure access under section 15 of the Northern Ireland (Emergency Provisions) Act 1987. While Lords Bingham and Steyn, dissenting, considered that the breach should have been actionable per se because the right of access is a constitutional right at common law, the majority of the House of Lords disagreed. Reaffirming the requirement that all the elements of the tort must be made out, their Lordships considered that damages should not be awarded, both because there had been no concrete loss to the plaintiff and because other remedies had been available at the time of the denial (viz judicial review proceedings). By adopting this approach, the House of Lords thus appeared to prevent the emergence of common law constitutional torts that would allow damages to be awarded even without proof of harm (see too [8.29]).

Misfeasance in Public Office

[8.28]   The tort of misfeasance in public office offers a remedy to individuals who have suffered loss as a result of the abuse of power by a public officer[113] (the vicarious liability of the employer authority will depend on whether the actions or inactions of the officer were unauthorised and so unconnected with the officer's authorised duties as to be outside those duties[114]). The tort is actionable where: (a) the public officer has, with malice, acted or failed to act in a way that has the object of injuring the plaintiff; or (b) the public officer has intentionally done or omitted to do something that he or she did not have the power to do or omit to do and which he or she knew would probably injure the plaintiff.[115] The House of Lords has since held that bad faith inheres in both (a) and (b), albeit that the two limbs are to be regarded as alternative rather than cumulative elements of the cause of action.[116] Bad faith is thus present in element (a) in the sense that a public power will here have been exercised for an improper purpose and with the specific intention of injuring the plaintiff (so-called 'targeted malice'[117]). In respect of element (b), bad faith will be present where the act or omission was done or made intentionally by the officer in the knowledge that it was beyond his or her powers and that it would probably cause the plaintiff to suffer injury (an absence of an honest belief that the act or omission was lawful will here be sufficient for the requirement of bad faith, which can be demonstrated by knowledge of probable loss on the part of the public officer). Bad

rather for the benefit of the public at large); and *Metcalfe v Chief Constable of the RUC* [1995] NI 446 (exercise of Director of Public Prosecution's powers under art 5(1) of the Prosecution of Offences (NI) Order 1972, SI 1972/538 (NI 1), could not give rise to a claim for damages because of 'compelling considerations rooted in the welfare of the whole community').

[111]   *O'Rourke v Camden LBC* [1998] AC 188.
[112]   [2003] NI 375.
[113]   *Watkins v Home Office* [2006] 2 AC 395 (unlawful interference with a prisoner's mail).
[114]   *Racz v Home Office* [1994] 2 AC 45.
[115]   *Bourgoin SA v Ministry of Agriculture, Fisheries and Food* [1986] QB 716.
[116]   *Three Rivers District Council v Bank of England (No 3)* [2003] 2 AC 1; on bad faith see [5.47]–[5.48].
[117]   *Three Rivers District Council v Bank of England (No 3)* [2003] 2 AC 1, 191, Lord Steyn.

faith will alternatively be present for the purposes of (b) where the officer was aware that there was a serious risk that the plaintiff would suffer loss due to an act or omission which the officer knew to be unlawful but where the officer wilfully chose to disregard that risk. Under those circumstances, the requisite bad faith is demonstrated by the officer's recklessness in disregarding the risk.[118]

[8.29]   Claims for misfeasance in public office are rare in the case law, largely because of the difficulties in making out an argument of bad faith.[119] Moreover, while the House of Lords has emphasised that the out-workings of the tort should not be constrained by rigid distinctions,[120] it has at the same time held that an action for misfeasance in public office cannot be sustained where a public officer has acted in bad faith but where the individual has suffered no special damage. In *Watkins v Home Office*[121] the House of Lords thus held that a prisoner could not succeed under the tort as he had suffered no special damage when prison guards had interfered with his correspondence with his lawyer. Although the Court of Appeal in England and Wales had held that bad faith per se was here sufficient as the officers had interfered with the prisoner's common law constitutional right of access to a court,[122] the House of Lords held that that proof of special damage had been expressly or implicitly central to the cause of action for over 300 years.[123] Such long-standing rules, it was held, should be disturbed only where there are compelling reasons to do so, and no such reasons were present in the instant case. The House of Lords also held that a reinvention of the tort in the light of common law constitutional rights was unnecessary as plaintiffs would in the future be able to make a claim for damages under the Human Rights Act 1998 (on which see [8.43]–[8.45]).

The 'Holding of Public Office' and 'Sentences in Criminal Cases'

[8.30]   The Judicature (Northern Ireland) Act 1978 finally provides for discrete remedies in respect of, first, persons acting in a public office without being entitled to do so and, second, sentences passed by a court that had no power to pass the sentence. In terms of public office, the relevant provision is section 24, subsection 1 of which provides:

> Where a person is acting or has acted in an office to which this section applies without being entitled so to act, the High Court, on an application under this section, may (a) grant an injunction restraining him from so acting; (b) declare the office to be vacant.

---

[118] *Three Rivers District Council v Bank of England (No 3)* [2003] 2 AC 1, 247, Lord Hope.

[119] On which see [5.47]–[5.48]; and for an example of the tort being argued in the case law see *Metcalfe v Chief Constable of the RUC* [1991] NI 237, and *Metcalfe v Chief Constable of the RUC* [1995] NI 446.

[120] *Kuddus v Chief Constable of Leicestershire Constabulary* [2001] 3 All ER 193 (the power to award exemplary damages should not be limited to cases where it could be shown that the cause of action had been recognised as justifying such damages before the House of Lords judgment in *Rookes v Barnard* [1964] 1 All ER 367, which case established that exemplary damages should be available where the plaintiff has been the victim of oppressive, arbitrary, or unconstitutional action by servants of government).

[121] [2006] 2 AC 395.

[122] [2005] QB 883.

[123] See now, eg., *Karagozlu v Metropolitan Police Commissioner* [2007] 2 All ER 1055 (Court of Appeal in England and Wales allowing an appeal against a striking-out order when holding that special damage for the purposes of the tort can, as argued here, include the loss of liberty that follows from a prisoner being moved from open conditions to closed).

Subsection 2 then provides that the 'section applies to any substantive office of a public nature and permanent character which is held under the Crown or has been created by or under a statutory provision or royal charter'. RSC Order 53, rule 11 relatedly provides that the Order 53 procedure is to be used where an individual seeks the remedy.

[**8.31**]   The relevant provision in respect of a sentence passed by a court that had no power to pass the sentence is section 25. The section, which is not dissimilar in its effect to section 21 of the Judicature (Northern Ireland) Act 1978 (see [8.15]), reads:

> (1) Where a person has been sentenced for an offence by a magistrates' court or, on appeal, by a county court and an application is made to the High Court for an order of certiorari to remove the proceedings of the magistrates' court or the county court into the High Court, and the High Court determines that the magistrates' court or county court had no power to pass the sentence, the High Court may, instead of quashing the conviction, amend it by substituting for the sentence passed any sentence which the magistrates' court had power to impose.

Subsection (2) in turn provides that any substituted sentence runs from the time when it would have begun to run if passed in the original proceedings, unless the High Court directs otherwise.

THE EUROPEAN COMMUNITIES ACT 1972

[**8.32**]   Section 3 of the European Communities Act 1972 requires that UK courts give effect to the remedies case law of the ECJ in cases that come under the Act[124] (the relevant principles and practices may thereafter 'spill over' into the domestic law of remedies[125]: and see [8.34]–[8.35]). That body of case law, which has been developed on the basis of the supremacy[126] and direct effect[127] doctrines and of Article 10 EC,[128] imposes significant remedial obligations on national courts hearing disputes involving EU law rights. Although the ECJ has long emphasised that EU law rights are to be protected through national procedures and practices (subject to the requirement that the protection is effective and equivalent to that given to rights under national law[129]), it has since also introduced a number of specific remedies requirements that have sought to heighten the standards of protection of individuals throughout of the EU.[130] The case law has thus

---

[124] 'For the purposes of all legal proceedings any question as to the meaning or effect of any of the Treaties, or as to the validity, meaning or effect of any Community instrument, shall be treated as a question of law (and, if not referred to the European Court, be for determination as such in accordance with the principles laid down by and any relevant decision of the European Court)'. See further [5.06]–[5.10].

[125] See [1.18].

[126] Case 26/62, *Van Gend en Loos v Nederlandse Aministratie der Belastingen* [1963] ECR 1; Case 6/64, *Costa v ENEL* [1964] ECR 585; and Case 106/77, *Amministrazione delle Finanze dello Stato v Simmenthal SpA* [1978] ECR 629. On UK courts' acceptance of the supremacy doctrine see [5.04]–[5.07].

[127] Case 26/62, *Van Gend en Loos v Nederlandse Aministratie der Belastingen* [1963] ECR 1, 13.

[128] 'Member States shall take all appropriate measures, whether general or particular, to ensure fulfilment of the obligations arising out of this Treaty or resulting from action taken by the institutions of the Community. They shall facilitate the achievement of the Community's tasks. They shall abstain from any measure which could jeopardise the attainment of the objectives of the Treaty.'.

[129] See, eg, Case 33/76, *Rewe-Zentralfinanz eG and Rewe-Zentral AG v Landwirtschaftskammer für das Saarland* [1976] ECR 1989; Case 47/76, *Comet v Produktschap voor Siergewassen* [1976] ECR 2043; and Case 158/80, *Rewe Handelsgesellschaft Nord mbH v Hauptzollamt Kiel* [1981] ECR 1805.

[130] See, eg, Case C-213/89, *R v Secretary of State for Transport, ex p Factortame* [1990] ECR I-2433 (national courts and tribunals are obliged to disapply rules of national law that are contrary to EU law); Cases C-6/90, *Francovich and Bonifaci v Italy* [1991] ECR I-5357 and Joined Cases C-178–179 & 188–190/94, *Dillenkofer v*

seen the ECJ develop more fully its understanding of what 'effective protection' of the individual requires,[131] with the corresponding objective being the attainment of more uniform protection throughout the EU irrespective of variations in national legal practice.[132] The emergence of an enhanced remedies regime at the national level is at the same time understood to have the potential to facilitate a fuller process of the enforcement of EU law in the sense that enforcement is no longer a matter primarily for the European Commission acting through the Article 226 EC enforcement procedure.[133]

[8.33]   There are three principal points about EU law's remedies regime and the remedies available on an application for judicial review.[134] These are concerned with: the availability of injunctions against Ministers of the Crown; the availability of damages; and the question whether remedies are to be regarded as discretionary in the EU law context.

Injunctions and Ministers of the Crown

[8.34]   The availability of an injunction as a remedy in proceedings involving a Minister of the Crown as respondent has its origins in the EU law requirement of the effective protection of the individual. The point famously came to the fore in the *Factortame* case[135] in which the ECJ held that national rules of procedure that militate against the effective protection of EU law rights should cede to the prior force of EU law and the corresponding need for such protection.[136] The case had arisen when a group of Spanish fishing boat operators sought an injunction to prevent the Secretary of State for Transport enforcing the terms of the Merchant Shipping Act 1988, which the operators challenged as contrary to the nationality, establishment, and capital provisions of the EC Treaty.[137] An Article 234 EC reference to the ECJ had in turn been made as the House of Lords considered that it could not grant the injunction because of the domestic rule that prevents

Germany [1996] 3 CMLR 469 (national courts must award damages where there has been a sufficiently serious breach of an individual's EU law rights by the State); Case C-213/89, *R v Secretary of State for Transport, ex p Factortame* [1990] ECR I-2433 (national courts must provide interim protection to EU law rights); Case C-312/93, *Peterbroeck van Campenhout SCS & CIE v Belgium* [1995] ECR I-4599 (national courts and tribunals are obliged to introduce into proceedings relevant provisions of Community law in the absence of either party to those proceedings doing so; cf Cases C-430–431/93, *Van Schijndel & Van Veen v Stichting Pensioenfonds voor Fysiotherapen* [1995] ECR I-4705); Case C-208/90, *Emmott v Minister for Social Welfare* [1991] ECR I-469 (national courts and tribunals are obliged to ensure that the operation of national time-limits does not prejudice the effective protection of EU law rights; cf Case C-338/91, *Steenhorst-Neerings v Bestuur van de Bedrijfsvereniging voor Detailhandel, Ambrachten en Huisvrouwen* [1993] ECR I-5475); and Case 199/82, *Amministrazione delle Finanze dello Stato v San Giorgio SpA* [1983] ECR 3595 (national courts and tribunals are obliged to provide for recovery of charges which are levied contrary to EU law).

[131]   Case C-213/89, *R v Secretary of State for Transport, ex p Factortame* [1990] ECR I-2433; Case 326/88, *Anklagemyndigheden v Hansen & Sons I/S* [1990] ECR I-2911; and Case C271/91, *Marshall v Southampton and South West Hampshire Area Health Authority (No 2)* [1993] ECR I-4367. And see, in the NI courts, *Johnston v Chief Constable of the RUC* [1998] NI 188.

[132]   See generally P Craig and G de Búrca, *EU Law: Text, Cases and Materials*, 4th edn (Oxford, Oxford University Press, 2008) ch 9.

[133]   On which see P Craig and G de Búrca, *EU Law: Text, Cases and Materials*, 4th edn (Oxford, Oxford University Press, 2008) ch 12.

[134]   On EU law's related obligations see [1.17]; [3.45]-[3.46] & [3.77]-[3.78]; & [5.09]-[5.10].

[135]   *R v Secretary of State for Transport, ex p Factortame Ltd* [1991] 1 AC 603.

[136]   Case C-213/89, *R v Secretary of State for Transport, ex p Factortame* [1990] ECR I-2433.

[137]   Viz, ex Art 7 EC (now repealed); Arts 43 and 48 (ex Arts 52 and 58) EC; and Art 294 (ex Art 221) EC.

the grant of injunctions against Ministers of the Crown in civil proceedings (viz section 21 of the Crown Proceedings Act 1947). However, the House of Lords subsequently granted the injunction in the light of the ECJ's ruling on the need for effective protection of the individual, with the result that the Act of 1988 was disapplied. This was an outcome that was widely understood to have contradicted the UK constitution's fundamental precepts of parliamentary sovereignty and implied repeal, as the European Communities Act 1972 had enjoyed priority over a later domestic statute.[138]

[8.35]   The availability of the remedy in purely domestic proceedings was subsequently established in the House of Lords judgment in *M v Home Office*,[139] which is the seminal instance of EU law 'spilling over' into domestic law.[140] Thus, while the judgment of the House in *M* was centrally informed by its finding that section 21 of the Civil Proceedings Act 1947 did not apply to judicial review proceedings because those proceedings are not civil proceedings (see [8.05]), the House also noted that there was a need to ensure parity of protection for the rights of individuals irrespective of whether the rights have their origins in domestic law or EU law. *Factortame* had therefore given rise to an 'unhappy situation'[141] that *M* had resolved.

Damages

[8.36]   It is a central feature of the ECJ's remedies regime that an individual may, as a matter of EU law, seek an award of damages in a national court where the State acts or fails to act in breach of his or her EU law rights. This doctrine of 'State liability' was originally of application only where the individual suffered loss as a result of a State's failure to implement a Directive in domestic law,[142] but it has since been developed to cover potentially any breach of an individual's rights by any of the branches of the State.[143] Case law has thus established that a State may be liable at the behest of an individual where its legislature has enacted legislation that is contrary to EU law rights,[144] where it has failed to repeal legislation that is contrary to EU law,[145] or (as per the origins of the doctrine) where it has failed to introduce legislation to implement a Directive.[146]

---

[138] See [1.28]–[1.29] and [5.04]–[5.07].

[139] [1994] 1 AC 377.

[140] On 'spill-over' see [1.18]; and, eg, *Woolwich Building Society v Inland Revenue Commissioners (No 2)* [1992] 3 WLR 366, HL ruling in the light of, among other factors, the EU law approach to restitution that individuals should have a prima facie domestic law right to the repayment of unlawfully levied monies. On the EU law approach see, eg, Case 199/82, *Amminstrazione delle Finanze dello Stato v San Giorgio SpA* [1983] ECR 3595.

[141] *M v Home Office* [1994] 1 AC 377, 407, Lord Woolf.

[142] Cases C-6/90, *Francovich and Bonifaci v Italy* [1991] ECR I-5357; and see, eg, *Re Burns' Application* [1999] NI 175 (declaration granted that the UK had been in clear breach of EU law because of its failure to transpose Directive 93/104 EC (the 'Working Time' Directive) into NI law and that such breach gave rise to liability for any damage thereby suffered by the applicant).

[143] Cases C-46 & 48/93, *Brasserie du Pêcheur SA v Germany, R v Secretary of State for Transport, ex p Factortame Ltd* [1996] 1 ECR 1029.

[144] *R v Secretary of State for Transport, ex p Factortame* [2000] 1 AC 524 (enactment of Merchant Shipping Act 1988 was an actionable breach of EU law).

[145] Cases C-46 & 48/93, *Brasserie du Pêcheur SA v Germany, R v Secretary of State for Transport, ex p Factortame Ltd* [1996] 1 ECR 1029 (Germany's historic beer purity laws were contrary to EU law and could thereby sound in damages).

[146] Cases C-178–9/94, 188–190/94, *Dillenkofer v Federal Republic of Germany* [1996] ECR I-4845 (Germany's failure to implement Directive 90/314 EC—the 'Package Holidays' Directive—was an immediate breach of EU law).

The case law has likewise established that liability may sound where administrative discretion is exercised contrary to EU law rights[147] or where those rights are breached by a judicial act or omission.[148]

[8.37]   The corresponding EU law test for liability has three elements, namely:

(1) is there an EU law provision that confers enforceable rights upon individuals?
(2) has there been a 'sufficiently serious' breach of the provision by the State? and
(3) has the individual suffered loss as a direct result of the breach?[149]

Of these elements the most important in many cases is that concerned with 'sufficient seriousness', as the ECJ has emphasised that the question of liability must be resolved with reference to the context to any State action or inaction. Hence, where a Member State authority has a wide discretion in a particular area, for example the national legislature introducing national legislation, liability will rest only where the State 'manifestly and gravely disregards the limits of its discretion'[150] ('manifest disregard' is also the threshold for liability in the context of judicial acts and omissions[151]). By contrast, where a Member State has only very limited or no discretion, for example making an administrative decision in a policy area closely regulated by EU law, the 'mere infringement' of an EU provision may be enough to occasion liability.[152] Cases between these two examples, for instance where a national legislature is introducing legislation to give effect to an EU Directive,[153] must then be resolved with reference to the ECJ's suggested list of criteria for identifying a sufficiently serious breach: was the EU law provision that was breached clear? Was the breach/damage intentional? Was any error of law on the part of the State excusable? Had the Member State been adopting or retaining practices contrary to EU law?[154]

[8.38]   Where an individual makes a claim for damages under the State liability doctrine, it is for the national court to decide which domestic cause of action is best suited to facilitating the claim. This is broadly consistent with the ECJ's historic emphasis on the role of national procedures and remedies (see [8.32]), albeit that the ECJ has said that the tort of misfeasance in public office would not lend itself to the effective protection of the individual[155] (on misfeasance in public office see [8.28]–[8.29]). The corresponding approach of the UK courts appears to favour an action for breach of statutory duty, with

---

[147] Case C-5/94, *R v Ministry of Agriculture, Fisheries and Food, ex p Hedley Lomas (Ireland) Ltd* [1996] ECR I-2553 (UK's refusal to grant licences for the export of live sheep to Spain was contrary to EU law).

[148] Case C-224/01, *Köbler v Austria* [2003] ECR I-10239 (ECJ reaffirming that the State may be liable for judicial acts or omissions, including those of its final court of appeal).

[149] Cases C-46 & 48/93, *Brasserie du Pêcheur SA v Germany, R v Secretary of State for Transport, ex p Factortame Ltd* [1996] 1 ECR 1029.

[150] [1996] I ECR 1029, 1150 (para 55). The formulation is based upon the *Schöppenstedt* formula used in the context of Art 288(2) (ex Art 215(2)) EC actions against the EU institutions: see Case 5/71, *Aktien-Zuckerfabrik Schöppenstedt v Council* [1971] ECR 975.

[151] Case C-224/01, *Köbler v Austria* [2003] ECR I-10239.

[152] Case C-5/94, *R v Ministry of Agriculture, Fisheries and Food, ex p Hedley Lomas (Ireland) Ltd* [1996] ECR I-2553 (para 28).

[153] See, e.g., Case C-392/93, *R v HM Treasury, ex p British Telecommunications plc* [1996] ECR I-1631.

[154] Joined Cases C-46 & 48/93, *Brasserie du Pêcheur SA v Germany, R v Secretary of State for Transport, ex p Factortame Ltd* [1996] I ECR 1029, 1150, para 56. And for further guidance from the ECJ see, eg, Case C-118/00, *Larsy v INASTI* [2001] ECR I-5063, and Case C-150/99, *Stockholm Lindöpark Aktiebolag v Sweden* [2001] ECR I-493.

[155] Joined Cases C-46 & 48/93, *Brasserie du Pêcheur SA v Germany, R v Secretary of State for Transport, ex p Factortame Ltd* [1996] I ECR 1029, 1154, para 73.

the duty being taken to arise from the European Communities Act 1972 as read with the relevant provisions of EU law.[156] However, there is also academic authority to doubt whether it is even necessary to fit the elements of the State liability doctrine within a pre-existing domestic tort. The alternative suggestion is thus that claims could be made within the framework of a free-standing 'Euro-tort' that simply transposes the case law of the ECJ directly into national law.[157]

Discretionary Remedies?

[8.39]   The final point to be made about remedies and the European Communities Act 1972 is that EU law's effectiveness principle is likely to entail that the remedies available on an application for judicial review cannot be regarded as discretionary in the EU law context (on their otherwise discretionary nature see [8.08]–[8.09][158]; and on the position under the Human Rights Act 1998 see [8.42]). Although the ECJ's case law originally emphasised that the protection given to EU law rights need only be equivalent to that given to rights under national law,[159] the failure to grant a remedy where an argument of illegality has been made out under the European Communities Act 1972 would be likely to run contrary to other core precepts of the EU order. In other words, while it is possible for the courts to decline to grant a remedy on an application for judicial review in the domestic context, that same approach under the European Communities Act 1972 would mean that a domestic decision, act, or other measure that is contrary to EU law would in effect enjoy primacy over the EU law provisions at issue. Such an outcome would, in turn, be inconsistent not just with the doctrine of the supremacy of EU law but also with the complementary logic of cases like *Factortame* (on which see [8.34]).

THE HUMAN RIGHTS ACT 1998

[8.40]   The Human Rights Act 1998 is structured around the twin objectives of (a) giving domestic effect to the provisions of the ECHR that are contained in Schedule 1 to the Act while (b) preserving the domestic constitutional doctrine of legislative supremacy.[160] In terms of remedies, the Act thus sub-divides between those provisions that enable the

---

[156] *R v Secretary of State for Transport, ex p Factortame (No 7)* [2001] 1 CMLR 1191.

[157] P Craig, *Administrative Law*, 5th edn (London, Sweet & Maxwell, 2003) p 934.

[158] And [3.81]–[3.87].

[159] See, eg, Case 33/76, *Rewe-Zentralfinanz eG and Rewe-Zentral AG v Landwirtschaftskammer für das Saarland* [1976] ECR 1989; Case 47/76, *Comet v Produktschap voor Siergewassen* [1976] ECR 2043; and Case 158/80, *Rewe Handelsgesellschaft Nord mbH v Hauptzollamt Kiel* [1981] ECR 1805.

[160] On the design of the Act see further [5.11]–[5.20]. The provisions of the ECHR in Sch 1, in numerical order, are: the right to life (Art 2); the prohibition of torture and inhuman or degrading treatment (Art 3); prohibition of slavery and forced labour (Art 4); the right to liberty and security (Art 5); the right to a fair trial (Art 6); no punishment without law (Art 7); the right to respect for private and family life (Art 8); freedom of thought, conscience and religion (Art 9); freedom of expression (Art 10); freedom of association and assembly (Art 11); the right to marry (Art 12); prohibition of discrimination (Art 14); restrictions on the political activities of aliens (Art 16); prohibition of abuse of rights (Art 17); limitation on use of restrictions on rights (Art 18); the protection of property (Art 1, Protocol 1); the right to education (Art 2, Protocol 1); the right to free elections (Art 3, Protocol 1); abolition of the death penalty (Art 1, Protocol 6); and death penalty in time of war (Art 2, Protocol 6).

courts to grant binding relief to individuals who make out an argument of illegality in a particular case (sections 6–8) and those that do not permit of binding relief because of the absence of a domestically recognised illegality (principally section 4, which provides for 'declarations of incompatibility'[161]). In practice, a clear majority of cases will fall under sections 6–8, and the courts will thus decide whether there has been or would be an illegality and, if so, whether a remedy should issue. However, it is also possible for cases to raise issues under both sets of provisions, and the remedies granted by the court may therefore be a mixture of both those with legal effect and those without.[162] Other cases may simply fall under the provisions that do not have binding legal effect, and the position of the parties will remain as was before the proceedings were initiated.[163]

Binding Remedies

The Relationship between Sections 6–8

[8.41]   The starting point in respect of binding remedies is section 6(1), which makes it unlawful for a public authority to act in a manner which is incompatible with the rights contained in Schedule 1 to the Act[164] (an act, for these purposes, includes a failure to act, save in relation to the legislative process in Parliament[165]). Although the term 'public authority' has arguably been given an unduly narrow interpretation by the courts,[166] section 6 is intended to allow individuals who are 'victims' within the meaning of section 7 of the Act to enforce their rights vertically against the State and all of its manifestations[167] (subject to the facts giving rise to the proceedings post-dating the Act's coming into force on 2 October 2000[168]). Section 7 thus provides that a person who claims that a public authority has acted (or proposes to act) in a way which is made unlawful by section 6(1) may (a) bring proceedings in the appropriate court or tribunal or (b) rely on the provisions in Schedule 1 in any legal proceedings so long as he or she is, or would be, a victim of the unlawful act. Where those proceedings are in the form of an application for judicial review, section 7(3) provides that the applicant is to be taken to have a sufficient interest in relation to the unlawful act only if he or she is, or would be, a victim of the act.[169]

---

[161] See too s 6(2); and [5.20].

[162] The most high-profile example is the judgment of the HL in *A v Secretary of State for the Home Department* [2005] AC 68 (Anti-terrorism, Crime and Security Act 2001, s 23 declared incompatible with the ECHR; and Human Rights Act 1998 (Derogation Order) 2001, SI 2001/3644, quashed).

[163] Eg, *Re McR's Application* [2003] NI 1 (Offences Against the Persons Act 1861, s 62 declared incompatible with Art 8 ECHR).

[164] Subject to s 6(2): 'Subsection (1) does not apply to an act if (a) as the result of one or more provisions of primary legislation, the authority could not have acted differently; or (b) in the case of one of more provisions of, or made under, primary legislation which cannot be read or given effect in a way which is compatible with the Convention rights, the authority was acting so as to give effect to or enforce those provisions.'. See [5.20].

[165] Human Rights Act 1998, s 6(6).

[166] *YL v Birmingham City Council* [2007] 3 WLR 112; and see [2.22]-[2.25].

[167] See [3.67]–[3.70].

[168] Sections 7 and 22; and, eg, *R (Hurst) v London Northern District Coroner* [2007] 2 WLR 726; *Jordan v Lord Chancellor* [2007] 2 WLR 754; and *In Re McKerr* [2004] 1 WLR 807. And see [1.32].

[169] Human Rights Act 1998, s 7(3); and on 'sufficient interest' see [3.30] and [3.64]–[3.66].

[**8.42**]   The central provision on the binding remedies available under the Act is section 8, subsection (1) of which provides:

> In relation to any act (or proposed act) of a public authority which the court finds is (or would be) unlawful, it may grant such relief or remedy, or make such order, within its powers as it considers just and appropriate.

In the context of judicial review proceedings, this means that each of the remedies available under sections 18–25 of the Judicature (Northern Ireland) Act 1978 and RSC Order 53, rules 1 and 7 are at the disposal of the court in proceedings under the Human Rights Act 1998. Moreover, while those remedies are traditionally regarded as discretionary (see [8.08]–[8.09][170]), it can be doubted whether they are discretionary in the same sense in cases under sections 6–8. This is because sections 2 and 8 of the 1998 Act require courts to 'take into account' all relevant ECHR case law in proceedings before them, including that on remedies.[171] It is thus arguable that remedies should be declined in cases of illegality under sections 6–8 only where there is ECHR authority to support that conclusion (see, eg, [8.44] on damages). Any other outcome would surely run contrary to the first objective of the Human Rights Act 1998 and to the ECtHR's related understanding that 'the ECHR is intended to guarantee not rights that are theoretical or illusory but rights that are practical and effective'.[172]

Damages

[**8.43**]   The requirement that courts take into account all relevant ECHR case law is particularly pronounced where a court is considering whether to make an award of damages for a breach of section 6 of the Act. Here, section 8 provides that a court is to make an award of damages where it is satisfied that the award is necessary to afford 'just satisfaction' to the person in whose favour the award is to be made[173] (the term 'just satisfaction' corresponds directly with the language of the ECHR[174]). In determining necessity, the court must take account of all the circumstances of the case including any other relief or remedy granted, or order made, in relation to the act in question (by that court or any other court) and the consequences of any decision (of that or any other court) in respect of that act.[175] Section 8 also provides that the court must here 'take into account the principles applied by the [ECtHR] in relation to the award of compensation under Article 41 [ECHR]'.[176]

[**8.44**]   The corresponding body of domestic case law has pointed towards a restrictive approach to awards of damages under the Act, at least in cases that do not involve breaches of the individual's absolute rights.[177] The leading authority on the point is

---

[170]   And [3.81]-[3.87].

[171]   On the nature of the s 2, and by analogy s 8, obligation see [5.11].

[172]   *Airey v Ireland* (1979) 2 EHRR 305, 316, para 26.

[173]   Human Rights Act 1998, s 8(3).

[174]   Art 41 ECHR reads: 'If the Court finds that there has been a violation of the Convention or the protocols thereto, and if the internal law of the High Contracting Party concerned allows only partial reparation to be made, the Court shall, if necessary, afford just satisfaction to the injured party.'

[175]   Human Rights Act 1998, s 8(3).

[176]   Human Rights Act 1998, s 8(3).

[177]   On which see, eg, *Van Colle v Chief Constable of the Hertfordshire Police* [2006] EWHC 360 and [2007] EWCA Civ 325 (police liable in damages for the death of a witness whom they had failed to protect in the light of threats from the person against whom evidence was to be given). On the nature of absolute rights see [1.21].

R (Greenfield) v Home Secretary,[178] which concerned the question whether a prisoner whose Article 6 ECHR rights had been violated by a prison disciplinary procedure should receive damages in addition to a declaration that the respondent had acted unlawfully. In holding that a declaration was sufficient in the context of the case, the House of Lords emphasised that the ECtHR itself frequently does not make awards of damages in Article 6 ECHR cases and that it tends to do so only where it finds a causal connection between the violation of Article 6 ECHR and any non-pecuniary loss for which the individual claims compensation. The House of Lords also emphasised that the Human Rights Act 1998 should not, in any event, be regarded as a tort statute that automatically gives rise to a remedy in damages, as the Act's objectives of ensuring compliance with human rights standards can in many cases be met simply through the finding of a violation. The Act, it was said, is not intended to give individuals access to better remedies than they would have were they to go to Strasbourg, but rather to incorporate in domestic law the ECtHR's case-by-case approach and to require domestic courts to have regard to that approach. On the facts of the instant case as read with the Strasbourg jurisprudence, there were thus no special features that warranted an award of damages. A similarly restrictive approach has since also been in evidence in the Northern Ireland courts in cases concerning violations of qualified rights in the prison context.[179]

[8.45]   It should finally be noted that the Human Rights Act 1998 also provides for damages in respect of judicial acts, albeit that they are available only where the judicial act is not done in good faith or where an award is necessary under Article 5(5) ECHR to compensate someone who has been detained in breach of his or her right to liberty under Article 5 ECHR.[180] Where such damages are sought, the appropriate respondent is the Crown, and the Minister responsible for the court or tribunal (or person nominated by him or her) must be joined as a party to the proceedings.[181]

Declarations of Incompatibility

[8.46] The Human Rights Act 1998's prioritisation of the core constitutional doctrine of legislative supremacy (or parliamentary sovereignty) is most evident in section 4, as read with the Act's section 3 interpretive obligation.[182] The combined effect of these provisions is that a court should try 'so far as it is possible to do so' to interpret legislation that interferes with rights in a manner that is compliant with the ECHR but that, where such interpretation is not possible and the legislation is primary legislation, the court may make a declaration that the relevant provision or provisions of the legislation are incompatible with the ECHR[183] (primary legislation here includes Acts of Parliament but

---

[178]   [2005] 2 All ER 240.

[179]   See, eg, *Martin v Northern Ireland Prison Service* [2006] NIQB 1 (High Court granting declaration that sanitary conditions in prison violated Art 8 ECHR but refusing a claim for damages: while the authority had acted unlawfully, an award of even a modest amount of damages could have a knock-on effect in terms of claims by other prisoners and this would run contrary to the public interest. The granting of declaratory relief was thereby the best way to reconcile the rights of the prisoner with the public interest in the continued funding of a public service).

[180]   Human Rights Act 1998, s 9(3).

[181]   Human Rights Act 1998, s 9(4).

[182]   On which see [5.12]–[5.14].

[183]   See, eg, *Re McR's Application* [2003] NI 1 (Offences Against the Persons Act 1861, s 62 incompatible with Art 8 ECHR).

excludes Acts of the Northern Ireland Assembly and Northern Ireland Orders in Council[184]; the courts that may make declarations are listed in section 4(5)[185]. That the doctrine of legislative supremacy is to remain unaffected by the Act is apparent from section 4(6), which provides that a declaration '(a) does not affect the validity, continuing operation or enforcement of the provision in respect of which it is given; and (b) is not binding on the parties to the proceedings in which it is made'. Primary legislation in that way remains sovereign and it is for Parliament to choose whether to repeal or amend the legislation or to leave it in force.[186]

[8.47]   Declarations of incompatibility may sometimes also be made in respect of subordinate legislation and, where they are made, this is a further outworking of the doctrine of legislative supremacy. Although it is implicit in sections 3 and 4 that subordinate legislation that is incompatible with the ECHR may be struck-down as ultra vires[187] (subordinate legislation here includes Acts of the Assembly and Northern Ireland Orders in Council[188]), section 4(4) makes an exception where the legislation has been 'made in the exercise of a power by primary legislation' and 'the primary legislation concerned prevents removal of the incompatibility'.[189] Under those circumstances, the courts may merely make a declaration that the subordinate legislation is incompatible with the ECHR and it is for Parliament to decide whether to repeal or amend the legislation or to leave it in force.[190] The doctrine of legislative supremacy similarly underlies section 6(2) of the Act, which provides that an act of a public authority will not be unlawful where:

(a) as the result of one or more provisions of primary legislation, the authority could not have acted differently; or

(b) in the case of one of more provisions of, or made under, primary legislation which cannot be read or given effect in a way which is compatible with the Convention rights, the authority was acting so as to give effect to or enforce those provisions.[191]

[8.48]   Where a court is considering whether to make a declaration of incompatibility it must give notice to the Crown in accordance with section 5 of the Act and corresponding rules of court.[192] Under those circumstances, a Minister of the Crown (or person nominated by him or her), a Northern Ireland Minister, and/or a Northern Ireland department is entitled to be joined as a party to the proceedings on giving notice in accordance

---

[184]   Human Rights Act 1998, s 21; and see [5.12].

[185]   'In this section "court" means (a) the House of Lords; (b) the Judicial Committee of the Privy Council; (c) the Courts-Martial Appeal Court; (d) in Scotland, the High Court of Justiciary sitting otherwise than as a trial court or the Court of Session; (e) in England and Wales or Northern Ireland, the High Court or Court of Appeal.'

[186]   Section 10 and Sch 2. And see, eg, the Prevention of Terrorism Act 2005, which was enacted in the light of the House of Lords finding, in *A v Secretary of State for the Home Department* [2005] 2 AC 68, that the Anti-terrorism, Crime and Security Act 2001, s 23, was incompatible with the Arts 5 and 14 ECHR.

[187]   See, eg, *A v Secretary of State for the Home Department* [2005] 2 AC 68, quashing the Human Rights Act 1998 (Derogation Order) 2001, SI 2001/3644, as incompatible with Arts 5 and 14 ECHR.

[188]   Human Rights Act 1998, s 21.

[189]   Section 4(3)–(4).

[190]   Section 10 and Sch 2. And see, by analogy, the Prevention of Terrorism Act 2005, which was enacted in the light of the House of Lords finding, in *A v Secretary of State for the Home Department* [2005] 2 AC 68, that the Anti-terrorism, Crime and Security Act 2001, s 23, was incompatible with the Arts 5 and 14 ECHR.

[191]   Human Rights Act 1998 s 6(2); and *R (Hooper) v Secretary of State for Work and Pensions* [2006] 1 All ER 487. And see further [5.20].

[192]   RSC Ord 121, rr 2 and 3A; and see [3.22] and [5.14].

with the rules of court.[193] Notice, for these purposes, may be given at any time during the proceedings.[194]

CONCLUSION

[**8.49**]   This chapter has considered the remedies available where an applicant has made out one or more of the grounds for review. There are four points that may be made by way of conclusion:

i.   The five main remedies available under the Judicature (Northern Ireland) Act 1978 and RSC Order 53 are an order of mandamus, an order of certiorari, an order of prohibition, a declaration, and an injunction (see [8.11]–[8.20]). While each of the remedies has different historical origins and, moreover, was subject to different rules and technicalities, they have been consolidated under the governing legislation. This means that the same procedural requirements should be observed irrespective of the remedy sought.

ii.   The remedies are discretionary and the courts may refuse to grant a remedy for a wide range of reasons (see [8.08]–[8.09]). On the other hand, where rights under EU law and/or the ECHR are in issue, it may be that the remedies cannot be regarded as discretionary within the domestic law sense. This is because EU law and the ECHR both require that rights are given effective protection, which may be lost where a court refuses a remedy where a decision or other measure is shown to be unlawful. In such an event, under the European Communities Act 1972 or the Human Rights Act 1998, it may therefore be that remedies may be refused only where this is consistent with the case law of the ECJ or ECtHR respectively (see [8.39] and [8.42]).

iii. Damages are also available as a remedy, albeit that awards of damages are very infrequent in the public law context ([8.21]–[8.29]). This is not just because of the rule that an ultra vires act will not per se give rise to a claim for damages (the public law illegality must at the same time be actionable in private law); it is also because of a restrictive body of case law on public authority liability. Moreover, while damages are available for violations of EU law and the ECHR, case law here may also be restrictive. However, all will depend on context and on the corresponding approach of the ECJ and ECtHR (see [8.36]–[8.38] and [8.43]–[8.45]).

iv.   The Human Rights Act 1998 contains its own remedies regime that distinguishes between cases in which the courts may grant binding relief and those in which no such relief is possible because of the absence of a domestically recognised illegality ([8.40]). This thus means that there may be cases in which an individual's rights have been 'violated' (for instance where primary legislation is contrary to the ECHR) but where the formal legal position of the parties remains the same (viz, where the remedy granted is a declaration of incompatibility). This is consonant with the Human Rights Act 1998's twin objectives of (a) giving domestic effect to the provisions of the ECHR that are contained in Schedule 1 to the Act while (b) preserving the domestic constitutional doctrine of legislative supremacy.

---

[193] RSC Ord 121, r 2 and 3A.
[194] Human Rights Act 1998, s 5(2).

Index